Texts in Philosophy
Volume 17

Mimesis: Metaphysics, Cognition, Pragmatics

Volume 7
Hugh MacColl: An Overview of his Logical Work with Anthology
Shahid Rahman and Juan Redmond

Volume 8
Bruno di Finetti: Radical Probabilist
Maria Carla Galavotti, ed.

Volume 9
Language, Knowledge, and Metaphysics. Proceedings of the First SIFA Graduate Conference
Massimiliano Carrara and Vittorio Morato eds.

Volume 10
The Socratic Tradition. Questioning as Philosophy and as Method
Matti Sintonen, ed.

Volume 11
PhiMSAMP. Philosophy of Mathematics: Sociological Aspects and Mathematical Practice
Benedikt Löwe and Thomas Müller, eds.

Volume 12
Philosophical Perspectives on Mathematical Practice
Bart Van Kerkhove, Jonas De Vuyst and Jean Paul Van Bendegem, eds.

Volume 13
Beyond Description: Naturalism and Normativity
Marcin Miłkowski and Konrad Talmont-Kaminski, eds.

Volume 14
Corroborations and Criticisms. Forays with the Philosophy of Karl Popper
Ivor Grattan-Guinness

Volume 15
Knowledge, Value, Evolution.
Tomáš Hříbek and Juraj Hvorecký, eds.

Volume 16
Hao Wang. Logician and Philosopher
Charles Parsons and Montgomery Link, eds.

Volume 17
Mimesis: Metaphysics, Cognition, Pragmatics
Gregory Currie, Petr Koťátko, Martin Pokorný

Texts in Philosophy Series Editors
Vincent F. Hendriks   vincent@hum.ku.dk
John Symons   jsymons@utep.edu
Dov Gabbay   dov.gabbay@kcl.ac.uk

Mimesis: Metaphysics, Cognition, Pragmatics

edited by
Gregory Currie,
Petr Koťátko,
and
Martin Pokorný

© Individual author and College Publications 2012.
All rights reserved.

ISBN 978-1-84890-056-1

College Publications
Scientific Director: Dov Gabbay
Managing Director: Jane Spurr
Department of Computer Science
King's College London, Strand, London WC2R 2LS, UK

http://www.collegepublications.co.uk

Original cover design by orchid creative   www.orchidcreative.co.uk

Printed by Lightning Source, Milton Keynes, UK

All rights reserved. No part of this publication may be reproduced, stored in a retrieval system or transmitted in any form, or by any means, electronic, mechanical, photocopying, recording or otherwise without prior permission, in writing, from the publisher.

Contents

Preface vii

Lubomír Doležel
1 Mimesis and Contemporary Criticism 1

Göran Rossholm
2 Mimesis as Directness 14

Fredrik Stjernberg
3 Truth is Stronger than Fiction 40

David Davies
4 Fictionality, Fictive Utterance, and the Assertive Author 61

Gregory Currie
5 Characters and Contingency 86

R. M. Sainsbury
6 Representing Unicorns: How to Think about Intensionality ... 106

Martin Pokorný
7 Characters as Someonewhos 132

Petr Koťátko
8 Radical Narration 178

Anders Pettersson
9 The Idea of Fictional Worlds 194

Karel Thein
10 The Beginnings: Mimesis and Human Mind
in Some Early Theories of Representation 220

Contents

Tomáš Koblížek
11 Representation: A Phenomenological Point of View 257

Anežka Kuzmičová
12 Fidelity without Mimesis:
   Mental Imagery from Visual Description 273

Peter Alward
13 Varieties of Photographic Fiction 316

James R. Hamilton
14 Mimesis and Showing 343

Alberto Voltolini
15 How to Reconcile Seeing-as with Seeing-in
   (With Mimetic Purposes in Mind) 383

Jerrold Levinson
16 Sound in Film: Design versus Commentary 408

Jon Robson – Aaron Meskin
17 Videogames and the First-Person 435

Enrico Terrone
18 Connecting Worlds: Mimesis in Narrative Cinema 465

Index of Names 481

Index of Topics 485

Preface

The concept of mimesis is a multi-faceted one, and the authors who have contributed to this collection have made no attempt to arrive at a unitary definition. Still, there is an area of core problems standardly associated with the term, especially in connection with literature, drama and the visual arts: typically, mimesis refers to the assumed relations of identity, equivalence, or genetic lineage between entities within a literary or dramatic fiction or an image and entities outside of it. It is the ambition of the present volume to survey the central issues that such an of inquiry can address.

Variation in approach is also feature of the philosophical aspects of this inquiry. While the majority of the essays exhibit shared influences, there is also significant variation. The editors, rather than trying to suppress these contrasts, have sought to present them in a manner that would be informative and stimulating. The volume's subtitle highlights the key differences in methodology and choice of emphasis that one can adopt: "metaphysics" provides a focus on the issues of ontology and existence, "cognition" refers to the mental realms of thought and imagination and "pragmatics" stresses the manner in which we handle and employ literary, dramatic and visual artifacts.

The eighteen papers may be grouped into six groups of three.

Papers 1-3 focus, with a relatively general scope, on the very concepts of mimesis and/or fiction. Lubomír Doležel argues that a clarification of the concept of mimesis and its utility — or lack of it — is a pre-requisite for an intellectually responsible literary criticism. Göran Rossholm starts by looking at the classical formulation of the concept of mimesis in Aristotle's *Poetics*, compares it with Nelson Goodman's theory of representation, and lays out a new theory of mimesis as directness. Fredrik Stjernberg examines whether, and to what degree, the advocate of a plurality of truth-perspectives is bound to admit that even fiction is true.

Papers 4–6 as well as papers 7–9 focus on the relationship between fictional entities and linguistic expressions. The first three place a relatively strong emphasis on some general issues in the philosophy of language, whereas the latter three focus more on issues linked to literary expression. David Davies defends a view of the nature of fictive utterances in the light of the latest contributions to this widely discussed topic. Gregory Currie focuses on an equally crucial as well as controversial issue: the problem of proper names in fiction, introduced by way of (apparently) necessary attributions. Mark Sainsbury analyzes the broader category of representations—including fictional entities—in its connection with intensional verbs and intensional attitudes. The latter three begin with Martin Pokorný's argument that literary characters are not individuals in any standard sense. Petr Koťátko presents a distinction between radical and immune narration as providing us with two ways of representing the fictional world by means of narrative. Anders Pettersson raises some doubts concerning the functionality of the concept of a fictional world for the process of literary reading.

Papers 10–12 cross the boundary between linguistic and visual representation. Karel Thein surveys some key theories formulated in Greek Antiquity regarding mimesis as an imaginative capacity. Tomáš Koblížek, taking cues from Ingarden, gives a phenomenological description of the mimetic, or representational, link. Anežka Kuzmičová offers a detailed inquiry into the activity of mental imaging as accompanying literary texts and its correspondence with perception.

Papers 13–15 are devoted to the space of a theatre scene and the space of a photographic frame. Peter Alward argues that photographs are fictional in a strong sense. James R. Hamilton analyzes the roles of narration and showing in theatrical performances. Alberto Voltolini, in re-interpreting certain dicta of Richard Wollheim's, argues for a double grounding of seeing-in in seeing-as.

Papers 16–18 share the topic of "moving pictures" — in videogames as well as in films. Jerrold Levinson analyzes the role of sound in movies, with a special focus on Jean-Luc Godard's *Masculin-Feminin*. Jon Robson and Aaron Meskin describe the role of first-person identification as induced by the process of participating in a video-game. And Enrico Terrone inquires into the modality of our encounter with narrative films.

Mimesis is certainly not a topic that could be exhausted in a single volume. Still, we feel we can claim for the present collection of essays that there is no key issue that it neglects, that it provides a fair idea of the mutual links between the various approaches and problems and that it offers stimulating historical, thematic and methodological excursions. We hope that, as such, it will inform and provoke.

Two of the included papers are reprinted: Lubomír Doležel's "Mimesis and Contemporary Criticism" (reproduced with slight modifications and an added second paragraph) first appeared in *Comparative Criticism* 11, 1989, pp. 253–61; Gregory Currie's "Character and Contingency" first appeared in *Dialectica*, 57 (2), 2003, pp. 137–48.

Preface

We are grateful to Tomáš Koblížek for having compiled the indexes. This publication has been made possible by the financial support provided by the Academy of the Sciences of the Czech Republic within its grant program of international cooperation. We thank the Academy for its support.

The Editors

MIMESIS AND CONTEMPORARY CRITICISM

Lubomír Doležel

ABSTRACT: Even after the challenge mounted by Modernist and avant-garde artistic practice, aestetic thinking remains to be dominated by the doctrine of mimesis, i.e., the view that artworks are secondary with respect to the represented reality (nature) and "worlds of art" are derivatives or transforms of the actual world. This state of affairs is documented by taking a close look at Nuttall (1983) and Prendergast (1986). The outcome of the analysis is that contemporary literary criticism is a hybrid genre with unclear, unspecified truth-conditions — which accounts for its cognitive failure.

Television cameras should have been around when Socrates visited the workshops of the painter Parrhasius and the sculptor Cleiton. An event of historical significance was about to happen: occidental culture would get its definition of the nature and purpose of art. We are not told what the artists themselves thought about the aims of their activity; Xenophon reports only that Cleiton was "puzzled" by Socrates' probing. Having no ready answer, the artist had to accept Socrates' teaching: "It is by faithfully representing the form of living beings that you make your statues look as if they lived." The doctrine of mimesis was born.

Two aspects of this foundation myth deserve emphasizing. First, it is the philosopher who teaches the artist what he, the artist, is doing. Second, the myth originates in ancient Greece, the source of our, occidental aesthetics. Aesthetics of other cultural domains — such as Chinese, Indian (Sanskrit) or Islamic — is not affected by this doctrine.

The doctrine dominated occidental aesthetic thinking for more than two millennia. During this long time, the concept of mimesis was subject to many reinterpretations and, consequently, has become polyvalent and vague (see Sörbom 1966; Tatarkiewicz 1980; Spariosu 1984). Much intellectual effort has been spent on explaining the differences between the Platonic conception—mimesis as *copying* of reality, and the Aristotelian conception—mimesis as *representation* of reality. These differences, however, are overshadowed by the common basis of all the varieties of the doctrine: whether copies or representations, reflections or models, artworks are secondary with respect to the represented reality (nature). "Worlds of art" are derivatives or transforms of the actual world; their genesis, structures and interpretation are determined by an asymmetrical (uni-directional) relationship of imitating.

The first serious challenge to the idea of art as mimesis came in the eighteenth century. The liberation of the poetic imagination from the straitjacket of the neo-classicist canon was justified by many innovative aesthetic ideas.[1] The literary historian John Neubauer, in his 1986 book on *The Emancipation of Music from Language*, explores the role of musical theory in this process. Neubauer disputes the well-known claim that eighteenth-century British critics contributed significantly to the new aesthetics by presenting powerful objections to musical mimesis. Nevertheless, he gathers rich material which demonstrates how the rise and blossoming of instrumental music furthered the formulation of a non-mimetic musical aesthetics. One of the eighteenth-century intellectual strains, an aesthetics and poetics inspired by Leibniz's doctrine of the plurality of possible worlds and formulated by J. J. Breitinger,

---

[1] This process has been traced in many monographs and surveys; Abrams (1953) still offers the most complete picture.

J. J. Bodmer and A. G. Baumgarten, provided a viable alternative to mimesis: the poet armed with his "flaming imagination" penetrates beyond the actual world and describes possible worlds, as the scientist aided by his microscope discovers the invisible microworld. Imaginary worlds ("figmenta") are possible worlds parallel to, rather than derived from, reality.[2]

The stimulus of Leibnizian poetics was forgotten during the nineteenth-century resurrection of the doctrine of mimesis due to the twin manifestations of a new cult of actuality—literary realism and aesthetic positivism. The inevitable modernist onslaught on the doctrine of mimesis was launched from many different theoretical positions extending from the reversal of the mimetic relationship—life (and even nature) imitates art, to the idea of "self-referentiality"—literary works are self-contained aesthetic structures representing nothing outside themselves. Modernist and avant-garde artistic practice found the idea of imitating reality retrograde and counter-productive; when this practice was allied with the structuralist theory of self-referentiality the doctrine of mimesis seemed to have been dealt the final blow.

However, mimesis was bound to be recalled from limbo in the post-modernist and post-structuralist reaction, and numerous books have attempted to revive the idea and reintegrate it into contemporary critical theory. I have selected two of them—A. D. Nuttall's *A New Mimesis. Shakespeare and the Representation of Reality* (1983) and Christopher Prendergast's *The Order of Mimesis. Balzac, Stendhal, Nerval, Flaubert* (1986)—as a representative sample, "representative" in the sense that it represents two opposite strategies available to today's defenders of the doctrine of mimesis: (a) to reanimate the pastorale of realist poetics by simply reasserting that the concept

---

[2] For a detailed discussion of Leibnizian poetics see Doležel (1990).

of mimesis captures adequately the relationship between literature and reality: both the existence of reality and the representational function of arts are unproblematic; indeed, they are their natural and essential features;[3] (b) to rescue mimesis by the same strategy which had brought about its demise: reversing the post-modernist paradoxes, turning the tables on the Cretan liar.

Nutall's book despite the promise in its title pursues the first, conservative strategy. Nuttall facilitates his restatement of realist poetics by putting down the theoretical challenge of modernism and structuralism. To this effect, he employs two well-known rhetorical tricks: (a) taming discomforting ideas by superficial and distorting interpretations so that they can be handily (and haughtily) explained away, and this distortion gives a defender of mimesis the reassuring feeling that most of the twentieth-century explicit or implicit criticism of mimesis came from half-wits, such as Freud, Saussure, Jakobson; (b) setting up a gallery of straw men, imagined, anonymous "spokesmen" of the anti-mimetic position: "merely literary"/ "metaphysical" structuralist, a "hard" / a "soft" formalist, etc. These ridiculous caricatures are engaged in a sort of Socratic dialogue where the defender of mimesis easily proves his intellectual superiority. In fact, the entire theoretical position of the antagonist (structuralist-cum-post-structuralist-

---

[3] The return of Realist poetics was presaged in the "classic" work of post-modernist mimetism, Auerbach's celebrated *Mimesis. Representation of Reality in Western Literature* (1957, German original 1946). Ignoring the challenge of modern artistic practice and eschewing deliberately any theoretical reflection, Auerbach adopted the traditional method of universalistic mimetic interpretation. Literature is assumed to represent reality in universal (typological or ideological) categories. For a critical analysis of Auerbach's method, see Doležel (1988).

cum-formalist), summarized in chapter I, is an arbitrary collection of five fictive "theoremes" lacking historical or logical cohesion. Their "authors" range from Vico through Saussure to Derrida. These thinkers are selected for the collage of the composite straw men only because they have one thing in common—the rejection of a simplistic, reified concept of reality which Nuttall is trying to resuscitate.

Having disposed of the modern critique of mimesis, Nuttall does not have to spend much time on refining the doctrine. He repeats the traditional and predictable slips of mimetic argumentation: speaking confidently about mimesis and mimetic art without providing us with a definition or an analysis of the concept; nonchalantly confusing mimesis and realism (e. g., Nuttall 1983: 87–88); stretching realism to include impressionism—"exaggerative visual realism" (Nuttall 1983: 79 and 88), etc. To be sure, Nuttall does not identify fictions with reality, does not claim that fictional characters are "real people". However, since no logical, semantic or aesthetic consequences are derived from the asserted ontological difference, the ontological difference can be shelved and the mimetic critic is free to treat fictional persons as real people or perceive only those of their characteristics which they share with real people. Nuttall openly admits what detractors of mimesis have known and deplored for many decades: the mimetic critic's thought is set "in terms of people rather than artistic conventions" (Nuttall 1983: 84).

Disappointed by Nuttall's theory, we turn hopefully to his practice of mimetic interpretation. Unfortunately, we are disappointed again, this time for a different reason: while the theorizing was radical, the interpretation is rather timid. In some cases, in the analysis of *Othello* for example, the mimetic approach is totally abandoned and Nuttall practises a formal-cum-philological investigation: Shakespeare's Venice is not a real city, but "an anthropological laboratory". "Itself nowhere, suspended between sea and sky, it receives and utilizes all kinds of people" (Nuttall 1983: 141). Such a perceptive observation which penetrates beyond the actual reference of the proper name to the atmosphere of the imaginary place might indicate that Nuttall is a mimetic critic *malgré lui*.

Nevertheless, Nuttall's prime analytical tool is mimetic interpretation. To be sure, he forgoes the most primitive mimetic method—matching fictional persons with historical prototypes; he cultivates the Auerbachian method of universalistic interpretation: fictional individuals are representations of actual universals ("types"). Unfortunately, Nuttall's application of this method—especially with respect to Shakespeare's historical tragedies—does not alleviate, but rather confirms, scepticism about the validity of mimetic interpretations.

Thus, Nuttall's search for Coriolanus' "type" is totally confusing; three interpretations are proposed and never reconciled: (a) he is the type of a Roman warrior (Nuttall 1983: 113); (b) he is an Elizabethan image of man constructed by hermetism (Nuttall 1983: 117); (c) he is an atemporal image of man as presented by twentieth-century existentialists (Nuttall 1983: 116). Where then is Coriolanus anchored historically, mimetically? Well, very nearly everywhere, because he is, after all, a conjunction of two perennial types: "at one and the same time a sort of Titan and a baby" (Nuttall 1983: 113). (Let us add that Nuttall's Coriolanus displays also a Stoic streak and that in his relationship with his mother might be amenable to a Freudian categorization.)

Similarly confusing, but for different reasons, is Nuttall's mimetic interpretation of Brutus. He is "a conscious Stoic", but this typological assignment is hedged on two sides: (a) the image of the universalist prototype is constructed on such a level of abstraction that "Stoics" can be found in any period of human history; (b) the image is blurred by the admission that "any actual Stoic Roman will have within him un-Stoic elements" (Nuttall 1983: 105). Under these circumscriptions, it is easy to prove that Brutus is a Stoic. The failure of this interpretation has serious consequences, since it was to provide an argument for a rather strong thesis: "Shakespeare did not merely distinguish Romans from English, he distinguished early Romans from later Romans" (Nuttall 1983: 102). Shakespeare's alleged historical authenticity is, in fact, a product of the mimetic critic's dubious interpretive strategy.

Ultimately, Nuttall's mimetic analysis is sustained by a minimalist justification. Fictions have to be interpreted as mimetic because: (a) they cannot be described "without referring to the things which are described as happening in them" (Nuttall 1983: 84); (b) they become intelligible only by "recourse to real human behaviour" (Nuttall 1983: 158). But such minimal postulates of representation do not necessitate a resurrection of the mimetic doctrine; they can be discerned at the foundation of any post- formalist fictional semantics.

Prendergast, in contrast to Nuttall, pursues a progressive strategy for defending mimesis. He is intimately familiar with the most fashionable anti-mimetic arguments, especially those formulated in the cognitive anarchism of contemporary French philosophical, social and aesthetic thought (Derrida, Lyotard, Deleuze and Guattari). The "nomadic" strategy rests on the image of human society and culture as a pack of hidden authoritarian conspirators who turned not only mimesis but all semiotic, cognitive, interpretive activity into a tool of ideological domination, "a matter for the police". In such a *polis* the anarchist attack on mimesis and, more generally, on the representational capacity of language can be feigned as a liberating act. Having a perfect understanding of the convoluted and obscure "texts" of the "nomadic culture", Prendergast at times succeeds in penetrating through their rhetoric to their conceptual nakedness. This happens when he resorts to "common sense" and, particularly, when he associates himself with the philosophical alternatives to epistemological anarchism (Wittgenstein, Ricœur, contemporary analytic philosophy). More often, however, Prendergast is curiously passive or indecisive in his epistemological critique, as if he was fascinated by the enemy's display of splendid armour. Trying to meet the enemy on his own ground he has to accept the enemy's rules of the duel.

Prendergast's position is predicated already in his locating of the elusive problem of mimesis. Mimesis is not formulated as a specific problem of the theory of art; rather, it is placed in the framework of philosophical aesthetics. The history of mimesis was written by Plato, Aristotle, Hegel, Lukács, Ricœur. Prendergast spends much time with Aristotle, especially with the *Poetics*, but strangely (or symptomatically) never consults the meticulous modern commentaries on the classic (such as Else 1957; Dupont-Roc and Lallot 1980), preferring "free interpretations" of literary critics.

The dearth of philological probing is a symptom of a general lack of conceptual analysis. Prendergast's engagement with analytic philosophy is nothing more than flirtation; actually, he does not accept the possibility of conceptual analysis, claiming that "some actually or potentially available canonic vocabulary" is an illusion. When formulating his epistemic strategy, Prendergast seems to accept fully the position of the post-modernist critics of mimesis: "What is historically and culturally authorised as the agenda of mimesis is not cosily negotiated; it takes place within situations where some have more negotiating power than others, or indeed the power to deprive others from participating in the negotiations altogether" (Prendergast 1986: 248). If we live in such cultural conditions, then, of course, "the aesthetics of mimesis also entails a politics" (Prendergast 1986: 248). But, as was the case with analytic philosophy, Prendergast is not willing to embrace wholeheartedly such an epistemology: "The task of a politically critical articulation of the issues is not to show that, in terms of one representation, another is *unrecognisable*, but that, for reasons to do with interests and bad faith, it goes *unrecognised*" (Prendergast 1986: 249). Prendergast seems to believe that the cure is in the disease: if politics ideologized everything, it will also make us understand what is behind the ideologization.

What does this epistemological figure-skating ultimately tell us about the concept of mimesis? Nothing much that is certain. After Prendergast's sophisticated manoeuvres "mimesis" continues to fluctuate between the broadest sense of the term—"a general strategy for living in and negotiating the world" (Prendergast 1986: 24)—and its narrowest application—realistic method, "adequate", "vraisemblable" representation (Prendergast 1986: 32 and 34). But the progress from vagueness to vagueness does not seem to bother the contemporary critic. Without asking what mimesis is, what "mimesis" means, he asks grand questions about its "existence", possibility, modes, effects etc. But since the concept was not fixed in the first place, the formulations and the solutions of the grand questions allow for considerable "float". As the arguments slip and glide without warning from one meaning of "mimesis" to another, obscured contradictions multiply. No wonder the topic becomes "unmanageable" (Prendergast 1986: 213) and, in the end, the defender despairs: the idea of mimesis is of an "inherently ambiguous and unstable character" (Prendergast 1986: 214). What is a necessary consequence of the critic's lack of conceptual analysis is ascribed to the concept itself.

Our sense of puzzlement about Prendergast's theoretical position is explained when we move on to his readings of a select set of nineteenth-century French narratives. These readings clearly reveal a post-structuralist approach to literature in general, and to narrative fiction in particular: literary texts are, basically, language (discourse) games (such as Flaubert's "game of quotation" in *L'Éducation sentimentale*). Having absorbed the first part of Prendergast's book, we know that in this interpretive hypothesis the concept of mimesis as representation of reality is dispensable, indeed, obstructive; what remains is its primitive (Presocratic) sense of "imitation of the Other" (Prendergast 1986: 196). And Prendergast leaves no doubt that he has mastered the lingo of post-structuralist "mimesis" to perfection. Madame Arnoux "is a substitute-representation for what are themselves the substitute-representations with which the stereotyped linguistic and cultural models of desire have furnished Frédéric's imagination" (Prendergast 1986: 197).

I have presented Nuttall's and Prendergast's books as opposite reactions to the modernist and structuralist scepticism regarding the idea of mimesis. I have come to the conclusion that both have avoided an analysis of the concept and thus advanced little our understanding of the issues. Could it be that this disappointing result has some common, underlying cause? I am convinced that it has, in the general character of contemporary literary criticism and of its discourse.

(i) The need to reconsider "mimesis" as a viable theoretical concept is a result of contemporary criticism's basic view of literature, pragmatic determinism. Pragmatic factors are presumed to impose on literature their utilitarian requirements and goals. Literary discourse, having lost its formal and semantic autonomy, its generic specificity and the continuity of its tradition, becomes a formless, pliable object of pragmatic manipulation. The only difference between the various systems of pragmatic determinism is that they place different actual or fictive entities in the role of the pragmatic prime mover (race, class, history, language). "Nomadic" anarchism is just a feigned escape from deterministic pragmatism; trying to repudiate determinism it constructs a theory of human culture precisely on the theoretical assumptions which are to be repudiated: human culture is derived from the power of a Kafkaesque supreme controller.

(ii) Being committed to deterministic pragmatism, contemporary criticism is, necessarily, a non-technical discourse on diverse cultural and philosophical topics. The aim of this discourse is not analytical clarification of issues, but elegance of texture and rhetorical effectiveness. Whether its rhetoric is traditional (as in the case of Nuttall), or post-modernist (as in the case of Prendergast) the result is the same: iteration of terminological vagueness and conceptual confusion. At the moment when our epistemological "anxiety" is not caused by the "experience of breakdown in the representational system", but by "a worry which turns on the uncertain status of representation as such" (Prendergast 1986: 14), any conceptual analysis is precluded. Instead, a host of "theoretical" and "interpretative" texts is produced and launched against the target: literary critics bombard literature with their essays and books hoping to hit the target by chance, since they cannot hit it by method.

As a result, contemporary critical discourse is neither the poetic criticism of romantic aesthetic idealism, nor the scientific discourse of the formalists and inter-war structuralists. It is a hybrid genre with unclear, unspecified truth-conditions. In the post-modernist spirit, the discourse is marked by a high degree of intertextuality, but the set of its "prototexts" is limited to a few "sacred" scripts. The authority of these scripts is less in their theory formation or analytic insight than in their embodying in a maximal degree the ideal of the hybrid text type.

The hybrid character of contemporary critical discourse accounts for its cognitive failure. After reading many pages of elegant prose and forceful rhetoric, after listening to many brilliant lectures, we are no wiser about issues of literary theory than we were at the beginning of the show. Having accepted an epistemological stance which undermines the very foundation of theoretic enquiry, contemporary literary criticism can do no more than *pretend* to posit and advance cognitive problems. It is—despite its loud attacks on "power" and "authority"—the voice of the academic establishment in a time of serious epistemological crisis.

University of Toronto (Emeritus)
lubomir.dolezel@utoronto.ca

REFERENCES

Abrams, Meyer H. 1953. *The Mirror and the Lamp*. Oxford–New York: Oxford University Press.

Auerbach, Erich. 1957. *Mimesis. Representation of Reality in Western Literature*. Trans. Willard Trask. Princeton: Princeton University Press.

Doležel, Lubomír. 1988. "Mimesis and Possible Worlds." *Poetics Today* 9 (3): 475-96.

– – –. 1990. *Occidental Poetics. Tradition and Progress*. Lincoln: University of Nebraska Press.

Dupont-Roc, Roselyne, and Jean Lallot. 1980. *Aristote. La Poétique. Texte, traduction, notes.* Paris: Seuil.
Else, Gerald F. 1957. *Aristotle's Poetics: The Argument.* Cambridge, MA: Harvard University Press.
Neubauer, John. 1986. *The Emancipation of Music from Language. Departure from Mimesis in Eighteenth-Century Aesthetics.* New Haven–London: Yale University Press.
Nuttall, Anthony D. 1983. *A New Mimesis. Shakespeare and the Representation of Reality.* London–New York: Methuen.
Prendergast, Christopher. 1986. *The Order of Mimesis. Balzac, Stendhal, Nerval, Flaubert.* Cambridge: Cambridge University Press.
Sörbom, Göran. 1966. *Mimesis and Art. Studies in the Origin and Early Development of an Aesthetic Vocabulary.* Stockholm: Svenska Bokförlaget.
Spariosu, Mihai (ed). 1984. *Mimesis in Contemporary Theory.* Philadelphia and Amsterdam: Benjamins.
Tatarkiewicz, Wladyslaw. 1980. *A History of Six Ideas. An Essay in Aesthetics.* The Hague: Martinus Nijhoff–Warsaw: Panstwowe wydawnictwo naukowe.

Mimesis as Directness

Göran Rossholm

ABSTRACT: Aristotle applies the term and concept "mimesis" to different art forms, and he explicates it differently in different contexts. The purpose of this article is twofold: to formulate a common denominator for Aristotle's various uses of this key term of aesthetics, and to discuss its conceptual coherence and validity in aesthetics today. The latter aim is carried out by discussing a notion of iconicity, inspired by Aristotle's use of "mimesis" as primarily referring to a characteristic of literature and representational pictures in the *Poetics*, and a notion of expression, inspired by Aristotle's use of "mimesis" as characterizing music in his *Politics*. Both these senses are discussed in the light of Nelson Goodman's theory of symbols, and at the end of the article it is suggested that they have a common root: directness or immediacy.

Many discussions in literary theory of mimesis—the term, concept or phenomenon—are explicitly based on Aristotle's works. However, more often than not, the expositions by literary scholars contain either no precise text references or, at the most, one or two quotes from the *Poetics*. There is no effort to clarify the inconsequences—or at least seeming inconsequences—in Aristotle's text and to go beyond the *Poetics* as a source book; rather, the meanings of the two terms "mimesis" and "mimetic" are taken for granted. In what follows, I will discuss whether it is possible to present a mimetic concept that is fruitful in contemporary aesthetic theory—in particular, narrative theory—yet well in tune with Aristotle's use of μίμησις and related forms. However, I want to stress from the outset that I have no ambition to contribute to Aristotle scholarship. I don't claim to say what it was that

Mimesis as Directness

Aristotle meant by "mimesis"; I am aiming at a concept along Aristotelian lines, rather than at a concept that he himself intended.

On the first page of the *Poetics* Aristotle lets the term "mimesis" bridge the three art forms of literature, visual art and music:

> Now, epic and tragic poetry, as well as comedy and dithyramb (and most music for the pipe and lyre), are all, taken as a whole, kinds of mimesis. ... [T]here are people who produce mimetic images of many things in the media of colours and shape... (*Poetics* 1447a13-19; Aristotle 1987: 31)

A few lines below he then adds a fourth mimetic art, dance. Thus, from the very start the term "mimesis" is given a trans-medial and trans-artial role. Let's start with the references to pictorial representation and the analogies between the arts of images and of words. At the beginning of chapter 4 Aristotle explains the importance of poetry in human lives partly by our natural disposition manifest since childhood "to engage in mimetic activities" — presumably he is referring to children's games — and partly by "the pleasure which all men take in mimetic objects". To illustrate this pleasure he turns to the mimetic art of representative pictures:

> for we take pleasure in contemplating the most precise images of things whose sight in itself causes us pain — such as the appearance of the basest animals, or of corpses. (*Poetics* 1448b10-12; Aristotle 1987: 34)

At the beginning of chapter 25 he once more brings out the mimetic parallel between poetry and visual art: "Since the poet, like the painter or any other image-maker, is a mimetic artist..." (*Poetics* 1460b8-9; Aristotle 1987: 61).

This use of "mimetic" is in accord with the tradition that existed before Aristotle. Stephen Halliwell (2009: 112ff) lists five uses of the word during the period before Plato: 1) "formal mimesis" ("direct correspondence between the mimetic object and its model"), 2) "behavioural imitation", 3) "impersonation" (differing from 2) by "intention and effect"), 4) "vocal imitation", and 5) "metaphysical imitation" (for instance, Pythagorean ideas about correspondences between numbers and the sensible world). The first four may easily be put under the semiotic umbrella "iconic", a term usually explicated by the relational words "similarity" and "resemblance". But what about literature (or "poetry", or, more precisely, "epic and tragic poetry, as well as comedy and dithyramb")? In what sense is it iconic? (I take it that the inclusion of dance is no problem with respect to iconicity.) In addition to the analogies to music and pictorial art, Aristotle points to one more aspect of mimesis, an aspect relevant for literary and theatrical narratives (and also to narrative artforms unknown to the Greeks, such as film) in chapter 24 of the *Poetics*. Here he motivates his high esteem for Homer:

> For the poet should speak as little as possible, for when he does so he is not engaging in mimesis. Now, other poets participate persistently, and engage in mimesis only to a limited extent and infrequently. But Homer, after a short preamble, at once "brings onto stage" a man, a woman or some other figure... (*Poetics* 1460a7–11; Aristotle 1987: 59–60)

This sounds like twentieh-century prose fiction aesthetics as presented by Percy Lubbock: "the art of fiction does not begin until the novelist thinks of his story as a matter to be shown, to be so exhibited so that it will tell itself." (Lubbock 1968: 62) Even though the literary techniques celebrated by Lubbock were unknown to Aristotle, we can easily imagine that narrators in antiquity were well aware of the choice between on the one hand telling a story in a manner that accentuated the fact that the words are mediated by an author, or at least a rhapsode, and on the other hand trying to conceal this circumstance and, metaphorically speaking, to let the story "tell itself". The 1965 Loeb edition of the *Poetics* proceeds along this track. The translator, W. Hamilton Fyfe, comments on the just-quoted passage in a footnote:

> Homer represents life partly by narration, partly by assuming a character other than his own. Both these "manners" come under the head of "Imitation". When Aristotle says "the poet speaks himself" and "plays a part himself" he refers not to narrative, of which there is great deal in Homer, but to the "preludes" ... in which the poet, invoking the Muse, speaks in his own person. (Aristotle 1965: 96-97)

This narrow interpretation of the phrase "the poet speaks himself" makes Aristotle a precursor of those twentieth-century narratologists who order narratives along a gradual line with two extremes, one completely dominated by the voice of the narrator (as in the openings of the chapters in Fielding's *Tom Jones*) and one harbouring narratives composed with "the camera eye" technique (as in Hemingway's "Hills Like White Elephants") or as streams of consciousness (as in the last chapter of Joyce's *Ulysses*). However, Halliwell does not trust this reading. He notes that Aristotle uses similar phrases as Plato in the dialogues of the *Republic*, where Socrates condemns poets who don't "speak themselves", that is, poets who let their characters speak directly. "To bring characters onto stage" means, according to Halliwell, to quote them and nothing more. This yields an interpretative problem: how to assimilate this restricted view of the mimesis of epic poetry to the much more inclusive and categorical one (for instance, the statement "epic and tragic poetry ... are ... kinds of mimesis", as quoted above). Halliwell clearly acknowledges this problem in his comments: "If such an interpretation were pressed rigorously, it would commit Ar. to an intolerable contradiction" (Aristotle 1987: 171; cf. Halliwell 2009: 126).

Fortunately, to make my point I don't have to take a stand here. Both readings are image-oriented interpretations of literary mimesis, interpretations which are well in accord with the inclusion of pictorial art within the realm of general mimesis and which motivate an exploration of mimesis as iconicity.

However, it seems to me that there are two serious major problems following from the iconic line of reasoning. Firstly, with respect to Aristotle, how is one to accommodate music as a mimetic art form? Music is generally not conceived of as a representational art, and consequently not as an iconic one. The second difficulty does not concern Aristotle exegesis, as it is a problem of general aesthetics and general semiotics: how do we proceed to determine what "iconic" means, or should mean, and could mean? I will approach the second question first, in order to prepare the ground for a discussion of the first one afterwards.

Charles Sanders Peirce established iconicity as a technical term of semiotics, and he gave several different definitions and typologies of it. One thing is common to all his theorizing about icons: they are to be characterized by similarity to what they stand for—sometimes by carrying some shared properties, sometimes by resembling it in some other respect. This relation—similarity or resemblance—is the core of traditional semiotic iconicity, but it is also its most evident weakness. The strictest criticism of the concept of similarity is spelled out by the champion of modern iconoclasm, Nelson Goodman (see

Goodman 1972; Goodman 1981: ch. 1). It might seem odd to take Goodman's position as a vantage point for exploring iconicity, yet I don't think there is any way *around* his criticism.

Goodman rejects any definition of representation in terms of resemblance or similarity; indeed, he rejects any use of these terms in serious scientific discourse.[1] Similarity is no sufficient condition of representation: two cars of the same model and the same colour do not ordinarily represent each other. Further, many things are less similar to what they represent than to something else—the two cars mentioned are more similar to each other than one of them is to a black and white photo that represents it. But the criticism cuts deeper still: similarity in the sense "having something in common" is a relation that holds between any two objects. This has the consequence that being similar is no significant relation in any definitional discourse. Of course, it remains a meaningful activity to use the term in a specific sense, e.g. "to have the same height", but there is little hope that we could find a specification applicable to all iconic pairs—visual, auditory, tactile, verbal, and whatever. (Still, common denominators play a crucial role in this context—I'll soon come back to that.)

In my opinion, Goodman has a strong case and provides substantial motivation for a search for a different approach to our understanding of iconic representation. Still, the very strength of our inclination to speak about representation in terms of similarity constitutes a reason to try and present an alternative approach such that it in some way helps explain this inclination of ours.

---

[1] Robert Hopkins (1998) has presented a resemblance theory of depiction immune to Goodman's criticism; however, his theory cannot be recast into a general theory of iconicity.

Goodman's well-known alternative (in my simplified version) runs as follows. Pictorial representation is a completely dense symbol system, which means that a) in between any given pair of pictures there is room for a third, between this third (which usually doesn't exist as yet) and the original two there is room for more pictures in between, and so on and so forth ad infinitum; and b) between any two portrayed things there is room for a third in between them, and so on ad infinitum. Pictorial representation is analogue (as against digital). It is not finitely differentiated: on the contrary, it is dense throughout, in contrast to finitely articulated symbol schemes and systems—the most important of which is, in the present context, language.

The concept of analogue systems in Goodman's sense applies to much more than representational pictures. Several kinds of gauges and diagrams are analogue, others are digital, and many established forms of representation have both analogue and digital features (for instance, drama texts taken as representations of performances). Films, theatre performances and representational dances are all wholly or partly analogue, they are uncontroversial examples of iconicity in semiotics in general, and they are also—in spite of the film anachronism— well in tune with what Aristotle says about mimesis. However, as noted above, these latter mimetic art forms are only partially analogue, and others, such as narrative literature, are in still sharper contrast to the analogicity of representative pictures. The two most obvious iconic phenomena in narrative literature are quotation and temporal matching. Both can be exemplified by "Veni, vidi, vici", first taken as a quote of what Caesar wrote, but also as an account of three events occurring in the same order as the proper reading of the text. Thus there seem to be non-analogue iconic phenomena. One might even go one step further and ask: is it really true that all representative pictures are analogue?

Goodman's theory of representation cannot consequently work as an explication of iconicity along Aristotelian lines. And I think there are problems with Goodman's approach also independently of the present effort to reconcile iconicity with Aristotelian mimesis. The first concerns ontology. Density implies infinitely many positions for in-between signs and denotata, and most of these positions are empty. No actual symbols ("inscriptions" and "characters" in Goodman's terminology) or actual denotata ("compliants" and "compliance-classes") are to be found there. We can only talk about them as possibilities. If the entities that there is room for actually show up, they are accepted by the system. This puts a heavy burden on what Goodman calls symbolic systems and schemes, even though, as can be seen from Goodman's discussion of digital pictures, this concept is very relative (for more on digital pictures see below, and Goodman 1988). There is nothing inconsistent in this, yet it would surely be preferable to have an account which supplies us with nothing more than actual symbols and actual denotata. Secondly and more importantly, Goodman's approach ignores the pre-theoretic notion of similarity between symbol and symbolized as an ingredient in pictorial representation. As suggested above, one would prefer an account which recognizes the inadequacies of the similarity terminology yet simultaneously gives us clues for explaining our habit of using that terminology whenever we try to clarify iconic relations.

I will briefly present an alternative approach to the definition of iconism, an approach which accommodates for Goodman's criticism of concepts of similarity as well as for what I consider to be two weak points in his theory. As will become clear, my alternative incorporates a large part of his theory—not only his criticism of traditional iconism in semiotics.[2]

My proposal is based on the observation that parts (or most parts) of representative pictures represent parts of what the pictures themselves represent; and this relation between parts and wholes distinguishes pictures from descriptions. One part of a portrait represents the forehead of the represented person; a part of that part represents the left half of that forehead; and so on. However, the parenthesis above indicates that this idea has to be made more specific. First, if every pictorial representation has a proper part, which in turn is a pictorial representation, then we have for every representation an infinite regress of representations. Second, we will have as a consequence an infinite number of representations that we are on principle unable to see. Third, many parts of a representative picture do not represent anything at all: the contour lines of a portrait may be divided into thinner lines which simply do not represent. Fourthly, if we take this part-whole relation as not only a necessary condition for pictorial representation but also a sufficient one, we will arrive at the consequence that all conglomerate portrait-parts—i.e. all parts unrecognizable as representations—are representative pictures, even if those conglomerates cannot be seen as such. Fifth, it is not clear how to widen this idea (if formulated as above) to apply to iconic symbols in general. And finally sixth, the term "represent" (if defined as above) cannot be used to cover fictional cases.

---

[2] This alternative is spelled out more in detail in Rossholm (1995) and Rossholm (2004: 155–79). Flint Schier (1986) has presented a theory of pictorial representation akin to my idea about compositionality; see Rossholm (2004: 159, n. 6).

Mimesis as Directness

The first two objections are no real objections: there is nothing wrong with infinite regresses or invisible pictures. Still, as will soon become clear, my ultimate proposal will imply neither (although on the other hand it will not legislate against infinitely small representations). For the rest, some Goodmanian tools are required. Pictures which represent existing objects *denote* what they represent (Goodman 1981: 5: "Denotation is the core of representation"), just like a denoting description. Pictures of non-existent objects do not denote anything but even so they are representative pictures: a picture of Zeus represents by being a Zeus-picture. This also parallels descriptions: a description of Zeus denotes nothing, but it remains a Zeus-description. In a short article (Goodman 1984), Goodman presents a more abstract category — what he calls "-ofs". Both a picture of Zeus and description of Zeus is a "Zeus-of". A fictional diagram of a non-existing process P is a P-of. The formulas *represent/describe … as* and *be x-descriptions/-pictures/-ofs* are not restricted to fictional symbols. A portrait of my cat, a Norwegian forest cat, depicts it as a Norwegian forest cat, and the portrait is a Norwegian forest cat-picture. The answer to How? often coincides with the answer to What? More Goodmania: every concrete sign in any medium is an inscription (so that consequently an "inscription" is not necessarily visual). Inscriptions form classes, and a class of equivalent inscriptions is called a character. Inscriptions and characters are either simple or compound; the quote "Veni, vidi, vici" is one compound inscription, belonging to one character, but it is also 12 inscriptions belonging to 6 characters and a number of compound inscriptions (such as "eni") belonging to corresponding characters.

Back to the remaining points of criticism. The final two objections are rather requests for clarifications than counter-arguments. My proposal concerns primarily the one-place-meaning of representation, which applies to both fictional and factual pictures. A portrait of Pickwick is a Pickwick-portrait, a Pickwick-picture and a Pickwick-of. A portrait of Churchill may be a statesman-picture, a soldier-portrait or a dog-picture depending on how he is portrayed. The qualification "primarily" is a reminder of the fact that when the picture is an x-picture of y, and this mode of representation is in accordance with what y actually is—for instance, a statesman-picture of Churchill—then my proposal applies to the relational sense of representation as well. The requested widening of the proposed concept of representation (in particular, wide enough to apply to literary iconicity) is easily met. The string of words "Veni, vidi, vici" represents a process, and parts of the string represent parts of the process; parts of a quotation of an utterance refer to parts of the utterance.

This leaves us with objections number three and four. They present substantial problems, requiring specifications and a supplementation of the preliminary version given above. The third objection—that not all parts of a representative picture represent anything—also applies in obvious ways to the just mentioned cases of literary iconicity. The fourth objection—that a whole representation can be composed of randomly spread partial representations—seems to ask for some constraints of the makeup of the whole representation, in particular with respect to the relations among the parts of the whole representation.

I suggest that the third objection can be handled by introducing the concept of level: the quotation "Veni, vidi, vici" can be taken as presenting parts at the level of sentences, which then refer to the three sentences uttered by Caesar, or again parts at the level of words, or syllables, or letters. The quoted text refers iconically to three events (I came, I saw, I conquered) at the level of sentences. The parts of a representative painting depict at a more general level — the level of reference in the non-relational sense, the level of "-ofs". A picture of a unicorn is a unicorn-of; parts of that picture are parts-of-unicorn-ofs. This does not mean that *every* part of a painting — or for that matter of a photograph — is *of* anything. Moreover, there is a difference between verbal and pictorial iconicity: Goodman's hallmark of picture, i.e. density, reigns also among part-whole-relations. If x represents y, and z is a part of x which represents a part of y, then there is another part of x which comprises z and represents a part of y plus whatever is represented by z. To give an example: when a part of the canvas represents a horse's nose and a smaller part of that part represents a piece of that partial nose then there is a pictorial part in between such that it represents less of the nose than the former part of the first two but more than the latter one.

In contrast, with the verbal medium, neither the quote nor the matching time order are dense: the words "vidi, vici" refer to a conjunction of events or states of affairs, and "vici" refers to one of them, yet "i, vici" does not refer to this latter event plus some portion of the previous one.

Let us call "compositional" all pictorial representations and iconic phenomena which can be analysed in this way, so that parts of the representation represent parts of what the whole representation represents (relative to a certain specified level). Generally put, a compositional relation R holds between an object or event and something else, and parts of that object or event stand in the same relation to parts of that "something else". Some relations are compositional with respect to a certain level, as illustrated above, and some are categorically compositional.³

In my answer to objection four I would like to re-introduce a concept rejected above, or at least something closely like it: common features. A picture of a green bottle may be green, and this colour-match counts. A Goodmanian twist upon common features is performed in two steps: you switch from talk about properties or relations to talk about terms, and you add the referential relation of Exemplification.⁴ The green bottle picture denotes a green bottle, and it does so partly by exemplifying (and consequently, by referring to) the label Green which in turn denotes the actual bottle. The referential structure becomes triangular: the picture directly denotes the object, but it also refers upwards to a term which denotes the same thing. (For illustrative reasons I have chosen a case in which the referred to object really exists. One could easily translate it into the more general, but also less habitual, terminology of x-ofs.) However, the term Green is one-place; what we primarily need as complements to compositionality are relational terms. If we change the word order (and thereby the order of sentences) in "Veni, vidi, vici", the words come to denote a different course of events. The order of the symbols refers iconically to the order of the partial denotata. And the part of the bottle picture which represents the bottleneck is placed above the rest of the bottle representation, as is the bottleneck itself in relation to rest of the portrayed bottle. The

---

³   This use of "compositional" and "compositionality" in the present article should not be confused with the standard sense of these terms in analytic philosophy.
⁴   Catherine Elgin discusses iconicity along these exemplificational lines in the chapter "Index and Icon Revisited" in Elgin (1997).

spatial order in the picture refers indirectly, via a mediating exemplified label, to the spatial order of the bottle.

As seen above, compositionality applies at different levels to different media, and these media can be analogue or digital or mixed. This actualizes one more question with respect to Goodman's semiotics: Are all pictures really dense? Isn't a chessboard diagram or — to use Goodman's example — a dotted picture of Abraham Lincoln a non-dense picture? Goodman himself has argued against the assumption that there exist digital — and consequently non-dense — pictures: "no symbol by itself is digital and none by itself is analog" (Goodman 1988: 127). Only symbol schemes can rightly be labelled digital or analogue (or mixed), and what constitutes one symbol scheme depends on how we group characters: when we insert our dotted Lincoln picture into a pack of cards consisting of "inscriptions of letters, words, numerals and so on", it belongs to a digital scheme, but inserted into a pack with representative pictures, it is part of an analogue scheme. And, obviously, the former pack is not generally considered to correspond to any well-entrenched category, as distinct from the latter. This much we get from Goodman. One might object that we can form a group of symbols consisting of nothing but digital pictures, and, more importantly, that in confining picture-like representations — icons — to dense representations we push out all non-pictorial (and not only verbal) representations.[5] To account for the iconicity of "Veni, vidi, vici" by applying Goodman's theory of symbols is impossible, whereas it is taken care of in my proposal, as the differences within this wide category of iconicism is at least partly recognized by the

---

[5] An example of a non-pictorially, non-verbally articulated iconic representation is a musical score.

specifications of the level up to which the symbol is compositional.

How does my proposal meet the two objections raised against Goodman's theory of symbols, i.e. the complaint regarding ontology, and the fact that a connection between iconicity and resemblance, while heavily criticized, remains ubiquitous?

The first objection concerned ontology. The crucial idea here is the infinity of places for characters in between and compliance classes in between, and, as I've said, these places are for the most part empty. Goodman never assumes anything else, the inscriptions and compliants are not there, the symbol scheme and system just "provide for" them. Still, a theory restricted to actual symbol tokens seems preferable, in particular from Goodman's own nominalist ontological vantage point. The compositional approach sketched above is such an account. The pictorial relations betweens parts and whole, and between parts and parts of parts, can be dense: a part of Leonardo's painting represents Mona Lisa's forehead, and a part of that part represents a part of her forehead, and so on ad infinitum. These pictorial parts, however small, are actually there. Other compositionally representative symbols, such as scores or quotes, are, as said above, non-dense, i.e. digital.

Finally, does this approach—in distinction to Goodman's—help explain the ubiquity of the concept of resemblance in most proposed definitions of iconic representation? I think there is a hint of such an explanation in the references to common properties and of compositionality. Even if we accept Goodman's critical examination of the relations termed "similarity" or "resemblance", the two words can be used meaningfully in a relative sense. It is possible to find out whether or not I can tell the difference between two objects on a certain occasion, and the same question with respect to different populations can be settled by tests. If I—or the majority of Swedes—cannot see difference between two objects A and B, we have strong reasons to believe that (a) A and B have common easily observable properties such that if we change these properties in A and not in B, the probability that I will be able to tell A from B increases, and that (b) A and B are similar in the admittedly weak common-property sense. Further, in this case we are certainly inclined to say that A resembles B and B resembles A (not because they share common properties but because we cannot tell A from B or B from A) in a very strong sense. And taken in this sense, the relation Resemble is compositional: if A is practically indistinguishable from B then perceptible parts of A are indistinguishable from certain perceptible parts of B, parts of these parts are indistinguishable from certain partial parts of A, and so on. If this compositional analysis comes to an end, A stops being indistinguishable from B. Thus, To resemble (or To be similar to) is a basic compositional relation, which constitutes a strong link between similarity and iconic representation.

Back to the main track: compositionality (at some level) plus triangular reference take care of the preliminary identification of mimesis to pictorial as well as literary iconicity. Aristotle's passing reference to dance can easily be incorporated in this configuration.

But what about music?

The mimetic concept occurs repeatedly in Aristotle's discussion of music presented towards the end (chapter 8) of *Politics*, from which the following two quotes are taken.

(1) Rhythm and melody supply imitations of anger and gentleness, (2) and also of courage and temperance, and of all the qualities contrary to these, and of the other qualities of character, which hardly fall short of the actual affections, (3) as we know from our own experience, for in listening to such strains our soul undergoes a change. The habit of feeling pleasure or pain at mere representations is not far removed from the same feeling about realities; for example, if anyone delights in the sight of a statue for its beauty only, it necessarily follows that the sight of the original will be pleasant to him. (Aristotle 1952: 545)

(4) Again, figures and colours are not imitations, but signs, of moral habits, indications which the body gives of states of feeling. (2) On the other hand, even in mere melodies there is an imitation of character, for the musical modes differ essentially from one another, (3) and those who hear them are differently affected by each. Some of them make men sad and grave… (5) The same principles apply to rhythms; some have a character of rest, others of motion… (6) Enough has been said to show that music has a power of forming the character, and should therefore be introduced into the education of the young. (Aristotle 1952: 545–46)

Mimesis in the first sentence of the first part presents a relation between music and emotion. The translator has chosen "imitation", but another candidate term would make it easier to fit these passages into contemporary aesthetics: expression.[6] In the sentence marked (by me) (2) in both parts, the mimetic relation holds between music one the one hand and "character" and the moral qualities that apply to character on the other hand. In (3) in the first quote Aristotle moves to the relation between music and listener—we share the feelings of the musical representation, and in a corresponding passage in the latter quote (also numbered (3)) we, listeners, become "sad or and grave". All this indicates an expressive reading of mimesis:

---

[6] See Rackham's translation (Aristotle 2005) where "representation" is chosen instead of "imitation" in the pertinent passages.

music expresses emotions, and by listening to it we are disposed to experience the very same emotions; in (2) the expressive relatum is widened to comprise not only emotions but also character and moral qualities. Such an interpretation is strengthened by the opposition between music and the characterization of literature as an art which only presents "signs", "indications" of the feelings and moral items that (according to my reading) are expressed by music. In (3) in both quotes Aristotle has turned from the expressed emotion of the work to the corresponding emotion in the audience. In (5) he demonstrates (like Goodman—see next paragraph) that the expressed content is not confined to emotions. Finally, in (6) Aristotle discusses the moral topic that motivates his whole discussion of music in this book: whether or not music should be part of education. This motivates the emphasis on the term "character" with its strongly moral connotations and on the listener's perspective: does music improve our moral character? The quotes seem to indicate that expression ought to play a central role in that context.

Thus, what to do with expression? Given that Nelson Goodman's *Languages of Art* is already with us, we may well adopt his exemplicational approach to this concept. According to Goodman, expression in aesthetic contexts is (or at least, yields) metaphorical exemplification. In less technical terms: a musical piece expressing sadness is sad, and furthermore it refers to this quality (this is the exemplification part), yet it is such and does so only metaphorically. Music is sound, and sound is, literally speaking, never sad. It has no feeling. What you possess is a metaphorical property, but your possession of it is literal.[7] It is there, and it is *as if* the literal property were

---

7   See Goodman (1981: ch. 2). For the sake of simplicity I deviate from Goodman's exposition by talking of expression and exemplification as

there. Most of Goodman's examples of expression are emotive, but he admits other expressive contents as well: Daumier's painting *The Laundress* expresses weight taken as metaphor (Goodman 1981: 87), a comment that corresponds to the inclusion of motion, rest, moral qualities and so forth in the quotes from the *Politics*.

If we accept such an extension of the concept of mimesis we have what might at first seem to be a heterogeneous composite, consisting of two distinct parts: iconicity (as compositionality plus trianguarity) and expression (as metaphorical exemplification). However, in doing so, have we accomplished anything more than created an ambiguity?[8] We may eschew the issue by stressing the fact that iconicity is not confined to visual art and literature and that expressivity is not confined to music; on the contrary, both are prominent in all art forms. But this obvious truth has no bearing on the fact that we are dealing with two distinct concepts.

To answer this question we have to turn to the statements numbered (3). In the first quote Aristotle may seem to mix up the question of how something is expressed with how it is taken up by the recipient; in the second part he passes from the variety of expression to the variety of uptake, and it may seem he does so for no particular reason. Further, at the end of the first quote he appears to contradict the opposition between literature and visual art, as declared in (4): in the passage now under scrutiny, pictorial art (statues) and music are on a par.

---

relations between a symbol and a property or something else which is extra-semantic; in his theory only labels are exemplified.

[8] Halliwell tries to combine mimesis as representation with mimesis as expression by appealing to Peirce's many-headed concept of iconicity. However, he does not elaborate on this interesting thought (see Halliwell 2002: 159–63).

Mimesis as Directness

Let me answer. First, there is no contradiction here. In (4) he states that representative pictures of humans permit inferences about feelings and "moral habit" but no direct expression of this content; at the end of the first part he only points out the fact that an emotion evoked by a statue of a man might be roughly the same as the effect of seeing the real man. No mention of expression here. The accusation of turning from discussing the expressiveness of music to treating the reaction of the audience for no explicit reason can of course be met by pointing to the overarching moral reason for taking up music in a book entitled *Politics*, but I think there is another course of defence, and a better (as well as, I admit, an obvious) one. The emotions expressed evoke similar emotions in the listener, and the emotions expressed are recognized as such by evoking similar emotions; as the emotions expressed vary, so do the emotions evoked. This is in parallel to the relation between iconic representation and uptake, as mentioned at the end of the first quote. The emotion evoked by the statue is similar to the emotion evoked by the represented object, and vice versa. Put in that way, the unity of a concept of mimesis defined along Aristotelian lines can be saved but at the price of some hopelessly naïve commitments, in particular the idea that expressed emotions are replicated in the listener, and the identification of make-believe uptake with its real-world counterpart. A reader, or listener, or spectator, may well react sympathetically, as presumed by Aristotle, but she may also react with a complementary feeling. Both the perception of the man and of the statue may fill me with pleasure, as in Aristotle's example, but the fear evoked by a tragedy differs in several respects from the fear evoked by an attacking tiger. However, I believe we can get around such details by adopting a more holistic view of Aristotelian mimesis. (Remember—we only seek to go along his account's lines!)

What unites expression and iconic representation is not revealed by an analysis of their respective semiotic basic structures—triangular reference plus compositionality and metaphorical exemplification, respectively. Let us call these basic structures and their dressed up versions "semiotic substrates".

What counts is the effect and the function. The spectator sees the statue as the man it represents. The reader experiences the speech made by the actor as a speech made by King Oedipus, and the reader of a narrative "follows" what happens and "looks forward" to what will happen, experiences herself as "dragged into" the process, and "identifies" with the protagonist. The spectator, the listener and the reader are *such as* experiencing something directly: a beautiful man, a miserable king, a sequence of events. This quality of directness is figurative—the recipients are all aware that they do not have the corresponding *literal* experiences—and it is gradual. The same goes for expression. I experience sadness directly, metaphorically speaking, because the music is not a sentient thing, but the directness is literal in the sense that the quality referred to is actually there; it is not just described or depicted (or inferred from description or depiction). Thus, mimesis is an artefact—musical, theatrical, literary or other—which has the effect of evoking such as-direct experiences. Sometimes the effect is not achieved, either due to the recipient or due to some features of the artefact, but on the whole the artefacts have that function all the same, and most probably they have it because it is expedient to having some further function.[9]

---

[9] One such further function may have to do with energy costs: taking in direct information is our most well entrenched and our most basic

Mimesis as Directness

The previous discussion of iconicity and expression concerns the semiotic substrate of the directness experience. However, this does not mean that in order to talk of directness—and of mimesis in this proposed sense—we must have a specific semiotic substrate and know its structure. When we do have one, we have something that contributes to the explanation of the mimetic experience, but directness can have other kinds of roots—and conversely, a semiotic structure does not guarantee directness, at least not to any high degree.[10] A very detailed and accurate chronological description of a man raising his arm can fail to evoke any strong sense of directness, and it can thus fail precisely due to its minuteness of detail and its lack of suspense and interest, although its iconic structure may be obvious.

This essay started with a reference to the use of "mimesis" among literary scholars, and it is primarily as a term of narratology that it has survived in aesthetic contexts. Percy Lubbock's *The Craft of Fiction*, mentioned above, plays a crucial role in the twentieth-century promotion of "showing"—or "mimesis"—in contrast to "telling"—or "diegesis"—in narrative theory; still more influential is Wayne C. Booth's *The Rhetoric of Fiction* in the opposite camp. Booth opens his book by reminding us of the authoritative voice of the pre-modern fiction writer/narrator:

> It is in a way strange, then, that in literature from the very beginning we have been told motives directly and authoritatively without being

---

epistemic attitude and habit—it is always "on", it is "easy". See Rossholm (2004b: 220f) and Rossholm (2010: 29f).
[10] A case in point: Anežka Kuzmičová (2012) uses the term "presence" about the reader's experience without any semiotic presuppositions.

forced to rely on those shaky inferences about other men which we cannot avoid in our own lives. (Booth 1961: 3)

However, for more than one and a half century a different mode of fiction writing has been prevalent:

> Since Flaubert, many authors and critics have been convinced that "objective" or impersonal" or "dramatic" modes of narration are naturally superior to any mode that allows for direct appearances by the author or his reliable spokesman. Sometimes … the complex issues involved in this shift have been reduced to a convenient distinction between "showing", which is artistic, and "telling", which is inartistic. (Booth 1961: 8)

Booth questions the assessment that Hemingway is proven better than Fielding by the show-tell test, and he also questions the very idea of narrative showing by emphasizing the fact that all narratives are mediated. This latter statement is of course true, but on the other hand no critic, writer or scholar has seriously questioned that. That a narrative shows what happens in the story is to be taken figuratively.

Does this mean that an interpretation of mimesis along Aristotelian lines, if applied to the art of narrative literature (or "epic"), ends by roughly identifying the Aristotelian concept with the concept of "showing", as current in the wake of Lubbock and Booth, and by identifying the Aristotelian assessment with Lubbock's? Not necessarily. If we return to where we started, i.e. to Aristotle's categorical assertion that epic *is* a kind of mimesis—not that *some of it* is—we can rephrase his position thus: the reading of narrative typically consists in experiencing (to varying degrees) the narrated events as the content of *direct, unmediated* experiences.

I believe that there are good reasons for maintaining this stronger thesis. The issue is too complex to be dealt with in any detail here—I will only point to some phenomena already touched upon. Direct speech and chronological match are two iconic features which contribute to directness in both modern and pre-modern literary narratives. There certainly are several examples of narratives lacking any quoted utterances (or texts), as well as of narratives with twisted temporal order. Still, most narratives contain some direct speech, and most of them on the whole respect the order of events. More importantly, we count matching chronology among the basic criteria of narrativity (see Stein 1982; Stein and Policastro 1983). Furthermore, even when the time order of events and the sequence of narration fail to match, we—and this includes both common readers and narrative theorists—tend to identify one or several temporal lines that we are disposed to call the "now" of the narrative and in relation to which other parts are "flashbacks" or "flashforwards" (see Rossholm 2004b). As mentioned above, iconicity isn't all: literary narratives which maintain broader interest usually do so by emotionally engaging the reader and making her feel suspense with respect what will happen—and both these phenomena increase the sense of directness. Again, this doesn't go for all narratives, but as these qualities are usually positively valued (in both modern and pre-modern narratives), they contribute to the explanation why these narratives continue to be read. If we turn to the narratological debate about telling and showing and take a closer look at the features representative for the negative extreme (with respect to directness, or "showing") on the scale referred to above, we find reflections, comments, evaluations, that is: words and sentences which don't push the story any further. Booth formulates the question "What, after all, does an author do when he 'intrudes' to 'tell' us something about his story?" (Booth 1961: 8); that is, on the "teller" pole we find things not belonging to the proper narrative (here: the (re)presentation of the story) at all. Thus, the occurrence of "telling" in novels and short stories does not constitute a counter-argument against the directness thesis—it means no more than admitting that novels and short stories may contain more than narrative.

Thus, to sum up in one word: mimesis, literary or not, is—directness.[11]

Stockholm University
goran.rossholm@littvet.su.se

REFERENCES

Aristotle. 2005. *Politics*. Trans. Harris Rackham. Loeb Classical Library. London—Cambridge, MA: Harvard University Press.
– – –. 1952. *Politics*. In *The Works of Aristotle*, vol. II, trans. Benjamin Jowett. Chicago—London—Toronto: Encyclopaedia Britannica Inc.
– – –. 1987. *The Poetics of Aristotle*. Trans. and commentary by Stephen Halliwell. Chapel Hill: The University of North Carolina Press.
– – –. 1965. *The Poetics*. Trans. William Hamilton Fyfe. Loeb Classical Library. London—Cambridge, MA: Harvard University Press.
Booth, Wayne C. 1961. *The Rhetoric of Fiction*. Chicago: The University of Chicago Press.
Elgin, Catherine. 1997. *Between the Absolute and the Arbitrary*. Ithaca, NY: Cornell University Press.
Goodman, Nelson. 1972. "Seven Strictures on Similarities." In *Problems and Projects*, 22–32. Indianapolis, NY: Bobbs Merill Company.
– – –. 1981. *Languages of Art. An Approach to a Theory of Symbols*. Brighton: The Harvester Press.
– – –. 1984. "Splits and Compounds." In *Of Mind and Other Matters*. Cambridge, MA: Harvard University Press.

---

[11] Research for this essay was supported by the Bank of Sweden Tercentenary Foundation.

———. 1988. "Digital and Analog." In *Reconceptions in Philosophy and Other Arts and Sciences*, Nelson Goodman—Catherine Elgin, 123-31. London: Routledge.
Halliwell, Stephen. 2002. *The Aesthetics of Mimesis. Ancient Texts and Modern Problems*. Princeton: Princeton University Press.
———. 2009. *Aristotle's Poetics*. London: Duckworth.
Hopkins, Robert. 1998. *Picture, Image and Experience*. Cambridge: Cambridge University Press.
Kuzmičová, Anežka. 2012. "Presence in the Reading of Literary Narrative: A Case for Motor Enactment." *Semiotica* 189 (1-4): 23-48.
Lubbock, Percy. 1968. *The Craft of Fiction*. London: Jonathan Cape.
Rossholm, Göran. 1995. "On Representation: An Iconic Supplement to Nelson Goodman's Theory of Depiction." *Semiotica* 103 (1-2): 119-31.
———. 2004a. *To Be And Not to Be. On Interpretation, Iconicity and Fiction*. Bern—Berlin—New York: Peter Lang.
———. 2004b. "Now's the Time." In *Essays on Fiction and Perspective*, ed. Göran Rossholm, 199-222. Bern—Berlin—New York: Peter Lang.
———. 2010. "Fictionality and Information." In *Fictonality–Possibility–Reality*, ed. Petr Koťátko—Martin Pokorný—Marcelo Sabatés, 19-31. Bratislava: Aleph.
Schier, Flink. 1986. *Deeper into Pictures. An Essay on Pictorial Interpretation*. Cambridge: Cambridge University Press.
Stein, Nancy. 1985. "The Definition of a Story." *Journal of Pragmatics* 6: 487-507.
Stein, Nancy, and Margaret Policastro. 1984. "The Concept of a Story. A Comparison between Teacher's and Children's Viewpoints." In *Learning and Comprehension of Text*, ed. Heinz Mandl—Nancy Stein, 113-155. Hillsdale, NJ: Lawrence Erlbaum Associates.

TRUTH IS STRONGER THAN FICTION.
ON ALETHIC PLURALISM AND TRUTH IN FICTION

Fredrik Stjernberg

ABSTRACT: According to alethic pluralism, truth can be many things that need not have one thing in common. Then we are perhaps free to say that fictional discourse is *true*, yet not be compelled to resort to Meinongian entities to explain these truths. This leads to a particular problem for the pluralist: Is there a principled way to hold onto the idea that *some* areas of discourse still are not suitable to be described in terms of truth? Take fiction as an example. If truth can be many things, would it not then simply be perfectly in order to add that fictional statements, for instance about Sherlock Holmes, can be true as well? My question is whether there is anything the pluralist can appeal to if she wants to draw the line somewhere. The monist about truth has it much easier: the monist can simply say that for instance fictional discourse is not truth-apt, since there are no fictional facts corresponding with the fictional statements, and that fictional discourse therefore fails to present truths. Is the alethic pluralist automatically forced to become very liberal, accepting that anything anyone calls "truth-apt" is in fact truth-apt, or is there some way to say that there are limits to truth-aptness without reverting to a monist position (perhaps being a "closet monist")?

> Truth is stranger than fiction, but it is because Fiction is obliged to stick to possibilities; Truth isn't.
>
> Mark Twain

Introduction

Truth may well be stranger than fiction, but I am here interested in a slightly different issue: is truth also *stronger* than fiction? By this question I mean whether claims about truth contain something above and beyond claims made in fictional contexts. In fictional contexts, we find that we are uttering sentences that on the face of it look like truth-stating sentences, and on the face of it commit us to things like Sherlock Holmes or Griffindor. But we also have strong intuitions pulling us in the other direction: Sherlock Holmes *doesn't* exist, Sherlock sentences are not true. Given this predicament, we seem to have three choices: explain away our apparent commitment to the existence of Sherlock Holmes; avoid the problematic vocabulary; acknowledge the commitment and introduce a new kind of being, fictional entities, as for instance Meinong did. Even though there are varieties of these strategies, they seem to exhaust the options. This kind of situation is not unique to fictional entities, but is to be found in other problematic cases as well. Quine found the apparent reference to abstract objects problematic from a generally physicalist point of view, but he accepted the existence of sets, because they had clear criteria of identity and were indispensable for mathematics, which in turn is indispensable for science. We can see some variations in the strategies. Paraphrases for explaining away the apparent commitment to the existence of Sherlock Holmes can take many different forms. The acceptance of the problematic entities can be more or less grudging. There is a connection here with truth. When reacting to the problematic sentences, we can paraphrase the sentence into something that is unproblematically true; say that the sentences really are false, as in error theories of ethics or mathematics; or accept the truth of the sentences and try to arrive at a suitable understanding of their truth.

There are many discussions of truth in fiction. What could it mean to say that a given fictional statement, such as "Sherlock Holmes is clever", is true? Some such statements may well be easy to accept, as when a Sherlock Holmes story states that London is the capital of Great Britain, or that London is foggy. But other cases are harder. Is it true to say that Sherlock Holmes was a good detective, or that he lived on Baker St 221B? No count of persons living in London at that times would have included Sherlock, and the address apparently never existed. So we would feel that some statements presented in the Sherlock stories are false, yet presented as true in the fictional setting of the story. It might then be tempting to think that if they are to be counted as true at all, Sherlock Holmes truths are truths *within the fictional setting* provided by the Holmes Canon.[1] But this suggestion doesn't seem to work too well without further supplementation. We can say things about Sherlock Holmes outside of the fictional setting, and some such things can very well strike us as being true: Sherlock Holmes is better known than Aurelio Zen, and perhaps Sherlock is Obama's favourite fictional character. Sherlock Holmes is perhaps the best known fictional detective of all. So appeals to truth *within* a fiction are at best part of a response to questions about truth in fiction. But denying that the Holmes statements can be true, or saying that all are false, seems problematic as well. Not all Holmes statements are in complete error, or they at least don't display the same kind of error.

Even if we don't think that Sherlock statements within the fiction are candidates for being true at all, it is clear that some statements about the Sherlock we find in the fictions are *better off* than others, in some sense of "better off" yet to be explained. Saying that Sherlock was a clever detective is better off than saying that Sherlock was a cross-dressing helicopter pilot, or a suburb of Prague. But what is "better off" here? If it is not the usual straightforward *true*, what is it then? Different attempts

---

[1] Walton (1991) is one example of this strategy.

have been made many times before to make sense of how we can manage to say something true in a fiction.[2]

In this paper, I will be considering another variation of this, by assessing what impact alethic pluralism might have on the special problem of truth in fiction. The alethic pluralist can be seen as attempting to liberalise the talk of truth in different settings, by accepting that truth can be many things. If there is room for letting truth be many different things, there may perhaps be room for saying that fictional statements can be true as well, without having to provide fictional objects or facts to make the fictional statements true. Perhaps truth in fiction works in some different way.

Before we look at what the alethic pluralist is saying, we shall consider a few examples where the appeal to truth is debated. In the following sections, I will briefly describe the alethic pluralist's position and argue that it can be used to provide a setting for truth in fiction. There is a price for doing this, however, in that this kind of move can turn out to be too liberal: if we start accepting truth in a fiction, is it not the case that anything goes? There is something to this worry, but I will argue that there are some means for the alethic pluralist to hold on to a substantial core notion of truth, so that it is not the case that everything goes. Truth in fiction is just one kind of case where greater conceptual pressure is being put on the notion of truth, and if we start our grasp on the notion of truth with simple empirical cases, this will not fully determine what we should be doing about truth in fiction. So questions about truth in fiction (and other more problematic cases, such as morals, mathematics, and other debated cases) are more a matter of

---

[2] Walton (1990) and van Inwagen (1977) are but two in a large set of references. There are far-reaching differences between these views, and Friend (2007) gives a useful overview.

deciding how we should handle truth in the area than *discovering* that this or that area "really" has such and such a character.

Alethic pluralism

The alethic pluralist thinks that truth may be many different things, depending on what kind of things we are talking about:

> The proposal is simply that any predicate that exhibits certain very general features qualifies, just on that account, as a truth predicate. That is quite consistent with acknowledging that there may, perhaps must be more to say about the content of any predicate that does have these features. But it also consistent with acknowledging that there is a prospect of pluralism — that the more there is to say may well vary from discourse to discourse. (Wright 1992: 38)

The usual arguments for alethic pluralism are taken from the poverty of a single theory of truth — correspondence theories don't work very well in some areas, even if they appear to be suitable for empirical statements about matters of fact. The notion of a fact is in itself hard to explicate further without making tacit use of the concept of truth, or of a true sentence, and in that case, we have not given enough explication of truth by appeals to correspondence and to facts. The different cases where we feel inclined to talk about truth are of a wide variety, and no existing theory of truth seems to be well equipped to cover all these cases in a uniform and useful manner.

It is hard to come up with a useful understanding of facts or correspondence that can do work for conceptual truths, or for moral or aesthetic truths, if we think that there are such truths. This is to be explained by saying that truth in the moral case doesn't require facts of the kind that truth in the empirical case requires — perhaps truth in the case of moral or conceptual truths is a matter to be settled by coherence. In this way, the temptation to opt for an error theory for a given discourse is reduced: Mackie's error theory for moral (Mackie 1977) goes from arguing that moral facts — whatever they might turn out to be — are "queer", and cannot be among the furniture of the universe. And as long as we accept some kind of correspondence view of truth, moral truths will require the existence of truthmaking moral facts. Field's case against mathematics (Field 1979) has a similar rationale: if mathematical truths require mathematical facts, and there is no way to account for mathematical facts within a physicalist setting, this spells trouble for thinking that there are arithmetical truths. But if the correspondence view of truth is given up in the mathematical and moral cases, the alleged queerness of mathematical or moral facts may not be too much of a problem: after all, no facts of that kind are invoked to explain truths in that area.

It would at least be worth examining whether something similar can be argued for the case of fiction as well. If we think that there are no fictional facts or entities (which, given the by now well-rehearsed problems with such things, seems reasonable), then there could still be fictional truths, as long as we provide an explanation of the nature of such truths. We could as a tentative starting point think that a kind of coherence theory would serve the case for fictional truth better, and think that it is true that Sherlock Holmes is a detective, because that is what coheres best with the Holmes stories. Nowhere are helicopters to be found in those stories, so we can therefore feel safe in saying that claims about Holmes being a helicopter pilot are *false*.[3]

---

[3] I am not necessarily endorsing here the idea that we have to accept a coherence theory of truth for fictional truths; it is intended merely as an example.

This liberalizing of truth for the service of truth in fiction does not by itself mean that we are free to set up any new kind of truth we may want to, new kinds of truth for new specific areas of discourse. That would leave the road open to "truth in the lying sense" and other creatures of darkness. The various notions of truth are to be held together by an assortment of "certain very general features", to use Wright's description.

These very general features would comprise various platitudes, or truisms, concerning truth, as for instance some version of the disquotational schema "p" is true iff p (with suitable restrictions to avoid paradoxical results). Other examples include thinking that true beliefs are a worthwhile goal of inquiry.[4]

But such platitudes concerning truth will not settle once and for all whether a given use of "true" is in order or not. Given a set of alleged platitudes about truth, there will be space for disagreement about the centrality of the truisms. Such disagreements arise when the truisms are put under pressure, as for instance when there is disagreement about how Liar sentences are to be handled.

One useful definition of a paradox is Sainsbury's in *Paradoxes*:

> This is what I understand by a paradox: an apparently unacceptable conclusion derived by apparently acceptable reasoning from apparently acceptable premises. Appearances have to deceive, since the acceptable cannot lead by acceptable steps to the unacceptable. So, generally, we have a choice: either the conclusion is not really

---

[4] Lynch (2009: ch. 1) presents a list of such truisms about truth, singling out a privileged group, the *core truisms* (Lynch 2009: 13ff), as especially central for the notion of truth. Some claims are more peripheral to the nature of truth than others. That it is difficult to arrive at the truth about a given subject may be correct, but that is not an instance of a core truism.

unacceptable, or else the starting point, or the reasoning, has some non-obvious flaw. (Sainsbury 1995: 1)

A paradox will thus leave us with a few options. When confronting Liar sentences, we can for instance choose to accept the conclusion (the dialetheist view, that there are some true conclusions) or revise the logic used in deriving Liar sentences. But it is by no means clear which of these options best covers what truth "really" is, or even if there is any such option at all.[5] Something similar can happen for the case of fiction as well. When considering questions about truth in fiction, we can get into similar discussions: are there differences in our understanding of the truisms of truth that leave room for differences in accepting the idea that at least some fictional statements can be true? If we had a very clear grip on what is entailed by our understanding of truth, it would perhaps be more straightforward to answer this question, but it turns out that it is surprisingly hard to pin down how we think about truth even in more everyday cases.

The next section will highlight a few cases where the use of "true" can lead us into problems. The cases are not as clearly difficult as Liar sentences, but they will put pressure on our understanding of what is involved in saying that a given sentence is true. In these cases, the truisms don't really seem to capture what we may think of as difficult in judging the cases at hand.

---

[5] Beall (2009) and Field (2009) differ on how the Liar is to be handled, and one specific issue is, which of the preferred options causes the least amount of damage to our concept of truth.

Fredrik Stjernberg

A few different cases
Literal truth can be compared with the vague notion of a statement being "better off" than another in other areas than fiction. We can consider a few examples, including a few not from fiction, showing how our reactions to the supposedly literal truth of various statements can differ:

1. A very fat man goes to the doctor. The doctor examines him and says: "You shouldn't eat between meals."
2. The sun rises.
3. Tomatoes are red.
4. It is (morally) wrong to torture small children as entertainment.
5. There are at least seven primes between 5 and 100.
6. Sherlock Holmes is clever.
7. Rubber is harder than diamonds.
8. Elton John is a faggot.

Many of the above statements can occur in ordinary circumstances, though (7) is usually seen as false, and (8) is best avoided. They pose different problems, centred on the notion of truth. The cases (2)–(6) have in common that it is easy to find people, including philosophers, who think the statements are true, yet it is also easy to find people, including philosophers, who give various arguments why such sentences are not true. But even if they are not held to be true, or even truth-apt, most would agree that they, given some dimension of assessment for the sentence, are in order. The denial of (4) is for instance at best silly, even if there can be philosophical reasons for denying that (4) expresses a *truth*. Even if we are undecided about the truth of the colour of tomatoes, saying that they are red is much better than saying that they are blue. Calling Sherlock stupid misses the point of the Sherlock stories. Saying that there are exactly two primes between 5 and 100 is much worse than (5) — even if we are undecided about the truth-aptness of (5).

The first case is probably very common, something that happens in doctors' examining rooms every day, but for once, something odd happens. The fat man protests, and says "I can't stop eating between meals! Every meal I take, apart from my very last, takes place between some other meals. My breakfast this morning came between my dinner last night and my lunch today. Not eating between meals means not eating, *period*. Are you trying to kill me?" Still, the doctor's advice appears to be pretty good — if taken in the right way.

As for (2), we don't think that the sun literally rises, but we are usually in agreement that this kind of statement, although literally false, manages to get some things right at times, so it is OK to speak like this in the morning, wrong to say such things in the afternoon and evening. Many will say that it is true in the morning, false in the evening, to say that the sun rises, although we all at some level know that the sun does no such thing at all, so strictly speaking it is always false.

Saying that ripe tomatoes are red is usually acceptable, it is for instance better than saying that they are green, yellow, or blue. Many philosophers and scientists, however, hold onto an error-theory of colour — *all* colour statements are false. In that case, it is simply false to say that ripe tomatoes are red, and hence not really much better than saying that they are blue. A pregnant formulation of this view is for instance:

> [W]hen someone calls something red, in an everyday context, he is asserting a falsehood. Indeed, our account of colour experience, when joined with the plausible hypothesis that colour discourse reports the contents of colour experience, yields the consequence that all statements attributing colours to external objects are false.

> One would be justified in wondering how we can accept this consequence, for two related reasons. First, we will clearly want to retain a distinction between "correct" and "incorrect" colour judgements, distinguishing between the judegement that a fire-hydrant is blue and the judgement that it is red. And it seems a serious question what point we error-theorists could see in such a distinction. Second, it seems perfectly obvious that colour discourse will continue to play an indispensable role in our everyday cognitive transactions. Yet how are we error theorists to explain this indispensability, consistently with our claim that the discourse in question is consistently false? (Boghossian and Velleman 1989/2008: 311)

This quotation presents a very close analogue to our question: even if we don't want to say that fictional statements are true, what are we to do about "correct" and "incorrect" statements? Boghossian and Velleman's second reason—the indispensability of colour talk—doesn't carry over as smoothly to the question about fiction, but different arguments have been proffered for the claim that the use of fiction is indispensable for acquiring certain cognitive skills.[6] Boghossian and Velleman try to handle the problem of "correct" and "incorrect" colour talk by referring to "harmless falsehoods", using (2) above as an example:

> Consider one of the many harmless falsehoods that we tolerate in everyday discourse: the statement that the sun rises. When someone says that the sun rises, his remark has the same content as the visual experience that one has when watching the horizon at an appropriately early hour. That is, the sun actually looks like it is

---

[6] Williams (1993) presents one kind of case for such a claim, Boyd (2010) another. Yet another kind of argument can be made by holding that our ability to reason counterfactually—an indispensable cognitive skill—is essentially intertwined with our ability to use fictional statements in an intelligent way.

moving, and that the sun moves in this manner is what most people mean when talking about sunrise. So interpreted, of course, talk about sunrise is systematically false. When someone says that the sun rises, he is wrong; and he usually knows that he is wrong, but he says it anyway. Why? When one understands that talk about sunrise is false, one also understands that its falsity makes no difference in everyday life. We do not mean that nothing in everyday life would, in fact, be different if the sun revolved around the earth, as it seems to. ... Talking about horizon-fall rather than sunrise would thus be downright misleading, even though it would be more truthful. Only an undue fascination with the truth could lead someone to reform ordinary discourse about the sun. Talk about colours is just like talk about sunrise in these respects. (Boghossian and Velleman 1989/2008: 311–12)

Given this diagnosis, (1) and (2) might seem similar: only an "undue fascination with the truth" could make someone discard the doctor's advice. But there can be differences. A natural reaction to (1), when confronted with the fat man's reaction, would be to say that the fat man *misunderstood* the doctor's advice, not that the doctor uttered a harmless falsehood. What is said in the doctor's room is something completely in order, and not a "harmless falsehood", at least if taken in the right way.

Moral statements, to give another kind of example, have been given all kinds of statuses, including true. People like Field deny that there are numbers, and such a denial makes (5) false (Field 1979). The different Sherlock Holms examples are cases where we appear to be referring to fictional entities, and such cases present various problems. It is natural to say that (6) is to be analyzed in the same way as a more pedestrian statement, such as "Barack Obama is clever". The latter sentence is clever because someone, Barack Obama, is clever. Proceeding from this cue, we find ourselves bound to say that (6) is true because someone, Sherlock Holmes, is clever. But how are we to find Sherlock? If we explain the truth of (6) in the same way as we explain the sentence about Obama's cleverness, we find that Sherlock had better exist. But many disagree here, wanting to give completely different analyses of (6). There are several suggestions. One is that there is an implicit operator, *According to a story...*, which should be prefixed to all fictional statements, and since there are stories depicting Holmes as clever, (6) comes out as unproblematically true.[7] Another idea is to say that Holmes is *created* by the telling of the fiction.[8]

The statement about rubber and diamonds, (7), is usually held to be unproblematically false. There are, however, cases in engineering where (7) is seen as unproblematically *true*. This is because the meaning of "hard" is not completely settled by our everyday understanding of the term (probably tied with how something feels to the touch), and the more sophisticated uses of the term, developed for engineering purposes, in certain cases will make it natural to say that rubber is harder than diamonds (for certain purposes, hardness is a matter of retaining the original shape after a shock, and rubber is harder in that specific way, since once a diamond is broken, it will never get back to its original shape) (Wilson 2006: 335ff). So in some areas, the meaning of "hard" is not sufficiently settled to make our ordinary judgements of hardness a meaningful measuring rod, but the new, more specific, meaning will retain enough of the original meaning to make it useful *for the practitioners* to think of the word as still expressing the original concept. *The Metals Handbook* of the American Society for Metals tells us the following about hardness:

---

[7] Walton (1990) would be one inspiration for such accounts.
[8] van Inwagen (1977) would be one example of this strategy.

> The definition of hardness varies depending upon the experience or background of the person conducting the test or interpreting the data. To the metallurgist, hardness is the resistance to indentation; to the design engineer, a measure of flow stress; to the lubrication engineer, the resistance to wear; to the mineralogist, the resistance to scratching; and to the machinist, the resistance to cutting. (*Metals Handbook*, 9th ed., quoted from Wilson 2006: 337)

There will be a significant overlap between these different ways of judging hardness (otherwise, talk of hardness would probably have fallen by the wayside), but the cases can come apart at times. In certain cases, the demands for judging hardness are systematically different from our everyday ways of judging hardness, and we should be careful in assuming that our everyday grasp of the notion of hardness will settle the more sophisticated cases.

Discussion of cases like (8) has been very extensive lately, and I will not enter into that debate here (Richard 2008; Predelli 2010). The example has been included simply to highlight that the question whether that sentence is true or not concerns only one of the possible dimensions used for assessing the sentence.

So the numbered cases present us with a widely differing assortment of cases where judgements about the truth of the statement are problematic. Just claiming that a given statement is true, or that it is not true, or even not a statement of the kind that aspires to being true, doesn't tell us all that much. We should at least not expect that one and the same view of what it means to say that something is true, false or meaningful will settle all the above cases in a single way. Different diagnoses will work for different cases.

An idea, which has gained some currency lately, is to take a closer look at the notion of truth involved in different cases.[9] The alethic pluralist says that truth can come in many varieties: there is not just one notion of truth that fits all the cases where we talk of a statement being true. This idea can appear to be well suited to aid us in understanding what is going on in the numbered cases. One lesson from the above cases is that the contrast we want to make between *true* on the one hand, and *useful/suitable/etc* on the other, can be made in different ways in different cases. Taking a stand on the truth-aptness of (3) won't tell us all that much about the truth-aptness of other cases. The discussions vary, and the diagnoses will also vary accordingly. The idea that what it is to be true also can vary is perhaps a promising move.

But before we move on to considering alethic pluralism, let me just say a few things about another influential conception of truth, the deflationist view.[10] The deflationist says that truth has no underlying nature, and that it is a tool for semantic ascent: to say that "*p*" is true is not to do anything above and beyond saying that *p*. Truth is a device that makes it possible to talk about sentences in a way that is not possible without the extra machinery provided by talk of truth. Truth talk makes it possible to talk about large groups of sentences in an ordered way: "Everything Carl said yesterday was true" stands in for

---

[9] Talk of a "notion of truth" is not quite precise, but in this usage I am following Richards (2008: 104ff). Certain terms — like "true" — can be used in widely different contexts. The notion of truth is something common to these different uses, making it possible for us to say that the word has the same meaning in these various contexts. A notion can be an assortment of truisms concerning truth. Richards: "What is common to different uses of 'true' is (something like) accepting the claims that it is true that snow is white iff snow is white, ... and so on" (Richards 2008: 104ff).

[10] As presented in e.g. Horwich (1990).

Truth is Stranger than Fiction

"If Carl said that the Earth is round, then the Earth is round, and if Carl said that Prague is in Europe, then Prague is in Europe, and if ...", making for much simpler expressions, but not adding anything of substance. It would also help us to understand logical rules, as when we say "All sentences of the form *p or not p* are true", but, again, no substantial property is connected with truth. Truth is a device for disquotation and nothing more.

Deflationist views of truth don't help us much here. They may have their strengths, but they don't show us why there would be a *point* in talking about truth in the various cases above. If talk of truth is just a shorthand marker, then such discussions are inexplicable—what are the parties disagreeing about, when they are disagreeing whether a given statement qualifies as true or not? If the deflationist thinks that the *only* reason for talk of truth is to facilitate talk about properties of groups of sentences, the issues concerning the numbered sentences are inexplicable. The deflationist will typically deny that truth has any explanatory role to play, and the discussions about the numbered sentences above were all at least framed as if there was some important difference resting on whether we should think of the sentence in question as true or not. So the main option for the deflationist would be that there is nothing substantial being discussed in the allegedly problematic cases. Perhaps no one will treat *all* the above sentences in the same manner, or think that there is a live issue concerning the truth or truth-aptness of all of them, but some instances will remain. And in the face of one such instance, the question of the truth and truth-aptness of the sentence will be held to depend on something beyond the pure deflationary schema. The different positions concerning whether it is true, false, or senseless to say that the sun rises are not handled by just invoking a deflationist view of truth.

Truth in fiction
Questions concerning truth in fiction have now taken on a more complex character, as in fact all cases where we are interested in the truth-aptness of a given area of discourse. It has turned out to be trickier than we thought to give a clear demarcation between truth-apt sentences and those that are not truth-apt. We may perhaps try to appeal to a distinction between literal and the figurative uses of language: it is only figuratively that "The sun rises" is true, though it is literally false. The fat man is only given figurative advice, not to be taken literally.

The division between the literal and figurative uses of language is not as clear as we might have wished. Whether a given sentence is literally or figuratively true, or even truth-apt, is more something we have to decide than something we discover. In view of this, our judgements concerning truth in fiction are not especially secure. Appeals to a unexplained literal-figurative distinction don't work too well in the Sherlock Holmes case: we are not saying figuratively that Sherlock is a detective; the intention would instead be to say something that is as literal as you wish. Saying figuratively that someone is a detective is perhaps saying that this person is good at figuring out things about people. For many, Sherlock Holmes stands out as a paradigmatic example of a good detective, not as someone who does things that in some way are *like* the things that detectives do.

So the distinction literal/figurative is not only insufficiently explained, it seems that it in any case is the wrong kind of distinction to make full use of in handling problems about truth in fiction.

Truth is Stranger than Fiction

Can we instead get a good explanation of truth in fiction by looking at our starting truisms about truth, and working our way from there? A fuller discussion of this issue is best left for another occasion, but there are a few things to be said here. If we try to delimit the notion of truth through appeal to a set of truisms concerning truth, there will always be room for disagreement about tricky cases, and issues concerning truth in fiction are among these. The situation is in many ways similar to that which obtained in the case of hardness above. We have a good enough grasp of what hardness is from everyday cases, just as we have a good enough grasp of which sentences are truth-apt, and what truth amounts to, from everyday cases. It is likely that this starting point for judging truth and truth-aptness is some kind of correspondence intuition, just as the starting point for judging hardness was probably connected to touching things and trying to deform them, noting how much they resisted our touch. But this kind of command of the simple cases will not tell us enough about the difficult cases, and cases of alleged truth in fiction put more strain on our everyday conception of truth. Simple intuitions will not suffice to settle questions about the truth of Sherlock sentences, and the more complex task of judging truth-aptness of these sentences will leave room for different judgements, without it being settled beforehand how we should judge them.

But the room for maneouver is limited here. Not anything goes. The starting truisms about truth provide an anchor for further explorations of the tricky cases. But one person's truisms need not coincide completely with another person's. Some will think that *p is true iff p corresponds with a fact* is one of the truisms of truth, while someone else will stress the law of non-contradiction instead. The dialetheist is prepared to give up the law of non-contradiction is particular cases, and many will be ready to give up the correspondence intuition. The perhaps most basic truism about truth—*"p" is true iff p*—is not sufficient to settle all the cases where people have different views about the truth-aptness of a given sentence. Saying that "Sherlock Holmes is clever" is true iff Sherlock Holmes is clever doesn't tell us enough to settle the questions we may have about the truth-aptness of that sentence, and it will not tell us whether there has to be a fictional Sherlock, or facts about Sherlock Holmes for the sentence to come out as true.

The anchor provided by the starting truisms will serve to settle some issues—no one will be expected to agree that "Sherlock Holmes is clever" is true iff Sherlock Holmes is not clever.

Conclusion: closet monism?
Does all this amount to a kind of "closet monism"? After all, it may seem that we have completed a full circle. The first issue, concerning truth in fiction, was supposed to have been handled by appealing to the idea that truth could be many different things, depending on context and on what kind of discourse we are looking at. This seemed particularly promising for the case of fiction, since some of our ordinary views about truth don't seem to be very well adapted to saying something about whether a given Sherlock Holmes statement should be seen as true or not. A kind of fictionalism regarding fictional talk was the result. This does not amount to downplaying the importance of truth; it just highlights how the very division between literal and other uses of language can quickly become complicated.

Then this opening up of the notion of truth was in danger of reverting to a kind of monism, since we wanted to still be able to say that *some* statements were not true. We couldn't liberalize the notion of truth to an extent that made every statement potentially true in some sense of true—that would make the whole notion of truth pointless. So we tried to anchor the use of the notion of truth in a few central truisms concerning truth. Would this then not mean that we were after all back where we started, with alethic monism, but without admitting it? No. These truisms are not sufficient to guarantee *one* notion of truth that is common to all the various cases in which appeal to a notion of truth is made. There is therefore still room for calling the resulting position an alethic pluralist view, since the truisms will leave it undecided how we should think of the truth-aptness of problematic sentences, like the ones numbered above.

Linköping University
fredrik.stjernberg@liu.se

REFERENCES

Beall, J. C. 2009. *Spandrels of Truth*. Oxford: Oxford University Press.
Boghossian, Paul, and James D. Velleman. 1989/2008. "Colour as a Secondary Quality." Originally in *Mind* 98 (389): 81–103. Reprinted in Boghossian, Paul. 2008. *Content and Justification*. Oxford: Oxford University Press. Page references to the reprinted version.
Boyd, Brian. 2010. *On the Origin of Stories: Evolution, Cognition, and Fiction*. Harvard: Harvard University Press.
Currie, Gregory. 1990. *The Nature of Fiction*. New York: Cambridge University Press.
Field, Hartry. 1979. *Science without Numbers*. Oxford: Oxford University Press.
– – –. 2009. *Saving Truth from Paradox*. Oxford: Oxford University Press.
Friend, Stacie. 2007. "Fictional Characters." *Philosophy Compass* 2 (2): 141–156.
Horwich, Paul. 1990. *Truth*. Oxford: Oxford University Press.

van Inwagen, Peter. 1977. "Creatures of Fiction." *American Philosophical Quarterly* 14 (4): 299–308.

Lamarque, Peter. 2003. "How to Create a Fictional Character." In *The Creation of Art: New Essays in Philosophical Aesthetics*, ed. Berys Gaut—Paisley Livingston, 33–52. Cambridge: Cambridge University Press.

Lamarque, Peter, and Stein Haugom Olsen. 1994. *Truth, Fiction, and Literature: A Philosophical Perspective*. Oxford: Clarendon Press.

Lynch, Michael P. 2009. *Truth as One and Many*. Oxford: Oxford University Press.

Mackie, John L. 1977. *Ethics: Inventing Right and Wrong*. Harmondsworth: Penguin.

Predelli, Stefan. 2010. "From the Expressive to the Derogatory: On the Semantic Role for Non-Truth Conditional Meaning." In *New Waves in Philosophy of Language*, ed. Sarah Sawyer. Basingstoke: Palgrave MacMillan.

Sainsbury, R. M. 2000. "Semantic Pretense." In *Empty Names, Fiction and the Puzzles of Non-Existence*, ed. Anthony Everett—Thomas Hofweber, 205–32. Stanford: CSLI Publications.

– – –. 2008. *When Truth Gives Out*. Oxford: Oxford University Press.

Thomasson, Amie. 1999. *Fiction and Metaphysics*. Cambridge: Cambridge University Press.

– – –. 2003. "Speaking of Fictional Characters." *Dialectica* 57 (2): 205–23.

Walton, Kendall. 1990. *Mimesis as Make-Believe: On the Foundations of the Representational Arts*. Cambridge, MA: Harvard University Press.

Williams, Bernard. 1993. *Shame and Necessity*. Berkeley—Los Angeles: University of California Press.

Wilson, Mark. 2006. *Wandering Significance. An Essay on Conceptual Behavior*. Oxford: Oxford Univeristy Press.

Wolterstorff, Nicholas. 1980. *Works and Worlds of Art*. Oxford: Clarendon Press.

Wright, Crispin. 1992. *Truth and Objectivity*. Cambridge, MA: Harvard University Press.

Fictionality, Fictive Utterance, and the Assertive Author

David Davies

ABSTRACT: Fictive utterance theories of fictionality hold that a text that includes a narrative is the vehicle for a fiction only if it is the product of an act of fictive utterance, a kind of speech act that invites the receiver to make-believe rather than believe what is narrated. I briefly outline and motivate a version of the fictive utterance theory that I have defended elsewhere according to which the further requirememt for fictionality is that primary constraint on the construction of the narrative not be what I have termed the "fidelity constraint". Critics, however, have charged that fictive utterance theories cannot account for the place of *non-fictive* utterances in the generation of fictional works. I argue that such objections can be countered if we do two things. First, we must take proper account of the way in which fictional narratives in general are supposed to work. I argue here that we need to take account of the distinct attitudes prescribed by the author of a fictional narrative to the *setting* of a fiction and to its *fictive content*. This also allows us to clarify the scope of the non-fidelity condition on fictionality. Second, we must respect the distinction between (a) considerations bearing upon the fictionality of a *narrative*, and (b) considerations bearing upon the fictionality of a *work*. Fictive utterance theorists are properly read as concerned with the former, but their critics argue — rightly — that fictive utterance cannot be sufficient for the latter.

I/ The view defended in Aesthetics and Literature

Fictive utterance theories of fictionality standardly hold that a text that comprises a narrative is the vehicle for a fiction only if it is the product of an act of fictive utterance. Fictive utterance is a kind of speech act to be understood in broadly Gricean terms, requiring that the utterer of a text have a complex set of nested intentions bearing upon the intended effect of the text on intended receivers. But fictive utterance, while it structurally resembles assertion, differs in that the attitude prescribed is not belief but pretence or make-believe or imagining (I shall for the purposes of this paper treat these notions as interchangeable).

Fictive utterance theorists like Currie (1990), Lamarque and Olsen (1994), and myself (2001; 2007) have maintained that fictive utterance is necessary to produce a fiction, but have also held that it is not sufficient. There is disagreement, however, as to the further condition that must be satisfied if an act of fictive utterance is to produce a fiction. Currie, for example, maintains that, if the receiver is asked to imagine something that is actually true, it must be only accidentally true. I have argued for what I take to be a more fundamental requirement that underlies Currie's proposal — that, while an author *may* include things she knows or believes to be true in a fictional narrative, her overriding motivation in constructing the narrative must be some story-telling objective other than the desire to relate what is true.

Since I want to defend what I hope is a more subtle version of my earlier view, let me briefly spell out both the motivation behind and the details of this view. I have argued that, in addition to being the product of an act of fictive utterance, what is required for the fictionality of a narrative is that, whether or not, for a given a narrated event p, it is true that p, or known or believed to be true that p, what the author A wishes to achieve in having readers make-believe that p does not *depend upon its being true that p*. Its being (believed to be) true that p is not the reason for p's inclusion in the narrative. This is a claim about the constraints under which narrative construction takes place in acts of fiction-making. These constraints are reflected in the ways in which reading a text as fiction differs from reading it as non-fiction. As a reader of a narrative, I posit a writing process in which certain events are chosen and ordered by an author for some purpose. As a critical reader, I ask, "why I am being told about *these* events in *this* order?" To read a narrative as non-fiction is to assume that the selection and temporal ordering of *all* the events making up the narrative was constrained by a commitment, on the narrator's part, to be faithful to the manner in which actual events transpired. We assume that the author has included only events she believes to have occurred, narrated as occurring in the order in which she believes them to have occurred.[1] We may term this the "fidelity constraint".

To read a narrative as fiction, on the other hand, is to assume that the choices made in generating the narrative were not governed in the first instance by this constraint, but by some more general purpose in story-telling, such as entertaining the reader. If considerations of fidelity are taken to enter into the construction of a fictional narrative—where, for example, an author wants to set the narrative in London during the Blitz—we assume that this consideration is subordinated to the more general purpose. My claim, therefore, has been that the fictionality of a narrative generated with the intention that receivers make-believe the narrated events depends neither on (a) whether the narrated events correspond to some actual sequence of events, nor on (b) whether the author of the text knew of, or was unconsciously guided by, the actual sequence

---

[1] This is not to say that the order of the narrative must inflexibly follow the believed order of the narrated events—flash-back and flash-forward must obviously be permitted in a non-fictional narrative. What is required is that the author of a non-fictional narrative be constrained by the requirement that the narrated events be *represented as occurring* in the order in which the author believes them to have actually occurred.

of events in question. It depends, rather, on (c) what constraints were taken, by the author, as the ones that the selection and ordering of events in the narrative must satisfy. This allows an author to select, as the narrative content of a fiction, a sequence of events she knows or believes to have actually occurred, as long as it is the satisfaction of some other constraint by this sequence of events that governs her choice. To summarize: I have argued that an utterance of a text comprising a narrative produces a fiction iff 1) it is a fictive utterance—term this the "fictive utterance" condition; and 2) the overriding constraint on the construction of the narrative is not the fidelity constraint—term this the "non-fidelity" condition.

One should always eye conjunctive analyses of this sort with a measure of suspicion, however, since one might worry that the analysis is somewhat ad hoc, adding a second condition to try to plug the holes in the first. Could we, perhaps, get by with a single criterion of fictionality, either by taking fictive intent to be both necessary and sufficient for something to be fiction, or by taking it to be both necessary and sufficient for fictionality that the construction of a narrative not be guided by the fidelity constraint? Kathleen Stock is working on the first kind of proposal, and Harry Deutsch can be seen as offering a version of the second. In section 2, I shall offer some brief suggestions as to why I think that fictive utterance by itself cannot be sufficient for the fictionality of a narrative, and I shall comment at greater length on Deutsch's suggestion. But a more serious source of resistance to fictive utterance theories of fictionality is that they cannot account for the place of *non-fictive* utterances in the generation of fictional works. This concern has been raised in particular by John Gibson (2007: ch. 5) and Stacie Friend (2008) and, in some unpublished work, by Kathleen Stock, and it will be the focus of the bulk of my paper.

Fictionality, Fictive Utterance, and the Assertive Author

Gibson, Friend, and Stock stress different ways in which the author of a fictional work must be seen as asserting at least some of the things explicitly comprised by her text, and thus, it would seem, as intending that the receiver believe, rather than (or in addition to) make-believe, such things. Friend also argues that fictive utterance is widely employed in works of non-fiction, further undermining the idea that fictive utterance is at the core of fictionality. The objection to fictive utterance theories, then, is that, while works of fiction may indeed call for readers to imagine certain things, (a) this is also the case for works of non-fiction, and (b) authors of works of fiction, in intending that readers believe certain things they place in those works, are to that extent engaging in assertion rather than fictive utterance.

I want to argue for two related claims. First, I think fictive utterance theorists are right in thinking that fictive utterance is a necessary but not a sufficient condition for the fictionality of a narrative. I also continue to think that the right way to cash out the further requirement for fictionality is in terms of constraints operating upon the process whereby a narrative is constructed, although this will call for more careful wording of the fictive utterance requirement itself. Second, I think that the objections presented to fictive utterance accounts only undermine infelicitous formulations — of which I myself have been guilty — that fail to take proper account of the way in which fictional narratives in general are supposed to work. Closer attention to the latter will allow us to specify more accurately how fictive utterance enters into the narrative process, and thereby to undercut the kinds of objections brought against fictive utterance theories in general.

But, in arguing for these two points, I think it is crucial to distinguish between (a) considerations that bear upon the fictionality of a *narrative*, and (b) considerations that bear upon the fictionality of a *work*. In my earlier treatments of these issues I failed to clearly make such a distinction and, as a result, failed to properly integrate my account of fictionality (Davies 2007: ch. 3) with my account of the cognitive values of fiction (Davies 2007: ch. 8). In this paper, I shall restrict myself to questions about the fictionality of narratives, postponing to another occasion questions about the fictionality of works.

II/ Do we need a conjunctive analysis of fictionality?
I have proposed two conditions that are individually necessary and jointly sufficient for the fictionality of a narrative—the "fictive utterance" condition and the "non-fidelity" condition. To motivate such a conjunctive analysis of fictionality, we must consider why neither condition taken by itself is sufficient. Consider first a narrative that satisfies the fictive utterance condition but not the non-fidelity condition. Suppose an author A at a time t generates a narrative N, where the construction of the narrative is governed by the fidelity constraint. A includes in the narrative only those events she believes to have actually occurred, narrates them as occurring in the order in which she believes them to have occurred, and takes this to be the overriding constraint on narrative construction. Suppose further that A's intention is that readers believe what is narrated. However, at $t+n$, having run out of traditional bedtime stories to read to her children, A decides to read them N, inviting them, as usual, to make believe the narrated events. In such a case, it seems appropriate to say that we have a non-fictional narrative that the audience is being asked to *treat* as if it were fictional. The narrative does not become fictional by being used, in this way, as a prop in a game of make-believe on a given occasion.

But now suppose that *A* generates *N* fully in accordance with the fidelity constraint *simultaneously* with her telling the story to her children with the intention that they make believe what is narrated. On this occasion, she meets the fictive utterance condition, and she no longer intends that her audience believes what she is narrating. But she brooks no departures from what the fidelity constraint demands in the interests of any more general story-telling motivations—she allows no alterations in the facts in the interests of entertaining her audience, for example. It seems, to me at least, that fictive utterance here is no more productive of a fictional narrative than in our earlier example where the acts of construction and of fictive utterance occur at different times. The reason for insisting on the non-fidelity condition is to reflect our strong intuition that, in some sense, the narrative content of a fictional narrative is determined by the creative decisions of the teller rather than by the dictates of the facts.

For some, it is the creative element in fiction that is its defining feature, to the exclusion of the need for fictive utterance. The most forthright presentation of such a view can be found in Harry Deutsch's defence (2000) of the idea that "a document or other form of communication is fiction if it is a token of a type that was made up out of whole cloth, perhaps with generous amounts of the fabric of fact woven in as well" (Deutsch 2000: 167). Where fact is woven into what is "made up out of whole cloth", this is because facts are themselves part of what Deutsch terms "the fictional plenitude" which he believes is what works of fiction describe. The fictional plenitude is defined by a logical comprehension principle. It contains "every sort of object and event imaginable, and then some" (Deutsch 2000: 155). According to Deutsch, it is because the author of a fiction is describing such a plenitude that she is immune from various kinds of error because *whatever* description she records will be equally correct.

Deutsch contrasts his account of fictionality with Currie's "fictive utterance" approach which, he claims, does not do justice to our sense of fiction as something that requires the creativity of the author in "making up" a story. He also claims that authors of fictions need not have fictive intent. He cites, in defence of this claim, Janet Cook's Pulitzer Prize winning articles on a purported child heroin addict, which were published as fact even though they were in fact made up. "Obviously," Deutsch maintains, "Janet Cook's articles were fiction, but she did not have 'fictive intent'" (Deutsch 2000: 170). Her articles are "obviously" fiction because "Janet Cook did everything a storyteller would do" (Deutsch 2000: 171) in making up various details of events and characters. In response to the objection that to try to get people to believe what you yourself take to be false is to lie rather than to produce a work of fiction, Deutsch maintains that Cook's lie is precisely to pass off what is fiction (i.e. what is made up) as if it were fact.

Deutsch's paper is puzzling, and it is easy to simply dismiss his claims—as some have done—as question-begging and inconsistent with our ordinary ways of classifying things as fictional or non-fictional. His claims seem to be question-begging since it is only if being made up is sufficient for being fictional that Cook's lie involves passing off fiction as fact, rather than merely passing off something made up as fact. And they seem to be inconsistent with normal ways of classifying things since, prior to encountering Deutsch's paper, I assume that few of us would have classified passing off what one believes to be false as if it were true as fiction-making. As Currie himself points out (Currie 1990: ch. 2), there is a long tradition according to which the producer of fiction does not lie.

Fictionality, Fictive Utterance, and the Assertive Author

But I think we can draw at least two valuable lessons from our brief consideration of Deutsch's paper. First, he is expressing, albeit in an overstated way, the intuition that a narrative's being fiction has *something* to do with its being "made up" or constructed by an author. But he is wrong in thinking this constructive dimension to our concept of fiction cannot be captured by the fictive utterance theorist. For this is precisely what the non-fidelity condition is intended to capture. Even if we allow that the events in a fictional narrative may not be "made up" in Deutsch's sense—they may be events that the author knows to have actually occurred—the fictionality of the narrative still requires that it result from the constructive activity of story-telling guided by constraints other than a desire to faithfully reflect the facts.

The second lesson we can glean from Deutsch's paper is that methodological difficulties confront us in our attempts to provide an account of fictionality. Deutsch takes it to be "obvious" that Cook's article is fiction, and we might ask where the burden of proof lies in such claims and the evidential force of an appeal to our contrary intuitions. This difficulty becomes even more acute when we consider the accountability of a proposed theory of fictionality to some of the more transgressive examples in recent narrative practice. Clifford Geertz coined the word "faction" to describe narratives whose departures from a concern with fidelity to what we believe to have occurred are motivated by a desire to more clearly "make out" reality, rather than to "make up" an alternative reality. At least some examples of what Capote called "the new journalism" seem to fit Geertz's description, and those writing on the nature of fictionality often try to hold theories of fiction accountable to such narratives. What is ironic is that we find the very same transgressive narratives cited in the literature as being clearly fictional and clearly non-fictional *works*! So John Gibson (2007: ch. 5) takes *In Cold Blood* to be a work of fiction, while Stacie Friend (2008) takes it to be a work of non-fiction that challenges fictive utterance theorists because it calls for make-believe!

III/ The problem of the assertive author

Critics of fictive utterance accounts of fictionality raise a number of issues relating to assertional roles that may be played by the author of a fictional narrative. One kind of authorial assertion relates to real world events incorporated into a fictional narrative — for example, the Napoleonic invasion of Russia which provides the historical background for Tolstoy's *War and Peace*, the German flying bomb attack on London which provides the background for the opening scenes in Pynchon's *Gravity's Rainbow*, and the geography of London which provides a framework for many of the Sherlock Holmes stories. A second kind of authorial assertion relates to more general truths or principles explicitly asserted within the text of a novel or implicitly endorsed, it would seem, by the general structure of the narrative. Much cited examples include the opening lines of Tolstoy's *Anna Karenina* and insights into human moral agency supposedly contained in works like Henry James' *The Golden Bowl*.[2]

A third difficulty is supposedly posed by the kinds of works of "biographical fiction" cited above, where the general aim is taken to be to tell the truth about certain events even though, in the narrative, certain of those events are creatively

---

[2] In an unpublished manuscript, Stock cites passages in *Vanity Fair* where the narrator's voice is taken to be a mouthpiece for the author's own beliefs.

reconceived or reordered for various kinds of literary effect.[3] Such works are taken to pose a problem for fictive utterance theories of fiction because, it is claimed, such theories provide us with no principled way of determining whether these *works* are fiction or non-fiction. We seem to finish up with what has been termed a "patchwork" theory that, even if it enables us to separate fictive and non-fictive utterances, leaves most works as "patchworks" with no clear principle to decide whether the work as a whole is fiction or non-fiction. As noted above, I shall restrict myself in the present context to the fictional narratives that a work, fictional or non-fictional, may comprise. But, as we shall see, critics of fictive utterance theories have tended to conflate issues about the fictionality of narratives and issues about the fictionality of works.

An example of this conflation is John Gibson's argument presented against fictive utterance theorists in his *Fiction and the Weave of Life* (2007). Gibson takes the issue about fictionality of concern to fictive utterance theorists to pertain to *fictional works* rather than to fictional narratives. He sets out to challenge the idea that make-believe is "the *basic* imaginative stance we take toward the content—*all of it*—of works of literary fiction" (Gibson 2007: 158) and that this is the stance that the work prescribes. It is crucial for the fictive-utterance theorist, he maintains, that make-believe is "a *comprehensive* attitude used to preface … our involvement with the entirety of novel" (Gibson 2007: 163). This is necessary if the fictive utterance theory is to be, as it claims, a theory of the stance we take towards fictional *works*. Otherwise, he claims,

---

[3] For example, Edmund Morris's *Dutch*; John Berendt's *Midnight in the Garden of Good and Evil*; Norman Mailer's *Armies of the Night*; Seamus Deane's *Reading in the Dark*; and Blake Morrison's *And When Did You Last See Your Father?*

> it would function only to explain our attitude towards those sentences occurring in literary works that are not true of the world, thus leaving the many accurate geographical, historical, psychological (and so on) descriptions we find in literary works unaccounted for. Since virtually every work of literature has many such descriptions, this would amount to a failure to offer a theory of what it means for something to be a work of fiction and instead reveal itself to be just a theory of fictional sentences. (Gibson 2007: 163)

The problem with the fictive utterance theory, according to Gibson, lies precisely in the comprehensiveness of the attitude that it asks us to bring to literature—its bringing of the entire content of a literary narrative within the scope of the prescribed make-believe. For the content of a work of literary fiction contains much that we believe to be true of the world. The problem for the fictive utterance theorist arises because, given the comprehensiveness of the prescribed attitude of make-believe, it must also encompass the things that we believe to be true. But, Gibson maintains, we can make no sense of the idea that we make-believe material in a work of fiction that we take to be true of the world:

> If I say that I am making-believe a certain proposition, it implies that I do *not* believe the truth of the proposition; in other words it implies that I will assent to the claim that it is false. (Gibson 2007: 166)

There is, he maintains, an air of Moorean paradox in the idea that we can make-believe what we know or believe to be true.

Critics of Gibson's argument have challenged this claim. Stacie Friend (2008), for example, points to empirical research by Alan Leslie that seems to show that children are able to both believe and make-believe the same thing at a given time. Any air of paradox disappears when we recognize that there need be no conflict between occurrent imagining and non-occurrent belief. Indeed, she further argues, it is crucial to our engagement with works of fiction that we can make-believe that which we take to be true. For we must import various beliefs about the real world in filling out the *fictional world* of a work of fiction, "the content we are supposed to imagine when we correctly interpret a work—that is, whatever is 'true in the fiction'" (Friend 2008: 155). Only through such importation can we supplement what is explicitly stated in the fiction so as to make proper sense of what is going on in the story. For example, we must import geographical knowledge of London to understand the movements of Holmes in the Sherlock Holmes stories. Conan Doyle simply takes for granted the reader's ability to "import" such knowledge. Friend offers, as one model of how this is done, the idea that we begin with a mental representation of the real world and modify it as required by the story:

> The resulting representation contains all the relevant beliefs about the real world that remain consistent with what is fictionally the case. If we imagine what is fictionally true, and what is fictionally true includes what we believe, then we imagine what we believe. (Friend 2008: 156)

Friend therefore, while challenging Gibson's claims about the impossibility of both believing and making-believe the same thing, agrees with him as to the comprehensiveness, in Gibson's sense, of the attitude prescribed to the narrative content of works of fiction, on the fictive utterance theory. Her objection to the theory is that there is no way of characterising the nature of the imagining prescribed by works of fiction that can distinguish works of fiction from works of non-fiction. She takes the most plausible candidate to be what she terms "mere-make-believe", an attitude of imagining-but-not-believing those things that are explicitly narrated in the text. The idea seems to be that what is explicitly narrated is what is "made up", and what is made up calls for mere-make-believe rather than for belief. The further conditions placed on fictions over and above being the product of an act of fictive utterance—in my case, the non-fidelity condition—are then seen as motivated by the need to ensure that works of fiction do indeed *have* something which is made up which can be the object of mere-make-believe—as Friend puts this, what such conditions ensure is that a work of fiction contains *fictive content*. For such supplemented fictive utterance theories,

> the content of non-fiction narratives is determined by what really happened ... while the content of fictional stories is determined by their authors. In this sense fictional content is "made up" and thus invites mere make-believe. (Friend 2008: 159)

Friend then offers a range of examples which supposedly discredit any such account of fictionality. In the first place, she maintains that we should reject outright the claim that fiction invites no belief but only mere-make-belief in its explicit content. Citing the opening of an Ian Fleming novel describing the Bahamian setting of the opening scenes, she writes: "This statement is not only true, it was intended to be true, and any informed reader of Fleming will believe it" (Friend 2008: 159-60). She then argues that many works of non-fiction contain story elements that are simply made up and that therefore prompt mere-make-believe. Some of these are controversial examples of "new journalism", but more clear-cut cases are talk of idealised entities such as frictionless planes in scientific texts, and the philosophical dialogues of philosophers like Berkeley. She takes the clearest examples, however, to be works by classical historians that incorporate invented speeches and tentative insights into the psychology of characters by "inner speech". She assumes that these are works of non-fictional history which nonetheless prompt mere-make-believe because some elements of the story are made up and are assumed to be so by intended readers. She takes this to show that

> mere-make-believe cannot be specific to fiction. Even if we accept the authorial intention to invite mere-make-believe as a necessary condition for fictionality, it cannot be sufficient. (Friend 2008: 161)

She further maintains that such examples pose acute problems for fictive utterance theorists like Currie and myself who propose necessary and sufficient conditions of fictionality in terms of mere-make-belief.

There are, I think, more and less insightful ways of responding to these criticisms. Let me briefly offer a less insightful (but I think effective) response, before turning to a more insightful and constructive way of taking such criticisms on board. The "quick and dirty" response is to point out that in fact neither Currie nor myself propose "necessary and sufficient" conditions of fictionality in terms of mere-make-belief. The second requirement for fictionality—in my case, the non-fidelity condition—is not, as Friend seems to think, merely a way of ensuring that the "fictive content" necessary for mere-make-believe is provided. It is indeed intended to ensure that the narrative is constructed by an author to satisfy story-telling objectives other than those served by the fidelity constraint. But—and here we come to a second point—nothing in either Currie's or my account requires that all of the explicit narrative elements in a work of fiction call for mere-make-believe. Currie certainly allows that readers may be intended to both believe and make-believe the kinds of stage-setting elements that

Friend locates in the opening sentences of the Fleming novel. Indeed, one of his objections to Searle's "pretense" account of fiction is that it cannot allow for an author to both assert and pretend to assert the same thing at a given time, whereas an author can coherently intend that a reader both believes and makes-believe the same thing.

The examples cited by Friend of works of non-fiction that call for mere-make-belief raise a different issue. For philosophical thought experiments and classical histories to pose a problem for the fictive utterance theorist, as Friend assumes is the case, the fictive utterance theorist must be seen as offering an account, in terms of fictive utterance calling for "mere-make-believe", of the distinction between fictional and non-fictional works. But if, as I have presented matters thus far, the primary aim of the fictive utterance theorist is to distinguish between fictional and non-fictional *narratives*, this leaves open the question which works that comprise fictional narratives count as fictional works. If it is at least a necessary condition, for something to count as a fictional work, that it contains a fictional narrative, this order of approaching matters is required if we are to make any progress in developing an account of what makes a *work* fictional. But we might hope to deal with the kinds of examples cited by Friend in a theory of fictional works that identifies further necessary conditions that must be met if a work comprising a fictional narrative is itself to be a fictional work.

This response also bears upon Gibson's claim that any interesting fictive utterance account of fictionality must meet the "comprehensiveness" requirement by specifying an attitude we are prescribed to adopt to everything contained in a fictional work. Gibson's claim, noted above, is that we otherwise have no more than an account of what makes a statement fictional, and thus we fail to illuminate what is distinctive of fictional works. I am suggesting, however, that the primary objective of the fictive utterance theorist is to provide an account of the fictionality of *narratives*, not of individual statements. And if, as suggested above, comprising a fictional narrative is a necessary but not a sufficient condition for being a fictional work, no understanding of the latter is possible without a prior understanding of the former.

In developing an account of the fictionality of narratives that takes seriously the challenges posed by Friend and others, we must look more carefully at what it is that the reader is prescribed to make believe by a fictional narrative, on the kind of fictive utterance account that I am proposing. What we should question, in fact, is something upon which Gibson and Friend—and indeed Stock—are in agreement—what Gibson calls the "comprehensiveness" of the prescribed response not merely to the fictional *work* bust also to the fictional *narrative* comprised by such a work. The assumption is that the fictive utterance theorist must furnish us with an account of a single attitude we are prescribed to take not merely to what is "made up" in some sense by the author but also to those features of the actual world upon which, as Friend rightly points out, narratives rely for their intelligibility.

I want to approach this question slightly obliquely by noting how Friend herself, in an earlier paper (2000), deals with what I think is a closely related question: how are we to understand the fictive content of works of fiction containing the names of real people and real places? Friend is attempting to make Walton-like theories of our emotional responses to fictions look more plausible. Rather than focus on the traditional cases, such as our capacity to pity Anna Karenina, she considers cases where a fiction contains names that have a referring use outside the fiction, such as Napoleon or London. She calls such names "connected" names, contrasting this with "unconnected" names like "Anna Karenina" that occur in fictions but lack an extra-fictional referring use.

The question is whether connected names *remain* connected when they occur in a work of fiction. The challenge is to explain how, if they do, we can explain our emotional responses to the referents of those names in the fiction if those responses rest upon things that we do not believe to be true of the real person who is the extra-fictional referent of the name. Friend argues that, in fictional contexts, connected names do usually refer to their ordinary referents, and that this is the case not only in statements about what is true in the fiction, but also in reports of our attitudes. Our attitudes, like our imaginings, are directed towards the real people mentioned in the story.

What is of interest to us here is that Friend suggests that there are at least two options open to us in our attempts to understand our imaginings relating to fictional narratives that contain a connected name like "Napoleon":

(1) We imagine, *of the actual person Napoleon*, that he is as described in the story.

Friend claims that this would be a form of *de re* imagining, so that in a report of our imagining, as in a report of our beliefs, "Napoleon" can be replaced by any co-referring expression *salva veritate*.

(2) We imagine that a fictional character, "Napoleon of the story", is as he is described in the story.

Fictionality, Fictive Utterance, and the Assertive Author

On this account, we treat the connected name "Napoleon" as it occurs in the story no differently from the way in which we treat unconnected names of other fictional characters, and we tell the same story about our imaginings of Napoleon that we do about our imaginings of these other characters — for example, that the objects of our imaginings exist as abstract artifacts or that we pretend that the names satisfy the normal conditions for reference.

Friend argues, with considerable ingenuity, for the first of these options. Her principal argument is that, if we take connected names to be disconnected in fictional contexts, we cannot grasp much of what the author is trying to achieve by including such names in the fiction in the first place. In the example that she gives, much of the humour intended by the author requires that we take the names to remain connected in the fictional context. But more generally it seems that the role ascribed to "imported" knowledge in Friend's later paper — its capacity to fill in the background necessary to generate the "fictional world" of the novel given what is explicitly narrated — requires that we import what we take to be true of the extra-fictional referents of connected names into the story. It doesn't seem to make much sense here to say that the object of our imaginings is a fictional character having just those properties possessed by the real referent of the connected name that are compatible with what is narrated of that character in the story.

Notice that, on the *de re* construal of the object of our imaginings, the *existence* of Napoleon is not itself part of our imaginings, nor is his possession of those properties that we import into the fiction. This is what is brought out by the *de re* characterization, which syntactically separates the content of our imaginings—which occur in the intensional context specifying what is to be imagined and is characterized *de dicto*—from the thing of which such things are imagined—characterized *de re*. It is what the story narrates *of* the real Napoleon that we are prescribed to imagine, again *of* the real Napoleon.

My proposal is that we see this as a general way of thinking about the nature of the fictive content that readers are prescribed to make believe by the authors of fictional texts. What holds for the connected names of real people in fictional contexts also holds for what we may term the "real settings" for fictions. Arguably, all intelligible fictional narratives require a real setting of some kind, since their fictional worlds presuppose that the reader locates what is explicitly narrated in a wider framework. This may in certain cases be supplied by other works in a given tradition—for example, the tradition of fairy tales in which magical things can occur and there are fire-breathing dragons—but even here much will still rely on what the reader imports from her understanding of the extra-fictional world—for example, that things made of wood ignite when subjected to fire. Given such a real setting for a fiction, we are prescribed to imagine something *of* that setting, but we are not prescribed to imagine that the real setting itself exists—this is something we are assumed to believe, not something we either imagine or are prescribed to imagine. Thus both Gibson and Friend are wrong in thinking that the make-believe prescribed by a fictional narrative is comprehensive.

IV/ The refined fictive utterance view of fictional narratives defended
What does this kind of approach get us? In the first place, it provides a principled way of accounting for the manner in which belief and make-belief are incorporated into our

engagement with fictions. We should not be discouraged from endorsing a fictive utterance view of fictional narratives by the fear that we will finish up with a mere patchwork of things asserted and things fictively asserted. In reading a fictional narrative, of course, we may have difficulty telling where the line between real setting and fiction is to be drawn. But this is an epistemological rather than a conceptual problem. While a reader may be uncertain where real setting ends and fiction begins, to the extent that she take part of the explicit narrative to belong to the real setting of the fiction, she will adjust, if necessary, her beliefs rather than her make-beliefs.

I think this point is masked, in much of the literature both for and against the fictive utterance view, by ambiguous talk about a prescription to imagine "what is true in the story". We see this, for example, in Friend's talk, cited above, about "the content we are supposed to imagine when we correctly interpret a work—that is, whatever is 'true in the fiction'", and in her claim that "if we imagine what is fictionally true, and what is fictionally true includes what we believe, then we imagine what we believe". In one sense, the things that are true in the Sherlock Holmes stories, for example, include that there is a place called London and that it has a certain geography. These things are "true in the story" not only in the sense that London provides the setting for the fictional events, but also in the sense that there could be fictional worlds in which no such city ever existed.

But it is crucial that we distinguish between what is "true in the story" in this sense and what we are prescribed to make believe. While it is true in the Sherlock Holmes stories that there is a city called London with a certain geography, this doesn't mean that we are prescribed to make-believe that there is a city called London with such a geography. Rather, this serves as part of the real frame for the fiction—we are prescribed to make-believe *of Victorian London* that a given sequence of events involving a given range of characters occurred. Compare: as I buy a ticket for the lottery I imagine that my ticket wins. It is true, as part of the real frame for my imagining, that I buy a ticket, but this is not something I make-believe—I make-believe, of the ticket I have just bought, that it wins the lottery, not that I buy a ticket for the lottery and it wins. These are different imaginings.

This allows us to clarify the non-fidelity condition on fictionality. I said in the introduction that

> to read a narrative as fiction ... is to assume that the choices made in generating the narrative were not governed in the first instance by [the fidelity constraint], but by some more general purpose in storytelling. If considerations of fidelity are taken to enter into the construction of a fictional narrative—where, for example, an author wants to set the narrative in London during the Blitz—we assume that this consideration is subordinated to this more general purpose.

The non-fidelity condition, we may now say, applies to those things included in the narrative that the reader is intended to make-believe—that is, those things that enter into the *de dicto* component of what is true in the story. Schematically, if a narrative relates, of setting S, that events E occur therein, the fictionality of the narrative requires not merely that its author intends that we imagine, of S, that E occurs therein, but also that the author's selection and ordering of the events making up E not be governed by the fidelity constraint. This has interesting implications for the kinds of cases to which I originally appealed in arguing for the non-fidelity condition on fictionality—cases where an author may draw upon events that she knows or believes to have actually happened in constructing a fictional narrative. In such cases, the author's satisfaction of the non-fidelity condition in the generation of the narrative effectively "disconnects" the real events that we are prescribed to imagine. To understand such a work is to treat these events as part of the content of the fiction, rather than as part of the real setting for the fiction. For, in such cases, if one took them to be part of the "real setting", there would be no fiction to be the object of our make-believe. For the constitution of *S is* governed by the fidelity constraint.

There is much that needs to be said to defend the view I have just sketched. Let me close by flagging one issue that merits further consideration. As noted earlier, Friend assumes, in her account of connected names in fictions, that the contexts in which such names occur are fully extensional—this is another way of saying that the names are used *de re*. It isn't clear, however, that this applies, strictly speaking, to the real settings for fictional narratives on the account I have proposed. While the linguistic context does indeed allow for substitution *salva veritate* of other extensionally equivalent expressions for those that occur in the characterisation of *S*, these substitutions may be constrained by the *author's* (or the fictional author's) beliefs about the world rather than by our own. This is most easily seen if we consider, for example, the theory of the humours which is plausibly taken to be part of the real setting for Shakespeare's plays. While Shakespeare prescribes that we imagine, of a real setting in which behaviour is explicable in terms of humours, that certain actions and events take place, we do not share his beliefs about such matters included in the real setting for the plays, and would misrepresent what is true in the story if we substituted our own understanding of psychological matters for his. In this sense, our engagement with a fiction may require imaginings on our part over and above the imaginings prescribed by the author. While the play does not itself prescribe that we imagine that behaviour is governed by humours, we must imagine this in order to understand the plays. This calls for careful consideration of the ways in which such imaginings interact in our engagements with fictions,[4] but it adds further support to, rather than undermines, the distinction between believings and prescribed imaginings in fictional works.

IV/ Conclusion

The account of fictionality developed in this paper departs in two significant ways from my earlier treatments of these issues. First, it corrects the conflation, in the latter, of the fictionality of narratives and the fictionality of works. Second, it clarifies the fictional content of a fictional narrative—that which we are intended to make-believe—by distinguishing the latter from the narrative's setting—that *of which* we are to make-believe such things. Nonetheless, the two core commitments of the earlier account are preserved: the idea that fictive utterance and non-fidelity are the key elements in a theory of the fictionality of narratives. While critics of fictive utterance theories of fictionality pose some significant challenges relating to the assertional roles played by authors, those challenges can, I think, be successfully countered by the more sophisticated

---

[4] In developing an account of such matters, a useful resource would be Robert Brandom's discussion, in the later chapters of his 1994, of the manner in which communication is possible despite differences in "simple material substitution-inferential commitments" across speakers who intuitively share a language. Brandom argues that the distinction between *de re* and *de dicto* content ascriptions is tailored to deal with precisely this feature of our communicative situation.

account of fictive utterance developed or canvassed in this paper.[5]

McGill University
david.davies@mcgill.ca

REFERENCES

Brandom, Robert. 1994. *Making it Explicit*. Cambridge MA: Harvard University Press.
Currie, Gregory. 1990. *The Nature of Fiction*. New York: Cambridge University Press.
Davies, David. 2001. "Fiction." In *The Routledge Companion to Aesthetics*, ed. Berys Gaut—Dominic McIver Lopes, 263-74. London: Routledge.
— — —. 2007. *Aesthetics and Literature*. London: Continuum.
Deutsch, Harry. 2000. "Making Up Stories." In *Empty Names, Fiction, and the Puzzle of Non-Existence*, ed. Anthony Everett—Thomas Hofweber, 149-81. Stanford: CSLI Publications.
Friend, Stacie. 2000. "Real People in Unreal Contexts, or Is There a Spy Among Us?" In *Empty Names, Fiction, and the Puzzle of Non-Existence*, ed. Anthony Everett—Thomas Hofweber, 183-203. Stanford: CSLI Publications.
— — —. 2008. "Imagining Fact and Fiction." In *New Waves in Aesthetics*, ed. Kathleen Stock—Katherine Thompson-Jones, 150-169. New York: Palgrave Macmillan.
Gibson, John. 2007. *Fiction and the Weave of Life*. Oxford: Oxford University Press.
Lamarque, Peter, and Stein Haugom Olsen. 1994. *Truth, Fiction, and Literature: A Philosophical Perspective*. Oxford: Clarendon Press.

---

[5] Earlier versions of this paper were presented at the Prague conference on *Fictionality* in April 2011, and at the University of Maribor. I am grateful to all those who provided me with critical feedback on those occasions. I would also like to thank the Social Sciences and Humanities Research Council of Canada for a research grant which helped to fund the research for this paper.

CHARACTERS AND CONTINGENCY

Gregory Currie

ABSTRACT: One way creatures of fiction seem to differ from real things is in their essential properties. While you and I might not have done many of the things we did do, Anna Karenina could not, surely, have been other than a lover of Vronsky. Is that right? Not straightforwardly: while it is true that "Necessarily, someone who was not a lover of Vronsky would not be Anna", it is also true that "Someone who was necessarily a lover of Vronsky would not be Anna". I use a framework developed by Stalnaker to explain this, and to shed light on the semantics of fictional names.

Nietzsche disbelieved in the substantive self and thought that all there is to a person's identity is qualitative history. Any change in your history would be a change in your identity. Alexander Nehamas suggests we see this as an assimilation of life to literature, for we accept that literary characters do not support counterfactuals like "Anna Karenina might not have fallen for Vronsky". Someone who did not fall for Vronsky just would not be Anna (see Nehamas 1985: 164–65).[1]

Nehamas acknowledges how problematic this assimilation is. But is it right to think of fiction as a home for super-essentialism, however inappropriate that model is for the genuinely human? I think it makes good sense to say that Anna

---

[1] I am not sure how seriously Nehamas means us to take this idea; some of the time he seems to be offering a much less controversial doctrine, and one of less obvious relevance to essentialism: that, as he puts it, "every detail concerning a character has, at least in principle, a point" (Nehamas 1985: 165).

Characters and Contingency

Karenina might not have fallen for Vronsky. Indeed, we all think that it is true that she might not have. The contingency of events in this and other stories is important; the story would affect us in a quite different way if it were thought to be the working out of a necessity.

It is not, strictly speaking, true that Anna might not have fallen for Vronsky; we get a candidate for truth only by putting the *In the fiction* operator at the front. But it is also not true, without the operator, that Anna did fall for Vronsky. In the only sense that it is true that Anna did fall for Vronsky—namely, with the operator applied as a prefix—it is also true that she might not have.

Notice that what is at issue here is what is true in the story, not what is actually said by the author in the text. Tolstoy made it explicit that Anna fell for Vronsky, and perhaps did not make it explicit that Anna might not have fallen for him. The relationship between these two things—textual content and story content—is complex, and highly sensitive to background.[2] But that relationship is not our topic. For present purposes I am taking the idea of truth-in-a-fiction for granted.

---

[2] The first systematic attempt to work out a theory of truth in fiction is David Lewis, "Truth in Fiction" (in Lewis 1983). Nehamas says: "Literary characters are exhausted by the statements that concern them in the narratives in which they occur." I think this is false, but even if this were true, it would *undermine* Nietzschean scepticism about contingency, since an author may actually say that a character has a property only contingently. What is true is that what the author says, together with relevant background, will never determine a complete set of properties. But where the story does determine that the character has a property, the character's possession of that property contingently can usually be inferred from background. An unusual story may stipulate that super-essentialism is true of its characters, but this is not the norm in fiction.

Given that our concern is with truth-in-a-fiction, it is strictly speaking wrong to suppose that there is one doctrine — Nietzschean super-essentialism — which can be applied to both real and fictional people. We have to understand Nehamas' claim in something like the following way. Take the two sentences:

(1) Nietzsche wrote *The Birth of Tragedy*.
(2) Nietzsche might not have written *The Birth of Tragedy*.

Nietzschean super-essentialism, applied to real things, says that (1) is true and (2) is false. I take it that this is false, because both (1) and (2) are true. Now take:

(3) Anna fell for Vronsky.
(4) Anna might not have fallen for Vronsky.

Nietzschean super-essentialism as applied to fictions says, on one reading, that (3), when prefixed by the *In the fiction* operator, is true, and that (4) when so prefixed is false. I am claiming that this, also, is false and not, as Nehamas invites us to believe, true. I say that both (3) and (4), when prefixed, are true.

There is another reading of the doctrine. Often we utter statements like (3) and (4) without using the prefixes, and without being merely elliptical. On those occasions we speak in pretend mode; we are not asserting these things but uttering them as part of an imaginative pretence (Walton 1990). So instead of contrasting unprefixed with prefixed sentences, we could keep all the sentences unprefixed and contrast kinds of utterance. That way, Nietzschean essentialism claims that (1) is assertable while (2) is not, and claims that (3) is appropriately utterable in a game of make-believe generated by *Anna Karenina* (which we may shorten to "is pretend-assertable") while (4) is not. This way of approaching the question of how to understand statements about fictional characters does a better job of unifying the two versions of essentialism. Let us say that a statement is *legitimate* if it is either (i) true or (ii) appropriately utterable in a game of make-believe. Nietzschean essentialism now says that the first but not the second member of both pairs is legitimate. Again, this is wrong. Both members of both pairs are legitimate.

One reason we cannot treat our two pairs of sentences (1,2) and (3,4) as on a par is that (3) and (4) are problematic in that they contain expressions that don't refer to anything. We could appeal to the view that expressions like "Anna Karenina" do refer—but to fictional characters, considered as abstract objects of some kind, and not to people. This would require us to think of (3) and (4), not as sentences pulled from the text of the novel, but sentences that might be asserted in a metafictive context: a serious discussion, the possibility of which is created by the initial act of novel writing (Currie 1990, section 4.8). If we are prepared to believe in these abstract objects, then (3) and (4) cease to be problematic from the point of view of reference failure, but they become problematic in another way. If "Anna" names an abstract object, it is not true that Anna fell for Vronsky—that is something only a person can do. So now (3) and (4) would need reworking along new lines; we would have to understand the attribution of *falling for Vronsky* happening in two possible ways. The first, ordinary way would be in the assertion that the object concerned possesses this property, while the second would be in the assertion that the object is a character from a fiction according to which the corresponding fictional person possesses this property.³

With (3) and (4) understood so as to contain references to abstract characters, super essentialism would say that (1) is true and (2) is false, when both are understood as involving ordinary attribution, while (3) is true and (4) is false, when both are understood as involving the extended sense of attribution. But this is no more plausible a doctrine. Both (1) and (2) are true, and so, on this new way of understanding them, are both (3) and (4). In the extended sense of attribution, *possibly not falling for Vronsky* is attributable to the abstract character, because that character is one from a fiction according to which the corresponding person fell for Vronsky merely contingently. Indeed, this way of reading the relation between the two pairs of propositions is particularly unhelpful, since the point of Nehamas' comparison was to compare real and fictional *people,* and that is not what we are now doing. There are, of course, no fictional people—other than those that are also real. The best approximation to the incoherent idea of comparing real and (unreal) fictional people is achieved either by comparing what is true with what is fictionally true, as with the two pairs (1,2) and (It is fictional that (3), It is fictional that (4)), or by comparing what is assertable with what is pretend-assertable. When we properly understand the options for saying things

---

³ This is the formulation of Nathan Salmon, discussing a view of Kripke (Salmon 1998: 295). Salmon proposes to extend this idea so as to make characters the referents of fictional names, as those expressions are used by the authors of the stories in which they appear. On this account, while Anna is presented by Tolstoy as being a person, she (it) is in fact an abstract object (Salmon 1998: esp. 300). Note that we should now understand Tolstoy as endorsing both (3) and (4), where the relevant properties are being attributed in the extended sense.

about fictional characters, super-essentialism is not an attractive view.

Am I missing the point? What I have said does not seem to do justice to the intuition that underlies Nehamas' use of the fictional case, which might be put as follows:

(5) Necessarily, someone who did not fall for Vronsky would not be Anna Karenina.

There is a sense in which this is true. But the sense in which it is true is consistent with it also being true that:

(6) Someone who necessarily fell for Vronsky would not be Anna.

(5) is true in the sense that anyone who did not fall for Vronsky would not satisfy the conditions for filling the Anna-role defined by Tolstoy's story. Think of the Anna-role as a function from worlds to individuals such that it picks out an individual in world ω just in case she is the unique individual in ω who did all the things Anna is said to do in the story. One of the things she is said to do is fall for Vronsky, and that is why no one in any world who resists Vronsky's charms in that world (or never meets him) would be Anna. But what is here a requirement on being Anna is that you fall for Vronsky, not that you fall for him *of necessity*. In fact it's a requirement on being Anna that you fall for him *merely contingently*; you have to be someone who falls for Vronsky in some worlds and not in others.

Now I will make three simplifying assumptions. The first two concern the particular case we are examining, and the third is quite general. First, I shall assume that Anna is the only fictional character in the work and that all the other characters are in fact real people, referred to by their usual proper names (as with Napoleon in *War and Peace*). Secondly, I am going to regard the story's content as entirely devoted to telling us things about Anna, rather than about any other person or thing. This will allow me to move quickly and easily between statements about Anna and statements about the story. These are, of course, unrealistic assumptions, but while dropping them would introduce complications into the exposition, it would not affect the claims I shall be making. And it will allow us to make a clear and simple distinction between the qualitative content of the story—what it tells us about Anna, her actions and sufferings—and the identity of its protagonist. One thing I am claiming here is that the story is determinate only up to qualitative content: it does not, and does not need to, tell us who Anna is. Thirdly, I will consider only consistent fictions, because I want a non-trivial notion of the world of the story. I want to consider stories true in some worlds and not in others. Some stories contain inconsistencies which we can easily remedy, because the inconsistency is due to obvious inattention on the part of the author. Other fictions seem to require of us that we incorporate the inconsistency into our imagining. I will not try here to decide whether this is the right view. But it does seem reasonable to adopt an approach to the semantics of fiction that is perspicuous and helpful in standard cases, even though it may turn out not to work for all cases.[4]

---

[4] On repairing inconsistent stories see Hanley (2004); Hanley offers a wide-ranging defense of Lewis's theory of fictional truth. On imagining inconsistency see Gendler (2000) and the contrary argument of Stock (2003). There are in fact other assumptions here, though perhaps not so controversial. I am assuming that fictional truth does not admit of degrees,

Characters and Contingency

Now consider Jane, a respectable inhabitant of the actual world. In the actual world she does not fall for Vronsky; in fact she never meets him. But, given what I have said just now, it may well be the case that Jane in some other world does fall for Vronsky; in that other world, Jane occupies the Anna-role. Does that make Jane, in this world, Anna Karenina? No. Being Anna is, according to me, something that happens to you in some worlds and not in others. It happens to you in worlds where you occupy the Anna-role. In any world in which Jane occupies that role she is Anna. But that does not make her Anna in this world.

Being Anna is not at all like being Jane. The person who is Jane in one world is Jane in all worlds. Being Jane is a matter of being a certain individual; being Anna, on the other hand, is a matter of occupying a certain role. Moving up a semantic step we can say that "Jane" is a proper name of an individual, whereas "Anna", where it is the proper name of anything, is the proper name of a function from worlds to individuals. Of course when Tolstoy says that Anna did this or that, we are not, from the point of view of our imaginative engagement with the work, to understand this as meaning that a role did this or that. This is because it is part of the fiction that "Anna" is the name of a person. But "Anna", as used by Tolstoy, is not in fact the name of a person, nor does it purport to be. Names are expressions used in order to pick out individuals, and Tolstoy does not use "Anna" in order to do this, nor does he expect us to believe that he is. "Anna", as used by Tolstoy, is not a name.

This is a controversial view, but I think that opposition to it rests on a mistake. For example, Adams, Fuller and Stecker say that "Ivan Ilych" as it occurs in Tolstoy's novella is a name

---

that it is not vague, and that it is not subject to indeterminacy. For relaxation of the first of these assumptions see Currie (1990, section 2.8).

because "It functions inside the fiction as a proper name" (Adams, Fuller, Stecker 1997: 131). We need to be careful in understanding the claim that "Ivan Ilych" functions inside the fiction as a proper name. What is true is that part of the pretence that the fiction encourages us to engage in is that "Ivan Ilych" is a proper name; we are to imagine that there is a certain person and that this is his name. But this does not mean that the expression really functions as a name in the text of the story; we cannot point to uses of that expression in the text and truly say of them that here the expression functions as a name. In a broad sense of character, the expression "Ivan Ilych" is a character in the story, as Moscow is. The story invites us to imagine things of Moscow which are not true—that Anna Karenina lived there, for example. Similarly the story invites us to imagine things of "Ivan Ilych" which are not true—that it is a proper name, for example. Because we are mandated by the story to imagine this, we can say that it is true in the fiction that "Ivan Ilych" is a proper name. But in general, it being true in the fiction that a is F does not entail that a (really) is F. "Ivan Ilych" is a fictional name, but that means that it is fictional that it is a name, not that it is a special, fictional, kind of name.[5]

Now recall:

(5) Necessarily, someone who did not fall for Vronsky would not be Anna Karenina.

This is true in the sense that someone who did not fall for Vronsky in world ω would not occupy the Anna role in ω. And recall:

---

[5] In this I follow Lewis (1983: 267). Similarly, I claim, contra Corazza and Whitsey (2003), that apparently indexical expressions used in the context of a fiction are often not really indexicals at all.

(6) Someone who necessarily fell for Vronsky would not be Anna.

This is true in the sense that someone who fell for Vronsky in every world would not be Anna — and in fact there is no such person anyway, because falling in love is not something you can do of necessity.

There is a useful framework for representing these ideas. The framework has complex antecedents in work on temporal operators, and was first clearly stated by Robert Stalnaker in a classic paper called "Assertion".[6]

I shall speak of intensions and extensions as associated with expressions. The intension of an expression is the function which takes a world to the extension of the expression at that world. I treat proper names as rigid designators: expressions which refer to the same thing in all possible worlds. So the intension associated with a proper name is a constant function from worlds to objects; the name has the same extension in every world.

Recall that I said that Tolstoy's use of "Anna" is not the use of a proper name, because Tolstoy is not using that expression intending to pick out an individual for our attention and to say something about it. What, then, is Tolstoy trying to do? Many things, perhaps, but one particularly relevant thing is to tell a story, the direct content of which (rather than, say, the moral message behind it) he does not expect us to believe. We are, as I have said, to imagine the content of that story. Part of

---

[6] Reprinted in Stalnaker (1999). See Jackson (1998: ch. 2) for discussion of natural kind terms and so-called a posteriori necessity using this framework, and for references to earlier work in this tradition; see also Chalmers (1996: 61–65).

what we imagine is that there is a particular person called "Anna", and that other characters are using "Anna" as a proper name of that person. But it is no part of what we are doing that we should identify a particular such person, which is just as well since there is no person. Nor is it a presupposition of our engagement with the story that there is such a person—as it might be a presupposition of our engagement with a certain scientific theory that there is something which is the reference of "Vulcan". In the case of the theory, a fatal flaw is discovered when we discover that the term in question is empty; interest in the theory collapses at that point. That is not in the case with Tolstoy's story; we assume from the start that there is no such person as Anna, and this fact does not detract from whatever value the story has. This suggests that the semantics of fictional names and the semantics of non-denoting terms in scientific and other kinds of theories are different.

What Tolstoy does by means of his story is to draw our attention to a class of worlds: the worlds in which someone—it does not matter who—does and is the things that Anna is said to do and be in the story: call these story-worlds.[7] Tolstoy does not draw our attention to a particular world, because a world is a maximal state of affairs; we specify a world fully only when we have determined the truth value in that world of every proposition. Tolstoy cannot be expected to offer us so detailed an account, and the attempt to do so would be a distraction

---

[7] Story-worlds are worlds where everything true in the story is true. They are not worlds in which only things true in the story are true, because stories leave much undetermined. Also, story-worlds need to be distinguished from Lewis's worlds where the story is told as known fact (Lewis 1983: 268). Lewis uses the this idea to define what is true in the story. My project starts, as I indicated at the beginning of this essay, only at the point where we take the notion of truth in a fiction for granted.

from what is relevant in the story. So the story-worlds differ in various ways from one another. One of the ways in which Tolstoy's activity is incomplete is that he fails to specify an identity for Anna; in world ω_1 it is A who does these things, in world ω_2 it is a different individual, B, who does them. Nothing in the story, and nothing in the most attentive and sensitive reader's response to the story, makes one of these worlds a better candidate for being the world of the story than the other. What Tolstoy's story invites us to imagine is, in effect, that some or other story-world is actual—it does not matter which. It does not invite us to imagine, of some particular story-world, that it is actual. What is true in the story is what is true in all the story-worlds, and nothing that identifies the story's protagonist is true in all these worlds.

However, we readers cannot afford to concentrate our attention on story-worlds alone; we have to take into account certain other worlds as well, if we are to understand what makes (6) true. It is at this point that Stalnaker's ideas become useful to us.

The reader imagines that what is actual is a world in which "Anna" really is a proper name which refers to someone, indeed to someone who is as the story describes. If ω_1 is such a world, we can represent the intention of "Anna", as it is used in that world, in the following way:

	ω_1	ω_2	ω_3
ω_1	A	A	A

Here ω_1 appears twice; once (on the left) in its role as world of utterance and once (above) in its role as world of evaluation. Since ω_1 is a world of the story, "Anna" really does serve there as a proper name, and hence as a rigid designator. As uttered in

ω_1, "Anna" refers to A in ω_1; as so uttered, it also refers to A in ω_2 and ω_3. Also, as used in ω_1, "Anna" refers in ω_2 and in ω_3 to A irrespective of whether these are story-worlds; the story may serve as a reference-fixing description for "Anna", but once introduced, the name picks out the same individual in all worlds, irrespective of whether the description is true of that individual in that world.

Assume, in addition, that ω_2 is a story-world and ω_3 is not, and that "Anna" does not refer to anyone in ω_3. Using this very restricted set of three worlds, we can construct a two dimensional concept for "Anna Karenina" as follows:

K	ω_1	ω_2	ω_3
ω_1	A	A	A
ω_2	B	B	B
ω_3	x	x	x

where "x" indicates no value. In all these worlds, "Anna" is used as a rigid designator. As used in ω_1 and ω_2 it picks out different individuals; hence the difference between rows 1 and 2. But as used in ω_1 it picks out the same individual in each world, and similarly for ω_2; hence the uniformity of cells within a row. As used in ω_3 it fails to pick out any individual in that world, and so picks out no individual in any world; it has the null intention. The worlds directly of interest to the reader of the story are ω_1 and ω_2, for these are story-worlds. They differ with respect to the identity of the person called "Anna" who does the things Tolstoy's story tells us about. So there is nothing that is true in the story concerning the identity of that person; recall that what is true in the story is just what is true in all story worlds. It is true in the story that that person is A or B, but not true in the story that person is A, and not true in the story that that person is B (remember that we are assuming, artificially, that ω_1 and ω_2 are the only story-worlds).[8]

However, the reader must also be sensitive to the existence of worlds like ω_3. The reader is not concerned with ω_3 as world of utterance, but as world of evaluation for utterances made in ω_1 and ω_2. In ω_1, the story is true, and a use of "Anna" in that world refers to A, who is the person of whom the story is true. But an utterance of "Anna" in ω_1 also picks out the very same person in ω_3, i.e. A, even though in ω_3 the story isn't true. Let's assume that in ω_3, A does not meet Vronsky. In that case a speaker in ω_1 can truly say that, although Anna did meet Vronsky, she might not have. For the speaker in ω_1 uses "Anna" to refer rigidly to A, and that speaker is able to refer to A in a world (i.e. ω_3) where A does not meet Vronsky. Let us also assume that in ω_3 B does not meet Vronsky.[9] So the speaker in ω_2 can say, similarly, that although Anna did meet Vronsky, she might not have.

Now go back to our two dimensional matrix, K. The matrix distinguishes, as I have said, between the role of a world as world of utterance and as world of evaluation. In the first row we are to consider ω_1 as the world of utterance, and the first cell gives the value of "Anna" at that very world; so on down the rows. In general, the *i*th cell in the *i*th row tells us what the extension of "Anna" is in the world of utterance. The sequence of all such cells is represented by the leading diagonal of the matrix. We may call this the diagonal intension

---

[8] This is no ad hoc stipulation; it is a quite general fact that the *In the story* operator does not distribute over disjunction (see Currie 1990: 74).

[9] We need to assume this only because we are working with a very restricted class of worlds; all we really need, given more realistic assumptions about the space of worlds, is a world in which A does not meet Vronsky, and a world in which B does not.

associated with "Anna". I suggest that we think of this intention as the Anna role or character; it is the function which picks out at a world the individual of whom Tolstoy's story is true if there is such a person, and is undefined otherwise. Now consider again

(5) Necessarily, someone who did not fall for Vronsky would not be Anna Karenina.

What makes this true is that, in the leading diagonal, cells are filled only in worlds where the story is true, and part of the story is that Anna falls for Vronsky. But to see the truth of

(6) Someone who necessarily fell for Vronsky would not be Anna.

we need to examine not just the diagonal intension. We start with the diagonal, and identify its filled cells. If the jth cell is filled, we know that ω_j is a story-world; it is a world where the story is true. We then look at filled cells in the jth row; all cells filled in that row will be filled by the same object, A_j; after all, "Anna", as used in ω_j, refers rigidly.[10] We need to find a filled cell in that row corresponding to a world where A_j does not fall for Vronsky. What makes (6) true is that we can do this for every filled cell in the diagonal. Generally, the ith cell in the diagonal intension is also the ith cell in the ith horizontal intension; let us say that all the other cells in that horizontal intension are *siblings* to the cell in the diagonal. It is true in the fiction that Anna falls for Vronsky merely contingently because,

---

[10] I say "Look at *filled* cells in the jth row" to accommodate those who think that some things exist in some worlds and not in others. Against this view see Williamson (1999).

for every filled cell in the diagonal, there is a sibling cell the occupant of which does not fall for Vronsky.

I have insisted that fictional names like "Anna Karenina" are not really proper names. In that case what account should we give of their semantics?

Stalnaker ends his paper with an idea about the interpretation of negative existentials that suggests a certain treatment of this issue. Stalnaker says that a conversation involves what he calls a "presupposition set": the class of worlds which are live options from the point of the conversation. What an orderly conversation does is to reduce the size of the presupposition set as the conversation goes on. And Stalnaker suggests that there are some rules that need to be observed if a conversation is to proceed in this way. One of them is that anything said in the conversation needs to be interpreted so as to express the same proposition in each of the worlds of the presupposition set. If this is not so, then someone may utter S in the conversation, but we shall not be able to use this to reduce the size of the presupposition set. Suppose that S expresses P in ω_1, and expresses Q in ω_2. In that case we would have to get rid of either ω_1 or ω_2 before we could disambiguate S so as to use it to reduce the presupposition set. So now we are stuck; before we can reduce the presupposition set we need to know what S says; before we can know what S says we have to reduce the presupposition set.

Think of story-telling as a rather one-sided conversation; it can certainly be thought of as an activity which progressively reduces the size of a presupposition set. By the end of the telling, the teller has reduced the size of the set to the set of story-worlds: the set of worlds where what is true in the story is true. I have said that the story worlds are just those worlds identified by filled cells in the leading diagonal; if cell j in the diagonal is filled, then world ω_j is a story world. Suppose now that at a certain point in the story telling, the teller says "Anna fell in love with Vronsky". It is of course part of the fiction's pretence that "Anna" here is a rigid designator. But when we consider what "Anna fell in love" conveys to a listener, we see that the listener cannot really treat "Anna" as a rigid designator, because if he did he would have to interpret "Anna fell in love" as expressing some singular proposition. But which one? Relative to ω_1 it expresses the proposition that A loves Vronsky, relative to ω_2 it expresses the proposition that B loves Vronsky. Thus we have violation of the maxim that the proposition expressed be the same one relative to each world in the presupposition set.

Stalnaker says that this requirement of conversational exchange sometimes pushes us into interpreting a speaker's words in such a way that we associate with them a diagonal concept.[11] Recall our two dimensional matrix for "Anna":

K	ω_1	ω_2	ω_3
ω_1	A	A	A
ω_2	B	B	B
ω_3	x	x	x

When we read Tolstoy's story, we want to interpret his utterance of "Anna fell in love" in such a way that it expresses the same proposition in every world in the presupposition set. We can do this by applying to the matrix the two dimensional

---

[11] Stalnaker's own account focuses on operators on propositional concepts, but he notes its generalisability to other cases (Stalnaker 1999: 83 n. 7).

modal operator dagger, which collapses the concept into the diagonal, for all worlds of utterance:

†(K)	ω_1	ω_2	ω_3
ω_1	A	B	x
ω_2	A	B	x
ω_3	A	B	x

We readers imagine that what is actual is a story-world. But we now do not have to make a decision about which one is actual, for the intension associated with "Anna" is the same in all worlds. What does that mean for our understanding of "Anna" as Tolstoy uses it? It means that "Anna" refers in each world to the person in that world, if there is one, who satisfies the qualitative conditions of the story and otherwise to no one. "Anna", so understood, has the same intention as would normally be assigned to the expression "The woman called Anna Karenina who was married to Karenin, who fell in love with Vronsky, who…", and so on for all that is true in the story.[12]

Stalnaker says that we apply the dagger operator to a range of serious utterances involving names and indexical expressions. It might therefore be replied that nothing I have said here about the application of the dagger operator to a fictional name distinguishes it from an ordinary proper name. But the difference is this: in the case of an ordinary referring proper name or indexical expression used assertively, there are many situations in which we do not need to diagonalise in order to maintain the integrity of the conversation. Those are situations in which speaker and hearer share knowledge of the

---

[12] For a defense and elaboration of this view see Currie (1990: ch. 4).

reference of the name or indexical. For ordinary proper names and indexicals, we can, perhaps, look on the use of the dagger as a response to an aspect of the pragmatics of these expressions, and not as telling us anything about their semantics. But with fictional names things are different. We accept from the start that there is no possibility of knowing who is being referred to, and it would betray a misunderstanding of the imaginative context of the story to worry that this was some sort of failure. So in the case of fictional names within the fiction, the use of the dagger operator can be said to have semantic significance.[13]

University of Nottingham
gregory.currie@nottingham.ac.uk

REFERENCES

Adams, Fred, Gary Fuller, and Robert Stecker. 1997. "The Semantics of Fictional Names." *Pacific Philosophical Quarterly* 78 (2): 128–48.
Chalmers, David. 1996. *The Conscious Mind*. New York: Oxford University Press.
Corazza, Eros, and Mark Whitsey. 2003. "Indexicals, Fictions, and Ficta." *Dialectica* 52 (2): 121–36.
Currie, Gregory. 1990. *The Nature of Fiction*. New York: Cambridge University Press.
Evans, Gareth. 1982. *The Varieties of Reference*. Oxford: Oxford University Press.

---

[13] This paper was given at the conference "Do ficta follow fiction?", University of Eastern Piedmont, Vercelli, June 2002. Thanks to members of the audience on that occasion for their comments. Thanks especially to Eros Corazza who read and commented on an early version, and to a referee for *Dialectica*.

Gendler, Tamar S. 2000. "The Puzzle of Imaginative Resistance." *Journal of Philosophy* 97 (2): 55–81.

Hanley, Richard. 2004. "As Good as it Gets: Lewis on Truth in Fiction." *Australasian Journal of Philosophy* 82 (1): 112–128.

Jackson, Frank. 1998. *From Metaphysics to Ethics*. Oxford: Oxford University Press.

Lewis, David K. 1983. *Philosophical Papers*. Oxford: Oxford University Press.

Nehamas, Alexander. 1985. *Nietzsche. Life as Literature*. Cambridge, MA: Harvard University Press.

Salmon, Nathan. 1998. "Nonexistence." *Noûs* 32 (3): 277–319.

Stalnaker, Robert. 1999. *Context and Content*. Oxford: Oxford University Press.

Stock, Kathleen. 2003. "The Tower of Goldbach and Other Impossible Tales." In *Imagination, Philosophy and the Arts*, ed. Matthew Kieran—Dominic M. Lopes, 107–24. London: Routledge.

Walton, Kendall. 1990. *Mimesis as Make-Believe: On the Foundations of the Representational Arts*. Cambridge, MA: Harvard University Press.

Williamson, Timothy. 1999. "Existence and Contingency." *Proceedings of the Aristotelian Society*, suppl. vol. 73: 181–203.

Representing Unicorns:
How to Think about Intensionality

R. M. Sainsbury

ABSTRACT: Intensional verbs raise a number of questions. For example, how can we think about unicorns, and so think about something, given that there are no unicorns, and so nothing to think about? Why should wanting red shoes entail wanting shoes, whereas fearing rabid dogs does not entail fearing dogs? I argue that such questions can be resolved by drawing on three resources: (I) an intensional or non-relational notion of representation, (II) the notion of "putting a representation on display" and (III) attention to the different ways in which the truth conditions of sentences containing intensional verbs depend upon the representations put on display.

When we think about unicorns, we are thinking about something, namely unicorns. But as there are no unicorns, we aren't thinking about anything, that is, it's not the case that we're thinking about something. One feature of intensional verbs is that they seem to generate this kind of contradiction.

Such verbs also generate problems of a seemingly entirely different kind. One example is this:

How can it be that, although "She wants red shoes" entails "She wants shoes", "She's afraid of rabid dogs" does not entail "She's afraid of dogs"?

In this paper, I suggest that the problems share a solution, insofar as they arise in connection with intensional verbs that ascribe mental states. The solution involves three elements. (I) A properly intensional or non-relational notion of representation. (II) A notion of "putting a representation on display". (III) A study of specific intensional verbs, to explain how the representation that is put on display connects with the specific meaning of the verb.

I/ Non-relational representation
A non-relational account of representation is one that rejects the following inference:

(R) from "x represents y" infer "there is something such that x represents it".

We are familiar with a non-relational notion of representation when we discuss representational painting. A painting may be *of a landscape* — as we say, it is a *landscape*-painting — without there being a landscape that it represents. It may be of a "purely imaginary" landscape. This is not a kind of landscape, for all landscapes are real. In describing a landscape as imaginary, we are simply saying that there is no such landscape, though the artist imagined that there was. We are not denying that landscapes the artist has experienced played some kind of causal role in the production. Even so, for any landscape, the painting is not, and is not supposed to be, of it; and it may well be that, for any landscape, the painting does not resemble it at all closely.

Natural as this non-relational conception of representation is for pictorial representation, it has been problematic both for perception and for language. In discussions of perception, it is associated with denials of the mind's capacity "directly" to connect with the world. Similarly, in connection with language, it has been associated with "descriptivism", and in turn with denials of "direct reference" theories. In fact, there is no such tension, as I'll illustrate with the case of language. The non-relational thesis is that the mere fact that some expression x represents y does not ensure that there is something, y, that x represents. This is consistent with there being species of expressions, object-involving ones, such that, for all such expressions, x, of this species, if x represents y then there is something, y, that x represents. The inference springs from the nature of some privileged subclass of expressions, and not from the very nature of representation. Representation in its own nature can be non-relational, even if, as cannot possibly be disputed, there are some things such that some representations represent them.

That the mind *represents* the world does not entail that its contact with the world is other than direct. Rather, the distinction between direct and indirect is a distinction within kinds of representation, not a distinction between representing something and accessing it in some supposed non-representational way. If John caused the mess, the representation *John* may count as a direct representation of John, and *the person who caused the mess* as an indirect representation of John. Specifying the distinction in general terms may be difficult, but here it is enough to stress that it is a distinction within kinds of representation. "Represented" does not entail "accessed indirectly".

One should start with a non-relational notion of representation, and then consider whether some representations are relational. Words like "unicorn" and "Pegasus" will not be good candidates for relational representations; ones like "red" and "London" will be better. But there is also another question: in describing the semantic properties of relational representations, should their relationality figure in the semantics? I think there are good reasons to think not. At one point the majority of users of "witch" took it to be a relational representation. The consensus now has gone the other way. This change is not a change of meaning or semantics. On the contrary, we have to mean the same by "witch" as the witch-hunters, when we say they were mistaken in believing that there were witches. Otherwise there is no real disagreement, merely a change of subject. It's probably a good division of labor to spare semantic theorists the task of determining whether or not there are things that "witch" or "Homer" represent. The default option for semantic description will thus be non-relational. This is consistent with adding a relational notion as an overlay, one that might emerge by reflecting on how words are learned, or on Twin-Earth cases. Whether the overlay is regarded as belonging to "semantics" or not seems largely terminological. Given the connection between semantics and understanding, and that one can understand an expression without knowing whether there is anything it represents, it seems best to say that the overlay would not belong to semantics.

What does "London" refer to? London. What does "Pegasus" refer to? Pegasus. This seems an unimpugnably correct answer, even in a context in which it is well-known that there is no such thing as Pegasus. A surprising moral: even reference, philosophers' preferred tool for describing word–world relations, is intensional, and so a non-relational notion.[1] Nothing of great moment follows, for one can define an extensional notion of reference (let us demarcate it reference*) by using the intensional one. One step on this road would be to stipulate:

---

[1] This claim can be found in Chisholm (1957: 174–75).

x refers* to y iff there is a z such that $z=y$ and x refers to y.[2]

Should we explain the semantics of names in terms of reference* or reference? A long tradition appeals to the former; but if you are moved by the point about witches, you should regard this as a mistake. We don't know whether there is any single person to whom "Homer" refers. Leverrier at one point falsely believed that there was such a planet as Vulcan. We go beyond what we know if we assign "Homer" reference*. We know we would be mistaken to assign "Vulcan" reference*. Yet the meanings of the words are stable and not in doubt, which is why we can raise questions about Homer, and can be sure that there is no such thing as Vulcan (a point on which Leverrier for a short period disagreed). We need semantic constancy between these variable epistemic states. This can be assured by saying that "Homer" refers to Homer and "Vulcan" to Vulcan, but cannot readily be assured if we have to use reference* as our central notion in the classical way.

In Davidsonian truth theory, the semantic clauses for predicates are non-relational, for example:

for all x, x satisfies "unicorn" iff x is a unicorn.

On some versions of truth-theory (e.g., McDowell 1977), axioms for names are different, for example

"Hesperus" stands for Hesperus,

where "stands for" is regarded extensionally. This disparity seems unjustified: names should be treated like predicates,

---

[2] Substitutivity can be added as a further stipulation: if x refers* to y and $y = z$, then x refers* to z.

predicates should be treated non-relationally, so names should be too.

It would not be desirable to implement this idea by simply helping oneself to a non-relational notion of reference within a truth theory. As Davidson said, the logic of intensional notions has not been worked out, and in working it out one might indeed encounter "problems as hard as, or perhaps identical with, the problems our theory is out to solve" (Davidson 1984: 22). However, one can use well-understood negative free logic. This enables us to exploit a relational notion of reference* to define (in effect) a non-relational notion of reference, as in this example:

(P) for all x ("Pegasus" refers* to x iff x is Pegasus).

Since nothing satisfies "x is Pegasus", the truth of the biconditional ensures that there is nothing to which "Pegasus" refers*. This is consistent with "Pegasus" referring to Pegasus as, intuitively, it does. We could understand (P) as in effect saying that the word refers* to Pegasus, if to anything.[3]

We have not yet surveyed, even at the most superficial level, all the resources this approach requires. The description of "Pegasus" just given by (P) is no more true than

(V) for all x ("Pegasus" refers* to x iff x is Vulcan).

But "Pegasus" does not refer to Vulcan. To address this lacuna, we could prefix the extensional description with some

---

[3] Worries about circularity may well arise. There is a conception of a semantic project upon which they are unfounded (see McDowell 1977). Treating names (and other referring expressions) as having irreducible semantics, as exemplified in (P) above, is recommended by Sainsbury (2005).

intensional operator. My preference is for "It is a matter of meaning alone that", which I'll abbreviate as "M". Prefixing this to (P) delivers a truth, but prefixing it to (V) yields a falsehood.[4] This is a basis for preferring (P) to (V) as a semantic axiom.

The overall plan is to use referential* free logical axioms of a kind which remain true even when M-prefixed. They feature unprefixed in the theory, in order to facilitate ordinary extensional logic. In the Davidsonian tradition, it is a familiar idea that keeping to appropriate theorems may require some restrictions in the proof-theory (one should restrict attention to "canonically proved" theorems). The ultimate test for correctness is that the theorems should fit harmoniously into an explanatory description of the behavior of the users of the language.

II/ Putting a representation on display

One element in Davidson's paratactic analysis of propositional attitude ascriptions is that they involve putting a representation on display. For Davidson, the way in which this is done is simply by referring* to an utterance. An utterance is a species of representation, so a representation is put on display by being referred* to.

I will suggest a variant on Davidson's idea.[5] Sentences express thoughts, and thoughts represent states of affairs (or

---

[4] Davidson considered a somewhat similar idea. Exaggerating its similarity with the present proposal, he suggested that axioms of truth theories should be understood as if prefixed by "It is a law of nature that" (Davidson 1984: xiv).

[5] For propositional attitude ascriptions, the idea can be found in Sainsbury and Tye (2012, section 6.4). There are similarities with the defense of Davidson by Ludwig and Ray (1998).

sets of worlds—the choice makes no difference for present purposes). When used assertively, a sentence is not merely displayed, but is used to claim, in effect, that the thought it expresses is true. When a sentence is embedded in an extensional context, what matters to the truth or falsehood of the whole is what the thought represents. When a sentence is embedded in a non-extensional context like "Galileo said that", what matters is the thought it expresses, and this thought is put on display. "Galileo said that the Earth moves" is true just on condition that Galileo said something expressing a thought suitably related to the one displayed by "the Earth moves".[6]

From this account it follows that you need to understand the embedded sentence in order to understand the whole: you need to detect what thought is being put on display. Hence the embedded sentence does not meet a certain (rather crude) condition for being mentioned but not used. Perhaps we should say, following Ludwig and Ray (1998), that it is both used and mentioned.

A similar idea can be applied to intensional verbs. If I tell you that Sally is thinking about unicorns, I put a *unicorns*-representation on display, and I tell you that Sally is exercising such a representation in thought. This is neutral about what public language, if any, Sally speaks: many public languages have *unicorns*-representations, and for all I know such representations can be used by subjects who do not speak any language. The representation is non-relational: it represents unicorns even though there are no unicorns it represents.[7]

---

[6] The "suitable relation" needs lengthy spelling out—identity is often, though not always, sufficient, and hardly ever necessary (see Sainsbury and Tye 2012, section 6.4).

[7] Completing the present account requires specifying the conditions under which two representations both represent unicorns.

The notion of displaying a representation features in at least three other familiar idioms. One is in certain uses of "as" exemplified by "She thought of the arsenic as a tonic" and "He saw the wren as simply some small brown bird". These sentences are true only if the subject in the former exercised a *tonic*-representation, and the subject in the latter exercised a *small-brown-bird*-representation. Another idiom is what is sometimes called "mixed quotation", exemplified by "The scratch on his new Mercedes made him 'totally, absolutely heartbroken'". In these cases, we are to suppose that not only is his broken-hearted mental state being affirmed, it is also said to be how he himself thought of his state. The primary function of the representation on display in the quoted words is to tell us how the subject was thinking about his emotions, rather than simply telling us what these emotions were. The thought of the person who thinks of arsenic as a tonic targets arsenic, but not in virtue of the exercise of a *tonic*-representation. Contrast with one who, on seeing a white powder, knowingly remarks: "Ah! Arsenic!" This thinker's use of an *arsenic*-representation ensures that her thought targeted arsenic; she thought of the arsenic, that is, her thought targeted arsenic, while also thinking of it as arsenic, and so using an *arsenic*-representation.

The third familiar idiom in which something like displaying a representation occurs is found in a use of "like" in some US dialects of English. For example, from "Alice went, like, I gotta get outta here" we can infer not only what Alice said (that she needed to leave) but also how Alice put it (the representation). Even if she did not speak English, the attribution is correct only if she spoke in a colloquial way and used a standard cliché in whatever language she spoke.

The value of the idea is to be tested by detailed applications, some of which are offered in the next section.

Before turning to these, I offer some comparisons. The thought that meanings are important in intensional contexts is neither new nor (so long as we keep the claim sufficiently vague) controversial. John Buridan, in the fourteenth century, said that when a phrase like "a unicorn" is dominated by an intensional verb, it *"appellat suam rationem"* — it invokes (or "appellates") its sense or meaning.[8] Appellation belongs to a complex theory involving a number of semantic primitives, including supposition, the closest to our contemporary notion of reference*. It is noteworthy that appellation is distinct from supposition: in our terms, the way in which a representation or its meaning figures in such contexts, according to Buridan, is not by being referred to.[9] Frege, by contrast, suggested that in opaque contexts, words are used to refer to their customary meanings; and Davidson, while deploring the supposed lack of semantic innocence involved in Frege's idea, took it that in such contexts an utterance was referred to, typically proleptically.[10] Different as these last two suggestions are in some respects, they both invoke the notion of reference as the relation whereby a meaning or utterance comes into salience. This contrasts with the present suggestion according to which the relevant relation is *displaying*.

Meanings or intensions also play a crucial role on approaches influenced by Montague, within a framework of

---

[8] *"[T]alia verba* [viz. intensional verbs] *faciunt terminos sequentes appellare suas rationes"* (Buridan 2001: 279).

[9] From Buridan's *Summulae de dialectica* (trans. G. Klima): "Appellation differs from supposition, for … there are terms that appellate and do not supposit, for example 'chimera' […]"; "terms [in intentional contexts] … appellate their own concepts by which they signify whatever they signify" (Buridan 2001: 294 and 226).

[10] The attributor of "Galileo said that the Earth moves" goes on to supply a reference for "that" by uttering "the Earth moves".

relational representation. Intensions, functions from worlds to objects, play the role of meanings, and every expression represents by being related to an intension. An immediate problem is that "unicorn" and "centaur" have the same intension, at least on many views,[11] whereas some difference is required in order to register the fact that one may think about unicorns without thinking about centaurs. On the non-relational account advocated here, the difference between such expressions is registered in a very direct semantic fashion: "unicorns" refers to unicorns but not to centaurs.

III/ Applications

A/ Specific/unspecific

A standard mark of intensionality in verbs is supposed to be that there are two "readings" of a sentence like this:

(1) John wants a sloop.

On one reading, (1) is true just if there is some sloop on which John has fixed his desires. On the other reading, (1) is true if John wants a sloop, but no sloop in particular. This reading, the unspecific reading, is sometimes characterized as "any old sloop will do".

I think the data on this issue have been distorted. First, we must distinguish the unspecific case from the case marked by "any old". It is very rare that anyone who wants an F wants any old F. John may want a sloop, and want no sloop in particular, yet not want a broken-down wreck of a sloop, or a wildly

---

[11] Kripke (1980: 156) argued that there could be no unicorns, and the arguments, if sound, would extend to centaurs. On this view, the intensions of "unicorn" and "centaur" coincide.

overpriced sloop, so he does not want any old sloop. "Any old" has no interesting role to play in characterizing the intensionality of desire.

Secondly, it is far from clear that sentences like (1) are genuinely ambiguous. The view that they are ambiguous is encouraged by a theory according to which intensional verbs "really" (or "upon paraphrase") don't take ordinary noun phrases in their second position. Rather, they take sentential complements of the form "that *s*", for a complete sentence *s*. When thus paraphrased, there is a possibility for an indefinite in *s*, treated as an existential quantifier, to have either wide or narrow scope relative to the main verb (e.g. "wants"). Then the alleged ambiguity is represented by the contrast between (1a) and (1b):

(1a) $\exists x(x$ is a sloop and John wants it to be the case that John possesses $x)$.
(1b) John wants it to be the case that $\exists x(x$ is a sloop and John possesses $x)$.

There is no doubt that (1a) and (1b) differ in truth conditions and that the difference is properly characterized as a difference of scope. But we can transfer this result to (1) only on the basis of the theory according to which it *needs* to be paraphrased as (1a) or (1b). One source of the belief that (1) is ambiguous comes not directly from linguistic data, but from the application of a controversial theory. Let's now return to the data.

If (1) is ambiguous, one should not count as having understood an utterance of it unless one has resolved the ambiguity. Yet it is plain that understanding imposes no such demands: one can know that John wants a sloop without knowing whether or not there's a sloop upon which he has

117

fixed his desire. (1) can be used to express what one knows, and so is neutral between the specific and the unspecific case.

The principle underlying this simple argument is that any ambiguity in "*p*" is resolved in any truth of the form "X knows that *p*". For example, if X knows that John went to the bank, what X knows must be either true just if John went to the river bank or true just if John went to a financial bank. It cannot be that X knows that John went to the bank, but does not know whether he went to a river bank or a financial bank.[12] But it can be that someone knows that John wants a sloop without knowing whether there is some specific sloop that is the object of his desire.

Different readings may amount to no more than different ways in which an unambiguous sentence can be true. There is more than one way for (1) to be true. There are many ways for "Jill runs" to be true, by running north or running south, running fast or running slow, running barefoot or running in trainers. This is entirely consistent with the fact that one can understand a specific utterance of "Jill runs" while not knowing anything about the further details of some truthmaker for the sentence. It's wrong to say that there are various "readings" of "Jill runs", if the existence of multiple readings is something that needs to be mirrored in the semantics.

What needs to be explained is the neutrality of "a sloop" as it occurs in (1). It characterizes a desire, but remains neutral on whether or not there's a sloop that it targets. Applying the theory of section II, the first thing to say is that (1) puts an *a-sloop*-representation on display. Now we have to say what the role of that representation is.

---

[12] X might know that the sentence "John went to the bank" is true without knowing how the ambiguity should be resolved. But that is a different issue.

Here are two examples of roles the representation does not play: (a) the representation is not the "object of desire", if an object of desire is an object that must be referred to in a correct answer to the question "what does John want?". John wants a sloop, not a representation of one. (b) It's not that his desire will be satisfied by anything of which the representation is true. That would be the "any old" case, which is rare, and is certainly not right in general.

In typical cases, the representation offers a necessary condition for the satisfaction of the attributed desire. It acts as a filter: as far as this desire goes, non-sloops are non-satisfiers.

The difference between specific and non-specific truthmakers for (1) is explained as follows. One truthmaking situation is that John's mental state of sloop-desire contains an indefinite but no definite *sloop*-representation. That will be the unspecific truthmaker. Another truthmaking situation is that the desire contains a definite *sloop*-representation: that will be the specific truthmaker.

This initial account, as we'll see in the coming section, offers only a sufficient condition for truth. It can be expressed thus:

X wants an F/the F/Fs if X has a desire centered on an *an F/the F/Fs*-representation; such a desire is satisfied only by an F/the F/Fs.

We'll shortly see various ways in which this sufficient condition may fail to be necessary.

B/ Wanting
Can we infer that if someone's desire for a sloop centers on a definite *sloop*-representation, the desire is also characterized by

an indefinite *sloop*-representation? Yes: a subject operating with a definite *sloop*-representation must also have an indefinite *sloop*-representation.[13] The "must" is not a logical "must", but closer to a psychological one. Let's consider only linguistic representations, and only languages which, like English, use separate lexical elements to mark indefiniteness and definiteness. In these cases, a definite *sloop*-representation is semantically complex, involving "sloop" and something like "the" or "that". One who understands "the" or "that" understands "a", and so understands "a sloop" and so has an indefinite *sloop*-representation. Typically, the indefinite representation will be psychologically active in behavior controlled by the subject's sloop desires. If the definite *sloop*-representation is "the sloop due to be auctioned tomorrow", a desire controlled by the representation will be one which will generate a response on these lines to the suggestion that the subject take an interest in a ketch: "I don't want that! It's not even a sloop." On this picture, the inference from "She wants the sloop due to be auctioned tomorrow" to "She wants a sloop" is reliable, but not logical.[14]

A *sloop*-representation is not a representation such that there is some sloop it represents. This condition would be both too strong and too weak. Too strong, since there may be nothing a *sloop*-representation represents, and too weak, since someone may represent something that is in fact a sloop without exercising a *sloop*-representation. Someone who stands in the relation of desire to a sloop may not have a *sloop*-

---

[13] A *sloop*-representation is not merely something that represents a sloop. It must represent something as a sloop.

[14] These issues are likely to take a different form for thinkers who use languages without the kind of definite/indefinite markers available in English.

representation of any kind. To illustrate: suppose that *The Mary Jane* is a sloop that John desires, but without knowing that it is a sloop. Then he has a definite representation that is in fact of a sloop. He might have no *sloop*-representation at all, yet he might still want *The Mary Jane*. Given that *The Mary Jane* is a sloop, it doesn't sound wrong to say he wants a sloop—the thing he wants is a sloop, even if he doesn't know it.

Theorists sometimes contrast "needs" with "wants" on this issue. For example, Graeme Forbes (2010: section 5) says that whereas the inference from "She wants a glass of water, water is H_2O, so she wants a glass of H_2O" is not valid, the corresponding inference with "needs" replacing "wants" is valid. On this view, we should simply tough it out, denying that John wants a sloop.

Although it might be nice to have a language with such a clear-cut distinction, English is not like that. Rather, we accept ascriptions of desires which put on display representations not used by the desiring subject (likewise for other intensional verbs for mental states). We accept that John wants a sloop, even though he has no concept of a sloop, no *sloop*-representation. We have to allow such ascriptions as correct, unless we are to be severely inhibited in our ascriptions of mental states. For example, we all want to allow that the dog Fido wants his bone and is looking for it under the sycamore tree. Yet we certainly do not wish to commit to the view that Fido has a *my bone*-representation or a *sycamore tree*-representation. Fido represents his bone and the tree somehow or other. But it would be foolish to have any confidence in the opinion that he exploits in his desires and searches the very representations that we exploit in our ascriptions of these states.

For a clear example among language-users: suppose you see a gnu at a zoo and sincerely say "I want that", yet you have no *gnu*-representation. (A *gnu*-representation is not just something that represents gnus; in addition it represents them *as* gnus.) Later in the day, your desire cannot be reported using the very representation that you used, since we now have no demonstrative access to the gnu you saw. You can be reported as wanting a gnu, or as wanting the gnu you saw, even though your desire has never involved any sort of *gnu*-representation. We must allow this mismatch between the representation used in the attribution and the representation at work in the subject's mental states, on pain of making it impossible to give a correct report of those states.

This suggests that a necessary and sufficient condition for truth of a sentence "X wants an F/the F/Fs" is on the following lines (for some relation R among representations):

X has a desire centered on a representation, Z, which is R-related to an *an F/the F/Fs*-representation; such a desire is satisfied only by a satisfier of Z.

Identity is a special case of the R-relation, providing a sufficient but not a necessary condition. In many cases, R obtains when the *an F*-representation (used in the ascription) is not Z (the representation in the subject's mental state) but is true of that of which Z is true. For example, R holds between the *The Mary Jane*-representation (Z) and an *a sloop*-representation when John wants *The Mary Jane*, which is a sloop though he does not know it (he has no *a sloop*-representation). This representation in John's mind, in this context, verifies the ascription "John wants a sloop".

The value of R is highly sensitive to context. The co-reference* condition mentioned in the previous paragraph is in many contexts insufficient. For example, Jane's desire for a unicorn cannot be reported as a desire for a centaur, even though an *a unicorn*-representation is true of just the things of which any *a centaur*-representation is true, that is, nothing.

In typical cases, straightforward inferences involving "wants" are easily accounted for. If Mary wants red shoes, she typically has a desire involving a *red shoes*-representation (here R is identity), which acts as a necessary condition for the satisfaction of the desire. If she were to be sorting through candidates for satisfying this desire, she'd reject things that are not red shoes; a fortiori, she'd reject things that are not shoes. In this case, compositionality in the *red-shoes*-representation ensures that she possesses a *shoes*-representation, and that she exercises it in her desire.

Preservation of such weakening inferences places a structural constraint on R. Let's represent adjectival modification by "+", and suppose that John has a desire centered on a representation of the form: $Z_1 + Z_2$. Then he has a desire centered on a Z_2 representation. Suppose that $Z_1 + Z_2$ is R-related to $X_1 + X_2$, so that we can correctly report his Z-desire as a desire for an $X_1 + X_2$. Given weakening, he desires an X_2. It follows that Z_2 is R-related to X_2. To illustrate with an example. Suppose John uses a *red shoes*-representation in his desire. In many circumstances we can report him as wanting fire-engine colored footwear. In the case, his *red shoes*-representation is R-related to the *fire-engine colored footwear* representation. Since it follows that he wants footwear, it also follows that his *shoes*-representation is R-related to the *footwear*-representation.

The present proposal, centered on the notion of putting a representation on display, does not apply to all intensional verbs. It does not apply to those which, like "needs", may not involve a mental state. In these cases, a report is not putting on display a representation that is (R-related to one) used in a truthmaking mental state. For example, "needs" allows non-specific indefinites, and so may be classified as intensional, even when there is no question of a contentful mental state being at issue, as in "The lily needs a stake". This can be true even if there is no stake it needs. The theory proposed here evidently cannot explain such cases: no representation is put on display. The phenomenon is, however, explicable drawing on familiar resources. Let's say that a sentence is non-specific iff it contains an indefinite like "a F", and can be true even if nothing is F. Negation and modals can evidently induce non-specificity as in:

It doesn't have a stake.
It ought to have a stake.

Needing is not having something one ought to have, and so its meaning already contains (twice over, in fact) material that explains the non-specificity without appeal to putting a representation on display.[15]

C/ Fearing
Mary can fear rabid dogs without fearing dogs. Weakening holds for the example of the red shoes, but fails in the example of the rabid dogs. The explanation is that, in the case of an ascription of fear, the representation that's put on display has a different job to do: it has to provide a *sufficient* condition. Having a representation of rabid dogs nearby, *as* rabid dogs nearby, should normally be enough to trigger fear in one who

---

[15] Other verbs belong with "needs", like "buys", "orders" (as in "ordered a bottle of wine") and perhaps even "resembles" ("the cloud resembles a unicorn") in having non-specific truth makers, but for which it is at least not obvious that the "displayed representation" approach will be appropriate. The taxonomy in this area remains frail.

fears rabid dogs. It does not follow that a representation of dogs nearby, *as* dogs nearby, should normally be enough to trigger fear in one who fears rabid dogs. By the same token, strengthening inferences will be valid: one who fears dogs fears rabid dogs too.[16] As before, these facts place structural constraints on the R-relation.

D/ Quantifiers

The inference from thinking about unicorns to thinking about something is correct. What is incorrect is to move to there being unicorns that are thought about. It would be nice if this was a simple matter of scope, governed by the rule: never apply external (wide-scope) existential quantification to the intensional place of an intensional verb. But that does not seem quite right, for it does seem acceptable to infer from "Mary is thinking about several unicorns" to "There is something Mary is thinking about — namely, several unicorns". The unacceptable conclusion is that there are several unicorns she is thinking about.

The singular quantifier form is appropriate in inferences from a premise involving the plural "unicorns". Similarly, an impersonal quantifier form can be appropriate in an inference from a premise involving a personal noun phrase: from "John and Peter want the same thing, namely a wife" we can properly infer "There's something John and Peter both want, namely a wife". We cannot properly infer "There's somebody/some woman John and Peter both want". These features make the

---

[16] How is "too" functioning here? The rabid dogs are dogs, so no further dogs are being adduced. What is added is a new representation.

"there is" expression "special" in some way.[17] It's not functioning as an ordinary quantifier phrase.

An explanation is that "there is" is picking up on the displayed representation. There is a representation Mary is exercising in thought, a *several-unicorns*-representation. The representation in its nature is singular, even though plural in what it represents. This is not a complete explanation, for it's not that Mary is thinking about a representation. Rather, she is thinking about unicorns, which are not representations. The relevant fact is that she is thinking *with* a representation, indeed, with a *unicorns*-representation; but there's no overt syntactic mark of this switch from "of" to "with". When "unicorns" occurs after "thinks about" it tells you what she's thinking about. When "something" occurs in "There is something she's thinking about", the *thing* in question is something she's thinking with, a representation, not something she's thinking about.

Similarly, John and Peter's desires both involve an *a wife*-representation. What they want is not the representation, but something it represents. Their desire uses that representation: they desire with it, even though not for it, rather as Mary thinks about unicorns with her *unicorns*-representation.

In some cases, just the right contrast is explicitly marked. For example, in

He thought of a sloop *as* a sloop.

the two occurrences of "a sloop" have manifestly different roles, the first to tell you what he thought about, the second to tell you how he thought about it, that is, what representation he

---

[17] These subtle distinctions first came to my attention in Moltmann's work (1997). She calls such phrases "special quantifiers".

used to think about it with. The second occurrence puts the relevant representation on display, a token of the very representation-type attributed to the thinker. We do not always separate these roles so clearly, whether we are using the more familiar intensional transitives, or are describing human action more generally — as suggested in the next section.

We are now finally in a position to explain away the contradiction offered in the first paragraph of the paper. We could reconstruct the argument for the contradictory propositions as follows:

1. We are thinking about unicorns (assumed).
2. We are thinking about something (from 1).
3. There is something we are thinking about (from 2).
4. There are no unicorns (assumed).
5. Hence there are no unicorns we are thinking about (from 4).
6. Hence there is nothing we are thinking about (from 5).

(3) and (6) are inconsistent, but seem to follow from the indisputable assumptions (1) and (4). We must accordingly show that one of the inferences as invalid.

One candidate is the inference from (2) to (3). But in fact, as just discussed, this inference is valid. (We need to be sure to distinguish the conclusion from "There are unicorns we are thinking about".) The remaining candidate is the inference from (5) to (6). The considerations of this paper show, perhaps surprisingly, that this is invalid. The most natural reading of the conclusion treats the "there is" as a special quantifier, one that relates to a representation. Even if there are no unicorns we are thinking about, we can be exercising a *unicorns*-representation in thought, and so be thinking about unicorns, and so there be something we are thinking about, namely unicorns.

IV/ The larger picture: actions

Our descriptions of our actions are subject to a similar kind of dual interest: sometimes we are concerned primarily with the representations the agents exploit in guiding what they do, sometimes primarily with the world with which they engage thanks to the representations they possess. We move between these interests with complete fluidity, and in ways that can easily be missed. Consider how the sentence

(1) They set out for Florence.

might be evaluated in each of the following scenarios:

— We are trying to trace a missing group of tourists and we want to know where we should look. If we know that (1) is true, we should check out the road to Florence.
— We are studying a group's psychology and powers of deduction. We leave various clues and messages in their environment. They pass the test if they figure out they should head for Florence. We know that if (1) is true they have passed the test, even if, due to an error irrelevant to our experiment, they are on the Rome road, wrongly thinking it is the road to Florence.

In the first scenario, we show a preference for the worldly side of the action, that is, with what the representation we use in the attribution represents; in the second case we show a preference for the representational side, that is, with the nature of the representation that guided the action we attribute. This corresponds to the tension we felt about whether John, who wants the sloop *The Mary Jane* without knowing what a sloop is, wants a sloop. If we are concerned with how he relates to the world, we are inclined to say he wants a sloop. If we are concerned with how he represents the world, we may be inclined to say he doesn't want a sloop. (As would be expected on the theory advanced here, the denial is more acceptable when heavy emphasis is placed on "sloop".)

The phenomenon is widespread. Someone is counting chickens and reaches the total 13. If we are primarily interested in this action from the worldly point of view, we will regard

(2) She counted 13 chickens.

as true only if there were 13 chickens to be counted. If we are more interested in her and her mental states, and are thus concerned with the nature of the subject's representations, we will treat (2) as true if she pronounced 13 to be the number of chickens, even if there were more or fewer chickens.

Another familiar example concerns the satisfaction of desires. There is room for two opinions about whether someone kidnapped in Columbia and forcibly transported to work on a US tomato farm has thereby satisfied her desire to travel. She traveled, and that's what she wanted; from a worldly perspective, her desire was satisfied. But of course she never wanted to travel under those conditions; this was not how, in her desire, she represented traveling.

Intentions involve representations, and the same worldly thing or state can be represented in different ways. (As Davidson famously said, it's one thing to fly one's spaceship to the Evening Star, another to fly it to the Morning Star.) Moreover, a representation may fail to represent anything. Those are the platitudes needed to explain the contrast between the divergent perspectives we may take on actions. If we are interested in the intentions, we are dealing with representations; representational grain is finer than worldly grain and may have no worldly correlate.

The upshot is that the kinds of considerations needed to make sense of intensional transitive verbs are required to make sense of our ascriptions of actions. Being human—acting, thinking, wanting or fearing—involves exercising representations. In describing these human states, we may well display the representations the agents used, and we transition seamlessly between a concern for what these representations were and a concern for the worldly situation in which they guided thought, emotion and action.[18]

University of Texas at Austin
marksainsbury@austin.utexas.edu

REFERENCES

Buridan, Jean. 2001. *Summulae de Dialectica*. Ed. and trans. Gyula Klima. New Haven: Yale University Press.
Chisholm, Roderick. 1957. *Perceiving: A Philosophical Study*. Ithaca: Cornell University Press.
Davidson, Donald. 1967. "Truth and Meaning." *Synthese* 17 (1): 304-23. Reprinted in Davidson 1984: 17-36.
———. 1984. *Essays on Truth and Interpretation*. Oxford: Oxford University Press.

---

[18] Material from this paper was presented at a colloquium in the Linguistics Department, University of Texas at Austin. My thanks to participants for comments, especially David Beaver and Alex Grzankowski. My thanks also to Petr Koťátko for comments on an earlier draft.

Forbes, Graeme. 2010. "Intensional Transitive Verbs." Online at http://plato.stanford.edu/archives/spr2010/entries/intensional-trans-verbs/.
Kripke, Saul. 1972/1980. *Naming and Necessity*. Oxford: Basil Blackwell.
Ludwig, Kirk, and Greg Ray. 1998. "Semantics for Opaque Contexts." *Philosophical Perspectives* 12 (12): 141–166.
McDowell, John. 1977. "On the Sense and Reference of a Proper Name." *Mind* 86 (342): 159–185.
Moltmann, Friederike. 1997. "Intensional Verbs and Quantifiers." *Natural Language Semantics* 5 (1): 1–52.
Sainsbury, R. M. 2005. *Reference without Referents*. Oxford: Clarendon Press.
Sainsbury, R. M., and Michael Tye. 2012. *Seven Puzzles of Thought and How to Solve Them: An Originalist Theory of Concepts*. Oxford: Oxford University Press.

CHARACTERS AS SOMEONEWHOS

Martin Pokorný

ABSTRACT: In the paper I argue that fictional characters are putative individuals under a description; and since putative individuals are no individuals, fictional characters are no individuals. However, developed fictional characters impress us as very singular natures. I argue that this is correct insofar as fictional characters are very distant from general types as we normally use them; nonetheless, it is a fallacy to conclude that if they are not types they have to be individuals. Yet the objection returns in a stronger form: fictional characters must be able to interact, and it seems evident that they interact as individuals (of a peculiar kind). In order to counter this impression, interaction among fictional characters is analyzed under the headings of plasticity, hierarchization, betting and "verbicture" (for "verbal picture"), and an alternative account is supplied.

The purpose of this paper is to defend a view of the status of literary, or fictional, characters.[1,2] My proposal will be fairly

---

[1] Throughout this text, I will use "fiction" and "fictional" in simple accordance with the general use and its ambiguities.

I have proposed a (fairly non-intuitive) definition of fictionality with respect to *texts* in Pokorný (2010); I do not assume that definition here and I am not building upon it. The problem of the fictionality of *texts* is distinct from the problem of the fictionality of text-based *entities*, such as characters. For more on this see below, Postscript II.

[2] This issue, as is well known, has been a much-debated topic for several decades; for a survey of the debate and further references see Schnieder & von Solodkoff (2009); Heidbrink (2010); Reicher (2010). Up to a point my proposal goes parallelly to Currie (1990: ch. 4), but there are several substantial differences. Also, I advocate the view, apparently

close to the naive understanding—for instance to the view that fictional characters do not really exist but some real people may be exactly like them.³ This is so due to my conviction that fictional characters are, in principle, doxastic entities: they are just what we think they are, as it is our thinking of them thus and so that actually makes them. So much in the way of a preface.

In part A, I will present my thesis. In part B, I will defend it against certain *prima facie* objections, and thus develop it. In part C, I will draw conclusions regarding criteria of identity, moral assessment, and the purpose of fiction.

A/ The thesis
Part A is divided into two sections. Section A.1 introduces the thesis, and the concept of a Someonewho. Section A.2 elucidates the use of proper names when applied to Someonewhos.

---

minoritarian in the debate, that names of fictional characters do not refer to individuals of any kind—but my approach differs from the various published explanations.

My own approach differs from most of this research in one key methodological point: for me, neither fiction nor its reception is, primarily or exclusively, a matter of correct thinking, i.e. of thought systematically judged by the criteria of correctness; and thus, I do not see any reason for assuming that the standard apparatus of logic should provide us with *all we need* in order to disentangle the status of fictional characters. (We are certainly capable, at least to a degree, of thinking correctly or incorrectly *about* fiction, including fictional characters; but that has no impact on whether fiction and/or fictional characters are *products* of correct thinking.)

3   It will also be close to Aristotle (*Poetics*, 1451b8–11; trans. Halliwell, modified): "'Universal' means the kinds of things [*ta poia*] which it suits a certain kind of person [*tô poiôi*] to say or do: … poetry aims for this, attaching names <to the agents>. A 'particular' means, say, what Alcibiades did or experienced."

A.1/
I will claim that fictional characters are Someonewhos. A preliminary definition of a Someonewho would run as follows:

(i) A Someonewho is someone who $x, y, z...$
(ii) A Someonewho is an entity such that it does not admit of any ontologically *stronger* characterization than the one given in the pertinent fill-in of (a) which is valid in a particular case.

An example: Leopold Bloom is someone who once wrote a poem as a boy, enjoys Burgundy, and has a wife and daughter. I, too, am someone who once wrote a poem as a boy, enjoys Burgundy, and has a wife and daughter. There is much more that could be said about both Bloom and myself, so the respective fill-in of (i) would be, in either case, very long, perhaps infinite (for Bloom as well as myself).[4] But there is one crucial difference. Take me and you can see that I admit of an ontologically *stronger* characterization: in particular, if you—for instance—observe me directly then you can state that I am *this* living being, thoughout its existence as a living being; or again, you can supplant the "*this*" by spatio-temporal coordinates; and so on. You cannot do any of this for Bloom: Bloom is, only and exclusively, someone who wrote a poem as a boy etc. etc. etc.; you can prolong the list but you cannot go beyond the list;[5] ontologically, this is the most you can do for him.

---

[4] See below, section B.5 on plasticity.
[5] That is, you cannot go beyond the list *as far as the character is concerned*. You can, in a way, go beyond it *as far as his/her story is concerned*. But it is not really going beyond: the story just is *not* a list—whereas the character is. Character and story may be intimately connected but they will remain different in this. For more on this point, see below, section B.6 on verbicture.

Characters as Someonewhos

Every person is also a someone-who—i.e. everybody is, necessarily, somebody who x, y, z...—but it is *not* the case that every person were a Someonewho in our sense: a Someonewho in our sense is, ontologically, *nothing more* than a Someonewho, and thus it is not, *de re*, a person;[6] there is nobody who actually *is* that Someonewho.[7] Yet a Someonewho need not be a fiction in the specifically artistic or literary sense. We talk about Someonewhos, and we, sort of, live with them, whenever we plan or hypothesize concerning unidentified individuals. Let it be given that one day I discover that my philosophical masterpiece, admired by the critics and wildly popular with the local public, has been translated into Schwitzerdytsch and that the publisher has failed to inform me and pay the outstanding royalties. My wife finds out and says, "Let's hire a lawyer. A Swiss lawyer." I say, "Sure enough, let's do that. But how shall

---

[6] On the sense in which it *is* a person see below, Postscript I.

[7] Here I introduce a distinction between a someone-who and a Someonewho which I will not attempt to formalize, as the distinction is a contextual one rather than one in content: a someone-who and a Someonewho differ precisely in this one respect, that with a someone-who there is a particular real entity that actually exhibits the features in question, whereas with a Someonewho there is merely a posited carrier, or rather, there is the positing of a carrier—but no real carrier. Intermediate cases are possible, and will crop up in our argument: even when there is no real carrier that we know of, we can still posit a carrier with the rider that, in fact, there is one (we are just unable to locate it), or with the wish that there be one; or again, there may be a real carrier yet we can consider the characteristics it possesses, i.e. its someone-who, as (say, for the sake of an argument) unrelated to any particular real carrier, and simply relate it to a merely putative carrier—to the general positing of a carrier. It did not seem advisable to introduce specific terms for all these cases; what matters for us is the difference between Someonewhos and individuals, not the difference between Someonewhos and someone-whos-considered-as-distinct-from-individuals. When one follows the argument, the shifts become clear.

we cover the initial fees?" My Lady Macbeth says, "Perhaps she will agree to be paid at the end; if she does her job, we are certain to get an indemnity, and she definitely ought to be grateful for every percent—I am sure she does not get such an amazing opportunity every day." Voilà, we have a Someonewho: our Swiss lawyer, eager for the task, bidding our wishes. Of course, in real life, the construction of a Someonewho is *geared* towards finding a someone-who, i.e. an actual person who actually is like that. Either we find her or we don't; in either case, once the search is finished, whether it is a success or a failure, the Someonewho is dismissed, or "dispersed"—and in the more advantageous case, a real person takes over the place that has been reserved for it in our talk.

What is, generally, a Someonewho? The "someone" part points to an individual; the "who" part points to a list of attributes; and the blending of the two bits that our neologism undertakes is to be taken as an iconic sign that in Someonewhos, the two moments blend, too, and the individuality of Someonewhos is indistinguishable from the list of their attributes.

However, here I have to go slow, and clarify what I mean by individuality in the special case of Someonewhos. A list of attributes creates a type; an individual, *sensu stricto*, is a token. But we can also consider the *relations* between types and tokens: for instance, we can consider a type *qua* related to a token. A type thus considered is not a token; indeed, it is not even *considered* to be a token, or to be embodied in a token; it is only considered *qua* related to a token, *qua* related to an embodiment.[8]

---

[8] In other words, a Someonewho is neither a complex of descriptions, nor a complex descriptive determination, nor an individual (unique or not) under that description. Rather, a Someonewho is a *putative* individual under a description: an individual *posited* as being under a description. Someonewhos

Characters as Someonewhos

(Whenever, in what follows, I say that a fictional character is a type, I always mean that it is a type considered *qua* related to a token. This consideration does not cancel out its being a type, so the reformulation, adopted for the sake of brevity, is legitimate; but the phrase would become confusing as soon as someone forgets about the rider and just adopts the plain letter of "a fictional character is a type". The point is this: a fictional character is a type; but it is a type considered in a manner distinct from anything that would be normally done with the type/token distinction; and thus, our standard stock of knowledge regarding types need not apply to it unreservedly.)

In passing from the consideration of a type to the consideration of a type *qua* related to a token, we gain fairly little. Certainly, we obtain no logical or directly cognitive profits, and we do not modify the ontology of the type in any way. However, we do gain an imaginative possibility: by considering the type *qua* related to a token, we arrogate the capacity to point to the type as embodied—even though there is no genuine embodiment to be found, so of course we cannot point to them in spatiotemporal reality. Yet, indeed, we can make up to point to them—in imagination, and in talk.

A.2/
In the kind of talk that is geared towards practical application, we refer to someone-whos (i.e. Someonewhos not meant to remain such) by anaphora: we say "the lawyer"—meaning "the one we are talking about". In fiction, we refer to Someonewhos by names: Oliver Twist, Emma Bovary. What is it, for a proper name, to refer to a Someonewho?[9]

---

are instruments of imaginative, rather than descriptive or classificatory, thought.

[9] Compare Roger White's remarks on what he calls "dummy names",

In the technical sense of reference, proper names refer to particulars. But in a weaker, non-technical sense[10] regarding both "refer" and "proper names", we can—and, in equivalent paraphrases, frequently do—say that proper names refer to someone-whos: Martin and John refer to a man, Emma and Joan refer to a woman, Alessandro refers to an Italian and Hermann von Bucht refers to a German noble. Overall, there is a formula that is valid for all proper names as names for—or with—a *potential* use: the proper name X, if meaningfully used, is the name of/for someone who is called X, with the phrase "is called" taken in the broadest acception, i.e. as stating that there is a group or, at the limit, an individual who calls (or else: can, would, might call) that particular someone by the name X.

As standard speakers, we are normally aware of the two functions of (liberally conceived) proper names and of the difference between them. It is this awareness that makes it possible for us to appreciate the witticism that the *Iliad* and the *Odyssey* were written either by Homer or by somebody else of the same name: in the former case, "Homer" is treated as a

---

such as the names "A", "B", "C" in a mathematical exercise concerning three workmen, A, B and C, who dig a ditch (White 1996: 111–12 and 283–84 n. 2). Such dummy names, he points out, "in many respects ... work in a completely different way from the familiar bound variables of quantification theory. It isn't just that we clearly cannot regard these sentences as if they were elliptical for quantified sentences... It is misleading to regard them as *bound* variables at all. They lack a fixed scope, and, once a dummy name has been introduced, it can continue to be used throughout a sustained narrative (or even for that matter, be used by two people in a *dialogue*); no standard way of binding variables can handle such an open-ended scope as this."

[10]   Non-technical, that is, as long as we accept the dominant story on proper names. For both a survey and a critique of the view that proper names—as they function in our language—refer to individuals see Algeo 1973.

genuine proper name, referring to an individual; in the latter case, it is a potential proper name, quasi-referring to anybody who is called Homer — an arbitrary member of a group, rather than an individual.[11]

How do we get from proper names, properly used, to Someonewhos? "Proper" proper names, i.e. proper names *sensu stricto*, are normally perceived as closely related, by association, to potential proper names; potential proper names are names for someone-whos; and someone-whos are almost (almost!) the same as Someonewhos[12] — so the final step is also an easy one to make. The net result is that we find it natural to apply proper names, or their potential analogues, to Someonewhos. What needs to concern us here is not the *formal validity* of these transitions but exclusively the *associative ease with which one can perform them*. We are not assessing the *legitimacy* of using potential proper names for Someonewhos;[13] rather, we are tracing the *structural motivation* for doing so.[14]

With respect to Fregean sense and Fregean reference, what I have said here agrees with the standpoint that the meaning of names is their reference and that fictional names have no reference: they refer to the empty x, a variable that can be supplied with no argument.[15] However, I point to another dimension of proper names and go on from there. If logic

---

[11] Certainly, there are other possible uses of the name "Homer", but it is these two that make the witticism funny (as the point is that the pretended "knowledge" concerning the individual who wrote the epics is, actually, no knowledge concerning an *individual*).

[12] See the previous note.

[13] Should we be called to assess it, we would claim it to be legitimate by default insofar as all tribunals are out of their jurisdiction.

[14] In other words: we are primarily concerned not with what is legitimate but rather with what is practicable.

[15] See, e.g., Adams — Fuller — Stecker (1997).

neglects it, that is perfectly fine—as long as one avoids thinking that if something remains outside the limits of logic then it cannot find a place in our experience anywhere.

B/ *Sources of singularization*

My thesis is that fictional characters, Someonewhos, are types *qua* related to a token; so that fundamentally, they are types—even though qualified ones, types "with a story" (in both senses!). Does this not run against the common intuition that fictional characters are individuals, and that we approach and perceive them as individuals?

This general objection can be unwrapped at several levels of complexity, and we will go through these options one by one. We will also split them into two groups. In section B.1, we will formulate it only in a simpler form, as related to characters looked at in retrospect, i.e. to already constituted characters that we look back on. This is then used in section B.2 to analyze away certain traditional semantic puzzles. Subsequently we proceed to the more difficult topic of the dynamic constitution of characters in the process of reading, and of the appearance of singularity that the process endows them with. In section B.3 we focus on the issue regarding the sense in which types can be seen as agents. Section B.4 points out certain differences of degree between the types that we normally use outside of fiction and the types specific for fiction. Both sections B.5 and B.6 treat of the mutual interaction of agents; however, section B.5 again focuses on the relatively more fixed results, whereas section B.6 proceeds to a more dynamical, processual analysis.

One general preliminary point is to be made. The vague intuition—and, with some, the defended thesis—that fictional characters just *are* individuals certainly does have some evidence on its side. My claim is that ultimately, I can explain this evidence away as reducible to the putative singularity exhibited by Someonewhos. But the stress is on "ultimately": as the following section will take up the issues one by one, there will certainly be moments where the reader may easily feel that I am tweaking the evidence (i.e. the evidence for individuality). My hope is that, at the end, it will become clear that all I am tweaking are the formulations—and the notions that we employ for explaining the evidence to ourselves.

B.1/
One part of the objection are emotional responses. It has been suggested that the object of our sympathy or disgust, love or hatred and so on are only individuals;[16] so if we are capable of emotional responses with regard to fictional characters, as we surely are, then fictional characters must be individuals. But the claim is incorrect. We can certainly admire people who devote their lives to noble causes, we can hate people who hurt animals, detest people who make loud phone calls in public and be sexually attracted to people who look thus-and-so. These formulations allow to be interpreted in the sense that, e.g., I actually admire a dozen actual individuals who, to my knowledge, devote their lives to noble causes; but a legitimate and actually a more natural construal of the phrase is, precisely, that I admire people who devote their lives to noble causes—that I admire them as a type. Does that mean that I admire *the type*? Well, not quite: we should rather say that I admire *that type of people*. Such a rephrasing does add and emphasize the relationship to individuals as part of the emotional attitude; in considering the type in this way, I consider it *qua* related to individuals; yet there are no particular individuals that I have to consider in order to feel the appropriate emotion—the

---

[16]   See e.g. Doležel (1988: 478).

emotion can be, and often is, constitutionally unattached to any particular individuals with particular histories. In a way, then, we do find confirmed the intuition that the proper target of emotions such as love and hate are individuals—yet it is not confirmed in its original, unreserved sense: emotions, I claim, can make do with putative individuals, posited only as an aspect of types; or perhaps, there are besides emotions related to individuals also emotions related to types, with putative individuals only as a structural addition.[17]

Another part of the objection concerns folk logic. In the kind of folk logic that we normally use in practical life, types have plenty of tokens—or at the very least, plenty of handily imaginable potential tokens. With the types that constitute famous fictional characters, this is not true: Oliver Twist simply does not work for us as a category under which we could subsume plenty of actually or imaginatively available embodiments. Thus it is fair to say that from the viewpoint of practical, folk logic, Someonewhos stand closer to individuals

---

[17] With regard to the well-known "paradox of (our reaction to) fiction", on which see e.g. the pertinent essays in Hjort—Laver (1997) and most recently Stecker (2011), my position then is that our emotions vis-à-vis fictions are emotions geared to types, and that these type-emotions are not limited to fictions but rather concern all kinds of representation—all cases where the "how" and "what" of a thing is captured or suggested, visually or otherwise, without the thing being actually present. In watching a horror movie *qua* fiction, the emotion I feel is the horror that *this kind of things* awakens in me; in encountering a real scary sight, I fear this real thing as the thing it is—which can be split, for the sake of argument, into saying that I feel both the horror with regard to types *and* the horror with regard to tokens or occurrences, even though of course I do not feel a mixture of two different emotions. Quite certainly, the type-emotion is genetically derived from the token-emotion, they remain very closely related, and it is psychologically easy to shift from one to the other and back again.

than to types. But there is no serious problem here. When we talk of types, we normally talk at the level of "poets" or "red wines" — whereas Stephen Dedalus is closer to 1986 Chateau La Tour Carnet 4ème Grand Cru Classe Haut-Medoc. But of course, that vintage is a type, too; and so (I claim) is Stephen.

The sole issue that I am handling at the moment is the apparent individuality exhibited by fictional characters maintained in our memory, in retrospective reflection. For the time being I am leaving aside the impression of particularity as frequently exhibited by the fictional events we encounter in the actual process of reading, and the ensuing impression of individuality of the persons involved.[18] Thus, limiting ourselves to the area of retrospection, we can conclude this section by taking up a joke which nicely documents the possible shifts in understanding as well as in emotional approach. In a Czech cartoon, a lady is approached by two men — one holds a rolled-up newspaper in his hand — and told: "Dear Miss, we have read your advertisement: Looking for a man, non-smoker, educated, cultured, reliable, tender, generous, tolerant, solid of comportment but young of mind, with a sense of humor and a liking of sports, a family type. We are obligated to inform you of the regrettable fact that this extraordinary person is no longer among us: he died in 1953."[19] The joke is in part on the "low quality" of men, but it is also, and perhaps primarily, a language joke, and the semantic point of the joke concerns the shifts between a someone-who, a Someonewho, and — distinct from the former two — a particular person who is such and such: the lady had assumed she was looking for a someone-who, i.e. for one person among the presumed many who would

---

[18] See below, sections B.5 and B.6.
[19] The author is Vladimír Renčín. I have not been able to locate the cartoon, so that this is not a word-for-word translation.

143

fit the description provided in the ad; the two men tell her that this was actually a category of one and that this one particular person is dead; and thus we, as readers of the cartoon, are forced to treat the person desired in the advertisement as a Someonewho—as, at present, a mythical being.

B.2/
There is a group of often raised problems which our analysis can treat very easily, and so we can go through them fairly quickly just to uplift our spirits, before we proceed to some more demanding issues.

A statement like "Sherlock Holmes lives on Baker Street", used purely retrospectively, i.e. to summarize a fiction, is analytical: it specifies a part of what Holmes is; not an attribute of a person, but a characteristics included in a type *qua* related to a token, i.e. in a Someonewho. But the sentence can also be used historically: it can be a response to the question as to where the author made Holmes live, or, more loosely, where the traditional story makes the character (say, Heracles) live. Then it is not tautological at all, and it clearly has a truth value: there is a fact of the matter which the statement can ascertain. Finally, of course, the statement can occur within fiction, as part of construing the fiction; and then it inserts one more item among the characteristics that collectively constitute Sherlock Holmes, a Someonewho.[20]

Another group of problems concern the presence, or impossibility thereof, of references to real entities in fiction. It is easy to see that all we have said about Someonewhos so far could be reformulated for Somethingthats—so that we do not have to distinguish here between persons and things, or

---

[20] However, for more on the process of accepting fictional instructions see below, section B.6.

Characters as Someonewhos

even liberally conceived "things in general", for instance events. Now, we have already pointed out that all real individuals are also someone-whos, and (we can add) all real things are also something-thats. Moreover, the only difference between Someonewhos and someone-whos, Somethingthats and something-thats is this: to Someonewhos and Somethingthats there is ontologically nothing more than the collection of characteristics, and the regarding them as related to an individual; whereas to someone-whos and something-thats there is much more — namely *the real person* (at least one) and *the real thing* (at least one). This does bring out a huge difference in the relationship between Someonewhos and real persons — yet the difference is rather tiny when we regard the relationship between, on the one side, Someonewhos, and on the other side, someone-whos *regarded as distinguishable from the real entities that exhibit them*.[21] The conclusion we can draw is there is no messaliance in mixing Someonewhos and Somethingthats with someone-whos and something-thats. Clearly, evidently, obviously, incontrovertibly, Sherlock Holmes cannot ever step on the pavement of London, the real, existing, bustling city; yet he (or "he")[22] is free to include among his characteristics innumerable walks on the (type-level) pavement of the kind of bustling metropolis that (the real) London is; with the existing city forever inaccessible, it is his/"his" sure prerogative to roam the corresponding Somethingthat at his/"his" (author's) pleasure.

---

21 I.e. someone-whos are, unlike Someonewhos, geared up towards finding a fulfilment in reality, and thus they are — in aspiration and purpose — linked to a real thing; nonetheless, they need not find the fulfilment, and even if they do, they can be distinguished from it for analytical purposes.

22 See below, Postscript II.

It is also easy to resolve the issue as to whether authors uncover their characters, or rather invent them, or something else again. Authors invent texts that allow the public to construe fictional characters *qua* Someonewhos. (To various degrees the authors can, and perhaps must, invent the Someonewhos before construing the texts, but that is a *matière de cuisine*.) Someonewhos pre-exist the texts that allow us to construe them (as well as the authorial notions that posit them at one or another stage) in the nominal sense that all possible[23] bundlings of available characteristics are nominally available as soon, and as long, as the constituent characteristics are available—which raises the interesting but perfectly separate issue of the temporality of general attributes.

A final group of problems concerns the issues of trans-work identity, identity across readings, identity across drafts, variants, intertextual allusions, rewritings and parodies etc. Of course, once we eliminate the assumption that fictional characters are individuals, the issues of identity become much less pressing, as the whole problematic area undergoes a transformation into (much more flexible) issues of *overlapping*. Two characters, bundles of characteristics as they are, are the same to a smaller or higher degree: the area of overlap is the area of sameness, the area of divergence is the area of difference. This does and does not solve the problem. It fails to solve it completely, insofar as the characteristics contained in the bundle are organized in a hierarchy—and we will get to the issue of hierarchization later.[24] Yet the inclusion of the principle of hierarchization will not change the basic finding: the degree of identity will remain constituted by the *overlapping* of the

---

23 Not logically possible; just possible—by combinatorics.
24 See below, section B.5.

(hierarchized) bundles, and the degree of difference will remain constituted by the *divergence* of the (hierarchized) bundles.

B.3/
Let us now return to the overall objection that we, as readers, just do not seem to perceive literary characters as types and to treat them as such. We have answered two more specific forms of the objection in section B.1 above. But we have limited ourselves there to what could be called static analysis: our sole topic were characters looked at in retrospect, i.e. already constituted characters that we look back on. Now we proceed to what could be called dynamic analysis: we shift and broaden our interest towards the dynamic constitution of characters in the process of reading, and towards the appearance of singularity that the process endows them with.

It is the specifics of a narrative, whether fictional or non-fictional, that it presents an interaction of agents (that may or may not be anthropomorphic).[25] A narrative is treated or presented as non-fictional when it is treated or presented as referring to existing persons or agents (and, by extension, things); a narrative is treated or presented as fictional when it is treated or presented as referring to Someonewhos and Somethingthats. As every existing person and thing is also necessarily a someone-who or a something-that, and as someone-whos and something-thats, taken in isolation, do not

---

[25] This is—unfortunately—not the way narrative is normally defined; standard accounts tend to focus on causality, eventhood, or the presence of a narrator. I believe the definition via interaction of agents, once understood, is unproblematic (i.e. it very easily captures all that we would normally classify as a narrative—and by adding "normally", I really wish to exclude only certain theorists of the minimal narrative) and puts these other features of narrativity in their proper place.

at all differ from Someonewhos and Somethingthats, it is easy to see how every non-fictional narrative[26] can be modified into a fictional one (whereas the contrary operation is much more demanding).

We know — well enough, in any case — how existing people interact in the real world; but it is far from obvious how bundles of characteristics can interact, and how well, if at all, such an interaction meshes with the way we experience fictional narratives. This is the question that we need to face now.

The issue of interaction among agents is easier to analyze if we — to start with — separate it from the issue of direct, live readerly experience, one that we are "engrossed in", and adopt an initial descriptive distance. Fictional characters, i.e. Someonewhos, interact by mutually ingressing into their constitutive bundles:[27] when the fiction is that Harry meets Sally, what happens is that Harry is modified into the kind of person who has met the kind of person that Sally is,[28] and Sally is modified into the kind of person who has met the kind of person Harry is.[29] If they just brush and go their separate ways, the ingressive consequences for the two bundles can be contained without any violence; however, if the two hook up, the potential consequences for the two bundles are, in degree if

---

[26] I.e. a narrative somehow, at some time and/or by some people either presented or treated as non-fictional. For more see below, Postscript II.

[27] Which is not to say that they are merely those bundles, and that their meeting is merely some conjuction of those bundles — since Harry and Sally are those bundles *plus a putative individual*. However, putative individuals are no individuals, and they cannot meet directly. The only way for them to meet one another is by the ingressing I talk about.

[28] Where for Sally, as a fictional character, this is the "is" of identity — not the attributive "is" it would be for real people (where I take it that "this kind of person" is, in our context, synonymous with "a person of this kind").

[29] And the same reservation applies.

not in quality, as fateful as is the corresponding step for any two human individuals—the huge ontological gap notwithstanding: for all that happens, or even has happened, to the Harry bundle (what he does, what he suffers, what relations he enters or entertains)[30] is potentially fair game for being seen as ingressing the Sally bundle. Here we encounter a mechanism for an interaction as rich as is the one between real people, even though in ontological terms the two spheres of occurrence are hugely different, and we can also see why such an interaction should draw our attention as soon as we pay attention to Someonewhos to start with—and in fiction we do.

Yet this is only an initial step. Of course, our readerly experience does *not* seem to mesh well with the idea that what we do is that we just calculate the transformations undergone by bundles of characteristics. My response is to remind ourselves that my full proposal is different: fictional characters are not types but Someonewhos; they are not mere bundles of characteristics but rather bundles of characteristics considered *qua* related to an individual (or, with things, a particular).[31] So when Harry meets Sally, it is not merely an operation at the level of types; it is more, though just slightly more.[32] From the quantitative point of view, it is *primarily* that—i.e. the *larger* part of what happens is that two types intertwine their constitutive characteristics. Yet it is not only and exclusively that, and the remaining bit, although small—a mere parameter—makes a big

---

[30] On whether the bundle is a "he" see below, Postscript II.
[31] I am simply following the common use here, without any grand claims: it is simply more natural to limit "individuals" to persons and "particulars" to non-human entities—"things" in the broadest sense.
[32] Given the further limitations imposed on this section, i.e. leaving aside the course of our direct readerly experience in encountering complex characters with complex stories, on which see below, sections B.4–B.6.

qualitative difference, at least for us humans, being what we are, i.e. being individuals that perceive individuals: in fiction, the intertwining of the two bundles is considered not in pure abstraction but rather *qua* related to an individual (or two individuals, in this case). The guiding questions of our readerly experience do not go along the lines of: What is the result of interaction between such a bundle and such a bundle? Rather, they go along the lines of: What is it, for a man like this, to meet a woman like this, and vice versa? From an external, analytic point of view, the difference between the two cases does not amount to much: in the former case, we consider two types *qua* types; in the latter case, we consider two types *qua* each related to a respective individual; and in neither case is there any individual whatsoever to be found anywhere. Yet from the internal point of view, i.e. regarding what it is that we enjoy doing—and thus, what we actually do when we read in virtue of our pursuit of enjoyment—the difference matters immensely.

B.4/
It is just as well to admit it: the assimilation of fictional characters to types as we encounter them outside of fiction may sound weird to many ears. One can easily suspect that something important—precisely the individuality that fictional characters often seem to exhibit—is being left aside. In what follows I will do what I can to demonstrate that the weirdness does not impact the proposal itself, and that it stems merely from the order of exposition, which needs to get clear about the easier aspects in order to gather the instruments necessary for outlining the more complex aspects. We have reached the point where we can pass over to those.

For the sake of continuity, let us start by raising possible objections at whose solution we have already hinted. First, the unease with which one will rather naturally perceive an effort to equate fictional characters with types stems, largely though not exclusively, from the fact that outside of fiction we simply never construe types this complicated and so finely grained: the best expert in fine wines, art criticism, anatomy, pathology, cosmology or finances will never adopt classifying instruments fine-tuned to the degree of complication of, say, Emma Bovary, who, irreducibly, grew up at a farm, met a doctor etc. etc. etc. In real life, the element of complication—in the original sense of "interweaving"—is provided for quite sufficiently by the messiness of the world around; overall, in expending intellectual energy, we tend to the analytical side; and even the most ambitious cognitive syntheses tend to be balanced by analytical partitions.

As I pointed out, we do come closer to fiction—indeed, we sometimes enter the realm of fiction—in hypothesizing and planning.[33] For instance, I sit and think of all I will do when I win that million; my wife and I passionately debate whether we dismiss or not the so-far-nonexistent lawyer if, in the middle of the suit, we happen on a more knowledgeable expert; and the entire broader family invents artifices for blocking the smells drafting from the kitchen to the children's quarters in the house we do not yet possess for the excellent reason that it does not exist. People say they got carried away precisely when they realize they forgot that the whole talk is, emphatically, in the as-if mode, and that there is no money, no lawyer and no house— at least so far (which is non-being enough). However, depending on the situation that the whole talk starts from, the planning can get relatively far afield without getting dreamy-eyed—with the crucial specification that it must remain geared towards reality: the individual that fits the characteristics is not

---

[33] See above, section A.1.

simply posited, fullstop; rather, the individual, or the thing, is provisionally posited in order to be looked for and found, or arranged for and made. These are, functionally, not Someonewhos and Somethingthats but someone-whos and something-thats; yet given that the pertinent entities are *so far* nonexistent (either absolutely, or for us, i.e. *qua* cognitively or practically inaccessible), the borderline between the two can become hazy.

If we skip the grey zone and go all the way to complex fictional narrative (for the moment leaving aside lyric),[34] it is clear that the bundles become immensely, almost incomparably richer, more complicated and nuanced. Up to a point we will be right to declare that this incomparability is merely an illusion, mistaking a different order of magnitude for a difference in structure; stating this does capture part of the truth. Yet this answer needs to be complemented by another. It is crucial to point out that characters in non-primitive narratives, fictional or not, mutually interact; and if the narrative is fictional, this interaction of characters gives rise to effects that cannot be observed elsewhere.

My response to the feeling of weirdness or unease, regarding an equation between fictional characters and types, is then this: I submit that it is true to say that fictional characters, and overall fictional entities, are types considered *qua* related to tokens, and nothing above that. However, the interaction of fictional entities, and of fictional characters in particular, gives rise to effects that are peculiar; and it is alright to feel that something crucial is being left out until these effects are addressed at least in an outline.

---

[34] On which see below, n. 45.

B.5/
For the purposes of our presentation, the effects created by narrative interaction can be segmented under four rubrics. For these we shall use the terms plasticity, hierarchization, betting and verbicture (i.e. a "verbal picture"). The former two, plasticity and hierarchization, are to be understood in an attributive manner: they are names for dimensions that characters possess. The latter two, betting and verbicture, are processual: they are not characteristics of fictional characters but rather processes by which characters are presented and frameworks within which they are accessible. It is not unlikely that in the final analysis the four rubrics might turn out to be various names of, and perspectives on, one and the same thing; but that need not bother us, as long as they prove helpful for structuring the presentation of our thesis.

By plasticity I mean that a character in a narrative is hardly ever identical with what is stated about it explicitly in the narrative text. The Someonewho that a character is (the "is" being the sign of identification here) is, then, not merely a chain of the textual segments, either cited to the letter or adapted, that explicitly concern the fictional person. We make deductions from what we hear or read, and the deduction need not have a strictly logical character. Much more often, it is of a quasi-pragmatic character: separated from any direct practical intent yet directly linked to the manner in which we normally resolve practical quandaries. When we accept to be led on by a narrative, the question that guides us is, "What is it for X to *y*", i.e. "What is it for such-and-such a person to behave/be treated/find itself etc. thus-and-so". True, in a fairy tale for very small children, it will be specified that the step-mother evicted her step-children *because* she was evil; but in any minimally complex narrative there will be cases when such an assessment as to what it means, for such-and-such a person, to do a thing, suffer a thing, or enter consciously or unconsciously into such-and-such a relationship, is left up to the listener or the reader. This attaching of further characteristics, ones that do not occur explicitly formulated in the oral or scriptural text, does not change the status of the fictional character as a Someonewho. However, it does make the character distinct *both* from the pragmatically geared someone-who ("the plumber we have to call") *and* from the common understanding-and-use of a type as constituted by a chain of characteristics: in either of the latter two cases, implicit, autonomously guessed characteristics play no role in their makeup. This, then, describes one specific feature of the fictional or narrative Someonewhos—and one possible source of resistance to calling them types (rider or no rider), even though, it is plain to see, the adding of textually non-explicit characteristics does not change their essential status.

By hierarchization I mean that a character in a narrative is *more relevantly* this and that and *less relevantly* something else and the other thing: Dr. Watson is very relevantly Holmes' friend and *confidante* and relatively less relevantly a physician, Emma Bovary is very relevantly a frustrated young wife and relatively less relevantly a nominal Catholic. The hierarchization of features need not be either unambiguously determined or generally decidable in all cases; it is sufficient to observe that *it exists*—fuzzy, messy, local and shifty as it sometimes may be. The crucial point is that the question "What is it for X to *y*" reflects on X and is capable of modifying it: if the narrative forces us to ask what it is for a mild-mannered honourable public servant to turn into a fierce Nazi, we may well end up concluding that he had never been that mild-mannered and honourable to start with; and in such a case, we not only modify the pertinent features but also add one more and insert it into a prominent position, as the character in question becomes (for instance) the incarnation of hypocrisy. This is, once again, a specifics of fiction: we can state there is a complete absence of structural plasticity *both* in the pragmatically geared someone-who ("the plumber we have to call") *and* in the common understanding-and-use of a type constituted by a chain of characteristics.[35] In neither of these latter two cases is it true that their makeup involves any hierarchization of their features.

Plasticity and hierarchization are two structural features very clearly lacked by the closest analogues that Someonewhos find outside of narrative or fiction; and by reason of this lack it may easily seem that literature has very little to do with either pragmatic imaginings or logical groupings, i.e. (to return to our terminology) that Someonewhos are *nothing like* either the pragmatically geared someone-whos or types. To be sure, a difference there is, it is an obvious one, and I am far from trying to deny it. However, the difference is not of such a kind that it would force us to abandon the view that fictional characters are types with a rider, i.e. that they are types considered *qua* related to a token.

---

[35] Although the absence is of a different nature in each case. With purely classificational types, there is simply no plasticity (in the sense pertinent here) to be found, and this is necessarily so. With pragmatically geared someone-whos, it is empirically true that they lack plasticity — but it is not a necessary feature: plastic someone-whos could be constructed, it is just that we never find ourselves in a situation that would provide sufficient pragmatic incentives for doing so. Our condition is such that non-plastic someone-whos pass over into non-plastic Someonewhos, and only then into plastic Someonewhos; the scenario where the grey zone is occupied by plastic someone-whos is imaginable but it simply does not conform to the fact of the matter.

Still, the possible objections are not exhausted here. We have cleared up the ground as far as characters *considered as separate* are concerned. However, there is also—and prominently so—interaction among characters, and our perception of it as readers/listeners. As common readers, we have perfectly good reasons to believe that within a story, characters fall in love, marry, commit adultery etc. *just once*; and it is fairly unclear how types, with or without a rider, could do/be/suffer something *just once* and within a perfectly singular configuration. Once we admit this, it obliges us to say more about the *process* of accessing narrative or fiction, as opposed to the restrospective view of characters *qua* already constituted.

B.6/
The transition from attributive to processual analysis is not a shift to a completely novel topic; rather, it will simply oblige us to complete and deepen the analysis we have provided for plasticity and hierarchization. We will do so under the two rubrics of betting and verbicture.

Betting is the modality under which we are being presented with the narrative issues of "What is it for X to y?"; indeed, it is *also* the modality under which we *select* (out of a potential infinity) the particular for-X-to-y-questions that we actually confront. That is to say: besides giving a certain response to the question of "What is it for X to y?", we do a little more—we *bet* on it that our response is the correct one; and besides simply selecting this or that particular for-X-to-y question out of a potential infinity, we do a little more—we *bet* on it that this is the question we ought[36] to ask ourselves. Let me take up these two options one by one.

First: betting (to say it once more) is the modality under which we are being presented with the narrative issues of "What is it for X to y?" Schematically, this translates into three types of resolution which can be viewed as coming one after the other.[37] One: we answer the question: for a step-mother to evict her little step-children is evil and cruel; for a flowergirl to be proposed by a millionaire is just an amazing stroke of luck. Two: we (may) let the answer reflect on (a) the character, (b) the event. In the case of the step-mother: since it was evil and cruel for the step-mother to do such a thing, we conclude that the step-mother, herself, is an evil and cruel person; and what she did was—in the sequence of the story—an utterly cruel deed. In the case of the flowergirl: since it was just an amazing stroke of luck for the flowergirl to be proposed by a millionaire, we conclude that the event of the proposition of marriage, itself, is an amazingly lucky turn of events (for the flowergirl, in any case); and the flowergirl herself is what we would call a lucky person. In drawing the conclusion (if and when we do draw it), we enrich the character and/or the event by a feature not explicitly stated in the text: we get engaged in the construal, we are invested in the form "things" are taking, we bet on it that this is so, that—say—the step-mother really is an evil and cruel person, that the proposition of marriage really is an amazing stroke of luck for the flowergirl. We make the best bet we can, based on our general knowledge of life and of literature as well

---

[36] Under what criteria the "ought" is made valid, is not a decisive issue here: *whatever* kind of reading we pursue, it remains true that we bet on its procedural steps.
[37] In actual practice, the three types can variously blend or else be skipped, so that the temporal sequence does not obtain.

as our specific knowledge of certain milieux, certain psychological types, certain genres or story-types, the particular teller/author etc.

Second: betting (to say it once more) is the modality under which we select (out of a potential infinity) the narrative issues of "What is it for X to *y*?" that we actually confront. For instance, the text tells us that the flowergirl which we know from the story was proposed by a millionaire. Such a state of narrative affairs pretty much leaves us no choice but to assess what it is for a flowergirl to be proposed by a millionaire—yet it also provides us with the open, facultative opportunity to raise for ourselves the issue what it is for a millionaire to propose to a flowergirl. If we actually choose to confront this issue, we thereby make a bet with certain consequences: we expend energy on believing that such a course of assessment is one that will "pay off" in the subsequent development of the story. Moreover, the raising of the issue opens yet other options to us, and to a degree even forces them upon us—since, for instance, our assessment of the motivation etc. of the millionaire's proposal will have to reflect back on our assessment of what it is for a flowergirl to be proposed by a millionaire; or perhaps more exactly, what is it for *this* flowergirl to be proposed by *this* millionaire, as each have become something more than just *a* flowergirl and *a* millionaire—they have become entangled in a web of mutual relations and reactions. Once again, we make the best bet we can, based on our general knowledge of life and literature as well as our specific knowledge of certain milieux, certain psychological types, certain genres or story-types, the particular teller/author etc. Our betting follows certain criteria—it is never a toss of the coin[38]—and in employing the criteria in the bet, we also put a stake on the criteria themselves.

Betting, as the modality of our subjective investment in the story, finds a kind of objective counterpoint in what I shall call verbicture—as an abbreviation for "verbal picture". Verbicture could be left aside for the great majority of fictional characters: either it is not operative for them at all, or else fairly marginally. However, it is to be expected that our thesis will be measured up against some of the finest examples of character-making: against Hamlet, rather than Horatio; against Emma, rather than Hommais; against Humbert Humbert, rather than Lolita. This forces us to go the whole way and provide a sketch of verbicture. I believe we may rightfully rest content with a sketch, as, first, verbicture concerns *more* the storytelling *than* the characters; second, complications notwithstanding, we do separate characters from their stories, at least to a measure—and we do so because we can; and consequently, a treatment of verbicture is *rather* an inroad into a different topic *than* a completion of our given topic.

The overall idea is this. Within a picture, motifs and patterns can gain a quasi-individuality thanks to an interplay of similarities and contrasts. Let me start with the most primitive example. For a blotch of red, we can claim a kind of material individuality; however, if there is a discontinuous but ordered—and sometimes even a disordered, quite playful—pattern of red blotches (and they do not have to share even the exact shade!), there is no ground for claiming a material or even

---

[38] If we *do* go for the toss-up, we do so in consequence of a conflict among our available criteria and the lack of a sufficiently clear meta-criterion which would resolve the impasse. In such a case, we actually use the toss-up *not* for directly selecting the outcome but rather for selecting the criterion to follow; so the role of criteria remains evident and crucial.

a specific individuality; and yet, under proper conditions, the pattern will be perceived as a kind of unity, a separate entity within the texture of the picture. (It does not concern us here whether, or to what degree, we do so legitimately; we merely need to observe that we regularly do so—that we *feel* legitimate in doing so.)

As I pointed out, the example given above is just the most primitive one. The phenomenon is certainly not limited to lines and blotches (even though, significantly, it will always remain *anchored* in lines and blotches—it would not occur if not for them). For instance, a face on a picture can acquire a certain expression thanks to the interplay of similarities and contrasts that it is engaged in within the picture. The face expression is not *drawn* or *painted* in the picture in the sense that it could be identified with certain lines and blotches; the interplay may include a very large area of the picture, at the limit its entirety.[39] Nonetheless, the face expression is there, in the sense that it stands out; and we would then speak of "the smile" or "the frown" as including this phenomenon of deep interplay.

Sophisticated narrative regularly awakens an effect similar to the pictorial one: a couple of lines "paints" a milieu "in front of our eyes", a phrase "sketches" a characterizing feature. (We do not have to assess how far the analogy with drawing really goes; it is sufficient that we easily grasp the analogy and that we get its point.) However, with narrative, the role of the interplay of similarities and contrasts as constitutive for a quasi-individuality can reach much further: it can enter the realm of action, its motivations and intentions, goals and real

---

[39] Or in fact, even more: it may include our long-term visual habits. This is important for the subsequent analogy with literature: the effects of verbicture may be created not only by the proximal context, i.e. the text, but also by the distal context, i.e. linguistic and stylistic norms, habits etc.

consequences; and also the realm of assessing one's own or another's action, and the motivations, goals and consequences *of such an assessment*. It is to the realm of narrated action that I will limit the term "verbicture".

A character in a narrative serves as a center of deixes: direct spatial deixes, cognitive and doxastic deixes, practical and orectic deixes and so on.[40] In other words, in a narrative a thing is always a thing for somebody: it is an entity that a character—normally, but not necessarily, an explicit intra-diegetic character[41]—sees or can see, knows or can know, desires or can desire, uses or can use and so on. We can speak of the *deictic field* of a character as the configuration of fictional entities that a particular character determines in the outlined manner. Of course, according to our thesis, all the characters and entities that we talk about here are types: when we read that the King was sitting on his throne, we read about a kind of man and a kind of chair. However, both types are considered *qua* related to a token—as, obviously, a type cannot sit on a type. But the sentence is not about tokens, it is not about an individual man sitting in an individual chair; what it presents is a certain type of a state of affairs—the type of a state of affairs when a king is sitting on his throne (and "his throne", here, does not refer to a particular throne).[42]

Narratives are defined by interaction of agents; complex narratives exhibit complex interaction of diverse agents; and

---

[40] My primary inspiration here is Bühler (1934: § 8). The topic is very well developed by Margolin (1991).
[41] For the purposes of this analysis, I would include narrators (of any kind) and even implicit authors among characters.
[42] See below, Postscript I.

agents are diverse due to the diversity of their deictic fields.[43] In the final result, this means that a complex narrative is, by the sheer fact of being an interaction of agents, also a series of interactions among deictic fields. Desdemona perceives certain things; Othello perceives some of the same things and some very different things; Jago, crucially, perceives not only things but also the ways things are perceived by Desdemona and Othello. Now, Desdemona, Othello and Jago are kinds of people: conceptually speaking, there could be many of them — and it is equally possible that there has never been a single one of them. But in order to grasp and follow the complexity of the verbicture that the play *Othello* suggests in employing them, we accept them as working units. This is nothing so very peculiar: in the same manner, a biologist will talk of the giraffe and a philosopher of the transcendental idealist. Yet whereas the talk of the biologist will maintain a direct link with the multitude of observable cases, and even the talk of the philosopher will strive to maintain at least the appearance of a link to at least some actually observable cases, the fictional talk is not constrained in this manner. The fictional talk, *qua* fictional, does not have to search for its tokens; it just stipulates a token and that's it. The stipulation does not make the token exist — but for the purposes of fiction that's indifferent.[44]

---

[43] For fictional characters, this is straightforwardly true: agents are distinguished *by means* of their deictic fields. Outside of fiction, agents also possess a material individuality that is independent from their deictic fields; nonetheless, *qua* agents, they are individualized by their deictic fields.

[44] Is my topic, then, the ontological issue of what Someonewhos are, or the semantic issue of how we talk about them? (I am grateful to Greg Currie for raising the point with me.) The former; but with the crucial addition that, for us, talk is a privileged — though perhaps not unique — venue of *access* to Someonewhos, and that once we limit ourselves to verbal fiction (as we do in the present consideration) the Someonewhos that interest us are *in fact*

Characters as Someonewhos

Characters are a bit like quantum particles: intellectually, we know that characters are nebulae of occupiable positions—yet whenever anyone (a character, a narrator, or ourselves) actually observes them, they collapse to a particle, a singular position. The analogy is meant to be playful but informative and it says this: When there is a rich man and a poor man, their typicality remains fairly clearly at the forefront; but when the rich man attempts to play a trick on the poor man and the poor man manages to slip out of the loop and outwit the rich man in his turn—in such a case we simply drop the typicality consideration and just think of stipulated individuals. In doing so, we certainly do not create (or encounter) any new individuals; overall, the shift to stipulated individuals is not a creative but rather an *economizing* move; as there is more and more happening among the characters, and among the deictic fields that they anchor, it is simply prudent to accept the working units—the characters—as *pro forma* individuals. But *pro forma* individuals are no individuals: they are analogies of individuals, created by the context and for the context—or more specifically, for the sake of a narrative.

When the narrative is rather simple, we find it fairly natural to revert to the nebulae-view: we tell a joke about the American, the Czech and the Russian—but everyone realizes that the joke is on and about Americans, Czechs and Russians, and/or the indefinite subset of them that fit the type. And the same will be true for narratives that remain simple with respect to their handling of characters (as hierarchized and, especially,

---

accessed by verbal artefacts. A more detailed analysis of the being of Someonewhos as *separable* from our talk about them is certainly a crucial task but it is one that can, and must, remain suspended within the present argument. To give at least a hint: the being of Someonewhos is to be seen as closely related to the being of states of affairs (*Sachverhalte*).

plastic; see above), even though they may get complex in other respects.⁴⁵ However, once there is complexity in the handling of characters, we commence to lean fairly distinctly to the particle-view, at least with regard to *those* characters that are plastic; in other words, we become increasingly resistant to separating the character from the story.

The ultimate reason for this resistance is, I suggest, verbicture. If we know the Shakespeare play well, we will find it practically impossible to separate the character of Othello from the way he lines up against Jago and Desdemona—as plastic agents that he is involved with and they with him; and we find no other access to this interplay but the story. The character is perceived as inseparable from the complex "verbal picture" through and in which he appears to us. The character

---

⁴⁵ Crucially, this rubric includes lyrical poetry. Lyrical poems are not primarily narratives, but they do possess a narrative aspect which we can focus on: the lyrical speaker—the *only* complicated character that is clearly functional in a lyrical poem—is always, in a non-trivial sense, an agent among agents, one who has been impacted by others, or perhaps yearns to impact others, etc. Now, it is obvious that this character can be very complicated in his or her feelings, memories, ethical makeup, and so on. But as long as we are talking about a genuine lyrical poem, the speaking voice will be *treated* fairly simply: trite and schoolboyish as it will sound, the truth is that it will just talk, remember, and have feelings; it will be *narratively* simple—not much will happen around it. I go to the lengths of pointing all this out because of the consequence which it has: *with lyrical speakers, we feel much less hindered to talk of them as types*. A lyrical speaker is, *prima facie*, a *kind* of person: an old man abandoned by his children, desperate of the world etc. etc. It is only when we follow some action that we start to feel that the story must be about something more than types. My contention is that this "more" involves only a shift in emphasis, not a structural modification: the lyrical speaker is perceived as individualized, too, but this individuality is, relatively speaking, much less important—whereas in following a story it becomes instrumental.

is a singular pattern in this verbicture, which provides him with a quasi-individuality.

Well, if he appears individual, are we not committed to say that he *is* individual?[46] No, we are not. For it is simply and unequivocally *not* the case that fictional characters appear to us as spatiotemporal individuals. The case is that they appear to us in a manner which we are inclined to see as fairly close to individuality—and this, in turn, induces us to adopt (and adapt!) for fictional characters expressions standardly referring to individual agents. Characters are agents—types of agents, that is; and the mutual intertwining of their deictic fields endows them with a contrastive quasi-individuality. Being agents (i.e., types of agents), and exhibiting quasi-individuality, does not make them into individual agents by any means. However, it does make them closer to individual agents than to anything else we normally talk about; and therefore we do what we always do in similar situations—we extend the available lexicon to the new cases (unless we have very strong reasons not to do so, and here we do not). Specifically, we talk and think of Othello as a determinate (not a generic) "he"; we say what he did and did not do; we attribute to him individual emotions, plans, mistakes and relationships; and any other talk would seem unnatural. Really, it would *be* unnatural—as any other talk, for instance a generic or an apersonal talk, would omit and deform something essential that the quasi-individual agent exhibits and that the standard determinate "he" talk captures very properly.

However, to repeat the same doubt with a different emphasis: if the character appears inseparable from its story (or from its verbicture), what gives us the right to separate them even for the purposes of analysis? The answer is this: Hamlet,

---

[46] See the first paragraph of this essay.

Emma Bovary, Humbert Humbert etc. are very special fictional characters; but as special as they are, they remain part of the set of fictional characters. Even though we may reserve for them a special place in our experience and our memory, it is equally necessary that we also, at a certain level, put them *in the same line* with all the second- and third-order characters within the story. Admittedly, this argument can pull both ways: theoretically, it can induce us to perceive all the second- and third-order characters as *just as complicated* as the few most prominent ones. But this possibility is very rarely, if ever, realized in actual readerly experience (for the simple reason that it would be amazingly costly in terms of maintained attention).[47] In the immense majority of cases, we perceive the story as including *some* very plain characters; and we are ready to admit that *at a certain level*, the finest-wrought characters share a way of being with the plainest ones. This is as much as to say that at a certain level, all characters, including the finest-wrought ones, continue to be perceived as mere Someonewhos separated from verbicture. And this conclusion is all we need for our purposes.

Verbicture is the ultimate foundational ground of the quasi-individuality of fictional characters: hierarchization and plasticity are only static dimensions of the dynamic verbictural environment; and betting is really the subjective correlate of verbicture as the quasi-objective storyworldline.[48] With most

---

[47] It is more likely that this option can become realized in an extended written analysis. We do call such analyses "readings" — but they are, at least in some respects, very distinct from actual processes of reading.

[48] It could be claimed that betting actually *creates* verbicture; and at a deeper level of analysis, this may well be true. But in our context it is better to say that betting *makes* verbicture *accessible*. What we are touching on here

characters, their "feel" of individuality (or at least non-typicality) can be sufficiently, and even more effectively, explained by means of the relatively simpler concepts of hierarchization, plasticity, and betting. It is only with the finest productions of character-making that we need to explain the special and prominent effect, established primarily by a collusion of plasticity and betting, and perceived as quasi-objective. It is this effect that we call "verbicture" and that we could no more but sketch—but were obliged to at least sketch, in order to elucidate the kind of quasi-individuality which the most memorable fictional characters exhibit.

C/ Some conclusions

Section C.1 unpacks certain consequences for the relationships between fictions mutually and between fictions and the real world, in moral as well as ontological terms. Section C.2 outlines a response to the query, why make the effort to create Someonewhos—which is the same as to ask, what is the purpose of fiction.

C.1/

Our thesis leads us to take up a rather liberal position concerning the overlap of fictional and real characters, the judging of fictional characters by extra-fictional morality, the notion that a fictional character can be "embodied" by a person, and so on.

   First: A real person is, necessarily, also a person of a kind. A Someonewho is a person of a kind, bar any actual person. In blending a real person with a Someonewho, we are not guilty of pushing two individuals into a single embodiment: there is just

---

is, of course, the problem of the objectivity of the literary artistic creation, and of the plurality of subjective readings.

one individual there, no more. What we do do when we compare a real character with a fictional one, is that we hypothetically endow a real person with an interweaved complex of characteristics, and observe both the misfits and the fits. There are separate reasons to think that with Someonewhos of any complexity, and, by extension, with Someonewhos fictionally interacting with Someonewhos of any complexity, the misfits will be fairly numerous and not negligible in relevancy, so that the comparison will become increasingly strained or imprecise. But whatever its other shortcomings, the comparison will involve no ontological sins, for generally speaking, an individual and a Someonewho fit (or not) like hand and glove: there may be huge misfits in particular cases but there is no general problem with *attempting* to fit them.

Second: It is alright to judge fictional characters by extra-fictional morality. Fictional texts do challenge us to employ our cognitive, pragmatic and moral—as well as cultural and literary—criteria in order to co-initiate the construal of the characters' plasticity and hierarchization. To limit ourselves merely to cultural and literary criteria might well be impossible; it is certainly neither needed nor desirable. We have no special morality-for-novels. True, in reading novels we blend our moral criteria with numerous other constitutive factors, thus achieving some very special effects indeed. Nonetheless, we do employ moral (as well as cognitive and pragmatic) criteria, *the very same ones* we employ out of fiction; and there is no *a priori* ontological messaliance in submitting fictional characters to moral judgments—especially given that those judgments are already "mixed into" those characters, having played a role in their constitution.[49] Certainly, there is the possibility that we find good literary reasons for witholding the moral judgment

---

[49] I.e. in betting; see above, section B.6.

that we spontaneously adopt, or for modifying it heavily—but then, exactly the same thing can, and often ought to, happen for other than literary reasons and out of fiction.

Last: A fictional character can really be "embodied" by a person. This is a pretty straight consequence of my initial point in this section, but it can be broadened to cover other interesting cases and to make a few additional points. To repeat: a real individual embodies a fictional character not by being identical, as a singular entity, with another singular entity, but rather by being someone who is such that she, in her being-someone-who, is either identical or close to a Someone-who. For somebody to embody a complex fictional character may be highly unlikely but there is nothing ontologically absurd or devious about it; and in any case, the embodiment can be seen as simply a mere part of the fact of the matter—and in this understanding it just occurs all the time. Real people embody fictional characters precisely in the way in which actors—who, after all, are real people, and definitely remain such during performances—embody fictional or even historical characters: for a time they behave like a person who is/suffers such-and-such, thus embodying either a genuine individual who is, also, such-and-such, or a Someonewho identical with being such-and-such. Paradox there is none—granted that, standardly, in talking about one person embodying another we do not expect the embodiment to be a true sharing or exchange of identity between two true individuals *qua* individuals; we expect it to be the complete or partial overlap of content between (a) someone-whos *minus* their singularity (which we subtract simply because we know it cannot be shared), or (b) a someone-who and a Someonewho (as when an actor plays Hamlet), or (c) a Someonewho and a Someonewho (when a fictional character, on stage or in a text, embodies another).

Once we mention partial overlap, however, we are facing the issue of plasticity and hierarchization.[50] My liberalism concerning the crossover between fiction and reality goes only so far as to state that there is no *fundamental* problem, no boundary that in principle one could not cross. Even so, there may be very many barriers of non-theoretical kind that hinder us in making the comparison between fictional and real characters effective, attractive, stimulating and so on. Complex fictional characters are very distinctly stratified, they exhibit plasticity regarding what we got to know about them and what we had to guess, they exhibit hierarchization regarding what is more and what is less relevant about them. It is rare for our acquaintance with real people to provide us with individuals that we experience with a plasticity and a hierarchization comparable in complexity to that of fictional characters. Yet even though it is rare, it is not impossible; and even though the drift of the present paragraph has been to point out that, after all, comparisons between complex fictional characters and real persons may be rather ineffective, our final verdict stands — such comparisons are perfectly legitimate as a matter of principle, and with relatively simple fictional characters we can certainly just go ahead and convincingly make them.

Even in cases where it might seem completely fruitless to compare some particular fictional characters with real persons, it remains true that our judgments concerning the fictional characters — judgments that we *have* to make, in order for the character to attain any plasticity and undergo hierarchization — are largely directed by criteria that are simply pragmatic, extra-fictional. And even with the criteria that are purely literary, such as are criteria bound to certain genres or particular authors, their use itself is meta-directed by our view regarding

---

[50] See above, section B.5.

the due position of literature in our lives—and this view, by itself, is not intra-literary; it is a pragmatic matter of our overall existence.

C.2/
What is the purpose of fiction? I will attempt an answer that builds upon the thesis I present. Let me sketch three schematic rubrics: In "realist" fiction, characters behave as they normally would: in following the actions, sufferings and relationships of characters, we learn, revive, deepen, or confirm what we know about people and the world. In "fantastic" fiction, characters behave differently from what people normally do yet the features they exhibit are features we know; the difference is in the exceptionality of combination or degree, not in their very existence: and thus, in following the actions, sufferings and relationships of characters, we learn, revive, deepen, or confirm what we know about distinct human characteristics, their causes and effects and their various interrelationships. Finally, in "artificial" fiction, characters exhibit features that just do not (or perhaps even cannot) occur in extra-fictional reality (for instance, the characters may embody intertextual resonances); yet the constitution of these characters is dependent on the criteria we employ in our betting, and these criteria are never purely intra-fictional, as even in liminal cases they are based on a conviction concerning the relationship *between* fiction *and* reality; and thus, in following the actions, sufferings and relationships of characters, we learn, revive, deepen, or confirm what we know about characteristics (whether human and real or fictional and artificial), their causes and effects and their various interrelationships. Now, the scare-quotes around "realist", "fantastic" and "artificial" are simply meant to highlight that within the context of our quick argument in this

section, these are no starkly divided rubrics: they can mingle within a single text, they can change between a reading and a re-reading, and so on. All I want to say is that, with characters being Someonewhos, it is easy to say what the ultimate expected (though, perhaps, not always realized) cognitive profit of each and any fictional practice may be: in a Kantian spirit, our perceptual and cognitive criteria enter into a free, purposeless interplay — and the very lack of an external purpose allows us to re-examine, sharpen, or revivify the criteria.

Postscript I: The predicative paradox
Our talk about Someonewhos exhibits a formulation ambiguity which may seem like a paradox but can be demonstrated not to be. In brief, the paradox is that there are things which one will deny about Someonewhos: Sherlock Holmes, one will say, is *not* real, *not* an individual, *not* a person; and also *not* a man, *not* a detective, *not* a Britisher whenever we take these terms in the standard acceptance that the context would suggest, i.e. as referring to a real singular man, detective, Britisher etc. But from a different perspective, all these various predicates can be ascribed to Sherlock Holmes: clearly, in a certain sense, Holmes is a detective, a Britisher etc.; he is also a person and an individual; and at the end of the day we also have to admit that in a certain sense, however qualified, he is real — as opposed to oneiric, phantastic, invented etc. beings.

The puzzle is not difficult to resolve. The distinction we have to draw is fairly close to the difference between "I want you to read a book" and "I want you to write a book": in the former case (and in the most common acceptance), there is an actual book that we are talking about; in the latter case, there is no book yet (and there may well never be) — we only wish for something to be there which will be a book plus written by XY.

With Sherlock Holmes, there is no detective either; we only *stipulate*, just like we have wished in the previous example, that there be an individual called Sherlock Holmes and that it be a detective. Now, in the former case, when I say "I want you to write a book", I definitely want you to write a *real* book—not, say, an optative one (although I could possibly have wishes about that, too).[51] And in the latter case, when I stipulate that Holmes be a detective, I stipulate that he be a *real* detective—not, say, a stipulative one (although I could possibly make stipulations along those lines, too—for instance in a novel including a literary theorist). But it still remains the case that there is no real book there, and that there is no real detective there. Nor is there any real paradox.

Technically, when I stipulate something concerning a Someonewho, what happens is that I enrich the characterizing content of the Someonewho. Someonewhos relate merely to stipulated individuals that they constitutively include, and nothing in the content of the Someonewho can change that. In order for Someonewhos to relate to real individuals, I have to directly or indirectly[52] *encounter* those—not stipulate them; just as no amount of wishing real hard will, by itself, make the wish true—the book we wish for just needs to be written, that's all.

---

[51] Say, I could wish that you wish that I write a book.

[52] Under indirect encounter, I subsume (a) encountering people and reporting sources such that I form the belief that such-and-such exists (has existed, will certainly exist); (b) encountering the surrounding world as a place such that I form the belief that such-and-such exists (has existed, will certainly exist).

One could also include conditional encounters: then the Someonewho relates to real individuals under a condition, precise or vague.

Martin Pokorný

Postscript II: Fictionality and narrativity
What about the difference between fiction and narrative that the previous argument seemed to confound? I certainly would not wish to imply that fiction equals narrative. However, the point can be made that in an important respect, a narrative is always fictional. My position is that fiction is the realm of Someonewhos and Somethingwhats, and narrative is the presentation of a mutual interaction of agents. Now, within a narrative, agents always act very prominently as someone-whos: their situation, their options of action, the impact of their acts is determined by what they (durably or momentarily) are, what characteristics they bear (or: are momentarily bearing). Once the narrative ends (or is interrupted), our attention may shift very decidedly from someone-whos and something-thats to individuals: as clients, detectives, lovers etc. we do not want just to hear stories, we want *the actual thing, the actual person* etc. However, as long as the narrative lasts (or: as long as, remaining continuous, it is followed attentively), the emphasis is borne by someone-whos and something-thats; and once someone-whos and something-thats gain functional dominance over individuals and particulars, they are basically identical with Someonewhos and Somethingthats. Thus, it is always possible to perceive a narrative as fictional, although the contrary is not true, i.e. not every narrative can be perceived as true; and as long as a narrative lasts and is continuously perceived, it is, in functional terms, always perceived as fictional (which is to say: as indifferent to reality—*not* as false)—yet at all times we are free to interrupt the narrative, either in actual fact or mentally, and to put it to a purpose. This is equal with saying that the processual fictionality has no binding power on us: it simply occurs—it does not oblige us to maintain it.

Of course, in common use outside of philosophy and theory of literature the term "fiction" is always understood more narrowly, as implying falsity, and perhaps even equivalent with it: whatever is fiction, is false—and (perhaps) whatever is false, is a fiction. In such a case, the pertinent Someonewhos and Somethingthats differ from actual entities—and from the whos and whats of actual entities—not only structurally and/or functionally but also in their content: it is simply not the case that there be an animal such that it is a unicorn; it is simply not the case that there be a woman such that it is an Emma Bovary. Yet even in this narrow understanding of fiction, the two terms—"fiction" and "falsity"—can be distinguished in their emphasis. Falsity is a negative term: it is the opposite of truth; it stresses that *there is no such thing or person* as to correspond to the proposed Someonewhos or Somethingthats. Fiction is a positive term: it is the capacity to spin; it stresses that *there is a speech creating Someonewhos and Somethingthats* – so that there is understanding but no reality. A lie you commit but a fiction you make. Simple fictions can be made by simple telling; but from a certain threshold of complexity, fictions can be created exclusively by narrating. Thus, our two-pronged argument of the last two paragraphs has shown that under any understanding of "fiction", the broader or the narrower one, fiction and narrative remain very closely related; and while they should not be simply confounded, in certain contexts and for certain purposes it is legitimate to see them as a pair.

Postscript III: Experience and fiction
In certain parts of the essay, the reader may be tempted to ask whether what I say could not be extended, beyond fiction, to much broader stretches of experience. In particular it could be

asked whether betting and verbicture are purely literary phenomena. My ultimate response would be that they are not. My general approach to fiction would be that it does not treat of other realms; it treats of the world as it is — it just treats it in a special manner. Aristotle was right, I believe, to say that in mimesis the possible matters more than the actual. Still, the possible is a dimension of the actual; it co-forms the actual; and even focusing on the possible, we still observe the actual — even though through a very special prism.

Betting and verbicture, as well as hierarchization and plasticity, are then in one important sense processes and effects that occur in all experience and constantly. However, in fiction they are focused upon the possible, whereas in reality they are focused upon the actual; and even though the difference is one of emphasis rather than an absolute one, it matters enough to make it profitable, and certainly legitimate, to separate the two areas. This is, then, what we have done: the key guidelines of the analysis could be pursued into all of experience — but to remain within the limited field of fiction is a legitimate undertaking.[53]

Charles University / Czech Academy of Sciences
martin.pokorny@ff.cuni.cz

REFERENCES

Adams, Fred, Gary Fuller, and Robert Stecker. 1997. "The Semantics of Fictional Names." *Pacific Philosophical Quarterly* 78 (2): 128–148.

---

[53] Work on this project was supported by a grant awarded by the Grant Agency of the Czech Republic, No. 401/09/P178 "Dimenze řečové události".

Algeo, John. 1973. *On Defining the Proper Name*. University of Florida Humanities Monograph 41. Gainesville: University of Florida Press.

Aristotle. 1995. *Poetics*, trans. Stephen Halliwell; together with Longinus, *On the Sublime*, and Demetrius, *On Style*. Loeb Classical Library. Cambridge, MA: Harvard University Press.

Bühler, Karl. 1934. *Sprachtheorie: Die Darstellungsfunktion der Sprache*. Stuttgart: Gustav Fischer Verlag.

Currie, Gregory. 1990. *The Nature of Fiction*. Cambridge: Cambridge University Press.

Doležel, Lubomír. 1988. "Mimesis and Possible Worlds." *Poetics Today* 9 (3): 475-96.

Heidbrink, Henriette. 2010. "Fictional Characters in Literary and Media Studies. A Survey of the Research." In *Characters in Fictional Worlds*, ed. Jens Eder—Fotis Jannidis—Ralf Schneider, 67-110. Berlin—New York: Walter de Gruyter.

Hjort, Mette, and Sue Laver. 1997. *Emotions and the Arts*. Oxford—New York: Oxford University Press.

Margolin, Uri. 1991. "Reference, Coreference, Referring, and the Dual Structure of Literary Narrative." *Poetics Today* 12: 517-42.

Pokorný, Martin. 2010. *Fictionality as Density*. In *Fictionality—Possibility—Reality*, ed. Petr Koťátko—Martin Pokorný—Marcelo Sabatés, 201-12. Bratislava: Aleph.

Reicher, Maria E. 2010. "The Ontology of Fictional Characters." In *Characters in Fictional Worlds*, ed. Jens Eder—Fotis Jannidis—Ralf Schneider, 111-33. Berlin—New York: Walter de Gruyter.

Schnieder, Benjamin, and Tatjana von Solodkoff. 2009. "In Defence of Fictional Realism." In *The Philosophical Quarterly* 59: 138-149.

Stecker, Robert. 2011. "Should We Still Care about the Paradox of Fiction?" *British Journal of Aesthetics* 51: 295-308.

White, Roger M. 1998. *The Structure of Metaphor*. Cambridge, MA: Blackwell.

Radical Narration

Petr Koťátko

> ABSTRACT: The author focuses on the type of narration in which the basic features of the narrated world are *exhibited* in specific performative parameters of the narration itself (in particular in the variety of ways in which the narration fails or collapses) rather than *described* in the narrator's utterances. This presupposes that the narrative performance, including the arsenal of tools available to the narrator, is consequently localized within the narrated world. The most prominent example is found in Samuel Beckett's late prosaic work. The characteristic features of this type of narration, labelled *radical*, are then generalized in the notion of a *radically conceptual* work of art.

In this paper I want to draw a contrast between two sources constitutive of the worlds[1] of narrative literary works:

— the *propositional contents of the narrator's utterances* and their imaginative fulfilment (wherein by the term "fulfilment" I refer to Felix-Martínez Bonati's elaboration of Husserl's idea of *Erfüllung* for the theory of fiction; see Martínez-Bonati 1981);

---

[1] Since I will speak, for short, about "fictional worlds", I should stress in advance that in this use I do not take "fictional" and "actual" as mutually exclusive. I do not see any reason to suppose that the role played by a fictional world in the construction (and in the functioning) of a literary work excludes, in general, its being identical with the actual world. And even if it is not, it is still possible for it to share entities with the actual world as coexisting with entities construed by the author. Moreover, these overlaps (or this identity) can play a substantial role in the construction of a literary work, so that a reading which fails to recognize them may stop the work from fulfilling some of its basic literary functions for the reader.

— the *narrative performance* itself, i.e. those parameters of it in which the relevant features of the fictional world are exhibited or demonstrated, rather than "merely" talked about.[2]

Narrative literary works can radically differ in the degree and manner of employing these two sources of the fictional world's construction, and this fact provides us with an auxiliary criterion for classifying narration types. In what I propose to call *radical narration*, the role of the narrative performance itself is amplified by the fact that the very capability of the narrator's utterances to express propositional contents which could jointly constitute a coherent fictional world is seriously challenged. In radical narration, the disturbances affecting this function of the narrator's performance do not serve as an indicator of her personal indisposition, but rather as a way of exhibiting the nature of the fictional world. This requires that the following two conditions be fulfilled:

(i) The very position from which the narration is performed, including the arsenal of narrative tools accessible to the narrator, is consequently localized within the world which the narration is about. (This is not to be confused with the narrator's involvement in the narrated story: it is neither

---

[2] There is another source deserving (and receiving) serious attention, namely the *interventions from the actual world* or from the reader's picture of it, which complete the fictional worlds in various respects over and above what is explicitely said or implied in the text.

The ways in which our beliefs about the actual world can participate in the construction of fictional worlds have been thoroughly discussed and these discussions resulted in valuable enrichments of the analytical devices of literary theory: perhaps the most prominent example is the notion of *truth-in-fiction*, as defined by David Lewis. But I will not go into this exciting issue here.

necessary nor sufficient for the narration's being *radical* that it be *homodiegetic*.)

(ii) Due to the specific nature of the relevant fictional world, the fulfilment of the condition (i) has the effect that the narrator's utterances cannot fulfil their functions, familiar from ordinary discourse, without serious disturbances.

(iii) As a consequence, the basic features of the fictional world which the narration is about are (to a large extent) not specified in the propositional contents expressed by the narrator's utterances (and "made vivid" by the imaginative fulfilment of these contents), but rather demonstrated in the specific ways in which expressing the propositional contents fails or is being disturbed.

A prominent example of radical narration is provided by the prosaic work of Samuel Beckett, in particular the novels of his "Trilogy" (Beckett 1979).[3] I do not know a better way of illustrating the intended function of this notion than applying it to Beckett's late prosaic texts—which is what I will attempt to do in the following paragraphs.

In a conversation with John Gruen, Beckett characterized the possible meaning of his work ("if it has any meaning at all," as he said) as follows: "I have perhaps freed myself from certain formal concepts" (Beckett 1969: 210). The problem with these "formal concepts", i.e. the principles governing the construction of literary works as they have developed in the history of Western literature, is not that they are unsuitable for literary experiments. Beckett rejects them as devices of presenting the world as an ordered whole, held together by causal links and providing space for a continuously identical subject and her

---

[3] Honestly speaking, the power of these texts is for me *the* reason why I find the notion of radical narration worth articulating.

meaningful action. From Beckett's position, summed up in his claim "I can't see any trace of a system anywhere" (Shenker 1956, section 2: 3; cf. Gontarski 1985: 11), it would be inconsistent, even dishonest, to use narrative devices which function in this way, i.e. which serve (according to Beckett) to create the illusion of order. The literary form acceptable for an author with such a credo must correspond to what we can experience, think and do in the situation of universal chaos.

The consequences for the position of the narrator and his narrative performance are easy to see. If there is no space for meaningful action whose unity would be guaranteed by causal relations and continuous awarness of the purpose, then there should be no space for coherent narration either, with its construction of continuous story lines and of communication between characters, with utterances matching one another in coherent dialogues. If, in the situation of universal chaos, we cannot rely on mutual coordination of our actions, and hence cannot expect to be interpreted as we have intended (and even if, from time to time, this happens to be the case, we have no chance to discover it), the question arises what are the sources of meanings that the Beckettian narrator could rely on in his utterances. In the world in which he is supposed to do his job, the linguistic conventions have no chance to be established — if we understand them, with David Lewis, as regularities in communicative behaviour fixed by a complex of common (i.e. shared and mutually reflected) beliefs and preferences of the members of a community. And if, following Davidson, we take the stand that utterance meaning results from a match between the communicative intention and the interpretation, then the chance that utterances aquire meanings, appears (in Beckett's world) to be negligible (cf. e.g. Davidson 1986).[4]

One cannot claim that Beckett's narrator operates consequently within the borders set by this picture of the human condition, as that would lead to a total resignation on all talk. However, as readers, we recognize—or rather experience—the trickiness and fragility of his position in the numerous collapses of his attempts to say something determinate or even to tell a story. Seen from the other side, we cannot, even as readers of Beckett's texts, resign in our attempts to make sense of his sentences by applying our interpretative routines—yet it is precisely the experience of the failures of these attempts and of our sustained efforts for continuous reading that gives us access to the world narrated in Beckett's novels.

Beckett's narrator from time to time reflects and comments on the precariousness of his position. The status of these comments is, to be sure, just as tricky as the status of the famous philosophical claims which fail to satisfy the criteria of meaningfulness declared in those very claims.[5] Admittedly,

---

[4] The classical version of David Lewis's definition of convention can be found in Lewis (1983).

[5] In the realm of philosophy, incoherence sometimes accompanies the most fundamental theoretical achievements. For instance, if we adopt the position of Kant's *Kritik der reinen Vernunft* , then we *must* and at the same time *cannot* think *das Ding an sich* , because the function of *Verstandesbegriffe* cannot be explained without reference to the thing in itself, while these very notions are applicable only within the sphere of possible experience (and hence not to the thing in itself). Similarly, the sentences of Wittgenstein's *Tractatus* do not satisfy the criteria of meaningfulness specified in these very sentences (this collapse is reflected in the metaphor of the ladder, *Tractatus* 6.54, impressive as a literary device). Similarly, the verificationist criterion of meaningfulness of the Vienna Neopositivists disqualifies the very sentences

precisely this fundamental incoherence is reflected and manifested in Beckett's narrator's comments in a very powerful way. For example:

> I who am here, who cannot speak, cannot think, and who must speak, and therefore perhaps think a little… (*The Unnamable*, Beckett 1979: 276)

> The fact would seem to be, if in my situation one may speak of facts, not only that I shall have to speak of things of which I cannot speak, but also, which is even more interesting, but also that I, which is if possible even more interesting, that I shall have to, I forgot, no matter. And at the same time I am obliged to speak. I shall never be silent. Never. (*The Unnamable*, Beckett 1979: 268)

> …impossible to stop, impossible to go on, but I must go on, I'll go on… (*The Unnamable*, Beckett 1979: 363).[6]

It should be clear that the situation which paralyzes the very ability to perform meaningful utterances includes, as one of its parameters, the collapse of the regulative force of rules. The Beckettian narrator reflects on this in formulations which evoke Wittgenstein's inquiries into rule-following:

> And if I speak of principles, when there are none, I can't help it, there must be some somewhere. And if always doing the same thing as it were is not the same as observing the same principle. I can't help it

---

in which it is declared. Any such kind of ineliminable incoherence creates a fatal problem for a philosophical system, but it certainly does not discredit everything that is said within the system. Much less, then, can incoherence disqualify an artist's achievement: however, it does introduce into her work a kind of tension which deserves to be reflected by the interpreter.

[6] In one of his dialogues Beckett puts it this way: "There is nothing to express, nothing with which to express, nothing from which to express, no power to express, no desire to express, together with the obligation to express" (Beckett–Duthuit 1965: 17).

183

either. And then how can you know whether you are observing it or not? And how can you want to know? (*Molloy*, Beckett 1979: 43)

All this being the case, the narrator's attempts at continuous narration must necessarily collapse, often in a manner resembling the communicative defect illustrated by Moore's paradox (cf. below, n. 7). The attempts are disqualified both *in general* (by pronouncements of the type quoted above) and by various ad hoc counter-moves. Here are some examples:

— A description which presents itself as a recollection of past events is immediately afterwards classified (by the narrator) as a mere invention — with the addition that what follows will not be any different: "For I weary of these inventions and others beckon to me. But in order to blacken a few more pages may I say I spent some time at the seaside, without incident." (*Molloy*, Beckett 1979: 63)
— The narrator classifies his own preceding utterances as a mere rhetorical exercise, whose only function is to keep the discourse going on: "And all these questions I ask myself. It is not in a spirit of curiosity. I cannot be silent. About myself I need know nothing. Here all is clear. No, all is not clear. But the discourse must go on. Rhetoric." (*The Unnamable*, Beckett 1979: 269)
— The narrator evaluates his own use of words as inappropriate, and so disqualifies his previous utterance: "One of these days I'll challenge him. I'll say, I don't know, I'll think of something when the time comes. There are no days here, but I use the expression." (*The Unnamable*, Beckett 1979: 268) Or again, the narrator declares to have no competence concerning some word he has just uttered, with the same effect: "I should mention before going any further, any further on, that I say aporia without knowing what it

means. I say aporia without knowing what it means."⁷ (*The Unnamable*, Beckett 1979: 267)

— The accumulation of contradictions is presented as a matter of (narrative) method: "What am I to do, what shall I do, what should I do, in my situation, how proceed? By aporia pure and simple? Or by affirmations and negations invalidated as uttered, or sooner or later? Generally speaking. There must be some shifts. Otherwise it would be quite hopeless. But it is quite hopeless." (*The Unnamable*, Beckett 1979: 267)

— The narrator's mind is presented as a space for interventions of other, more assertive and more efficient minds, so that the speaker of the narrative utterances vanishes and the literary function of first-person narrative collapses: "Is there a single word of mine in all I say? No, I have no voice, in this matter I have none. … But I don't say anything, I don't know anything, these voices are not mine, nor these thoughts, but the voices and thouhts of the devils who beset me." (*The Unnamable*, Beckett 1979: 319) Cf. also: "But enough of this cursed first person, it is really too red a herring, I'll get out of my depth if I'm not careful." (*The Unnamable*, Beckett 1979: 315)

---

[7] This corresponds to the following variation on Moore's paradox: "The cat is on the mat but I don't know what 'cat' means." Similarly one can construe Moore-like analogies for the examples mentioned above: "The cat is on the mat but this is just my invention." Or: "The cat is on the mat but take it just as a rhetorical exercise." All these sentences (when uttered) are performatively self-defeating in the same way: the speaker makes a certain move and immediately afterwards takes it back. (In the original version of Moore's paradox the speaker commits herself to certain belief, namely that the cat is on the mat, and immediately afterwards cancels this commitment by denying that she possesses that very belief.) In general, countless revocations of various kinds to be found in Beckett's text play the (desctructive) role of a counter-move analogical to the one responsible for Moore's paradox.

Petr Koťátko

It should be clear that the problems with the first person in Beckett's "Trilogy" (and the abandonment of the first person in later texts), as well as anything else responsible for the paralysis of the content and force of the narator's utterances, is not a side-product of the author's linguistic experiments, but rather a result of his sustained striving for consistency. The starting point is Beckett's sensitivity to those aspects of life which are incompatible with the picture of the world as an ordered whole and as a space for meaningful behaviour. The consequence is a never-ending search for a narrative form (and hence also for a way of construing the narrator's position and his performance) which would manifest the universal chaos instead of supporting the illusion of order: "To find a form that accommodates the mess, that is the task of the artist now" (Driver 1961: 23).

No matter how sceptical Beckett himself might have been about his achievements, one can hardly deny that the novels of his "Trilogy" not only speak about the absence of order: they let us experience it in the narrator's repeated attempts at continuous narration and in their failures, in permanent revocations, in accumulating contradictions, in suspending word-meanings and the illocutionary force of narrator's utterances, in the collapses of the referential function of the first person pronouns and hence of the literary function of first-person narrative. In these parametres of the narrator's performances I as a reader recognize the contours of his situation and of the world in which it is anchored. Or to put it better, I experience this situation myself in the collapses of my sustained attempts to apply my interpretative routines and in the failures of my striving for continuous reading.

The consequent inclusion of the narator's position and his performance into the narrated world or state of affairs is a radical move and a substantial literary achievement, provided that this world or state of affairs is incompatible with the commonly shared picture of the world, presupposed and ratified in everyday communication. This becomes well visible in a confrontation with cases where this move (i.e. the step specified in the condition (i) of our characteristics of radical narration) is *not* made—and in which it arguably would have had radical consequences, if it *were* made. This type of narration, which is unaffected (in its performance as well as in its tools) by the nature of the world which is narrated about, may be perhaps aptly called *immune*.[8]

For instance, the narrators of Jorge Luis Borges' stories often describe objects, events, states of affairs, and ways of acting and thinking which do not match our commonly shared picture of the world. They speak about a community with a radically idealistic worldview and form of life ("Tlön, Uqbar, Orbis Tertius"), about people with a radically different intellectual equipment ("Funes the Memorious") or with radically extended perceptual capacities ("Aleph"), to mention

---

[8] Just like in medicine, various types and degrees of immunity can be distinguished. Even the narrator's utterances in the novels of Beckett's *Trilogy* are immune against the universal chaos to that extent that they have the form of sentences with determinate syntactic structure. (Their abandonment in Beckett's later texts was a step towards a higher degree of consistency.) They do not resign upon devices which presuppose causal relations, such as verbs referring to acts based on these relations, e.g. in the sentence „...I put on my trousers, my greatcoat, my hut and my boots" (*Molloy*, Beckett 1979: 44), or compound sentences with purpose clauses; they do not resign upon mathematical calculations (see Molloy's ten pages long ruminations about the possible ways in which the sixteen stones in his possession should circulate between his four pockets and about the order in which they should be picked out for sucking, in order to guarantee that all of them, and not merely a subclass of them, will regularly appear in his mouth; *Molloy*, Beckett 1979: 64–69); etc.

just a few examples. The narrator is typically construed as an intelligent, well educated, sensitive, sometimes rather complacent intellectual, describing these phenomena in *our* common way of speaking, literarily cultivated and elegant, but firmly bound to *our* intellectual and perceptual equipment. For example in "Tlön, Uqbar, Orbis Tertius", the narrator speaks from *our own* standpoint about the consequences of the radical idealism of the inhabitants of Tlön for *their* language (for instance, substantives are replaced by verbal or adjectival constructions), for geometry and arithmetics as well as for the forms and functions of literature. It was not part of the author's aspirations to produce a text which would *exhibit* these consequences in its syntax, semantics and indicated literary aspirations. (The result of such an attempt would be an example of *radical* narration.) On the contrary, he construed the narrator and his performances as *immune* against these consequences, as remaining outside their scope.

The contrast I have in mind can be perhaps more prominently illustrated by another well-known Borges story, "The Book of Sand", as the difference between, on the one hand, *describing* an endless book, *speaking about the way it behaves* when we try to read it or to browse through it — and on the other hand, creating a *text which behaves that way* (an infinitely expanding text, text generating some kind of infinite regress, let us say due to some sort of self-reference). While the former is a standard literary aspiration, the latter is the most radical literary project one can be engaged in: not to describe some object or a state of affairs brought to the extreme from a standard, commonly shared position, but to *push the text itself to the extreme*, to create the text as an exemplar or product of that extreme states of affairs. This includes inducting the narrator into an *extreme position*, in which the linguistic conventions, the shared conceptual apparatus, the world-picture, patterns of behaviour, syllogistic figures etc., or at least some relevant parts of this arsenal, cannot provide their services to her without serious disturbances. We have *considered* the possible consequences of such a step in several Borges stories—and we have *seen* the consequences of this step powerfully *implemented* by the novels of Beckett's "Trilogy".

So much for the contrast between two kinds of narration which I propose to call *radical* and *immune*.[9] Let me now generalize this distinction, so that it is not any more restricted to the sphere of literary fiction. Both Beckett's and Borges' literary achievements in the texts referred to above have an important parameter which deserves to be called *conceptual*, due to the way in which it challenges our conceptual apparatus or other parts of our cognitive equipment. Let me call artworks producing such an effect *strongly conceptual* (adding "strongly" in order to avoid confusions with the term *conceptual* or *conceptualism* as it is used in the fine arts).[10] The *strongly conceptual work* of art can be then defined as follows:

---

[9] Those radically narative literary works which are construed as a picture of the actual world (or of some essential parametres of our life in it) deserve to be called "radically realistic", since in them the nature of the represented reality intervenes into the narative performance itself. As I have attempted to show here, Beckett should be interpreted as a radical realist in this sense; for a detailed argument see Koťátko (2010).

[10] See e.g. Lucy Lippard's statement: "Conceptual art, for me, means work in which the idea is paramount and the material form is secondary, lightweight, ephemeral, unpretentious, cheap and/or 'dematerialized'" (Lippard 1997: vii); or this statement on the website of The Tate Collection (Tate Glossary, Conceptual Art): "Conceptual artists do not set out to make a painting or a sculpture and then fit their ideas to that existing form. Instead they think beyond the limits of those traditional media, and then work out their concept or idea in whatever materials and whatever form is appropriate. They were thus giving the concept priority over the traditional media."

(i) It introduces its recipient into a situation which seriously challenges her conceptual apparatus or perceptual schemes or interpretative skills or patterns of behaviour: rather than providing her with an occasion to apply her cognitive or behaviorial mechanisms in a routine manner, it prevents them from running their usual course, or else puts them to excessive strain, thus showing their limits.

(ii) The main (not necessarily the only) effect it aspires to is that the recipient experiences this critical situation (and, possibly, reflects upon it).

As I have said, I take both Beckett's novels and the Borges stories referred to above as fulfilling these conditions, but not in the same way: what differs is the way in which they achieve the effect characteristic for strongly conceptual artworks. Let me call the entities whose reception and interpretation has the consequences described in the condition (i) *extreme*. In Borges' story "The Book of Sand" we are, by means of a description, confronted with an endless book, which certainly is an *extreme object* in this sense: its description challenges quite efficiently the conceptual schemes in which we are accustomed to think about material objects, as well as our imagination, both visual and motoric. Similarly, in Tlön we face, again by means of a description, a worldview and a way of life (shared by members of a fictitious population) which radically challenges our intuitively realistic way of thinking about the world. In "Pierre Menard, Author of the *Quixote*", we find a description of a literary work which radically challenges our intuitive account of the text-work relation.[11] In all these cases, the attack on our

---

[11] The implications of the Menard case have been thoroughly discussed in philosophy, aesthetics and literary theory. Some contributions to this debate are collected in Koťátko—Pokorný—Sabatés (forthcoming).

conceptual apparatus consists in a confrontation with *extreme entities described* in the text, not in a confrontation with a *text construed as an extreme entity*. On the other hand, Beckett's *texts themselves* are powerful examples of extreme objects, equal to Joyce's *Finnegans Wake* and certain dada and surrealist poems.

Let me call a work of art whose bearer (be it text, sounds, formations of lines or colour stains, three-dimensional objects, situations or events) is an *extreme entity* in the sense defined above *radically conceptual*. It should be clear from these definitions that every radically conceptual artwork is *ipso facto* strongly conceptual, but not the other way round. And all pieces of radical narration are radically (and hence also strongly) conceptual literary works: but not all conceptual literary works are radically narrative (as they need not be narrative at all — see some typical dada poems).

Let me conclude by illustrating these relations by some examples I have discussed above plus a few others. The novels of Beckett's "Trilogy" or Joyce's *Finnegans Wake* and all other pieces of radical narration are radically conceptual literary works (since, as I have pointed out, their texts are extreme objects in our sense): hence they are also strongly conceptual. Borges' Menard story is a strongly but not radically conceptual work, since its text is not an extreme object, but "merely" includes a representation of such an object (namely of Menard's *Quixote*). It attacks our concept of a literary work (and has inspired fundamental theoretical discussions about the text-work relation), but not in a radically conceptual way. Marcel Duchamp's *Fountain,* analogically, attacks our concept of a work of fine art (and it has inspired some substantial theoretical revisions of it), but unlike Borges' story it is a radically, (and hence also strongly) conceptual artwork: the act of exhibiting the urinal in an art gallery (or even the mere manifestation of such an intention) makes the urinal itself an extreme object in our sense, rather than a "mere" representation of such an object.[12] John Cage's famous composition 4'33'" is a radically, and hence also strongly, conceptual artwork: it drastically converts the very scheme of our perception of a musical composition by making us to listen to a continuous silence as a piece of music. The only thing which enters into our accustic field besides the silence are "disturbing" noices from the outside—or more precisely, it becomes unclear what is inside and what is outside the composition. Our listening then balances between two modes of perception, similarly to what happens with our vision when we look at Necker's cube. The situation which so radically challenges the accustomed way of listening to music and attacks so brutally our notion of a musical composition, is itself an extreme entity in our sense, rather than a representation of such an entity.

These are examples of what I regard as clear cases of strongly or radically conceptual works of art. Certainly there are dozens of cases which I would be unable to evaluate from this point of view, as they lie beyond my interpretative capacities—due to the limits of my intellect, sensivity, experience and technical skills. But there may be also cases in which even the most competent interpreter would be unable to decide whether they satisfy the concepts defined above or not.

---

[12] The question arises whether in our time, with galeries full of ready-mades, we can still insist that a urinal exhibited as an artwork satisfies our characteristics of an extreme object. The reply is certainly relative with respect both to time and to persons. Perhaps we should introduce categories like "historically extreme" (referring to the role the object played at the time of its creation), "extreme with respect to common sense" (referring to the role the object plays for typical laypersons) and also "simply (or timelessly) extreme" (which would apply to the text of Beckett's "Trilogy").

Their number would show the degree of applicability of these notions, and hence their value for the interpretation of the works of art.

Czech Academy of Sciences
kotatko@flu.cas.cz

REFERENCES

Beckett, Samuel. 1969. "Interview with John Gruen." *Vogue* (December), 210.
– – –. 1979. *Trilogy (Molloy, Malone Dies, The Unnamable)*. London: Pan Books Ltd.
Beckett, Samuel, and Georges Duthuit. 1965. "Three Dialogues." In *S. Beckett: A Collection of Critical Essays*, ed. Martin Esslin, 16–22. Englewood Cliffs: Prentice Hall.
Davidson, Donald. 1986. "A Nice Derrangement of Epitaphs." In *Truth and Interpretation. Perspectives on the Philosophy of Donald Davidson*, ed. Ernest Lepore, 433–46. Oxford: Blackwell.
Gontarski, Stanley. 1985. *The Intent of Undoing in Samuel Beckett's Dramatic Texts*. Bloomington: Indiana University Press.
Koťátko, Petr. 2010. "Beckett: hledání správné věty." In *Beckett: filosofie a literatura*, ed. Karel Císař – Petr Koťátko, 33–68. Praha: Filosofia.
Koťátko, Petr, Martin Pokorný and Marcelo Sabatés. Forthcoming. *Text and Work: The Case of Menard*.
Lewis, David. 1983. Languages and Language. In: *Philosophical Papers*, vol. 1, 163–88. Oxford: Oxford University Press.
Lippard, Lucy R. (ed.). 1997. *Six Years: The Dematerialization of the Art Object from 1966 to 1972…* Berkeley – Los Angeles: University of California Press.
Martínez-Bonati, Félix. 1981. *Fictive Discourse and the Structures of Literature*. Ithaca: Cornell University Press.
Shenker, Israel. 1956. "A Portrait of Samuel Beckett, the Author of the Puzzling Waiting for Godot." *New York Times* (May 6), Section 2.

The Idea of Fictional Worlds

Anders Pettersson

> ABSTRACT: The author explains in what sense a fictional literary work will always, metaphorically speaking, come to describe a "fictional world": because of its explicit and implicit meaning, the work will necessarily introduce a complex of represented states of affairs. However, the author denies that a piece of literary fiction is associated with a "fictional world" in any richer sense of that expression. Specifically, the author presents a number of arguments against the idea, common in the analytical philosophy of literature, that the reader has to fill out the "fictional world" of the work by adding content to it through acts of supplementation that are based on the reader's background knowledge of the real world.

In his *Philosophy of Literature* (2009), Peter Lamarque tells us that "every narrative fiction presents a 'world'" (Lamarque 2009: 197), and most of us would probably agree. However, the conception of a fictional world that Lamarque has in mind is developed within analytic literary aesthetics, and certain of its features appear problematic to me. My aim in this essay is to question standard literary-aesthetic thinking about fictional worlds and to point to another—to my mind, better—way of thinking and speaking about the imagined states of affairs that we encounter in a literary fiction.[1]

---

[1] I will draw very much on Lamarque's balanced and reliable presentation in *Philosophy of Literature* for the basic exposition of the literary-aesthetic idea of fictional worlds, but my discussion of the conception does not by any means concern Lamarque's views specifically.

The Idea of Fictional Worlds

The question of the nature of fictional worlds forms part of a large complex of issues concerning the nature of fiction, literary meaning and interpretation, and overall approaches to literature as an art form. This will become obvious in relation to several points in my text, but it will not be possible for me to pursue such wider implications of the subject here.[2]

I/
Franz Kafka's "The Judgement" ("Das Urteil", 1913) opens with the following scene:

> It was a Sunday morning in the height of spring. Georg Bendemann, a young businessman, was sitting in his own room on the first floor of one of the small, lightly built houses which stretched out in a long row beside the river, hardly distinguishable from one another except in height and colour. He had just finished a letter to an old friend of his who was now living abroad, toyed with it for a while as he slowly sealed it, and then, resting his elbow on his desk, he looked out of the window at the river, the bridge and the rising ground on the far bank with its faint show of green. (Kafka 1992: 37)

The peaceful Sunday morning letter writing will soon give way to an absurd confrontation between Georg and his elderly, widowed father, whose judgement is that Georg shall die by drowning. At the end of the story Georg actually lets himself fall into the river which we can glimpse through the window of his room. "The Judgement" is an important Kafka story, but in this connection I will simply be using it as a point of reference, an example of fictional discourse, and the few sentences already quoted form the only passage that I will consider more closely.

Is it true that we are presented with a fictional world when reading "The Judgement"? In a sense, yes. The talk of

---

[2] I would like to thank Martin Shaw for checking my English.

fictional worlds is inevitably metaphorical because, by definition, fictional worlds have no real existence—they would not be fictional if they had.[3] Still, we are being told that Georg Bendemann is sitting in his room, sealing a letter and looking out of the window. I do not mind saying that, metaphorically speaking, there is a fictional world in which Georg Bendemann is sitting in his room sealing a letter (and so on).

My main problem with the idea of fictional worlds in analytic literary aesthetics is that it makes fictional worlds contain very many things over and above the comparatively few states of affairs that are being explicitly or implicitly introduced by the author (or by the text, if you prefer to express yourself in non-intentionalist terms).[4] For the analytic aesthetician, there are yet many more fictional "facts" to be found when the verbal meaning of the text, and all that literary explication and interpretation can uncover, have been accounted for. Those additional fictional facts are established by means of something that Lamarque calls "supplementation":

> Reading fiction is an exercise in supplementing what is explicitly "given". There are connections, clearly, with both explication and

---

[3] Some philosophers hold that there actually are non-existent objects. For example, Terence Parsons has maintained that there actually are objects that do not exist, but has refrained from calling such objects real (see, e.g., Parsons 1980: 7 and 13). I choose to disregard such complexities; I do not believe that they are relevant for the main issues in my essay.

[4] As far as I can see, nothing in my paper hinges on whether you subscribe to an intentionalist or a conventionalist theory of interpretation (or, more realistically perhaps, to a considerably more complex analysis of meaning and interpretation), and I will avoid these contentious issues as much as possible. I will often refer to the author as a creator of meaning, but conventionalists should be able to translate my formulations into the kind of phrasing that they prefer.

> interpretation, for they too are concerned with drawing out what is implicit. But the supplementation of worlds is not a search for meaning—although it presupposes descriptive meaning in narrative—nor is it a search for a work's value as literature. All fictional narrative, whether literature or not, invites supplementation… (Lamarque 2009: 197)

Undeniably, there is implicit meaning in texts, also in fictional texts, and not only explicit meaning. For instance, Kafka does not explicitly tell us that the "faint show of green" on the other shore is the green of spring—not, for example, a partly hidden green poster or a green house gable—but that is no doubt the case in his fiction, and that would be obvious even without the many other references to new positive developments and new life in the earlier parts of "The Judgement". As there is implicit meaning in fictional texts, there are also fictional "facts" over and above what is immediately described. But according to Lamarque—and to standard thinking about fictional worlds in analytic literary aesthetics—a fictional world contains more fictional facts than those introduced via the explicit and implicit verbal meaning of the fictional discourse. A very simple example adduced by Lamarque is the putative fact that, in the world of the Sherlock Holmes stories, Holmes never travelled in a rocket (Lamarque 2009: 201). (Lamarque's contention is not simply that we are never told about travels in a rocket in the Holmes stories, but that it is a fictional fact in the stories that Holmes never undertook such travels.)

Lamarque does not think of supplementation as a subjective operation. If we perform supplementation competently, the things we supplement will be genuine elements of the "world" of the work. "It is helpful," he says,

> to distinguish between a supplementation that is purely whimsical or personal and one that is responsive to the work itself… It might not

always be clear what is 'authorized' by a work, but using the work as merely a prompt for private imaginings is not the way to try to comprehend the "world" being presented. (Lamarque 2009: 198)

Lamarque clearly holds that we can establish fictional facts over and above those created by the verbal meaning of the text, and that we can do this in a non-arbitrary manner. This is a belief which appears to be widely shared within analytic aesthetics, but there is no real consensus regarding the principles that we apply, or should apply, when supplementing fictional texts. Lamarque refers to two possible principles; in this, he follows the lead of Kendall Walton, who, in turn, builds on the analyses by David Lewis in Lewis' seminal article "Truth in Fiction" (1978).[5] The two principles are called (by Walton and, after Walton, by Lamarque) the Reality Principle and the Mutual Belief Principle.

The Reality Principle presupposes that "readers assume the fictional world to be as like the real world as is compatible with what is explicitly stated" (Lamarque 2009: 198). To choose an example that is not used by Lamarque: we know that the Earth's crust is made up of huge tectonic plates, so if we follow the Reality Principle, the fictional world of Kafka's "The Judgement" will be a world where the Earth's crust is made up of huge tectonic plates. However, the tectonic plates were unknown in Kafka's time, and we may feel that we should avoid ascribing anachronistic features to fictional worlds. One way of getting around such problems is to follow the Mutual Belief Principle instead. If we apply the Mutual Belief Principle, "it is not reality or fact that constrains our inferences but common shared beliefs at the time the narrative was written"

---

[5] For Walton's discussion of the two principles, see Walton (1990: esp. 144–61).

(Lamarque 2009: 199). The application of this principle will remove the tectonic plates from the world of "The Judgement".

Even if you find the Mutual Belief Principle more convincing than the Reality Principle, you will still face the problem that authors may not share the common beliefs of their time. Lamarque mentions Thomas Hardy as a case in point: several of Hardy's heroines act in ways that challenge contemporary moral beliefs, but it would be wrong to conclude that those heroines are therefore being portrayed as immoral. As a result of such reasoning, some have felt that an even more finely tuned principle than the Mutual Belief Principle is required, and Lamarque considers sympathetically a suggestion from Gregory Currie "according to which what is true in fiction is what it is reasonable for an informed reader to infer that the 'fictional author' believes"(Lamarque 2009: 200).[6] In the cases that focus on Hardy it will, presumably, be clear that the fictional authors do not morally condemn the heroines, and it will be the fictional authors' beliefs that determine the moral facts in the novels' fictional worlds.

II/

I have now offered a condensed account of standard literary-aesthetic thinking about truth in fictional worlds, an account based on Lamarque's short overview of the problems and suggested solutions.[7] My next step will be to introduce and

---

[6] Lamarque is referring to Gregory Currie (1990: 75-81).

[7] I have excluded Lamarque's brief evaluation (Lamarque 2009: 200-201) of the attempt to analyze fictional worlds in terms of possible worlds. Lamarque himself takes no definite stand in the discussion about the various proposed solutions, even though he appears sympathetic to Currie's analysis in terms of fictional authors and to Walton's feeling that maybe no single satisfactory principle can be found. In fact, Lamarque ends (2009: 201-2) by indicating that he finds the discussion too confined to what is true in

defend a different perspective on what is "true" in the "world" of a fiction.

When reading a fictional text, or any piece of linguistic discourse, you are presented with a material bearer of signs—traditionally, a sheet of paper that is marked by some kind of ink by means of handwriting or printing. You decipher the signs on the material surface, arriving at a sequence of sentences in a given language. These sentences carry explicit and implicit meaning when they are understood in the light of the semantics and syntax of the language used and of the general pragmatic principles of reading and understanding text. The conventions of reading will help you to establish explicit verbal meaning in a text like "The Judgement", but also implicit verbal meaning.

Texts are firmly associated with complexes of representations, that is, with descriptions of states of affairs—sometimes, as with "The Judgement", descriptions of fictional states of affairs. All of those who read Kafka's story competently and in accordance with the conventions of reading will construe the same complex of representations. (They will imagine that Georg Bendemann is sitting in his own room, sealing a letter, looking out, and so on.) Representations have content in the sense that they represent certain things as being in certain ways. (It is part of the representational content of "The Judgement" that Georg Bendemann is sitting in his own room, that he is seeing the green of spring on the other bank of the river outside the house he is in, et cetera.) Responding to a

---

fiction: according to him, critics must ultimately be interested in the work as an artifact and as a whole, not merely in its quasi-real world. (Walton, Currie, and others could reply that the discussion simply *is* about what is true in a fictional world, but that nobody claims that that is the deepest question we can ask about literary fiction.)

literary text, whether fictional or not, is to respond, intellectually and emotionally, to the representational content and to all the other aesthetically relevant features of the work (features which we can, for the purposes of this essay, simply call "the form").[8]

As already indicated, I do not mind saying that the representational content constitutes a fictional world, a world in which Georg Bendemann is sitting in his room on a certain Sunday, looking out of the window and seeing the green of spring across the river. Such metaphorical talk is innocuous and, in a way, attractive, because it is more vivid and less technical than talk of representational content. However, I differ from standard literary-aesthetic thinking about fictional worlds as soon as the idea of what Lamarque calls "supplementation" comes into play. In my view, we do not need supplementation. I cannot see how the reader can establish textually "authorized" content in any other manner than by following the conventions of reading, and I regard everything that the conventions of reading let us read into the text as forming part of the verbal meaning.

As a consequence, my fictional worlds contain much less than those ordinarily constructed in analytic literary aesthetics. I accept the (metaphorical) idea of fictional worlds in a "thin" sense, in which the content of the world is identical with the representational content, but I do not accept the idea of fictional worlds in the "thick" sense adopted in analytical literary aesthetics: the sense in which fictional worlds also contain supplemented material. For instance, Brazil will exist in the fictional world of "The Judgement" no matter what principle of supplementation you adopt among those that are currently

---

[8] I have worked out this perspective in considerable detail in other contributions, particularly in Pettersson (2000).

regarded as plausible, but Brazil does not form part of the story's representational content—there is no description of Brazil, either explicit or implicit, in Kafka's "The Judgement"—so I do not view Brazil as an element of the story's fictional world. As I do not countenance "thick" fictional worlds, the problem of finding the right principles of supplementation does not arise for me: we need no supplementation, and consequently no principles of supplementation.

I have now introduced an alternative to the view that fictional discourse presents us with fictional worlds: in my version, a piece of fictional discourse is associated with a representational content but not with a fictional world (unless you identify the fictional world with the representational content). For a number of reasons, I find my alternative a better way of understanding these matters.

First, it is obviously simpler to analyze the imagined states of affairs that we encounter in a literary fiction in terms of representational content than to analyze them as the contents of a thick fictional world. The analysis in terms of representational content takes care of the question about principles of supplementation by arguing that the question rests on mistaken assumptions. If the analysis in terms of representational content is indeed tenable, we should prefer it already because of its simplicity.

However, my main reasons for preferring my alternative analysis are more substantial. The idea that fictional discourse presents us with thick fictional worlds has certain counterintuitive consequences. Lamarque touches upon these when he points out problems with the Reality Principle:

> Modern theories of astronomy or nuclear physics or human psychology would generate fictional truths in the worlds of Sophocles or Chaucer totally at odds with the implied contemporary

> background. Not only are the truths anachronistic, but arguably there are too many of them, in too great detail. Do abstruse facts about quarks or quasars belong in the world of *Oedipus Rex*? Of course the idea of a "fictional world" is itself unclear, so how determinate or wide in scope the "contents" of such a world might be is debatable. (Lamarque 2009: 199)

The problem that there are too many fictional truths, and that they are too detailed, obviously affects the Mutual Belief Principle too, for if we apply that principle, all commonly shared beliefs at the time the narrative was written automatically become part of the fictional world. Furthermore, most of those purported fictional truths will be patently irrelevant to the aesthetic or artistic functioning of the literary work in question. It is difficult to see how the existence of Brazil, or the identity of the President of the United States in 1913 (first William Howard Taft, then Woodrow Wilson), is at all important for the experience of "The Judgement" as a work of art. Why should lots and lots of aesthetically irrelevant features be included in the world of the work? My analysis of the imagined realities in terms of representational content rids us, to all intents and purposes, of all the fictional truths that have not been actively installed in the work in order to form part of the basis of the reader's literary experience.

For me, it is an even more decisive argument that the view I recommend offers a comparatively literal and credible account of how we understand what is fictionally true in a piece of fiction. The reader encounters a material bearer of signs, interprets the signs in accordance with the normal practices of reading, and makes a literary experience take form in response to the signs and the recovered representations. The analysis has the additional merit of being applicable, mutatis mutandis, to all forms of verbal communication. By contrast, the view that fictional discourse presents us with thick fictional worlds has a fatal weakness—the difficult (to me: incomprehensible) idea that there is content in the work which is objectively present (not merely subjectively ascribed to the work by the reader) and still not established through the ordinary conventions of reading.

Those who believe in thick fictional worlds would perhaps want to respond that they see it as one of the ordinary conventions of the reading of fiction that readers should be performing supplementation. But it is an implausible idea that readers actually engage in supplementation when they establish what is true in the fiction they are reading. In order to be able to project onto a work everything that was commonly believed at the time of its production (or, for that matter, everything that is true in the actual world), the reader would first have to form and entertain an idea of what was commonly believed at the time of the production of the text, across the board (or of what is true in the actual world, across the board). The lack of sheer processing capacity would mean that the readers could never meet that initial demand: the task is just too immense.[9] We cannot, therefore, be performing supplementation when we are reading fiction.

---

[9] If readers were actually capable of forming and entertaining an idea of all that is true, or all that was commonly believed at the time of the production of the text, and of projecting those contents onto the work to define what is fictionally true in the text, they would then have to neglect practically all the fictional facts cumbersomely established, because those facts would be patently irrelevant for the story at hand. This is another strange aspect of the idea that readers of fiction are performing supplementation. Reading fiction may be an exercise in supplementing what is explicitly given, as Lamarque says, in the sense that much implicit meaning will have to be established by the reader, but not in the sense that readers will be performing what Lamarque calls supplementation.

Adherents of the theory of supplementation could reply that readers may well perform selective supplementation, projecting some circumstances onto the fictional work (Brazil, perhaps, but not the protagonist's not having travelled in a rocket), even though they cannot perform overall supplementation. That is true, but a theory of selective supplementation will be haunted by questions about what conventions readers performing selective supplementation are expected to follow. For example, are readers conventionally expected to project whatever commonly believed circumstances they choose onto the work (let us call that "spontaneous selective supplementation") or only certain specific kinds of such circumstances ("rule-governed selective supplementation"), and if the latter is the case, what kinds of circumstances would they be?

I do not find theories of conventional selective supplementation promising. It is easy to claim, but difficult to prove, that such-and-such more esoteric conventions for reading literature are in force, and, more importantly, the idea of selective supplementation lacks prima facie plausibility for me. Admittedly, however, statements about more esoteric conventions of reading are also difficult to disprove. Instead of embarking on an attempt at straightforward refutation, I will try to offer a better explanation of the reader's situation. In the next section, I will discuss the role of background knowledge in reading. In my opinion, the selective use of background knowledge that I describe presents us with a better alternative to selective supplementation.

The analytic aesthetician may feel that I make too much of the actual mental operations of real readers, and it is true that we can perform selective supplementation outside of the act of reading. However, if supplementation is not an element of the ordinary reading of fiction for enjoyment or aesthetic experience, what kind of relevance is supplementation, and the philosophical discussion about supplementation and possible principles of supplementation, supposed to have? Fictional worlds do not exist, so it is difficult to see how questions about the content of fictional literary worlds can make sense unless the questions are interpreted as queries about how such worlds are imagined, or should be imagined, by readers.

III/
Advocates of thick fictional worlds naturally adduce reasons for their conviction of the necessity of supplementation. As far as I can see, their deepest motive for the conviction is an intuition: the intuition that we read a work of fiction against a background of beliefs about the world, and that the contents of those background beliefs spill over into the work, as it were, filling it with extra states of affairs that are fictionally true. In this section and the next one, I will exemplify that stance, looking at another two analytic-philosophical discussions of truth in fiction. I will then devote a final section (section V) to certain phenomenological aspects of literary experience that may seem to speak in favour of the existence of thick fictional worlds, but do not, actually, give us reason to posit such worlds.

When David Lewis wrote his "Truth in Fiction", initiating the modern discussion about the topic, it appeared evident to him that truth in fiction is created through the application of cultural background knowledge (what Lewis called "a background of generally prevalent beliefs") to the representational content (the "explicit content").[10] Much as you apply the conventions of reading to the material carrier in order

---

[10]   Quotations from Lewis (1983: 272).

to recover the linguistic signs and the representational content, you apply your cultural background knowledge to the representational content in order to establish what is true in the fictional world. This seems to be Lewis' perspective, and it is clearly different from mine.

It is a true and important observation that fictional texts — and other texts too, for that matter — can only be properly understood against a background of relevant knowledge. We need linguistic knowledge in order to understand a text like "The Judgement", but also cultural knowledge of many kinds. It is not without significance for the comprehension of the story to know that Sundays are not working days in typical Western cultures, to know how the practice of writing, sending, and receiving letters works, and so on. Authors count on their readers having the relevant linguistic and cultural competence and they draw on this competence greatly and often in subtle ways. These circumstances are not controversial; I take all this for granted, and so do the advocates of thick fictional worlds. The difference between us lies in the function or functions ascribed to background knowledge.

In my view, cultural background knowledge can be said to assume partly different functions in the reading of fiction. Cultural background knowledge will often prove to be necessary for making sense of the text and establishing the representational content. For example, it becomes obvious later in "The Judgement" that Georg and his father both work in the family firm, and it would be incomprehensible that they did not work during the daytime if you had not known that Sundays are not working days in typical Western cultures. However, cultural background knowledge also plays a more general role. It affects our reading in a subtle, overarching way; metaphorically speaking, it supplies us with the light in which we see and understand the representational content. The representational content in "The Judgement" is sparse, but while reading the story we are considering the representational content against the background of our cultural knowledge. Our impression of the representational content, and our intellectual and emotional processing of it, will be influenced by our cultural knowledge and cultural expectations in ways that are subtle, undetermined, diffuse, and difficult to define.

The difference between Lewis' perspective and the one I am defending here does not, then, consist in the belief or disbelief in the importance of the reader's cultural background knowledge. The key difference between us is that Lewis projects our cultural knowledge onto the text, making the contents of our cultural knowledge part of the contents of the text, while I regard the contents of our cultural knowledge as an instrument for establishing and understanding the representational content, viewing only the representational content as forming part of the text. If we follow Lewis' analysis, we will have to say that it is true in Kafka's story that there is a country called Brazil. In my analysis, Brazil does not figure at all, at least not explicitly. I view the knowledge that there is a country called Brazil (and that the existence of Brazil was known to Kafka and his time) as forming part of the reader's cultural background knowledge, but that specific piece of knowledge will not have to be retrieved even implicitly during the reader's transactions with "The Judgement", because the existence of Brazil has no perceivable relevance for the understanding or experiencing of Kafka's story.

Apparently, Lewis thinks of his perspective as commonly adopted (without offering any evidence for its ubiquity) and obviously valid. "There are some," he writes, who never tire of telling us not to read anything into a fiction that is not there explicitly. I do not believe, however, that such a usage is at all common. Most of us are content to read a fiction against a background of well-known fact, "reading into" the fiction content that is not there explicitly but that comes jointly from the explicit content and the factual background. (Lewis 1983: 268)

As I said in the last section, I feel certain, partly for reasons that have to do with the psychology of reading and processing text, that we are not in fact performing such supplementation when reading fiction. (I agree with Lewis that there can be implicit content in fiction, so that part of his argument does not affect my position.)

Lewis also describes how we can project real-world facts onto fictional worlds, and he presents the resulting picture as being, intuitively, evidently correct. The Sherlock Holmes stories furnish him with one of his most conspicuous examples. Conan Doyle's stories do not tell us that Holmes lives nearer to Paddington Station than to Waterloo Station, but they do tell us that Holmes lives in Baker Street. The real Baker Street is nearer to the real Paddington than to the real Waterloo. Hence, according to Lewis, in the absence of any evidence to the contrary, it is a fictional fact in the Sherlock Holmes stories that Holmes lives nearer to Paddington than to Waterloo (Lewis 1983: 268). I do not share Lewis' intuitions on this point. If Conan Doyle were drawing on our real-world knowledge about the relative distance of the two stations from Baker Street, we would have to make use of that knowledge, forging fictional facts about the matter. (This is how it becomes a fictional fact in the world of "The Judgement" that Sundays are holidays.) But as long as fictional facts about the relative distances between Baker Street, Waterloo, and Paddington are not actually needed for the understanding or experiencing of any given Sherlock

Holmes story, I can see no reason to force such assumed facts on the stories.

IV/
A recent discussion of truth in fiction, published later than Lamarque's overview, is found in Gregory Currie's *Narratives and Narrators* (2010). Currie's book is wide in scope because its subject is the "philosophy of stories", and it also contains a number of remarks that are relevant to the present theme. Currie has obviously abandoned his previous idea that what is true in fiction is what it is reasonable for an informed reader to infer that the fictional author believes, because he no longer maintains that a fictional text necessarily contains a fictional narrator (Currie 2010: 68-69). Currie still appears to be closer to the Mutual Belief Principle than to the Reality Principle, though, as he indicates that he bases himself on "intention rather than truth" when deciding what forms part of the fictional story content (Currie 2010: 10).

The expression "story content" is worth noticing. Currie expresses his dissatisfaction with the talk of "worlds" and speaks, instead, of what is "part of the story content".[11] Yet that does not mean that Currie's position now coincides with the one I am defending here because the tenor of his remarks is that we can and should transcend what the representational content offers us. Like Lamarque, Currie stresses that such supplementation (a term Currie does not use) should be grounded in the literary work itself (Currie 2010: 198).

Currie points out that works contain more than is explicitly said. "The work itself reaches well beyond the text of

---

[11]   About "worlds", see Currie (2010: 10-11, n. 18). (Currie points to logical differences between worlds on the one hand, story contents on the other.) The quotation is taken from Currie (2010: 12).

the work," he writes, "and issues on which the text is silent cannot be assumed to be issues left undecided by the work"(Currie 2010: 197). Simplifying somewhat, one could say that by "text" Currie means the string of linguistic expressions as such, and by "work" he means the string of linguistic expressions when it is perceived as being produced by a specific author at a specific time.[12] This makes it easy for me to agree with Currie that works reach well beyond the texts of the works, and his observation does not represent an argument against my views. Formulated in Currie's terminology: I am speaking of the representational content of the work and denying that the work contains more fictional facts than those comprised in its representational content.

It is not easy to determine whether Currie's discussion in *Narratives and Narrators* introduces any new arguments for supplementation: it is brief, sophisticated, slightly evasive, and it is partly presented in a negative form—defensive rather than providing evidence for his arguments. Currie brings up questions concerning truth in fiction in association with the representation of character in literature. His immediate aim is to argue for the justification of what he calls "Character-speculation", and a point of departure is the classic topic of the children of Lady Macbeth. It is supposed to be fictionally true in Shakespeare's Macbeth that Lady Macbeth had—or had had— children, but nothing is said in the drama about how many those children might be. In literary criticism, the question "How many children had Lady Macbeth?" has become emblematic of futile speculation about fictional characters as if they genuinely existed. Translated into the terminology that I am using here:

---

[12] See Currie (2010: 10–11, n. 19) and Currie (2004: ch. 1, esp. 9–10 and 24–26). Currie's use of the two terms follows stipulations of his own; in this essay, I often use "work" and "text" as synonyms.

Shakespeare has not specified how many children Lady Macbeth has or had—the number of her children is not included in the representational content—and it would therefore be pointless to pursue the question of how many they might have been, supplementing the drama in that respect. Currie, however, argues that the matter should be viewed in a different light.

> There is no answer given by *Macbeth* to the question "how many children had Lady Macbeth?", but this is not simply because the text does not name the number. The text does not say that the number was less than 100, but we can be certain that it was. The text has always to be taken in conjunction with a set of background assumptions, and any reasonably chosen set of assumptions will tell us that the number was less than 100. As things stand, getting a precise figure would require a textual statement, since there is no particular number of children that a woman is overwhelmingly likely to have. But if human females were capable of having at most one child, and this was part of common knowledge in Shakespeare's society, there would be a strong argument for saying that the number was one (given the textual implication that the number was at least one). How many hands does Lady Macbeth have? A reasonable answer is "two", despite the text not being explicit on the question.
>   Deciding what the appropriate background is may be difficult. It may even generate unresolvable disputes. In such cases, we may have answers—more than one—that go beyond what the text itself tells us, where the choice between them can only be a matter of personal preference. (Currie 2010: 197–98)

Currie seems to share Lewis' intuition that we "read a fiction against a background of well-known fact, 'reading into' the fiction content that is not there explicity but that comes jointly from the explicit content and the factual background", because he obviously contends that our background assumptions do introduce fictional facts over and above those contained in the representational content. Sometimes such facts cannot be established—we cannot know the exact number of Lady Macbeth's children, for example—but that is an accidental rather than essential circumstance. We do know that Lady Macbeth had two hands, even though it is not stated in the drama.

I naturally agree with Currie that literary texts—and other texts too—can only be properly understood against a background of relevant knowledge.[13] (It is also a good point that the content of the relevant background assumptions is hard to specify.) Yet, as before, I cannot see that this observation opens up a space for supplementation. We must bring relevant knowledge about the real world to bear in order to establish the representational content, and the ordinary conventions of reading demand from us the application of such relevant knowledge. In my view, however, everything that can be objectively established by following the ordinary conventions of reading will form part of the explicit or implicit verbal meaning, and no fictional facts that go beyond the verbal meaning can be objectively established.

Currie does not make his argument for the validity of supplementation entirely explicit. I believe that the force that his observations may seem to have derives from two sources. For one thing, Currie demonstrates that questions like "How many children had Lady Macbeth?" are not simply meaningless. There is a principled way of answering such questions: they can be responded to in the light of appropriate background assumptions, even though we may not always

---

[13] I do not claim that a given text is, in itself, associated with a given set of background assumptions. To what extent such a claim would be true, is too complicated a question to be discussed here. My point is simply that, as a reader, you must possess relevant knowledge about the real world if you are to understand the text adequately.

be able to provide a precise answer. Currie is no doubt right in this, but I cannot see that his observation shows that supplementation is justified. The questions about Lady Macbeth come across as being meaningful, but that does not automatically mean that the work imputes an approximate number of children to Lady Macbeth or, even, a given number of hands. To me, the two questions are meaningful only when understood in a counterfactual vein: "If Shakespeare had specified how many children Lady Macbeth had — which he did not do — how many children would he have said that she had?"; "If Shakespeare had specified how many hands Lady Macbeth had — which he did not do — how many hands would he have said that she had?" Or: "If we were to imagine, as viewers or readers, how many children Lady Macbeth had — which we have no good reason to do — how many children would we have imagined that she had?"; "If we were to imagine, as readers, how many hands Lady Macbeth had — which we have no good reason to do — how many hands would we have imagined that she had?" These questions make sense, but they are purely hypothetical, not questions about what is true in the world of *Macbeth*.

The other seemingly significant point is Currie's remark that Lady Macbeth must be supposed to have two hands although nothing is said explicitly about that fact in the drama. For me, that argument, too, fails to demonstrate that supplementation is necessary or valid: even if we should find Currie's remark that Lady Macbeth must be supposed to have two hands entirely correct in itself, his observation does not prove that there is a space for supplementation. When reading the drama, we will conceive Lady Macbeth as an ordinary (fictional) human being, special only with respect to the features specifically attributed to her. We can perhaps therefore be said to understand Lady Macbeth, implicitly, as having two hands, but even if this is the case that is not an extra feature of the world of the work, established through supplementation. It is a feature implicit in the representational content, or implied by it, without being itself represented.[14] In reading the drama, we have no reason to pay any special attention to Lady Macbeth's hands. No matter how I twist and turn Currie's discussion of character speculation, I cannot find any convincing argument for the validity of supplementation.[15]

V/

We may believe in the necessity of introducing fictional worlds in the thick sense because we are struck by the existence and importance of background conventions, but phenomenological considerations can also come into the picture. Do we not seem to experience a thick fictional world, not just a thin representational content, when reading a piece of fictional discourse like Kafka's "The Judgement"? Judging by my own experience, that is entirely true. I would argue, however, that

---

[14] In a production of the play, Lady Macbeth can no doubt be expected to be impersonated by an actress with two hands, but that is another matter and not directly relevant for the question of how many hands Lady Macbeth had.

[15] However, I am certainly not opposed to reflection on the motives of Hamlet's actions or similar character-speculation (see Currie 2010: 198). Even if we are ultimately unable to pin down Hamlet's motives, we will have to reflect on them in order to understand what is going on in *Hamlet*, and reflections on Hamlet's possible motives may also enter into our more personal intellectual and emotional assimilation of the play. It is a little surprising, though, and especially in view of the well-known obscurity of Hamlet's motives, that Currie says (ibid.) that character speculation "should always be speculation we have reason to think *might* be settled by the work itself". I do not subscribe to that.

the objection is ambiguous, and that it loses its force as soon as the possible interpretations of the objection are separated from each other and submitted to closer investigation.

We cannot, of course, experience a fictional world in the ordinary, straightforward sense of experiencing: we cannot come into contact with it through our senses. If we have the impression of experiencing a fictional world in that sense, we must be the victims of an illusion because fictional worlds do not exist, except metaphorically. It may seem to us, in our literary experience, that we come into contact with a fictional world, but that experience does not permit us to infer the actual existence of a corresponding world. Indeed, we know very well that there is no such world.

Taking "experience" in a different sense, it is true that we do experience Georg Bendemann when reading "The Judgement" because we do have imaginative experiences while reading, and representations of Georg Bendemann are elements of those experiences. It is important to remember, however, that Georg Bendemann forms part of the representational content of the story, so when imagining him we are experiencing a fictional world in the thin, unproblematic sense. I would say that we do not normally, when reading, have imaginative experiences of things that we attribute to the fictional world but that do not form part of the representational content. To the extent that we do in fact have such imaginative experiences, I would say that we should avoid having them. I would deny, for example, that we normally have imaginative experiences that include representations of Brazil (as forming part of Georg Bendemann's world) when reading Kafka's text. And I would look with some suspicion on readers who entertained imaginings of Brazil as forming part of the world of "The

The Idea of Fictional Worlds

Judgement": to me, their behavior would appear strange and out of place.

One more thing needs to be said about the reader's experience. When we read the initial passage from Kafka, we will probably have the impression of encountering a world which stretches out from the represented scene in every direction—beyond the room, beyond the house, beyond the town or city. I protested, above, that such an impression must be illusory, and I made it clear that my discussion of fictional worlds is concerned with how things actually are, not with how they appear in the reader's experience. I will not go back to that, but one aspect of the situation deserves additional comment.

Only the things explicitly or implicitly introduced into Kafka's story form part of the representational content. That should not be taken to mean, however, that all the objects that are not explicitly or implicitly introduced into the story are to be understood to be nonexistent. Perhaps an author can succeed in making it fictional that he is describing a world where absolutely nothing exists except the things explicitly or implicitly said to be there. But that is not what Kafka is doing; that is not how we are expected to understand the world of "The Judgement". Nothing is said about how Georg Bendemann is dressed, about the wallpaper in his room, or about the exact measurements of his desk. However, without violating his contract with the reader, without launching into another mode of writing, Kafka could very well have made it fictional that Georg Bendemann is wearing such-and-such clothes in such-and-such-colours, he could have decorated Georg Bendemann's room with wallpaper with a specific pattern, and so on. As readers, we know that the author may at any moment introduce new fictional states of affairs, filling out

217

spaces in the complex represented situation that have so far been left empty. For that reason we experience the representational content, the fictional world in the thin sense of the word, as something which is expandable, capable of being added to in many different respects.

If you wish, you can therefore say that there is, in our imaginative experience, a wider, virtual fictional world beyond the fictional world in the thin sense. That circumstance is no doubt quite important for the reader's experience of the fiction. But the wider, virtual fictional world is, precisely, virtual. It has no content. It is there merely as an empty possibility, and we are not expected to fill it out through supplementation. If we know nothing about Georg Bendemann's clothes (well, we soon learn that they contain a pocket into which he puts his letter), that is because Kafka did not introduce any further information about his clothes into his story, probably because he did not find it relevant to do so. In that situation, we have no good reason to introduce this or that item of clothing ourselves, inferring their characteristics from background assumptions.[16]

Umeå University
anders.pettersson@littvet.umu.se

---

[16] Many readers are visualizers; they will see Georg Bendemann in their mind's eye, possibly also his clothes and his hands. I understand such visualization primarily as a way of aiding the comprehension of the situation described in the text. I find visualizing completely innocent; however, the reader's quasi-visual experience cannot, of course, introduce new content into the work itself.

REFERENCES

Britton, John. 1961. "A. C. Bradley and Those Children of Lady Macbeth." *Shakespeare Quarterly* 12 (1): 349–51.
Currie, Gregory. 1990. *The Nature of Fiction*. Cambridge: Cambridge University Press.
— — —. 2004. *Arts and Minds*. Oxford: Clarendon Press.
— — —. 2010. *Narratives and Narrators: A Philosophy of Stories*. Oxford: Oxford University Press.
Kafka, Franz. 1992. "The Judgement: A Story." In *The Transformation and Other Stories: Works Published during Kafka's Lifetime.* Ed. and trans. Malcolm Pasley. Harmondsworth: Penguin Books.
Knight. Lionel C. 1933. *How Many Children Had Lady Macbeth? An Essay in the Theory and Practice of Shakespeare Criticism*. Cambridge: G. Fraser, The Minority Press.
Lamarque, Peter. 2009. *The Philosophy of Literature*. Malden, MA: Blackwell.
Lewis, David. 1983. "Truth in Fiction." In *Philosophical Papers*, vol. 1, 261–75. New York–Oxford: Oxford University Press.
Parsons, Terence. 1980. *Nonexistent Objects*. New Haven: Yale University Press.
Pettersson, Anders. 2000. *Verbal Art: A Philosophy of Literature and Literary Experience*. Montreal: McGill-Queen's University Press.
Walton, Kendall L. 1990. *Mimesis as Make-Believe: On the Foundations of the Representational Arts*. Cambridge, MA: Harvard University Press.

THE BEGINNINGS: MIMESIS AND HUMAN MIND IN SOME EARLY THEORIES OF REPRESENTATION

Karel Thein

ABSTRACT: Offering a critical rereading of the early philosophical history of the notion of mimesis, the paper's double focus is on how, in the broadly speaking mimetic activity, human mind works and on how this working connects to the issue of human nature and its specificity. Despite dealing with ancient texts, the paper's aims are systematic rather than historical. The choice of four authors—namely Plato, Aristotle, pseudo-Hippocrates and Philostratus—allows for a sufficiently varied approach to a number of psychological and ontological issues connected with the representational power of human mind. More narrowly, the paper brings out the original tension between the naturalistic conception of imitation, which derives the properly human power to imitate (in the arts as well as philosophy) from a primitive framework of natural processes, and the emphasis on what we can label 'imagination', this notion being in fact in a much earlier use than many readers assume. Without trying to simply oppose these two tendencies (with the Hippocratic author of *On the Regime* and Aristotle on the one side, Plato and Philostratus on the other) I wish to analyze their respective treatment of the notion of image and the latter's relation to the apparently unavoidable talk about *mental* images.

In the history of Western culture, few concepts seem as ubiquitous as mimesis or, as the current and potentially misleading translation has it, imitation. This is no doubt because mimetic activity plays an essential role in both material and intellectual culture in their broad acceptations ranging from social habits and crafts to education, art and philosophy.

Mimesis: Metaphysics, Cognition, Pragmatics
ed. G. Currie, P. Koťátko, M. Pokorný
220–56. London: College Publications, 2012.

The Beginnings

At the same time, the contemporary philosophical treatments of mimesis tend to split into two possibly overlapping yet distinct discussions: one about the representational arts including literary fiction, another about the role of pretence and pretend play in the very structure of the human mindset.

To a degree, and in a sense that I will try to elucidate, it may well be this latter issue that comes closer to historical roots of mimesis as a process or activity whereby human beings both examine and reinforce their relation to the world at large.[1] In this perspective, the focus on mimesis in the arts (and the theorizing of arts) tends to go hand in hand with a narrowing of the original scope of mimesis. Rather than a straightforward reduction, however, even this evolution is a complex process with an internal logic of its own, one whose meanderings are hardly reducible to a forthright history. Instead, on the basis of its intervening into a wide range of human pursuits, mimetic activity seems to expose some quite durable beliefs about human condition starting with the variously formulated recognition of humans' special and undoubtedly intimate relation with image and image-making. In concrete terms, both Greco-Roman and Christian culture, precisely because they entertain a similarly ambivalent attitude towards human condition, tend to describe man as a reflection or image of some

---

[1] At the same time, the contemporary thematic split (with many overlaps) remains much similar to the twofold sense of mimesis in ancient times. See Ackerman (2001: 126): "Imitation was understood in two senses during antiquity and the Renaissance: the imitation of nature or human behavior, and the imitation of preceding writers and artists." While it is impossible to disagree with this summary, my interpretation of these two senses and their relation is not the same as Ackerman's. Also, the latter's focus is on the Renaissance, mine on Antiquity.

more perfect structure or agent, one that can (and should) become object of human representations and imitations.

Since we are not dealing here with the history of the concept of human nature we need not enter the varieties of this peculiar notion of human being as an image-making image. We should, however, recognise that even the most refined and abstract forms of our understanding of what images and representations are (and, by the same token, of what they are *meant* to be) bears at least a trace of the original anthropological dimension. The latter also explains why, since the earliest treatments of our issue, we are witnessing a competition between two opposite tendencies of either divinizing or naturalizing mimesis, a competition that goes on till, at least, Coleridge's romantic attempt at reconciling both tendencies.[2] In retrospect, we can see quite clearly how the apparently opposite gestures of grounding mimesis in what is taken for divine or of deriving it from what is considered a fully natural order of things belong to the similarly motivated efforts to explain how men stand in the broader scheme of things and what exactly they are capable of doing and creating. Still, the two tendencies are not exactly the same and, while clarifying both the mimesis" early scope and its possible meaning for contemporary discussions, we should stay alert to their differences as much as to their similarities.

In this context, one last methodological remark is in order. The above summarized tension that I will analyse in some detail (thus, again, the tension between the activity that intends to assimilate and appropriate, *also* but not exclusively by linguistic and intellectual means, what is divine, and the

---

[2] On Coleridge, and especially on his distinction between copy and imitation as well as his use of Schelling's *Naturphilosophie*, see Burwick (2001: 77–106).

activity that sees itself as a spontaneous expression of the all-pervading natural order of things) is clearly different from the later and more often discussed duality of imitating *natura naturata* (by reproducing the created nature or the results of divine creation) and imitating *natura naturans* (by creating, on a more modest scale, in the same way as nature does at large). This duality, historically more dependent on the specifically Christian metaphysics of creation and nature, comes close to my subject inasmuch as it informs, in various guises, some late Medieval and Renaissance descriptions of the artistic activity as *analogous* to either the inner working of nature or to the divine creation itself.[3] Still, to delve deeper into the similarities and possible historical filiations at issue here would mean to enlarge the scope of the material under scrutiny beyond reasonable limits.

It must also be added that the tension I am about to analyse is only tangential on the one between mimesis understood as a more or less straightforward imitation of nature and the idea of mimesis as leading to a different or perhaps an alternative world. It is to this latter sense of mimesis (whose product has been, since the first half of the eighteenth century, labelled "heterocosm") that most contemporary analyses and interpretations are devoted, even if they do not use this or any other neologism.[4] In these analyses, the older interest in how far a homology between a universe of discourse

---

[3] Boccaccio's treatment of Giotto and Vasari's treatment of Michelangelo are of course exemplary of these two options. For more on the duality in question see Białostocki (1963).

[4] Alexander Gottlieb Baumgarten's coinage "heterocosm", which owns its revival to Doležel (1998), is recalled in Halliwell (2002: 4). For more see Ruthven (1979: 1–15), Doležel (1990: 39–52).

and a physical universe can be pursued[5] gives way to the analytic, proposition-centred reworking of the very idea of "fictional worlds" into a field where make-believe games are won or lost in words. Acknowledging the importance of this theoretical development, of which Kendall Walton's *Mimesis as Make-Believe* is the most often discussed example (Walton 1990),[6] I will turn in a different direction and try to revive the other strain of the whole mimetic story, the one where mimesis, instead of being a way of building up fictional universes, serves to inscribe or perhaps re-inscribe its practitioners into the available world. At the same time, I hope that this reminder of what mimesis meant before and beyond textuality, be it a literary or a philosophical one, can shed some non-trivial if sometimes oblique light on the central issues discussed in this volume.

To make the following reconstruction of the early history of mimesis easier to grasp (and thus necessarily more schematic than it had to be), I will present a sample of texts that I take for representative of the two above-mentioned tendencies. Thus, on the one hand, I will turn to Plato's criticism of mimesis in the *Republic*, and also to a passage possibly related to this criticism in Philostratus" much later *Life of Apollonius of Tyana*. On the other hand, I will reread the relevant passages from the

---

[5] It is indeed this interest, which was very much alive in later Antiquity that gives substance to the eighteenth-century treatment of *heterocosmica*. It is not irrelevant that, for instance, Goethe's *kleine Kunstwelt* was traced back to some elements of Neoplatonic, more exactly Plotinian aesthetics. On the universe as discourse (and discourse as universe) see Coulter (1976), and also Brisson (1987).

[6] Here I intentionally simplify: for instance, Walton's emphasis on the issue of participation in games of make-believe offers a possible common ground for the new and the ancient theories of mimesis (see also the concluding paragraphs of this essay).

The Beginnings

Aristotelian corpus, including the metaphysical and physical writings, and also, much more briefly, the Hippocratic treatise *On the Regimen* whose several sections defend the thesis that all human arts and crafts are (mostly unconscious) imitations of natural processes. I take it that this theoretical breadth is needed especially in order to show how profoundly ambivalent is Plato's position as the "father" of theorizing about mimesis and *representational* art, and, by consequence, how ambivalent is this entire theoretical tradition.[7]

Now even with such a programme we can hardly hope to achieve a straightforward reconstruction of some allegedly lost continuity between natural and artistic activities. In fact, the genealogy of mimesis—whose repercussions are still felt, admittedly in hushed echoes, in contemporary discussions—suffers from an equivocation that we may never be able to resolve. This equivocation is due, ironically enough, to the very structure of the first textual effort at defining mimesis while *attacking* quite ferociously its allegedly common poetic use. For all its theoretical idiosyncrasy and metaphysical underpinning, this attack, as carried on in Plato's *Republic*, consists in narrowing down the broad use of mimesis *for philosophical purposes*; still, to hit his target, Plato is forced to partially rely on the perhaps original yet similarly narrow understanding of mimesis as a basis of poetic *performance*. Plato's criticism thus confirms that two equally original streaks of mimesis are present already in ancient thought: the term can be predicated either of acts that produce new, henceforward independent

---

[7] I will start with what is best known and most often commented upon: the doctrine in Plato and Aristotle. Only then I will proceed to the relatively less well known texts of the Hippocratic author and of Philostratus. This, I hope, is the best way to bring out the more general lesson as it connects with the overall scope of this volume.

objects, or of activities that modify the soul and behaviour of a person. What is peculiar in Plato's case is only the way he mixes the elements borrowed from poetic tradition with his novel metaphysics, all this with an intention to subvert *both* the poetic tradition *and* the broader discourse of natural philosophy.[8]

In order for us to understand such a compressed claim, we must start by recalling that, in all the ten books of the *Republic*, mimesis does not appear, as is often claimed, at two but rather at three different moments, all of which bring variously into focus Plato's emphasis on ethical issues, namely on the state of the soul. Now if Books 2–3 and also Book 10 deal with the imitative poetry's potentially noxious effects on the soul's inner harmony, it is also true that Plato, so to say along the way, in Books 6–7 appropriates for philosophy an important dimension that is originally proper to poetic performance: the effort at imitating and assimilating, through a well-ordained performance, what is taken for a higher or paradigmatic order of reality. When, at 500c2–5, Socrates recommends mental assimilation of an intrinsically perfect order (which, I take it, is the structure of celestial motions), he is actually presenting us with a version of the ideal of *homoiôsis theô* or "attaining a

---

[8] At this point, a caveat is necessary: I will not even try to do justice to the literature on Plato's relation to poetry and the poets. From among the most recent contributions, an inquisitive and more analytically minded reader will do well to consult Moss (2007) with a reference to Belfiore (1983). Destrée and Hermann (2011) appeared too late to be taken into account here. A recent contribution focused on Plato's psychology as a condition of his conception of mimesis is Harte (2010). In what follows, I focus mostly—and extremely selectively—on the *Republic*, leaving aside the issue of mimesis in the *Cratylus* and the *Laws*, as well as in the *Sophist*. The question of the difference between the *mimêsis eikastikê* and *mimêsis phantastikê*, so prominent in the *Sophist*, is beyond the scope of this paper; for a recent treatment see Nightingale (2002).

likeness to god".⁹ And while it is clear that this highly intellectual version is cognitively and linguistically articulate in a way which is intentionally different from the music of poetry, it still relies on a particular mode of mimetic activity and the language of mental assimilation (employed already in regard of the malleable children who are at the opposite pole of human condition in Book 2, 377b).¹⁰

This continuity in transformation, I submit, is important as part of the background to Plato's rejection of imitative poetry. It is certainly true that mimesis before Plato includes a relatively simple or straightforward imitation and that Plato *includes* such an imitation within the range of his attack. After all, the earliest attested use of the verb *mimeisthai*, in the Homeric Hymn to Apollo (v. 163), concerns the girls of Delos, Apollo's handmaidens, who "can imitate the tongues of all men and their clattering speech: each would say that he himself were singing, so close to truth is their sweet song" (trans. Evelyn-White). Yet besides its simple reading, this text offers another and more universal interpretative option, which would consist in assuming that Apollo's maidens do not ape the individual pitch of a given listener, but re-enact instead the very essence of human voice (its truth) so perfectly that every listener recognizes his participation in this essence. The plausibility of

---

[9] After a very long period of theoretical neglect, this kind of intellectual imitation has recently become one of the most discussed issues in ancient philosophy. See, e.g., Sedley (1999), Armstrong (2004), Russell (2004) and Morgan (2010).

[10] See Miller (2007: 335), and also Pelosi (2010: 42–43 n. 64). In contrast to these and other interpreters, I assume that the entities whose order is to be assimilated are not Platonic Forms but rather celestial motions as paradigms of just behaviour. On this reading, which I cannot properly defend here, *Republic* 6, 500c, is closely related to 9, 592b2–3, and *Timaeus* 47b5–c4 to 90c–d.

such a reading is reinforced by its reference to the actual practice of a complex poetic performance, organised so as to transport its audience into a community with the divine.[11] In this sense, *mimesis*, not entirely unlike the later category of fiction, re-enacts but also induces an imaginary experience and, by the same token, has a dimension of *both* a pretend play *and* a make-believe game: the performers touch the listeners by impersonating other voices than their own, and by doing it anew, with fresh variations, each time the poem or hymn is performed.

Here, I think, we touch upon the core of Plato's quarrel with mimetic poetry: not only does the latter turn towards the wrong divine, but it does so for the wrong reasons and by inappropriate means. In the *Republic* but also the *Laws*, Plato is very explicit about why he aims his criticism at the formal aspect of poetic and musical composition and performance: this is because the soul, whose education and virtue is at stake, is especially susceptible to particular metres, harmonies and rhythms, on which the *Laws* are more eloquent and analytic than the *Republic*, but whose general effects consist in distorting the potentially valuable message conveyed by a poetic text. It is up to poetry to present the majority of citizens with role models (cf. 2, 377e-378a), but the "wrong" mode of presentation of

---

[11] For more on this and some related issues see the commentary in Furley and Bremer (2001). See also the (rather more controversial) treatment of mimesis in Nagy (1996, esp. 59–86). It is fascinating to see to what degree the mimetic performance becomes itself the theme of some Hellenistic poems. Thus Callimachus's hymns describe and re-enact the occasions of their own performance. In a different register, but still concerning the mimesis of the divine, one is struck by the epigram where the same Callimachus celebrates four Graces—three real ones and a statue of a Grace that "has just been molded"; see *Epigram* 15 in Gow and Page (1965). For more on this poem and its wider context see Tueller (2004).

these models leads the audience to let down its rational guards and to open its soul to corruption—for which, under these circumstances, the members of the audience become co-responsible.[12]

At the same time, in order to drive his point home, Plato is remarkably selective about what the poets and other mimetic artists re-enact: in a summarising formula offered in *Republic* 10, he goes as far as to claim that "mimetic art represents human beings who carry out violent or voluntary actions" (603c4–5). Also, in Books 2-3, we have learnt that poets model their representations of *divine* actions on precisely this pattern of the worst of *human* violence and depravity. This means—although Plato does not use exactly this language—that poetic imitation subverts the very relation of men to the true and divine models that invite mimesis: instead of making humans to re-enact what is truly divine and peaceful, they represent divinities as evil and violent supermen. (Does Plato react here against the possible historical shift in the nature of auditorial response, as—in the fifth century and under the influence of tragedy—the previous modes which reconciled a more distanced perception with performative re-enaction gave way to an imaginative absorption of a new, self-reflexive kind? This is a question I am obliged to leave aside.)[13]

An important corollary of this critical view of poetry as the field of joint performative venture is the decisive role that

---

[12] For a new emphasis on this important point and its wider implications see Harte (2010). At the same time, it seems clear that poets are also victims of their actions, succumbing to the rhythms they use in composing their epic or tragic poems.

[13] On this issue and the parallels between the development of dramatic and visual arts see Elsner (2006). For the new "theatricalization" of the ancient poetic and mythic material see Wilson (2000).

Plato ascribes to the poetic form and to the harmful organisation of performance. In fact, the latter seems to determine, largely if not fully, the wrongness of the performance's content. This is why Plato can famously suggest that the remedy against poetic mimesis consists in reforming the current mimetic modes, more exactly those rhythms and harmonies that form the poem's musical and efficient *êthos* (see 398d8–399a1 or 400c7–d5, with a clear implication that harmonies should be made conform to words).[14] The very possibility to convert, say, the great epic poems into simple narratives or *diegeseis* suggests that what we take for poetry may have a surprisingly prosaic kernel. Indeed, at 392c-394e, the poetry is described as *not* mimetic in its nature; mimesis is only one of its compositional facets, one that the *audience* itself imitates while absorbing the performance.

In all, it is possible to conclude that Plato's treatment of mimesis in the *Republic* as well as in the rest of his oeuvre, exhibits a remarkable oscillation between a wider and a narrower understanding of mimesis. It is certainly possible to add that this oscillation can be found in the cultural context of Plato's times.[15] Thus the apparent ambiguities in Books 2–3 would follow, partly at least, from the continuity with both the broader understanding of mimesis as a sort of compositional-cum-performative complex and the narrow meaning of mimesis that would connect the latter, somehow more fundamentally, with the primarily musical form which affects the audience first

---

[14] I cannot deal here with the different meanings of "harmony"; in the passages relevant to my discussion, it is treated both as an organisation of pitches and as abstract structure. For references and comments see Petraki (2008).

[15] See the summary with references to other authors in Halliwell (2002: 51 and n. 35).

and foremost. What helps us to make sense of these two meanings of mimesis without reducing them entirely is Plato's focus on the soul and its musico-ethical *êthos*: it is the diversity of characters and their correlative tasks in human cities that explains the need to treat the very idea of a morally good music and poetry on different levels.[16]

It is thus obvious that Plato's theorizing of mimesis, determined as it is by his specific and revolutionary conception of the structure of the soul, must take exception both to the older practice of poetic performance and to the recent developments of the tragic spectacle. At the same time, since Plato is shifting the core of the "good" mimesis into the apparently more refined realm of philosophical inquiry where the point is to attain and re-enact the rational structure of the intellect itself, it is obvious that distinct parts or functions of the soul should be ideally correlated with different mimetic practices, ranging from stories designed so as to tame the lowest part of the soul all the way to the specific actions of the intellect that strives to grasp and mentally reproduce the universe as a whole. That much being clear, the great challenge for any interpretation of this layered scheme that repeatedly punctuates the *Republic*'s progress is to explain the apparently abrupt change of tone at the beginning of Book 10 where, before turning back to the issue of mimetic poetry and its dangers, Plato shifts from what mimesis *does* and how it is *used* to a question of what mimesis *is*.

---

[16] Koller (1954) defends the view that mimesis ("representation" rather than "imitation") was first limited to the sphere of music and dance; thanks to the (alleged) Pythagoreans, this original mimesis would then connect to the concept of a musical *êthos*. On the possibility to apply Koller's hypothesis to Plato see Pelosi (2010: 57–58).

The resulting text, Plato's only attempt at a definition of mimesis (cf. the introduction at 595b6–c7), leaves provisionally aside the structure of the soul and turns to the structure of reality instead.[17] What we get as a result is a brief and highly metaphysical excursus that defines mimesis as a reproductive activity removed, *by definition*, from the mode of being proper to what it imitates. Now we could discuss Plato's decision to rely, in these lines, on the explanatory model of painting rather than poetry (clearly, painting helps to describe more vividly the mutual *exteriority* of the model and its copy: both poetry and painting mould souls, but painters moreover create *things*). This, however, is less important than the basic assumption that determines the whole argument, namely that *all things*, including the standards that serve as models for human craftsmen-imitators, can be described as results of the alleged divine production (*poiêsis*). To put it briefly, it takes a fully artificial world, planned and created by a supreme divine craft, to turn the poets and painters into the imitators of the lowest kind.

It is here that we arrive, from a new direction, at the essence of Plato's quarrel with poetry which, on his view, seems to include almost all of the Presocratic thought as well. It is the elevation of the *divine* craft into an unprecedented height (Plato seems to be most serious in envisaging the world as divine *artefact*) that has for its corollary the relative contempt of *human* crafts that include the arts of poetry and painting. Since these crafts take no part in the design of the universe, there is an inverse proportion between them and the divine craft (cf.

---

[17] The argument will change its basic structure again at 601d1–2 where, instead of three degrees of reality, it starts to rely on three distinct crafts: "for each thing, suggests Socrates, there are these three crafts [*technai*], one that uses it, one that makes it, and one that imitates it" (trans. Reeve).

529d7–530c1). As a result, it is only the peak of human *theoretical* science—namely dialectic—that can understand what is divine and then help reproduce its basic features in human soul (484c-d with 500c-d; 540a8–b1 with Book 9, 592b2–3; and cf. *Timaeus*, 47b5–c4 and 90c-d).

In this perspective, largely independent of the detail of how we interpret the relation of Book 10 to Books 2–3,[18] Plato's quarrel with various conceptions of mimesis reflects his fundamental mistrust of nature (and, correlatively again, of human nature) as a self-governing force that *includes* divine forces re-enacted by the—broadly speaking—poetic performance and its pleasurable reception by the audience. Rejecting this re-enactment on the basis of a complex argument against both nature and pleasure, Plato rejects, in advance, exactly the two notions upon which will rest Aristotle's account of mimesis.

Before turning to the latter, we can thus conclude that there are two reasons for why Plato defines mimesis by turning it away from a widely conceived cultural practice and reducing it to a narrow scheme of either the low artistic production or the high and purely intellectual achievement. First and obviously, there is the political context in which his discourse about mimesis is situated and which brings into focus the states of individual soul that must conform to the good of a larger whole. Second and perhaps more importantly, there is Plato's overall rejection of the very idea of a spontaneous natural order of things of which, for other ancient authors, the mimetic activity makes part. Thus Plato, giving no credit to our capacities and actions that do not proceed from some fully explicit knowledge, swims against the philosophical current

---

[18] A recent reappraisal of the relations between Books 2–3 and Book 10 is included in Barney (2010).

that considers mimesis as the most natural way of insribing man into the material universe.

Before we notice how and on what exact conditions the Platonic reduction of mimesis became reintegrated into later (including modern) theorizing of art, it is important to take a brief look at two examples of an alternative attitude towards mimesis as an activity embedded, with a remarkable continuity, in nature as well as in human nature as nature's perhaps quite special yet still integral part. These two examples are the much read Aristotle and the much less read Hippocratic treatise *On the Regimen*. Although I contrast both these conceptions with Plato's rather narrow understanding of mimesis, it will be equally important to point out that they differ in some important respects that cannot be reduced to simple differences in style and the subject matter.

Like in Plato's case, Aristotle's best known statements about mimesis relate to poetry, more exactly tragedy. Tragic mimesis, however, is only one among many kinds of mimesis, and even this kind does certainly not consist in the oft-evoked "imitation of nature".[19] Aristotle explicitly states that tragic mimesis is "not of persons but of actions and life" (*Poetics* 6, 1450a16-17), and it is this formula that, while being at the heart of dramatic composition and performance, points towards a much broader horizon of what the Aristotelian mimesis truly is. All things considered, we can legitimately take *action* (*praxis*) and *life* (*bios*) for the keywords of Aristotle's understanding of mimesis. More exactly, the two words are the key to the specifically *human* activities, be they simply playful or moral

---

[19] This surprisingly common misreading is rejected in Halliwell (2002: 151), whose treatment of mimesis in Aristotle (Halliwell 2002: 151-206) is probably the most comprehensive one as far as arts and human activities are concerned.

ones;[20] later on we shall see that the full range of the Aristotelian mimesis includes activities (*energeiai*) and life (*zôê*) that occur beyond the sphere of human decisions and actions, and belong to the realm of natural or cosmic processes. Now if there is an important continuity in so many different manifestations of mimesis, it is due to the crucial fact that the Aristotelian mimesis is not *of nature* but *part of nature*, including—as I have said—human nature. Indeed, among the entries in Aristotle's notional catalogue of distinctively human features we find the description of man as "the most mimetic (*mimêtikôtatos*) among the animals" (*Poetics* 4, 1448b7), a description fit to characterize not just man's natural propensity to learn and to learn by playing, but also, by extension, the practical dimension of how moral virtues are, or indeed can be, acquired.

In this respect, three different strains of our mimetic propensity need to be brought together, which Aristotle does without any further argument. Clearly, for him, the appeal to human nature is sufficient to pick human mimesis out as the natural basis of learning (1448b8), and then, in the next sentence, to identify it with the equally natural pleasure (1448b9). Only a moment later, after having pointed out that we delight in representations of horrible things, he combines this psychological fact rather subtly with our pleasure in learning. Since Aristotle proceeds here in a way which, its apparent familiarity notwithstanding, is rather non-trivial, the text of *Poetics* 4, 1448b10–17, deserves a full quote:

---

[20] It is impossible to deal here with the issue of mimesis and character or *êthos* since it would require us to reread *Politics* 8.5 on the musical equivalents of characters. This important and complex text is scrutinised in Halliwell (2002: 158–63 and 237–49).

> Of those things we look at with pain (*lupêrôs horômen*), the most accurate images (*tas eikonas tas malista êkribômenas*) cause us delight when we contemplate them (*chairomen theôrountes*), such as figures of the most base animals or of corpses (*hoion thêriôn te morphas tôn atimotatôn kai nekrôn*). The reason for this also is that learning is most pleasant not only for philosophers, but for others alike—except that they take part in it briefly. It is for this reason that people delight in looking at images, because it happens that, by contemplating, they learn and they infer about what each one is, namely that this person represents that person.[21]

As the mention of accuracy implies, it is the *formal* features of representation that produce, simultaneously and spontaneously, delight *and* instruction. Pleasure, which is the natural goal pursued by every living creature including man (although it is not the latter's moral goal), is thus not opposed to but rather combined with learning that will ultimately, in the long run, transcend its quasi-appetitive natural origin. Emphasizing that this is true of every human being, Aristotle offers here a variation on the famous line that opens the *Metaphysics* by flatly stating that the *desire to learn* is equally innate to *all* human beings (980a21).[22] We are, to paraphrase Aristotle in less technical terms, naturally attuned to representations and pretend plays as ways of finding out more about our own place in the large scheme of things.

Prima facie, such a conception of the natural basis of education looks like a modern attitude that resonates in

---

[21] I borrow the translation by Peponi (2004: 310–311). On the pleasure that follows from contemplating the *representations* of fearful or disgusting things cf. *Parts of animals* 1.5, 645a11–15.

[22] Lear (1988: 1–14 and *passim*) offers a very persuasive interpretation of these lines in their Aristotelian context. I leave aside the proximity of this sentence to certain fragments of the younger Aristotle's *Protrepticus*.

contemporary studies in developmental psychology.[23] Especially striking is the contrast with Plato, or at least with the *Republic* which tends to describe small children as irrational beasts or cattle that needs to be "tamed'. On such a description, human tendency to indulge in tragic mimesis is of course a sign that this taming is rarely a fully successful one. Adopting the almost exactly opposite view of things, Aristotle prefers to assume that tragic mimesis is only the most elevated form of what comes naturally and without any formal codification to all kids who engage in this or that game of make-believe.[24] Insisting that we are keen *both* to imitate *and* to watch other people imitating, whether in theatre or elsewhere, Aristotle comes quite close to recognising the importance of human behaviour in the "as if" mode that enables us to assume a certain role without fully or entirely grasping all its implications. Indeed, the attitude of a *pretender* at virtue seems crucial to the whole scheme of our moral education: we need to acknowledge precisely this mode of behaviour in order to describe how we have *started* to acquire, and then been *progressively* acquiring, virtue and wisdom.

The reconstruction of possible connections between the early mimesis (that consists in various games of make-believe) and the adult progress towards virtue (where experience combines with imitation of moral examples) is beyond the

---

[23] In fact, the current debate tends to take one step further by analysing how children's early pretend plays include—due to the work of imagination—hypothetical and counterfactual situations. For perhaps the clearest exposition see Harris (2000).

[24] Here I am using Aristotle's analysis primarily in virtue of its making some important general points. We should not forget that, by the time the *Poetics* is being written, the great age of Attic tragedy is by and large over.

scope of this chapter.[25] It is however worth noticing that Aristotle's insistence on the pleasurable character of virtue (the latter is certainly *not* pleasure, but contains pleasure insofar as virtuous life is always an *active* life, see *Nicomachean Ethics* 1.8) is perfectly compatible with his explanation the pleasure we take in the representations of the exemplary human deeds. Like moral instruction, the successful mimesis of actions requires a rich imaginary participation on behalf of the spectators. Their relation to what is being imitated is itself an emotionally engaged mimetic attitude; after all, it is not for nothing that the Greek noun *mimêsis* means both imitation and emulation.

At this point, we can conclude that, compared to Plato, Aristotle's grasp on mimesis is quite naturalistic. As such, it not only conveys a strikingly different moral lesson, but it also implies an entirely different picture of mimetic processes in general. On the one hand, there is little doubt that human mimesis retains its special place inasmuch as it re-enacts the actions that follow from voluntary decisions, be they good or bad. On the other hand, if all human mimesis (not just its theatrical versions but its ethical instances too) is of action as *praxis*, there is also a broader mimesis not of *praxis* but of *energeia*. The latter is to be understood in its Aristotelian sense: it is a specific form of behaviour or process that defines all natural (and thus psychic) motions that *aim at a certain goal* and cease their activity only when they achieve it. To put it simply, Aristotle's broad understanding of mimesis gives the latter a fundamental teleological dimension; this teleology has a fully natural and immanent character that is specifically re-oriented but not fundamentally changed or even denied in human arts as based on the mimesis of action.

---

[25] For Aristotle's view on mimesis and becoming good or virtuous see Fossheim (2001).

The Beginnings

In fact, the letter of Aristotle's description of man as the *most* mimetic of all animals implies, in virtue of the superlative *mimêtikôtatos*, that some other animals are capable of at least some degree of mimetic activity too. This is undoubtedly true, yet here we must carefully distinguish between the rather superficial mimesis in its plainly imitative sense,[26] and a more fundamental activity that makes part of the natural teleology of which all animal actions are part. It is undoubtedly in this latter sense that we must understand Aristotle's claim that animals, including and especially those that are incapable of theoretical activity, *imitate* divine activity (or better actuality) through reproduction.

Firmly stated in two different treatises (*De anima* 2.4, 415a26-b2, and *De generatione animalium* 2.1, 731b24-732a11), this idea of an endless chain of mortal creatures as a substitute for individual perfection is certainly reminiscent of Plato's *Symposium* 208a-b, where Socrates describes human procreation as a sort of surrogate immortality. Aristotle, however, has a different scheme in mind, one where imitating in the sense of producing "another such as itself" (415a28) belongs to a much broader concept of final causation.[27] Thus, when he implies that animals including man are not the only natural entities that behave in some broadly speaking mimetic fashion, but that the

---

[26] See *Historia Animalium* 8.12, 597b23-26; 9.1, 609b19; 9.49, 631b9. I owe this last reference to Halliwell (2001: 104 n. 2), who quotes all three passages without adding that they all pertain to the mimetic (and especially vocal) abilities of various bird species.

[27] *Pace* Richardson Lear (2004: 80-83), who assumes affinity between Aristotle and Plato on this point and whose more general claim is that Aristotle models his "imitative form of final causation" upon Platonic love (80). A very good summarising interpretation of the texts in question is Johnson (2005: 146-149) who is careful not to personify Aristotle's idiom and includes some critical remarks (147) on Richardson Lear and other readings.

physical motions in our sublunary part of the universe "imitate" the perfect circular locomotion of the celestial sphere,[28] he sketches a whole hierarchy of motions whereby various natural things "imitate" a higher (and ultimately divine) form of activity or *energeia*, which is prior and superior to their own natural motion in every respect.[29] In other words, the object of natural mimesis is, first and foremost, a better way of being.

Nature, by contrast to everything that we read in Plato, is thus a source of its own aiming at self-transcendence. Most importantly, human arts and crafts find their place on this scale as well, albeit in a way which is proper to a thinking animal with the widest range of needs and interests. In this perspective, the famous dictum "art imitates nature" (*Physics* 2.4, 194a21-22) is not free of an often misunderstood equivocation. On the one hand, arts and crafts are, for Aristotle, not productive of substances in the full sense of the term: their products lack life and thus natural motion which they can, at best, represent and approximate. On the other hand, the "imitation" in question is certainly nothing like a copying of some firmly given natural pattern. Rather, it is an invention that makes this or that activity or its product structurally *analogous* to natural entities.[30] In fact, human art (including arts

---

[28] See *De generatione et corruptione* 2.10, 336b25-337a7, on rectilinear motion as continuous only insofar as it *imitates* the circular locomotion; and *Metaphysics* 9.8, 1050b28-30, with examples of earth and fire; these two texts concern the cyclical transformation of elements. For obvious reasons I cannot venture here into a detailed discussion of Aristotelian physics and cosmology.

[29] For a defence of this reading see Rudolph (1988: 236). I wish to thank Diana Quarantotto for her comments on this issue.

[30] This is firmly emphasised and explained in, for instance, Schummer (2001). Cf. Husain (2002: 22-23): "Aristotelian *techne* imitates the methods

in our sense of the term) also can, and often does, *perfect* or *supplement* this or that natural state of affairs. The thrust of Aristotle's account can thus be paraphrased by saying that arts are representative of nature's working. Hence Aristotle's apparently curious insistence that a natural house or a natural ship, were there any, would be exactly as the house or the ship made by art (cf. *Physics* 2.8, 199a8–20, b28–30). In a similar way, a well-crafted tragedy is structurally akin to disasters that befall good men and conveys a lesson about what naturally (albeit not commonly) threatens us.

Mimesis in fine arts is thus part of a larger web of mimetic relations. This is why its Aristotelian legitimacy differs so strikingly from Plato's much narrower connection between mimesis and intentional reproduction of a given pattern (be the latter a human or a divine one). Such a conclusion is only reinforced by the recent suggestion, made by Francis Wolff, that Aristotle invented the very concept of mimetic art (*technê mimetikê*) by newly combining two originally heterogeneous concepts, viz. that of art (*technê*) and that of mimesis.[31] This is especially plausible in the light of Aristotle's broad understanding of mimesis as a process that consists in the naturally teleological effort at assimilating and, if possible, further refining of what works best.

---

and processes of *physis* rather than the descriptive content of the products of *phusis*." And cf. Wolff (2007: 63): "'*Every art* imitates nature' does not mean that it reproduces it, it means that two modes of making are isomorphic. Without nature, it would be impossible to proceed artificially, without art it would be impossible to understand how nature naturally proceeds."

[31] Wolff (2007: 51-53). Wolff, who is interested in the relationship between mimesis and pleasure, brings out the similarities of the pleasure we take in artificial and natural objects.

At the same time, to stress the distance between Aristotelian and Platonic mimesis is not to range Aristotle within the camp of the "hard" naturalists, willing to take all mimesis for an aspect of natural processes and apparently leaving little or no place for mimesis as specifically connected to human mind. By contrast, the most illustrative expression of this position, which makes part of the Hippocratic treatise *On the Regimen*, insists on the material unity of human being whose "technical" performances (in other words arts and crafts) are identical to mimetic functions whose not necessarily explicit or even conscious object is the universe or some of its aspects.[32] Here the explanation of various arts is logically preceded by a description of human constitution as resulting from the mimetic activity of fire which "imitated" the universe in order to best arrange what is small in conformity with what is great (1.10). Interestingly enough, this variation on the theme of macrocosmos and microcosmos (utterly different from the Platonic assimilation of the numerical structure of celestial motions by human intellect) does not proceed by a simple derivation of human physiology (which includes the entirely material mind) from a larger natural framework. The mimetic relation is described as going in both directions: much as human constitution is said to "imitate" the structure of the

---

[32] The relevant portion of the text is *On the Regimen* 1.12–24. Among commentators, it continues to have rather bad press. For instance, Halliwell (2002: 15 n. 34), simply states that *On the Regimen* 1.10–18 is difficult to reconcile with Aristotelian mimesis, adding that it posits a wide range of mimetic relations "in the context of a pseudo-Heracleitean mishmash". Exceptions to this attitude are Pigeaud (1995: 180–82), and also Bartoš (forthcoming), who discusses the relation (and contrast) between the Hippocratic text and both the Platonic and the Pythagorean conceptions of mimesis, including the pioneering interpretation of these issues in Burkert (1972).

world, the latter can be described as "imitating" human constitution.

In the resulting scheme, mimesis is fully and non-platonically naturalized, and thus made entirely independent on *conscious* human intentions. It is at work in every craft, with *or without* the craftsman's conscious grasp of it. Indeed, most often, the craftsmen simply use the god-given capacity of imitating (*mimeisthai*) without any understanding for its underlying structure as shared by their own minds and bodies, and also the universe at large (see 1.11).[33] As a result, human things get done on the basis of the custom whose true foundation (viz., the natural mimesis) men ignore. The ramifications of this lesson are then developed in a series of thirteen chapters of various lengths. Ranging from seercraft through cobblery, carpentry or pottery to sculpture, the art of writing and the athletic training, these chapters are amazingly direct in applying the core premise to all kinds of human activity. Directness, however, does not exclude a refinement that reaches far beyond the obvious comparison between the potter's spinning wheel and the cosmic revolution that makes and forms all things (1.22). Who, after all, would have thought that the art of writing (*grammatikê*), which recalls the past and shows what must be done by putting together figures as symbols of human voice, reflects and makes truly manageable the foundation of all sense-perception in the outward and inward passages of hot and cold breath (1.23)?

---

[33] The beginning of chapter 11 presents us with a textual difficulty that I need not discuss in detail: it mentions "the mind (*noos*) of the gods" which taught humans to imitate *their* own function. "Their" can refer either to what gods do (gods are no different from nature here) or, more plausibly, to the functions of their human bodies.

It was suggested that this Hippocratic text could have influenced those who were dealing with mimesis in a narrow aesthetic sense, although its author is clearly not interested in this line of inquiry himself.[34] Still, some readers were even willing to detect its echoes in Aristotle, and that despite the fact that it offers no connection to what Aristotle says about mimesis in his *Poetics* and that, more importantly, the views expressed in *On the Regimen* are strikingly different from Aristotle's teleologically oriented understanding of both natural and cultural processes. In all, by repeatedly emphasizing the often unconscious dimension of all mimetic activity, the Hippocratic author arrives at an original explanation of arts and crafts that differs, by its sheer naturalism, from Aristotle's above-discussed and ambivalent dictum "art imitates nature." It goes thus almost without saying that it differs to an even higher degree from all efforts at using the arts as *explanans* of the nature itself, including Empedocles' famous analogy between zoogony and painting.[35] In Empedocles, painting is used to explain a natural process ("just as, when painters decorate, etc."); the Hippocratic author chooses to do the opposite and to show how our understanding of natural processes explains the whole range of human activities.

Fully naturalised, the activity of *mimesthai* thus becomes one of expressing — rather than "imitating" — the patterns that are firmly established in the world at large. In this context, the talk about mimesis points towards a very specific form of representation, one based on the possibility to correlate the descriptive contents of natural structures and human actions. Such a correlation will be used by many later authors and on

---

[34] See Joly (1960: 73), with discussion of other interpretations.
[35] Fragment B 23 Diels-Kranz. Among recent interpretations are Pigeaud (1995: 183–84), Sedley (2007: 58–59), and Porter (2010: 152–54).

the most various occasions, yet almost always with the addition of a teleological dimension, which is absent from the original Hippocratic presentation. It is probably the introduction or re-introduction of teleology that allows for what we might call individual initiative, and hence art in our sense of the term. Once we admit—together with Aristotle, the Stoics or a later medical author like Galen—that "nature is capable of foresight for the living being and of expect craftsmanship" (*On Natural Faculties* 2.2), we gain the possibility to discover a similar capacity in *our* nature: a capacity that turns the mimetic activity away from what is a simple natural given and towards what asks instead for an assimilation in more creative terms. Seen in this perspective, the history of mimesis appears as the constantly renegotiated access to what used to be described as divine: not because the ancient mimesis would have implied some explicitly posited theology, but because it was always tending, much like its modern counterpart will tend, *beyond* imitating and towards creating.

While this tendency is traceable back to the earliest descriptions of the mimetic activity as a fundamentally human endeavour, it gets certainly more prominent in those later texts that situate the simultaneously imitative and creative activity within the mind of both the artist and his or her audience. Although this conceptual move retains some formal similarities with, say, the imitation of the divine by a choral performance, it is far from being a revival. Rather, it uses new philosophical sophistication in order to transform the performance, which appropriates and re-enacts a divine source, into the almost authorial process of inspiration whereby it is the creator's own mind that becomes divine in its turn. Now given that Plato can be read as the greatest adversary of, loosely speaking, any creative element of mimesis, it is ironic that this influential shift seems to have occurred precisely through the mediation of Platonic legacy by various sophistic and rhetoric theories.

This story is too long and meandering to be recounted here in detail, but a double shift must be mentioned, whereby the Platonic Forms (originally described as unattainable or at least unattained by the poet) got transformed into divine thoughts and then relocated into the mind of the human creator.[36] As a result, true mimesis is not of natural objects, including human actions, but of the objects of thought. Suffice it to quote Cicero's *Orator*, 2.8–3.9, a text exemplary of this development and explaining how the author intends to produce a portrait of a perfect orator (trans. H. M. Hubbell, modified):

> But I am firmly of the opinion that nothing of any kind is so beautiful as not to be excelled in beauty by that of which it is a copy, as a mask is a copy of a face. Thus ideal cannot be perceived by the eye or ear, nor by any of the senses, but we can nevertheless grasp it by the thought and the mind (*cogitatione tantum et mente complectimur*). For example, in the case of the statues of Phidias, the most perfect of their kind that we have ever seen, and in the case of the paintings I have mentioned, we can, in spite of their beauty, think about (*cogitare*) something more beautiful. Surely that great sculptor, while making the image of Jupiter or Minerva, did not look at any person whom he was using as a model, but in his own mind (*ipsius in mente*) there dwelt a surpassing vision of beauty; at this he gazed and all intent on this he guided his artist's hand to produce the likeness of the god. Accordingly, as there is something perfect and surpassing in the case

---

[36] The first of these moves I need not discuss here. It may have originated with Antiochus of Ascalon who is a possible influence on Cicero (as quoted in the next sentence). For other sources see Wolfson (1961) and Watson (1988b). Both Christian Platonists and Neoplatonists, starting with Plotinus, will be crucial for the revival of this line of thought during the Renaissance. See Panofsky (1924), Cocking (1991), Halliwell (2002: ch. 11-12).

of sculpture and painting—an intellectual ideal by reference to which the artist represents those objects which do not themselves appear to the eye, so with our minds we conceive the ideal of perfect eloquence, but with our ears we catch only a copy (*effigiem*).

Subsequently we learn that these patterns of things (*rerum formas*) are indeed Plato's Forms. Such a statement is perhaps not valid for a truly orthodox Platonist, but this is less important than the presence, in the quoted lines, of a germ of an entirely new dimension of conceiving mimesis. On the one hand, any representation of perceptible things and actions is relegated, obviously and very Platonically, into the background. On the other hand, however, it is precisely by this relegation that Cicero anticipates a decisive break in the history of mimesis by saying that we, the spectators or listeners, can (indeed must) *imagine* what the artist was *imagining* while creating his works. Simply put, our mimesis is of the artist's non-mimetic invention.

The key lies in the phrase *cogitatione tantum et mente complectimur*, which describes both the great artist's mental fashioning of a perfect form and *our* reaction to the perceptible result of the artistic mimesis of such a form. Here, I submit, Cicero outlines a situation that will be described more clearly (albeit still rather fleetingly) in Flavius Philostratus' *Life of Apollonius of Tyana*, a much commented upon and almost novelistic biography of the first-century Neopythagorean sage.[37] Two passages from Books 2 and 6 respectively have been since long recognised as an important contribution to the history of Western thinking about art and the second passage of these passages has been read, with some justification, as one of

---

[37] For various state-of-the-art treatments of this 3rd-century narrative see Demoen and Praet (2009).

the earliest praises of imagination in the current sense of the term.[38] My aim is not to evaluate such a reading and even less to quarrel about the alleged historical priorities; I only intend to reappraise perhaps more neatly what connects Philostratus to some contemporary theories of mimesis.

When, at *Life* 6.19, Philostratus lets his hero contrast *mimêsis* (as representing only what has been seen) and *phantasia* (as able to represent what has not been seen), he uses the same example as Cicero (and, indeed, many other authors): Phidias' statue of Zeus. The point of this example is of course that the divine, so brilliantly sculpted by Phidias, could not have been fashioned after any model accessible to the senses. It could have only been produced by *phantasia*, "a wiser and subtler artist by far than *mimêsis*'. The nature of this wisdom and subtlety is not due to some allegedly ecstatic vision that transcends the sensible realm. Rather, it consists in the imagination's capacity of offering not a snapshot or a series of snapshots, but an expression of a well-articulated knowledge of what is being represented. It is thus not entirely exaggerated to say that Philostratus' Apollonius puts forward a sketch of the causal theory of pictorial meaning: "When you entertain a notion of Zeus you must, I suppose, envisage him along with heaven and seasons and stars, as Phidias in his day endeavoured to do, and if you would fashion an image of Athene you must image in your mind armies and cunning, and handicrafts, and how she leapt out of Zeus himself." Clearly, and as the subsequent scorn of Egyptian symbols makes even clearer, this is not about a

---

[38] Among the important (and mutually distinct) interpretations of *Vita Apollonii* 2.2 and 6.19 (taken together or apart) are Birmelin (1933), Schweitzer (1934), Cocking (1991: 43–48), Watson (1988a: 59–95), Manieri (1998: 60–66), Halliwell (2002: 308–10), Miles (2009), Schirren (2009: 175–77) and Platt (2009: 133–35).

symbolism representations of gods. It is about how the invisible divine fares in the observable universe at large. More exactly, it seems to be about how every well-crafted image is an image of a world.

That this theory underlies not only the images of the divine, but all kinds of truthful representations, is amply attested by Philostratus" other famous text, the *Images*, which consists in a series of detailed descriptions of the probably notional paintings, a series framed — surely not by chance — by the theme of seasons or *Hôrai*.[39] Moreover, it connects well with a point made much earlier in the *Life*, at 2.22, where the discussion between Apollonius and his companion Damis bears on the right understanding of the art of painting, and thus of mimesis. Here the main point is to preclude the identification of mimesis with the art of painting, an identification too narrow and inexact insofar as mimesis consists, first of all, in the natural capacity of human mind, a capacity irreducible to any particular craft, including the art of the painter. In concrete terms, the viewer's response to any image consists first and foremost in his or her conception of a mental image (labelled either *eidôlon* or *eikôn*), the latter being the proper medium whereby we judge the representation in question, including (and especially so) its intrinsic mimetic qualities.

Thus conceived, Philostratus' mental mimesis comes pretty close to an important and obvious aspect of what we call imagination. Various examples are supplied, ranging from how our natural mimetic capacity makes us see some definite shapes in the clouds (centaurs, goat-deer, wolves or horses) to how we mentally supplement, quite spontaneously, a simple line-drawing or a monochrome that we turn into a fully coloured figure endowed with precise expression. The point is not to

---

[39] On the importance of this framing see especially Elsner (2000).

simply state that it is impossible to disentangle what we see from what we know, and what we already know from what we are learning in the very process of looking at images. Rather, it is to stress that viewing is an acting process conditioned by the presence of the imitative faculty (*hê mimêtikê*) in every viewer. And it is not just about picturing some fancy beasts based on the floating clouds: no representation, whether of things known or unknown (the example of the former is a horse or a bull and its picture), cannot be appreciated without our re-creation of the mimetic act. This is further stressed and developed, by another crucial statement that Philostratus puts into Apollonius' mouth at 4.7, where the latter insists that literary presentation has natural advantage over a sculpture (or a painting). To quote Philostratus' own example, Homer's Zeus is superior even to the one of Phidias.[40] This is because of its imaginary location, in other words because — precisely as a mental image unconnected to a non-equivocal perceptible appearance (like, say, *this* particular statue) — the literary Zeus is situated, always and predominantly, in the mind.

It is rather easy to spot the possible conceptual link between such an imaginative mental mimesis (a truly participative activity) and many later, indeed contemporary theories of mimesis that emphasise its often intimate connection with imagination. For instance, to acknowledge that there is an ongoing mimetic activity in the mind of any reader or spectator who feels the so-called "fictional emotions" seems a precondition for fully grasping the nature of the latter. This sort of activity is not simply identical with personal imagining; necessarily, it invites us to rethink some core features of concept

---

[40] See Philostratus, *The Life of Apollonius of Tyana*, 4.7. Some accounts of mimesis in Philostratus tend to omit this passage; but see Watson (1994: 47–69), Miles (2009: 155), Platt (2009: 134).

formation as well.[41] Still, the concepts that we can form in this way are naturally "projectional" or expressive: rather than tools of analysis, they resemble tools of an interpretative search in the territory of artistic mimesis. This, after all, is how the Philostratean account was understood by Lessing, whose *Laocoon* became instrumental in spreading the view that no product of mimesis can be understood without the intervening imagination, and that imitation (*Nachahmung*) always combines with expression (*Ausdruck*).[42] It is this common ground shared, variously but equally firmly, by the artist and by his or her public that gives legitimacy to mimesis as something substantially wider than "imitation" of any and all sorts.

Clearly, Philostratus, Lessing or many contemporary theorists of mimesis put more in the eye and the mind of the common beholder than Plato or Aristotle did. At the same time, however, they have kept and keep alive one of the original streaks of mimesis as a mental and compositional activity aimed at *reconstructing* of what is truly there. To suggest that we are aware of mimesis when we participate in it by imaginary means need not imply that the world, whose invisible structures the ancient mimesis started to re-enact by assimilating them to something divine, is a world well lost. At least in this respect, the difference between the ancients (with their full blown cosmologies) and the moderns (with their attention to subtleties of linguistic meaning) may still be one of degree rather than kind. To put the same point in much simpler

---

[41] This is not to deny that any picture (in the large sense of the term) *authorises* personal imagining, as Walton (1990) is keen to submit and amply defend. For a succinctly formulated criticism of this view see Currie (1993). Fortunately, I need not adjudicate this quarrel in the present context.

[42] For more on Lessing and his reading of Philostratus see Halliwell (2002: 118-20 and 309).

way, the fictional worlds of modern art and theory are still, firsts and foremost, worlds. In fact, even when subtly (or painstakingly) fragmentary, they can be imagined only as such.[43]

Charles University / Czech Academy of Sciences
karel.thein@ff.cuni.cz

REFERENCES

Ackerman, James S. 2001. *Origins, Imitation, Conventions: Representation in the Visual Arts*. Cambridge, MA: The MIT Press.
Armstrong, John M. 2004. "After the Ascent: Plato on Becoming Like God." *Oxford Studies in Ancient Philosophy* 26 (Summer): 171–183.
Barney, Rachel. 2010. "Platonic Ring-Composition and *Republic* 10." In *Plato's* Republic*: A Critical Guide*, ed. M. L. McPherran, 32–51. Cambridge – New York: Cambridge University Press.
Bartoš, Hynek. Forthcoming. "The Concept of *Mimēsis* in the Hippocratic *De victu*."
Belfiore, Elizabeth. 1983. "Plato's Greatest Accusation Against Poetry." *Canadian Journal of Philosophy*, vol. 9 suppl. (*New Essays on Plato*, ed. F. J. Pelletier and J. King-Farlow), 39–62.
Białostocki, Jan. 1963. "The Renaissance Conception of Nature and Antiquity." In *The Renaissance and Mannerism: Studies in Western Art. Acts of the Twentieth International Congress of Art History*, ed. I. E. Rubin, vol. 2, 19–30. Princeton: Princeton University Press.
Birmelin, Ella. 1933. "Die Kunsttheoretischen Gedanken in Philostrats Apollonius." *Philologus* 88: 149–180, 392–414.

---

[43] Again, this does not diminish the *possible* variety of other conceptions that, according to Walton (1990: 67), *would* focus, probably, on taking fictional worlds for "classes of propositions". For such fictional worlds, perhaps some remote ancestry in Stoic dialectic and Stoic views of fiction could be claimed. But this would be the matter for a very different chapter in the history of mimesis.

Brisson, L. 1987. "Le discours comme univers et l'univers comme discours. Platon et ses interprètes néo-platoniciens." In *Le texte et ses représentations. Études de littérature ancienne 3*, 121–127. Paris: Presses de l'École Normale Supérieure.
Burkert, Walter. 1972. *Lore and Science in Early Pythagoreanism*. Cambridge, MA: Harvard University Press.
Butwick, Frederick. 2001. *Mimesis and Its Romantic Reflections*. University Park, PA: The Pennsylvania State University Press.
Cocking, John M. 1991. *Imagination. A Study in the History of Ideas*. London: Routledge.
Coulter, James. 1976. *The Literary Microcosm: Theories of Interpretation of the Later Neoplatonists*. Leiden: E. J. Brill.
Currie, Gregory. 1993. Review of Walton (1990). *Journal of Philosophy* 90 (7): 367–370.
Demoen, Kristoffel, and Danny Praet (eds). 2009. *Theios Sophistes. Essays on Flavius Philostratus'* Vita Apollonii. Leiden: E. J. Brill.
Destrée, Pierre, and Fritz-Gregor Herrmann (ed.). 2011. *Plato and the Poets*. Leiden: E. J. Brill.
Doležel, Lubomír. 1990. *Occidental Poetics: Tradition and Progress*. Lincoln: University of Nebraska Press.
– – –. 1998. *Heterocosmica: Fiction and Possible Worlds*. Baltimore: The Johns Hopkins University Press.
Elsner, Jas. 2000. "Making Myth Visual: the *Horae* of Philostratus and the Dance of the Text." *Mitteilungen des Deutschen Archäologischen Instituts, Römische Abteilung* 107: 253–276.
– – –. 2006. "Reflections on the 'Greek Revolution' in Art: From Changes in Viewing to the Transformation of Subjectivity." In *Rethinking Revolutions through Ancient Greece*, ed. Simon Goldhill – Robin Osborne, 68–95. Cambridge: Cambridge University Press.
Fossheim, Hallvard. 2001. "Mimesis in Aristotle's Ethics." In *Making Sense of Aristotle. Essays in Poetics*, ed. Øivind Andersen – Jon Haarberg, 73–86. London: Duckworth.
Furley, William D., and Jan M. Bremer. 2001. *Greek Hymns*, 2 vols. Tübingen: Mohr Siebeck.
Gow, Andrew S. F., and Dennys L. Page (ed.). 1965. *The Greek Anthology. Hellenistic Epigrams*, 2 vols. Cambridge: Cambridge University Press.
Halliwell, Stephen. 2001. "Aristotelian Mimesis and Human Understanding." In *Making Sense of Aristotle. Essays in Poetics*, ed. Øivind Andersen – Jon Haarberg, 87–107. London: Duckworth.

———. 2002. *The Aesthetics of Mimesis: Ancient Texts and Modern Problems.* Princeton: Princeton University Press.
Harris, Paul L. 2000. *The Work of the Imagination.* Oxford: Blackwell.
Harte, Verity. 2010. "*Republic* X and the Role of the Audience in Art." *Oxford Studies in Ancient Philosophy* 38 (Summer): 69–96.
Husain, Martha. 2002. *Ontology and the Art of Tragedy: An Approach to Aristotle's* Poetics. Albany, NY: State University of New York Press.
Johnson, Monte R. 2005. *Aristotle on Teleology.* Oxford: Clarendon Press.
Joly, Robert. 1960. *Recherches sur le Traité pseudo-hippocratique de Régime.* Paris: Les Belles Lettres.
Koller, Hermann. 1954. *Die Mimesis in der Antike. Nachahmung, Darstellung, Ausdruck.* Bern: A. Francke.
Lear, Jonathan. 1988. *Aristotle: The Desire to Understand.* Cambridge: Cambridge University Press.
Manieri, Alessandra. 1998. *L'immagine poetica nella teoria degli antichi.* Pisa: Instituti editoriali e poligrafici internazionali.
Miles, Graeme. 2009. "Reforming the Eyes: Interpreters and Interpretation in the *Vita Apollonii.*" In Demoen and Praet 2009: 129–160.
Miller, Mitchell. 2007. "Beginning the 'Longer Way'." In *The Cambridge Companion to Plato's* Republic, ed. G. R. F. Ferrari, 310–344. Cambridge: Cambridge University Press.
Morgan, Kathryn A. 2010. "Inspiration, Recollection, and *Mimēsis* in Plato's *Phaedrus.*" In *Ancient Models of Mind. Studies in Human and Divine Rationality,* ed. Andrea Nightingale–David Sedley, 45–63. Cambridge: Cambridge University Press.
Moss, Jessica. 2007. "What Is Imitative Poetry and Why Is It Bad." In *The Cambridge Companion to Plato's* Republic, ed. G. R. F. Ferrari, 415–444. Cambridge: Cambridge University Press.
Nagy, Gregory. 1996. *Poetry as Performance: Homer and Beyond.* Cambridge: Cambridge University Press.
Nightingale, Andrea. 2002. "Distant Views: Realistic and Fantastic Mimesis in Plato." In *New Perspectives on Plato, Modern and Ancient,* ed. Julia Annas–Christopher Rowe, 227–247. Cambridge, MA: Harvard University Press.
Panofsky, Erwin. 1924. *Idea: Ein Beitrag zur Begriffsgeschichte der älteren Kunsttheorie.* Studien der Bibliothek Warburg 5. Leipzig–Berlin: Teubner. English trans.: *Idea: A Concept in Art Theory,* trans. Joseph J. S. Peake. Columbia, SC: University of South Carolina Press. 1968.

Pelosi, Francesco. 2010. *Plato on Music, Soul and Body*. Cambridge: Cambridge University Press.
Peponi, Anastasia-Erasmia. 2004. "Initiating the Viewer: Deixis and Visual Perception in Alcman's Lyric Drama." *Arethusa* 37 (3): 295-316.
Petraki, Zacharoula A. 2008. "The Soul 'Dances': Psychomusicology in Plato's *Republic*." *Apeiron* 41 (2): 147-70.
Pigeaud, Jackie. 1995. *L'art et le Vivant*. Paris: Gallimard.
Platt, Verity J. 2009. "Virtual Visions: *Phantasia* and the Perception of the Divine in Philostratus' *Life of Apollonius of Tyana*." In *Philostratus*, ed. Ewen Bowie–Jas Elsner, 131-154. Cambridge: Cambridge University Press.
Porter, James I. 2010. *The Origins of Aesthetic Thought in Ancient Greece: Matter, Sensation, and Experience*. Cambridge: Cambridge University Press.
Richardson Lear, Gabriel. 2004. *Happy Lives and the Highest Good: An Essay on Aristotle's* Nicomachean Ethics. Princeton: Princeton University Press.
Rudolph, Enno. 1988. "*Energeia* in Aristotle and Theophrastus." In *Theophrastean Studies: On Natural Science, Physics and Metaphysics, Ethics, Religion and Rhetoric*, ed. William W. Fortenbaugh–Robert W. Sharples, 233-237. New Brunswick: Transaction Publishers.
Russell, Daniel C. 2004. "Virtue as 'Likeness to God' in Plato and Seneca." *Journal of the History of Philosophy* 42 (3): 241-260.
Ruthven, Kenneth K. 1979. *Critical Assumptions*. Cambridge: Cambridge University Press.
Schirren, Thomas. 2009. "Irony Versus Eulogy. The *Vita Apollonii* as Metabiographical Fiction." In Demoen and Praet 2009: 161-186.
Schummer, Joachim. 2001. "Aristotle on Technology and Nature." *Philosophia Naturalis* 38 (1): 105-20.
Schweitzer, Bernhard. 1934. "Mimesis und Phantasia." *Philologus* 89: 286-300.
Sedley, David. 1999. "The Ideal of Godlikeness." In *Plato 2. Ethics, Politics, Religion, and the Soul*, ed. Gail Fine, 309-28. Oxford: Oxford University Press.
– – –. 2007. *Creationism and Its Critics in Antiquity*. Berkeley: The University Of California Press.
Tueller, Michael A. 2004. "The Origins of Voice and Identity. Ambiguity in Callimachus' Epigrams." In *Callimachus II*, ed. Anette Harder–Remco F. Regtuit–Gerry C. Wakker, 298-315. Leuven: Peeters.

Walton, Kendall L. 1990. *Mimesis as Make-Believe. On the Foundations of the Representational Arts*. Cambridge, MA: Harvard University Press.

Watson, Gerard. 1988a. *Phantasia in Classical Thought*. Galway: Galway University Press.

— — —. 1988b. "Discovering the Imagination. Platonists and Stoics on *Phantasia*." In *The Question of "Eclecticism"*, ed. John Dillon—Anthony A. Long, 208–233. Berkeley: University of California Press.

— — —. 1994. "The Concept of *Phantasia* from the Late Hellenistic Period to Early Neoplatonism." *Aufstieg und Niedergang der römischen Welt* II.36.7: 4765–4810.

Wilson, Peter. 2000. "Powers of Horror and Laughter: The Great Age of Drama." In *Literature in the Greek and Roman Worlds: A New Perspective*, ed. Oliver Taplin, 88–132. Oxford: Oxford University Press.

Wolff, Francis. 2007. "The Three Pleasures of *Mimêsis* According to Aristotle's *Poetics*." In *Artificial and the Natural: An Evolving Polarity*, ed. Bernadette Bensaude-Vincent—William R. Newman, 51–66. Cambbridge, MA: The MIT Press.

Wolfson, Harry A. 1961. "Extradeical and Intradeical Interpretations of Platonic Ideas." *Journal of the History of Ideas* 22 (1): 3–32.

REPRESENTATION:
A PHENOMENOLOGICAL POINT OF VIEW

Tomáš Koblížek

ABSTRACT: Is it correct when we claim that text—as a specific type of representation—provides us only with instructions to obtain the image of the represented object? Can we conclude that text as a specific medium represents the border between us and the full image of what is represented? In this paper I try to argue that every text, as a representation, puts us in front of its object immediately and that we cannot experience any text without its object being presented. Such a perspective on textuality then brings out a reciprocal relationship between representation and its object: it is not the case that only representation determines what we know about the object—the object also determines the features of representation.

One way of approaching the question of mimesis is to define the relationship between two originally separated levels: (1) the level of reality and (2) the level of its representation.[1] From this point of view, one is expected to deal with questions such as, how elements of reality can be adequately represented, or to what extent representation forms an image of the represented object. The approach I have chosen in this paper differs from such a type of analysis. Instead of asking how an entity can obtain its representation or how a mimetic object is produced, I will focus on the issue of how we *perceive* "mimetic objects" or representations in general. In this regard it is plausible to

---

[1] To be more specific, Paul Ricœur, with his triple notion of mimesis, can be named as a modern exponent of this approach to mimesis (see Ricœur 1984).

designate the following descriptions as phenomenological. The descriptions will be presented in the following order: First, I will focus on the essential features of representation as a specific function. The analysis of this function will be developed in a subsequent analysis of "the implicit character" of representation and in a description of the phenomenon of ambiguity. The descriptions will end with an analysis of a specific "chiasm" which binds together the level of representation and the level of the represented object.

Representation as a function
In this section I will describe the essential features of representation by means of a model of written signs. Written representation reveals the general structure of representation with a particular clarity, and thus it can serve us as a starting point for phenomenological descriptions of more complex "representational objects". Throughout I will both follow and develop phenomenology of reading outlined by Roman Ingarden in the first chapter of his *Cognition of the Literary Work of Art* (§7 "Apprehension of the written signs and verbal sounds").

Let's focus on Ingarden's assertion that the reading of a written sign cannot be identified with a perception of individual perceptible "features". According to Ingarden, the perception of a graphical sign differs from the perception of mere spots of ink on paper. There are two possible ways of reading his argument. According to the first interpretation, Ingarden operates with two isolated acts which together constitute a complex act of reading: There is an act by means of which we conceive visual figures *as* expressions and a subsequent act by means of which we grasp the meaning. Thus, to conceive something as a sign or expression is distinct from a "simple" perception, since we ascribe to the perceptible "material" a specific identity: it is not only a spot of ink on paper but rather a figure that can express or signify something. Let's emphasize that, according to the first interpretation, this "ascription" concerns only the level of expression and it can be executed without conceiving any meaning.

This reading of Ingarden's argument is plausible insofar as he explicitly asserts that the perception of "the verbal body" is always accompanied by an apprehension which interprets the written text (the sensual data) *as* expression. Ingarden claims that there is an act which grasps "the verbal body" as "an expression of something other than itself" (Ingarden 1973: 21). We ascribe to these entities the character of "expressiveness" and we perceive them as expressions insofar as we attribute to them the quality of conveying a specific semantic content. This central thesis is elaborated further by means of a distinction between the notions of "expression" and "word". For Ingarden, "expression" refers to "the phonic or written form of the word" whereas "word" refers to the entity "which encompasses both the phonic form and the meaning" (Ingarden 1973: 22). This distinction indicates that there are two different objects corresponding to two different acts: a less complex object ("the written form") apprehended as expression and a more complex object perceived as a composition of form and its meaning.

All these distinctions indicate that, according to Ingarden, an expression as expression can be constituted *fully* as soon as we ascribe to the "verbal body" the quality of "being an expression". In other words, we are capable to comprehend the expression as an expression only by means of the act which grasps the graphical entities, that is, we are capable to identify an expression *independently* of an actual experience of a transfer of meaning. This interpretation is supported by Ingarden's assertion that only the preliminary apprehension of an entity as expression makes possible the subsequent consciousness of the transfer of meaning. The identification of something as expression lays the basis for the subsequent "consciousness" of reference to meaning.

Ingarden's descriptions culminate in the passage which brings into focus the phenomenon of incomprehension or "not-understanding". As Ingarden puts it, one can point to the exceptional cases

> when the word is, or seems to be, foreign to us, the apprehension of the verbal sound is not automatically connected with understanding. If we cannot grasp the meaning immediately, we notice a characteristic slowing-down or even a halt in the process of reading. We feel a certain helplessness and try to guess the meaning. Usually it is only in such a case that we have a clear thematic apprehension of the verbal sound and visual form; at the same time we are puzzled about not finding the meaning which should be immediately evident and nonetheless does not come to mind. (Ingarden 1973: 22)

Clearly, this passage builds upon the previous analysis. The phenomenon of incomprehension takes place whenever the primary act—which supplies the interpretation of an entity as expression—fails to be followed by another act by which we grasp the meaning. This is to say that in such a case, the understanding of an entity as an expression is no doubt constituted, yet we cannot extend this understanding any further and relate ourselves to the expressed meaning. It is evident that the element of a particular "in between" is crucial to this experience: we are able to conceive of a figure as an expression, yet meaning is entirely absent. From this perspective, the phenomenon of incomprehension is not limited to a degree of un-clarity pertaining to a partially clear meaning;

rather, meaning as such becomes entirely blocked. The reader goes through the experience of an empty expression, or the paradoxical experience of a sign which does not signify. It would seem that no other experience can reveal more persuasively the original division between the two acts — the act which grasps the expression and the act which grasps the meaning.

Beside the interpretation just presented I will attempt to develop an alternative reading of Ingarden's text. This reading will, I hope, induce us to a rather different description of experience of sign. The starting point of this second interpretation is provided by Ingarden's claim that "simultaneous with and inseparable from the described apprehension of the verbal sounds is the understanding of the meaning of word" (Ingarden 1973: 22). According to the first interpretation, this claim would still refer to the fundamental difference between the two acts we are dealing with: an expression may be comprehended *as such* even though the meaning is entirely absent. However, there is another way of interpreting the relationship between the sign and the signified content. The alternative approach becomes available if we avoid stressing the division of the two acts and if we rather focus on the claim that "an apprehension" (of sound) and "understanding" (of meaning) are in fact *inseparable*. To understand this claim properly we must take into account Ingarden's notion of *function*, more precisely, his notion of a "particular function of meaning" (Ingarden 1973: 21). This term indicates that the consciousness of an expression as such can in no way be isolated from an awareness of the "fact" that a graphical body *is actually* (at the present moment) expressing a particular meaning. In other words, the act by means of which we grasp an expression as expression is identical with an observation that the expression is actually expressing a concrete content. A "name" is conceived of as name only if it is actually "naming" something, a representation is perceived as representation only if it is actually representing an object. Thus, an entity never becomes representation by the mere fact that we name it "representation" (disregarding if it is pointing to any object or not) or that we presume that it might possibly become a representation of something. Sign or representation in general always and necessarily confronts us with a represented object and any talk of experiencing an "empty" representation or an "empty" sign without object ("a simulacrum") is, in fact, a contradiction in terms.

In the following part I will develop the alternative interpretation in more detail. However, from now on the analysis will proceed without any explicit reference to Ingarden's text.

Implicit and explicit character of representation

Let's start with some basic distinctions which characterize the relationship between the level of representation and the level of the represented object. Two poles that define this relationship can be singled out. The first pole corresponds to the fact that as regards the represented content, it is only ideally that it reveals itself with a clarity and distinctness such that it could be grasped as something absolutely present to the sight of reader or perceiver. The represented content always—at least to an extent—stays outside "the center" of representation, i.e. the area where it could be *fully* grasped or contemplated with all of its semantical aspects. There is always a deflection between what we know and what we could and might know about the represented object. Similarly, the other pole corresponds to the fact that the represented content always—at least to an extent—

reaches the center of the representation and that it never turns into entirely unreachable entity which escapes even minimal comprehension.[2]

These distinctions imply that the clarity and unclarity of representation must not be understood purely psychologically, as referring to the state of mind of a particular individual or to one's capacity to understand. The clarity and unclarity are primarily essential features of the representational object itself: the representation itself "exists" clearly or "unclearly". Given that, both characteristics must be included in the description of any representation. For example, an analysis of the representation of Oblomov must contain information on the clarity of its constitutive parts. We must bring into focus which ones of Oblomov's features are elucidated and which of them remain unclear in this particular image. An attempt to supplement the unclear parts while relying on personal or individual assumptions about the fictional character would put us at risk of overlooking these objective qualities of the representation.

The distinctions I have just singled out also point at some more general presuppositions concerning representation. On the one hand, these distinctions imply that representation cannot be defined as a discontinuous object. Representation as perceived is not composed of two self-sufficient levels which are bound together by means of the act of mimesis or by means of the act of representation. Rather, representation appears as a "movement" wherein a content "becomes" continuously

---

[2] This idea of two poles which determine the degree of "presence" of a phenomenon is inspired by Martin Pokorný's essay on language (see Pokorný 2008). In the beginning of his phenomenological analysis he interprets Husserl's "principle of all principles" (the self-givenness of objects) as a "regulative idea".

explicit or implicit—as a movement of "becoming clear" or "becoming obscure". On the other hand, these distinctions also imply that the interpretation of a representation ought not to be described as discontinuous, that is, as "a leap" from one autonomous level (representation) to another (the represented object). The perception of a representation occurs as a fluent motion toward a represented object.[3] This is also to say that whenever we decipher a sign or a representation, we do not ever remove the signifier completely and we do not ever come to contemplate solely the represented object. We always perceive both levels which are necessarily co-present in the field of perception. As we shall see, this fact will play a specific role in the phenomenon of chiasm.

Levels of representation

As I have indicated, the relationship between representation and the represented object, as described at the level of graphical signs, can also be observed between more complex levels of representation, that is, between contents that are constituted at higher levels of representation.[4] For every object which is

---

[3] The motive of continuity in sign as well as the notions of explication and implication are indicated in Gilles Deleuze's book on Proust (Deleuze 1964). In this context, Deleuze focuses on Proust's image of Japanese paper toys which can serve as a model for the movement of explication: "To the metaphors of implication correspond the images of explication. For the sign unfolds, unrolls as soon as we interpret them. The jealous lover unfolds the possible worlds which are locked in the soul. The sensitive man frees the souls implicated in things—it is similar to those pieces of Japanese paper which unfold in the water, they unroll or explicate themselves and form flowers, houses or persons" (Deleuze 1964: 110).

[4] The notion of "level" refers to the French notion of *niveau* as used by Émile Benveniste in his 1962 study "The Levels of Linguistic Analysis" (in Benveniste 1966). Even though Benveniste himself does not focus on the

represented can become a representation of another object; and by this process, a string of representation is constituted.

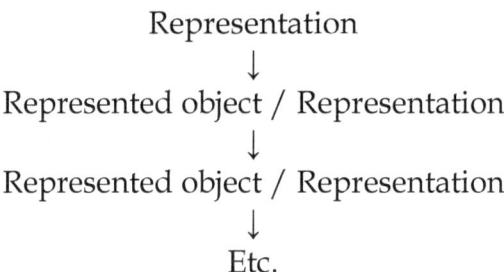

These higher levels of representation must be again described with the same categories I have distinguished at the level of graphical signs: representation as a function, clarity and unclarity of implications. For the sake of clarity, we can use the example of Oblomov's actions as representing or implying a psychological reality of this fictional character. Similarly to the case of a graphical sign and its content, a specific thematic complex — the actions — becomes a representation as soon as we conceive of its relation to the represented psychological reality. In this particular case, we can observe as Oblomov's inner personality (= level of the represented object) articulates itself through the actions of this fictional character (= level of representation).

This transition to higher levels of representation allows us to see more clearly the phenomenon of a specific "directedness" or "intentionality" as characterizing the relationship between

---

notion of representation, the phenomenon of "levels" can be very well described by means of his model of utterance. Especially, I refer to his idea that there are different levels "laid" upon each other in each utterance and that the lower level always represents the constitutive ground for the upper one.

representation and the represented object. This directedness can be described in aspects. The first aspect corresponds to the fact that the level of representation *constitutes* or *lays the basis for* the level of the represented object: Regarding the perspective of constitution, we can take the distinction between the representation and the represented object as a distinction between the constituting and the constituted level. For example, we can see that a specific layer of Oblomov's psychological makeup is *constituted* upon the layer of actions. One could not perceive these features if the level of actions was not present. Yet, at the same time, we can point to another aspect of this directedness of the representation to the represented content. The latter is not dependent on the former only with regard to its constitution but also with regard to its very identity. This is to say that such and such comprehension of the represented psychological features is possible only if one looks at these features "through" a particular representation—in this case "through" particular actions of the fictional character. For example, the particular nature of Oblomov (laziness), with all its individual aspects, comes up only if the readerly sight focuses at it through particular actions and utterances of Oblomov. Were this laziness represented only by the word "laziness", which would explicitly occur in the text, rather than by a description of Oblomov's actions, one would be confronted with a rather different content from the laziness indicated by actions. Such a principle implies that perception of a representation should not be understood as a mere penetration through the signifying level to the signified level which can then be contemplated in itself. It must be rather understood as "a looking through" the sign to its signified content—as "a looking through" which informs the sight of the reader.

Representation

Incomprehension and ambiguity
Regarding the descriptions of representation I have made so far, the phenomenon of incomprehension can be grasped anew. If we adopt the initial reading of Ingarden's analysis, the incomprehension of a sign takes place as soon as we do not automatically move from the apprehension of something as a sign to an understanding of its meaning. The moment of a particular hesitation or particular incertitude was explained as an incertitude directed solely at the level of expression. However, if we admit that the apprehension of a sign as such is identical with the awareness of "the particular function of meaning", then we must interpret the moment of wavering over the sign as wavering over the content which does not reach the particular degree of articulation or "semantical specificity". Thus, the phenomenon of incomprehension does not refer to the absence of meaning; rather, a degree of revealed meaning constitutes a necessary condition of "not-understanding".

In this particular context, we must point out that the phenomenon of incomprehension must not be confused with the experience of ambiguity. This is to say that a representation representing clearly its objects can be nonetheless ambiguous and that the maximally unclear representation can be free of ambiguity. The ambiguity constitutes its own axis of more or less numerous contents that do not share the same string of representations.[5] For example, the actions of Oblomov can simultaneously represent the laziness of this particular

---

[5] A similar image of two axis of representation—i.e., the axis of parallel series and the axis of implication—can be found in Deleuze's already mentioned monograph on Proust. In this context Deleuze uses the metaphor of a "box" for the series of explicated contents and the metaphor of a "vessel" for the group of parallel contents (see Deleuze 1964: 140ff).

character, the decline of old Russian aristocracy, and various other contents.

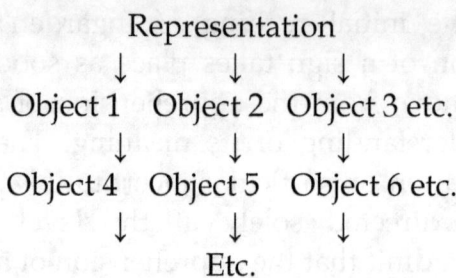

Similarly to the description of the axis of clarity, we can point to the fact that a representation presents one sole chain of represented objects only ideally, and that a representation falls apart into an immeasurable amount of chains of represented objects only ideally. The former case would correspond to the pole of pure unambiguity of representation, the latter would correspond to the pole of pure ambiguity of representation. At this point, we can put forward two claims about ambiguity similar to those about clarity and unclarity of representation. Firstly, I must point out that the notion of ambiguity accounts primarily for the basic poles between which the representation as such is constituted. Thus, the notion of ambiguity refers to the fact that every representation necessarily reveals itself as moving to one of the poles of ambiguity. To decide which of the poles is more characteristic for this or that particular representation is a separate problem. Secondly, insofar as the representation is constituted necessarily between these two poles we can assert that ambiguity and unambiguity becomes a quality of the representation itself. The phenomenon of ambiguity refers primarily not to the confused mind of the reader but rather to an objective quality of representation. The representations "exist" in themselves ambiguously or unambiguously and, consequently, the quality of ambiguity must be included in the description of every representational object.

Chiasm
In this concluding section I will attempt to sketch out a specific type of relationship which is characteristic for representation and cannot be reduced to the relationships discussed thus far. For this purpose I will introduce the notion of chiasm.

Let's start with an assertion: chiastic relationships are conditioned by the fact that representation and its represented object always reveal themselves together or simultaneously. The chiasm is constituted when the readerly sight grasps *at once both* the level of representation *and* the level of the represented object. The notion of chiasm should indicate that the relationships between these two levels of representation cannot be explained only in terms of "one-way" directedness, as described above. To be more specific, that the representation determines the identity of the represented object is not the whole story, since we can always observe that the represented object retrospectively determines the level by means of which it is represented. In other words, the represented object is no less "productive" for the level of representation than the level of representation for the content which is represented.[6] Thus, to recall the example of Oblomov, we can stand by the assertion that the level of action (= the level of representation) is constitutive for such and such a shape of Oblomov's psychology (= represented object). These features become apparent to the reader only through these and not through

---

[6]   A similar model of mutual determination can be found in Catherine Malabou's monograph on Hegel. Malabou operates with the notion of "plasticity" (Malabou 1996).

other actions. Yet, the represented object is also constitutive for the identity of the level by means of which it is represented: although one can grasp the represented contents only by virtue of the particular actions of the fictional character, the identity of these actions itself becomes specified by the represented psychological features. The actions appear to be of such and such nature if we take them as a representation of a particular type of laziness and if we direct them at this very series or string of represented objects. Oblomov's permanent tendency to fall asleep and his unwillingness to move appear as such a tendency and as such an unwillingness insofar as they represent the laziness of this particular individual. Yet the same actions could also turn up as a residuum of aristocratic customs. This would be the case if they became a representation of different contents—such as the decline of old Russian aristocracy.

We can assume that this is not the only type of mutual influence between the representation and the represented object once we bring into focus the other general distinctions made above. Firstly, the distinction between clarity and unclarity as the fundamental, non-psychological feature of represented contents imply that the "becoming clear" or "becoming obscure" of the represented object reciprocally determines the clarity or obscurity of the representation. For example, the more sharply Oblomov's actions reveal particular psychological features, the more sharply will appear the particular semantic aspects of his deeds or behavior. On the other hand, the more implicit or un-articulated are the represented contents of his behavior, the more un-articulated remains the nature of his particular deeds.

Similarly it can be noted that the reciprocal influence takes place not only in the case of identity and clarity of the representation but also in the case of ambiguity—a term which refers to the phenomenon of parallel strings of represented objects. As I have mentioned above, one can always point at a particular number of parallel objects that are present in the same representation: Oblomov can be interpreted as an individual, as an exemplary case of the aristocratic class, as an incarnation of Goncharov's philosophical views etc. However, if we stick to the principle of chiasm it becomes evident that the ambiguity concerns not only the level of represented objects; it also reciprocally contaminates the level of representation. To put it more clearly, as far as the parallel strings of represented objects reveal themselves in the process of reading, the level of representation simultaneously divides itself into mutually irreducible "semantical sectors". On the other hand, if the readerly sight spots only one or just a little number of parallel contents, then the level of representation becomes narrower or more concentrated. Re-employing Oblomov we can say that the higher the number of the series of contents that stem from Oblomov's actions, the higher the number of the images of his behavior that become articulated in front of our readerly sight.

Finally it must be emphasized that the notion of chiasm should not be understood as an attempt to surpass the observations made in the section dedicated to the "one-way directedness": rather, the two dimensions of representation that I have arrempted to sketch should be conceived as parallel. They are necessarily bound together or interwoven in every experience of representation since the reader always explicates the representation and simultaneously perceives the reciprocal transformation of the level at which the explication began. This is why it would be equally incorrect to take one of the dimensions as primary and the other as secondary. In fact, both dimensions are fundamental for representation and one always implicates the other. This then helps constitute an idea of "full reading", one which cannot be reduced to one of the dimensions I have designated. Rather, full reading would require sensitivity to both types of relationships and to the complexity that accompanies any experience of representation.

Charles University / Czech Academy of Sciences
koblt@post.cz

REFERENCES

Benveniste, Émile. 1966. *Problèmes de linguistique générale I*. Paris: Gallimard.
Deleuze, Gilles. 1964. *Proust et les signes*. Paris: PUF.
Ingarden, Roman. 1973. *Cognition of Literary Work of Art*. Trans. Ruth O. Crowley and Kenneth R. Olson. Evanston: Northwestern University Press.
Malabou, Catherine. 1966. *L'Avenir de Hegel. Plasticité, temporalité, dialectique*. Paris: Vrin.
Pokorný, Martin. 2008. "Řečové dění, výkon reflexe a psyché." *Svět literatury* 18 (37): 5–24.
Ricœur, Paul. 1984. *Time and Narrative*, vol. 1. Trans. Kathleen McLaughlin and David Pellauer. Chicago: The University of Chicago Press.

FIDELITY WITHOUT MIMESIS:
MENTAL IMAGERY FROM VISUAL DESCRIPTION

Anežka Kuzmičová

ABSTRACT: In this paper, I oppose the common assumption that visual descriptions in prose fiction are imageable by virtue of perceptual mimesis. Based on introspection as well as convergent support from cognitive science and other disciplines, I argue that visual description (and the mental imagery it elicits), unlike narrative (and the mental imagery it elicits), often stands in no positive relation to perceptual mimesis because it lacks a structural counterpart in perceptual experience. I present an alternative way of defining the kind of mental imagery elicited by visual descriptions, and propose a number of text variables underlying the imageability or non-imageability of any such description.

What does one really gain from the critically acclaimed visual descriptions in the novels of Dickens, Franzen, McEwan and hundreds of others? What do they add to mimesis?

When we read prose fiction, many kinds of mimesis are at stake. There is mimesis of conceptual thought generation, mimesis of emotions portrayed and aroused, mimesis of historical or scientific fact, mimesis of speech and so forth. One kind of mimesis particularly relevant to the non-scholarly reader, and particularly neglected by literary scholars in spite of the current cognitive boom, consists in emulated experience (e.g., Halliwell 2002: 22) of the world as apprehended pre-verbally, by the sensorimotor apparatus alone. For instance, if a narrative rendition of bright midday sunshine in high summer elicits the near-experience of needing to squint, then the passage in question is likely mimetic in the sense relevant for this paper. For lack of a better word, I will further refer to this kind of mimesis as *perceptual mimesis* (see also Scarry 1999: 6ff). It should be pointed out, however, that I assume perceptual mimesis to involve the entire sensorimotor array, including the proprioceptive and kinaesthetic modalities (e.g. the senses of limb and organ position, velocity, effort, acceleration and so forth) that are less frequently associated with perception proper.

It is generally assumed that the reader's mental imagery is a prime vehicle of perceptual mimesis. Insofar as a piece of fiction succeeds in eliciting sensorimotor (especially visual) images of its content, it is regarded as perceptually mimetic. In the common parlance of book reviewers, essayists and literary scholars, a particularly strong mimetic effect of the perceptual kind is usually attributed to visual description (Wolf 2004: 339; Nünning 2007: 113). To my knowledge, nobody has put this near-automatic association between perceptual mimesis, mental imagery, and visual description to closer scrutiny. Several authors (Esrock 1994: 38; Scarry 1999: 55; Grünbaum 2007: 311) have briefly countered the widespread assumption that there is a straightforwardly direct relationship between the amount of visual detail provided through description on the one hand and the imageability of a text on the other. A few attempts have been made to account for the mechanics of visual (Scarry 1999; Burke 2011: 56–85) or multimodal (Kuzmičová, forthcoming) imagery elicited by fiction at large and by narrative in particular, but there is no systematic account of the imagery elicited by visual description (when elicited at all). This paper aims at filling the gap.

In section 1, I will briefly specify what I mean by visual description and present a further rationale for describing the visual imagery it elicits. In section 2, I will proceed to the main body of my argument and make the following point: Unlike instances of narrative proper, visual descriptions and the mental imagery they elicit are not perceptually mimetic, because they lack an experiential correlate in the world as apprehended pre-verbally. In this stage of the argument, special emphasis will be put on the pre-requisite of experientiality and, to a somewhat lesser degree, on the closely related pre-requisite of suspending the verbal. In section 3, I will argue that even though these specific points of contrast preclude perceptual mimesis, they allow for a fruitful analogy between images from visual description and another kind of visual mental imagery, namely images from voluntary visualization (e.g., one's purposeful image of what a particular bike model looks like). This analogy will be based on the following: images from visual descriptions, just like images from voluntary visualization (and in contrast to those images that are perceptually mimetic), are always expected, feeble, and essentially finite. Finally, in section 4, I will further elaborate on the analogy in order to infer a tentative set of rules of imageability generally applicable to visual description. The proposed rules will be supported by introspective analysis, aided by extant analyses of voluntary visual imagery and by research on reading and language processing at large. References to other cognitive-scientific research, as well as to literary scholarship on the general topic of description, will be made throughout the paper when appropriate.

Reduced to the most basic questions and answers, the main argument of the paper can be summarized as follows: Is imagery from visual description perceptually mimetic? (No.) If it has no correlate in perceptual experience, what other sort of experience does it resemble, if any? (The experience of voluntary visual imagery.) What makes visual descriptions difficult to image in the first place, and what makes the imageable ones imageable? (Visual descriptions in general tend to run athwart the experiential makeup of visual mental imagery, exceeding the limits of what can be accommodated in a visual mental image. Visual descriptions only become imageable when they operate within these limits.)

1/ Why visual description?
One could go on forever trying to formulate a comprehensive definition of visual description. For the sake of brevity, I will instead refer to a prototypical example:

> An oval splayed out with whale-bone, [the cap] started off with three pompons; these were followed by lozenges of velvet and rabbit's fur alternately, separated by a red band, and after that came a kind of bag ending in a polygon of cardboard with intricate braiding on it; and from this there hung down like a tassel, at the end of a long, too slender cord, a little sheaf of gold threads. It was a new cap, with a shiny peak. (Flaubert 1995: 16)

This description of Charles Bovary's cap is by far the most frequently quoted one among literary theorists of description (see Bal 1982). Here are a few suggestions as to why this may be so: Firstly, the passage ascribes "properties to entities within a mental model of the world" (Herman 2009: 90). Secondly, the entities and their properties are represented "in stasis, in simultaneous relation, and (they) are organized by spatial markers like adverbs of place.[1] Verbs in the present, past, or past-progressive tenses depict states" (Mosher 1991: 442). Thirdly, references to the properties are post-posited with regard to the central entity, which thus constitutes the "global *introductory*

---

[1] Or, in this particular example, by temporal adverbs acting as spatial markers.

theme" of the description (Hamon 1982: 159; emphasis mine). Having recognized these generic features of literary description, let us now turn to the features that in my view are prototypical for visual descriptions in particular.

Firstly, the passage isolates an inanimate object rather than a person, animal, landscape or other kind of complex spatial configuration. Inanimate objects tend to be comparably insignificant in fiction insofar as they are the least likely to have direct impact on the story (see also Barthes 1989). An inanimate object cannot be readily imaged (like landscapes or other spatial configurations) or identified with (like people or animals) inwardly, by projecting one's body inside it, and with it one's mind. An inanimate object is as close as one gets to objectivity, and therefore also to a description that is purely sensory, visual. Secondly, the inanimate object described in the passage is a manufactured rather than a natural one, and like most manufactured objects described in modern prose, it is an object of daily use. Unlike natural objects, manufactured objects are fully dependent for their identity on how they happen to be instantaneously used (Atran 1990: 63). Thus lacking an objective essence, manufactured objects are little more than what they appear to be in a given situation. This makes them the perfect content for visual descriptions, the descriptions of appearance. All examples in this paper will consist in visual descriptions bearing significant family resemblance to the above prototype. Yet I believe that part of what I have to say about mental imagery from visual description may apply to descriptions quite remote in kind, visual or non-visual.

However, description is not only a type of text, but also, by virtue of its intuitive noticeability, an autonomous mode of text processing. That is to say, there is more to descriptions than their typical features encoded in text. There is also something it is typically *like* to be reading a description. This experience in turn, albeit subject to many variables in its final quality, may be correlated with specific cognitive processes prior to consciousness. Description can only exist against the background of other types of text and processing. In most cases, its other is narrative, the dominant text-type of prose fiction. As far as prose fiction is concerned, it is by contrast to narrative that description is usually defined, and rightly so; it is the contrast to narrative that makes it pre-reflectively noticeable in the first place. Description processing entails, first and foremost, a marked pause in a chain of events. More specifically, once narrative processing has given way to visual description processing, the reader temporarily loses track of, and any connection whatsoever with, the preceding story. An eclipse of awareness takes place as it were; the reader focuses on one type of content only, the basic content of visual description: "that something is there and like that" (Wolf 2007: 34). In real time, this could last a fraction of a second or several minutes.

What visual description processing entails apart from a clean-cut contrast to narrative temporality, and what is meant by narrative, will be explored throughout the rest of this paper. Importantly, it should be noted at this point that I do not assume my notion of visual description processing to cover all possible visual description experiences. Depending on context and the instantaneous focus of the reader, visual descriptions as a text-type can be experienced in a number of different ways. What I rather assume is a continuum of possible description experiences where my notion of visual description processing constitutes one of two extremes. The opposite extreme consists in description experiences indistinguishable, in terms of mental imagery and perceptual mimesis, from experiences of narrative. As for my examples of visual description as text-type, certain types of visual descriptions, such as descriptions of human characters, landscapes or other spatial settings, are disregarded exactly inasmuch they seem more likely to prompt experiences of a less distinctly descriptive, i.e. more narrative, kind.

For any account of perceptual mimesis of the visual kind, descriptions in general and visual descriptions in particular would seem the natural place to begin. While narrative proper may be equally, or in fact more, efficient in prompting visual mental images, visual descriptions alone (when imageable at all) secure the highest possible fidelity of mental image with respect to the text. For instance, upon reading about a "broom" with no further description, my mind may image whatever it pleases. Most often, it will image by default the kind of broom I am most familiar with from my firsthand experience of the world. Most often, this will be unproblematic. But what if the broom, or the story as a whole, turns out to be set in a foreign or otherwise distant context? In such a case my mental image may be proved incorrect anytime by a subsequent passage suggesting that the broom is to be ridden on by a medieval-style witch, or that it sweeps aboard a spaceship in zero gravity. Although my initial image is then by no means disqualified as mental experience, it fails to pertain to the story-world in question. On the other hand, should my "broom" be described when first mentioned, its visual description may perhaps delimit my freedom of imaging but it prevents me from conjuring incorrect images.

Although some of the mechanics of readers' visual mental imagery have previously been accounted for by literary scholars (Scarry 1999; Burke 2011: 56–85), none of the accounts has exposed or even acknowledged visual description's unique potential to stipulate bottom-up rather than top-down processing. Drawing implicitly on a romantic notion of imagination as essentially a free activity, these scholars have treated imagery without properly considering its prosaic debt to the specific wording of a text. Michael Burke, for instance, suggests that readers tend to furnish fictional interiors with visual images based on their childhood homes and that they often do so regardless of textual counter-evidence. Such "whimsical" top-down imaging may possibly be considered truly experiential in ways largely outreaching the domain of vision (e.g., in terms of its affective impact on the reader), but from the viewpoint of content fidelity, it could just as well be regarded as mere mind-wandering. To restate one of my opening formulations with a little more precision, a piece of fiction is perceptually mimetic insofar as it triggers mental images of the world as we pre-verbally apprehend it. But the images must also be images of certain fidelity with respect to the text. Otherwise there would be no way of determining that they really arose as an effect of a specific passage in a specific piece of fiction, rather than as an effect of fiction reading in general, or language use in general, or for no particular reason at all. This is why visual description would appear to be highly relevant to the study of perceptual mimesis.

An intuitive grasp of this unique ability to specify the visual is probably what makes the common association of perceptual mimesis with visual description so appealing. When checked against random intuitions about actual practices of reading, however, much of its appeal vanishes. Indeed, visual description might make us image far less frequently and far less vividly than suggested by the rhetoric of book reviews and book promotion materials. For instance, there must be a reason why non-scholarly readers, so notoriously keen on vicarious experiencing, show a tendency to skim, or even skip (Allington 2011), particularly lengthy descriptions. Furthermore, when I ask fellow literary scholars for book recommendations featuring vivid visual descriptions of, say, manufactured objects, they invariably cite passages in which manufactured objects are simply mentioned without being described. This may well arise from the fact that visual descriptions of manufactured objects occur less frequently than simple mentions do, but only to a certain point. I have established elsewhere (Kuzmičová 2012) that simple mentions often conjure imagery more reliably and more vividly than visual descriptions. My objective then was to account for the fundamental processes underlying the most multimodally saturated kind of perceptual mimesis, the one resulting in the reader's instantaneous sense of *presence* in the three-dimensional world of a story. Now is the time to explain wherein the main difference between descriptions and simple mentions lies, and to finally analyze the mental images prompted by visual description in their own right.

I now turn to the main difference between imagery from visual descriptions and imagery from simple mentions, which, I would like to argue, is not one of degree, but one of kind. That is to say, whenever my mind conjures up a visual image of an object based on my processing of its visual description, the resulting experience does not amount to some weak variety of my presence in the story-world, or a weak variety of perceptual mimesis for that matter. In fact, the resulting experience is not at all perceptually mimetic. Images prompted by visual descriptions are essentially different from other readerly visual imagery because they are generated differently. *While simple mentions and other narrative instances of fiction generate images by virtue of their experientiality, visual descriptions can only generate images by virtue of their imageability.*[2] The former part of this

---

[2]   When aesthetician Elaine Scarry (1999) subsumes all fiction-induced imagery under the (further undefined) notion of perceptual mimesis, she

assertion will be elaborated in the next section. The latter part will be elaborated subsequently.

2/ Why not perceptual mimesis?

Why is experientiality proper not at work in the processing of visual descriptions? A definition of perceptual experience is needed here. Underlying my assertion is an understanding of perception as preconditioned by bodily interaction. Continuous interaction with our immediate environment, be it overt (action, i.e. bodily movement) or covert (psychophysiological processes related to pre-conscious or conscious action simulation), has lately been identified at various levels of inquiry to be the basis of our sensorimotor apprehension of the world. A textbook example of the inextricable link between interaction and perceptual experience are the clinical cases of so called experiential blindness. Congenitally blind patients whose vision has been restored by surgery tend to take physical objects for blurs in their visual field as long as they remain unable to couple their visual sensations with relevant sensorimotor patterns of interaction. (Noë 2006: 5ff) At a pre-experiential level, there are indications that visual attention for objects involves neurophysiological processes inherent to action preparation (Rizzolatti and Gallese 1988). There are countless convergent sources like these, spanning vast areas and methodologies of inquiry from isolated brain imaging studies of visual and linguistic processing (see e.g. Martin 2007; Fischer and Zwaan 2008) to comprehensive enactivist phenomenologies of the self (Gallagher and Zahavi 2007). The growing body of interdisciplinary research pointing toward a centrality of

---

fails to isolate description as a distinctive text-type and mode of processing. Also, her examples of imageable prose are predominantly narrative rather than (visual) descriptive.

interaction in experience is commonly subsumed under the aggregate label of embodied (or grounded or situated) cognition. Given the strong definition of experience proposed by the framework of embodied cognition, visual description construed as stasis and as subsequent temporary detachment from the object described (see also Grünbaum 2007) has no purely experiential correlate in the actual world. For in visual description, interaction has come to a temporary halt.

That is not the case with simple mentions. Simple mentions of object names, unless we are dealing with a catalogue rather than with narrative, tend to be part of interaction insofar as they stand for grammatical subjects or objects attached to non-copular verbs, e.g.:

> In the kitchen closet I <u>found</u> a practically new broom[.] (Baker 1998: 20)

This is a matter of syntactic fact rather than necessity. In not-very-elegant prose, the broom in this sentence could be minutely visually qualified, e.g.:

> In the kitchen closet I found a practically new bright red ridged plastic broom.

The point is that simple mentions happen to adhere more closely to their referents as pre-verbally experienced. Upon the reading of the above sentences, the reader's embodied mind has no problem identifying an interaction to emulate (the firsthand act of opening a door and finding a broom in the penumbra of a closet), forming thus a multimodal sensorimotor image, an instance of presence, a mediated experience proper of a world out there.

Anežka Kuzmičová

One could argue that all descriptions, along with the objects described, are likewise embedded in interactive situations because they belong to larger narrative wholes that always feature such situations. However, as suggested by the introductory definition of visual description as a mode of processing (section 1), the surrounding story is relegated to outside the reader's consciousness as soon as a visual description is encountered and pre-reflectively identified as such. Visual description means per definition an instantaneously experienced lack of continuity with any narrative (and interactive) embedding, and consequently with any emulated firsthand experience.

One could further object that by token of the theories of embodied cognition, even the seemingly most passive observation of the world entails covert interaction, and that visual descriptions are in this respect no different from the firsthand experience of such observation. One could say, in other words, that visual description emulates in the reader an act of firsthand yet passive visual experience and that it is experiential in the same way as narrative renditions of overt interaction are, only less perspicuously. It may be particularly tempting to say so with regard to descriptive passages that are framed by explicit or very strongly implied references to acts of perceiving. For instance, the context of the visual description of Charles Bovary's cap strongly suggests that the cap is in fact being scrutinized by the boy's contemptuous classmates. Yet again, as long as the reader's mind remains aware of such framing, which seems particularly unlikely in a description of such flamboyance, we are not dealing with visual description processing proper. Should the same objection be raised so as to encompass all visual descriptions regardless of framing, it must be countered by the following clarification:

In the instant of switching, for a second or a fraction of a second, from narrative to the mode of visual description processing, the linguistic nature of reading robustly emerges toward the threshold of the reader's consciousness. The reader thus assumes, if barely reflectively, the cognitive stance of someone who is being informed that a certain object has certain visual properties. In line with this argument, several literary theorists (Hamon 1981: 21; Cobley 1986: 397) have noted that description in general entails an increased presence of the narrator. Importantly, the reader has no way of simultaneously maintaining the cognitive stance of someone who is approaching an object of certain properties pre-verbally, the stance of a perceiving experiencer. Instead, the properties are taken in as foregrounded information in a framework of communication.[3] Whatever the actual syntax of the description in writing, the mental propositional "syntax" (if there was such a thing) of visual description processing would follow roughly this pattern:

> There is a broom. It is practically new and made of bright red ridged plastic.

rather than:

> There is a practically new bright red ridged plastic broom.

Unlike in the processing of (certain instances of) narrative proper, it becomes impossible under such circumstances to

---

[3] This part of my argument seems to dovetail with Michael Riffaterre's. Speaking of description in general, literary theorist Riffaterre maintains that description's "primary purpose is not to offer a representation, but to dictate an interpretation" (Riffaterre 1981: 125).

bracket off this quasi-communicative dimension of visual description and achieve as it were a full, pre-verbal sense of presence. This results in the immediate noticeability of visual description in the course of reading, its autonomy as a receptive mode, as well as in the skimming or skipping of descriptions by impatient readers, which goes hand in hand with another typical attribute of visual description as text-type: its low memorability. Unless the wording or subject of a visual description is perceived as particularly striking, the reader is often left with a sense of amnesia as soon as the description is over, not to speak of one's minuscule chances of retaining the rough contents of a description beyond an immediately subsequent stretch of text.

In cognitive psychology, a pronounced tradeoff has been found to operate in the (English) lexicon and its processing between imageability on the one hand and phonological and orthographic uniqueness on the other (Westbury and Moroschan 2009). Words with the lowest number of direct phonological neighbors, i.e. words that differ the most in their structure from the rest of the lexicon, happen to denote referents with low or no imageability (e.g., "thought"). Conversely, words with highly imageable referents are the least conspicuous as to their structure (e.g., "broom") and thereby also the most easily confused with other words ("room", "boom", "brook" etc.). Suggesting that marked "verbality" somehow interferes with imagery, these findings can be taken in support of the above assumption that a sense of being verbally informed of perceptual facts is necessarily discontinuous with a sense of direct perception. Overall, they further disclose how treacherous visual description is by nature. It is intuitively known by the reader to denote something quite familiar and easy to image, yet in the end it is always found to consist in a unique, unfamiliar[4] concatenation of qualifiers.

Besides, unless the qualifiers in question situate the object in uncommon context, e.g. by suggesting the kind of twig broom used by witches and others in the Middle Ages, they also happen to be more or less tangential to any sort of interaction. In most visual descriptions they will be tangential by necessity, because those properties that really pertain to interaction are already encapsulated in the central object name itself. Empirical studies have shown that in the cognitive processing (and thereby also in the linguistic labeling) of manufactured objects, each object category — broom, cup or flower pot — is delimited exactly by the particular subset of its properties that are immediately relevant to interaction (Rosch et al. 1976). For instance, any container that can be used for planting flowers, qualifies as a flower pot. Thus it would make little sense to describe a flower pot by recounting the properties of being hollow and closed at the bottom. Indeed, few straightforwardly prosaic descriptions take such course.[5] In general, visual descriptions tend rather to exploit the countless accidental properties, those having no direct relation to how objects are essentially interacted with.

The above mentioned impossibility to bracket off the linguistic medium lies also in the very nature of isolated objects and their visual properties. In firsthand visual experience, as long as objects are principally apprehended as objects of interaction, visual properties are those that are self-evidently

---

[4] An interesting exception being visual descriptions by way of *epitheton constans*, which are always standardized within a corpus and thus largely familiar.

[5] The opposite cases generally signal an anti-representationalist authorial agenda, resulting in estrangement.

given. This may be why visual description seems to occur rarely in mundane oral narrative and conversation in general,[6] and when they do, they may mostly be meant to foreclose baseline misconception, rather than help the interlocutor walk in another perceiver's shoes. Unless I am describing an object for its purely aesthetic qualities, e.g. a work of art or a piece of clothing, the pragmatics of my infrequent spontaneous descriptions tends to be other than that of prompting imagery: I want the interlocutor to help me find my purse in the mess of my office, or to pick up the right kind of baby food at the grocery store. I want the interlocutor to know what these things look like, not necessarily to see them with the mind's eye.

Lastly, apart from being self-evident, the visual properties of an object given in firsthand experience are in most cases all simultaneous and one with the object itself. In comparison to narrative renditions of interactive situations, this puts visual description at a disadvantage vis-à-vis the inherent temporality of language and turns it once more into a gross abstraction from perceptual experience. Looking at the ancient broom in my childhood home kitchen, I can certainly conceive of its visual properties in a linear sequence, one by one. But I cannot do so without recourse to inner speech, without hearing my mind briskly articulate at least some of the sounds in "brown", "wooden", "shabby", "orthogonal".

To sum up, the aim of this section was to isolate two fundamental characteristics of visual description. The two characteristics taken together disqualify visual description from

---

[6] As discourse theorist William Labov (1972: 370) would put it, visual properties of static objects are seldom reportable, i.e., they tend to lack the quality of being inherently worth telling. Labov (1972: 389) also expressly notes the rarity of qualifying syntactic structures in his own material, the African American Vernacular.

perceptual mimesis. Ultimately, the two characteristics taken together bear a significant deal of responsibility for visual description's lower overall imageability when compared to narrative. Firstly, I have shown that visual description, unlike narrative, defies firsthand perceptual experience. Secondly, I have shown that mental imagery from visual description, when prompted at all, is significantly less pre-verbal in nature than mental imagery from narrative. While the latter characteristic is a matter of degree (at a certain level of awareness, the reader always knows that he or she is dealing with a piece of verbal fiction), the former is a question of imagery from visual description either bluntly being or bluntly not being experiential and perceptually mimetic. But to say that imagery prompted by visual description in a very particular sense is not experiential is not to say that it does not amount to experience. What sort of experience it amounts to will be suggested in the following section.

3/ What other sort of experience?
What do I mean by stating, at the end of section 1, that visual descriptions can only generate imagery by virtue of their imageability? In part I am referring to their dissociation from firsthand perceptual experience. There is no experience *in* them; there is only the experience *of* them. But I am also hinting at the one sort of experience to which imagery from visual description bears resemblance: the experience of (unseen) objects as visualized in a voluntary mental act of imaging. Voluntary mental imaging is the kind of imaging engaged in when one tries to image what an object (e.g., a particular bike model)

looks like based on one's memory or declarative knowledge, or when one fantasizes about a perfect something.[7]

It is not my intention to suggest that imagery from visual description is mimetic with regard to the above mental acts. Once again, unless the above mental acts are explicitly rendered in the text and retained as such in the reader's focus, i.e., unless the mode of processing inclines toward narrativity and fails to be one of visual description proper, the reader's experience is clearly dissimilar from voluntary visualizing or indulging in fantasies. For instance, the acts of voluntary imaging are temporally open-ended, the imager possessing the ultimate power to extend their duration endlessly. Imaging in visual description processing, on the other hand, is always framed by the reader's assumption that strict temporal constraints have been set beforehand. A visual descriptive stretch of text can easily turn out to feel somewhat lengthy to a reader, but a voluntary imager never continues imaging beyond what feels right for the moment. Furthermore, while in the act of voluntary imagery it is the imager alone who is the originator of the experience and who thus largely exerts control over its content, imagery from visual description arises upon external instruction, with all the rigor and lack of control this entails. Given these and other discrepancies, an important clarification must be made at this point: I am going to consider similarities between voluntary mental imagery and imagery from visual

---

[7] Unlike philosopher Evan Thompson (2007), I assume that it is *possible*, although not necessary, to image an object by an act of will without simultaneously enacting, on the level of consciousness, a firsthand perceptual experience of that object. Voluntary visual images involving emulated perceptual experience (e.g., images of what it is like to be looking at a particular object), perfectly common as they are, will be excluded from the present discussion for lack of analogy to imagery from visual description.

description pertaining only to how the *product* (the image), not the act of production (the imaging), is experienced. Separating the two phases of experience conforms with established phenomenological practice (Casey 2000: 38).

The following questions may arise: Why voluntary visual images in the first place? Why not consider other sorts of visual images, such as the far more frequent products of compulsive imaging, the fleeting yet intense mental images that can take us by surprise whenever we happen to think of, or talk or hear about, something highly imageable? One could even wonder whether these latter images really are not closer to images from visual descriptions after all, given their uncontrolled character. But they are not. They differ from voluntary visual images and from images prompted by visual descriptions in several respects. Firstly, they differ in that they can, and do, take us by surprise. Voluntary visual images, on the other hand, are always *expected*, and the same is true of images from visual description. As soon as a visual description has been encountered in a text and identified as such, the (modern) reader automatically assumes that visual imagery will somehow be addressed. This is not to say that one is never surprised by the specific contents of an image prompted by a visual description, just like one can sometimes be surprised by the specific turns one's voluntary imagery has taken. But one is never surprised that an image has arisen.

Apart from always being expected, voluntary visual images as well as images from visual description tend to be experienced as markedly *feeble* (see also Scarry 1999: 4; Casey 2000: 3). Their feebleness distinguishes them further from involuntary visual images. Surprise alone could be the reason why images of the involuntary, fleeting kind appear as much more saturated. However, the sheer possibility of surprise lies at the heart of a yet deeper difference, one that comes down to the question of perceptual mimesis.[8] For instance, why am I surprised by the compelling image of the handlebar of my bike suddenly emerging in my consciousness as I let my mind wander freely on a tired afternoon? Why do I experience the image as strikingly vivid? I am surprised because initially I was thinking of something else than my bike and the visual details of its handlebar. Otherwise the image would have been expected. And I experience the image as strikingly vivid because this something else that I was initially thinking about was in fact an instance of interactive perceptual experience: dropping off my son at daycare this morning, then biking to the station to catch the bus for the University. Consequently the involuntary image of my bike has experiential qualities comparable to the perceptually mimetic imagery prompted by certain instances of narrative. These qualities are absent in any visual image resulting from a voluntary attempt to visualize a static (see also Jajdelska et al. 2010) isolated object. At the same time, these qualities seem to be constantly in demand, visual imagery being reflexively assessed by the standards of perceptual experience. Hence the sense of enfeeblement inherent to images from visual description.

The third and last feature to be recounted in this section is *finitude*. This feature too is best conceptualized upon comparison with involuntary visual images and images from narrative. It too derives indirectly from the lack of perceptual mimesis, in the following respect: bearing traces of perceptual experience, involuntary visual images and images from

---

[8] By contrast, Elaine Scarry (1999: 104) contends that all fiction-induced imagery supersedes the feebleness of voluntary visual imaging. By way of explanation, she emphasizes that imagery in reading is involuntary inasmuch as it is constrained by external instruction.

narrative are residually dynamic. This is not the case for voluntary visual images or images from visual description, which are static through and through. Mental images of all kinds may be considered temporal insofar as they have a certain if minimal duration, yet only the dynamic ones contain a promise of something more than what is immediately presented. For instance, when I as a reader have experienced a visual image of a broom while emulating the experience of retrieving it from a closet, my broom image tends to recur for a little while before it fades away completely. Sometimes it changes slightly between the various stages of recurrence and then it is no longer, strictly speaking, the same image as before. Nevertheless, an image of a broom does recur without a broom being mentioned anymore. It echoes throughout the dynamic extension of my covert enactment of the bodily movements involved when stretching my arm, grasping the broomstick, retrieving the broom. When such enactment is particularly strong, perhaps outright noticeable in the muscles of my arm and hand (see also Kuzmičová 2012), the image can keep recurring for a considerable period of reading time.

Alas, images from visual description, similarly to voluntary visual images of isolated objects, do not have the same tendency to deliver promises of surplus visual experience, or to promise anything in the first place. They must be cued anew if they are to recur. In their static nature, they are destined to yield to other, dynamic and interactive experiences at the very next intersection with narrative. Here are a few examples of how this can happen:

> [The camera] was mounted on an altazimuth bracket above the back door. Its casing was of brushed aluminum. It had a purplish gleam in its eye. ¶ [1] Gary returned the bottle to the liquor cabinet, moved to the sink, and ran water in a bucket. (Franzen 2001: 230)

293

Anežka Kuzmičová

> By a pile of magazines was a coffee cup — tall, in thin white porcelain, one of a set of six [2] bought by Patrice at Henri Bendel's in New York. [3] Aldous raised it to his lips. (McEwan 2011: 97)

In cases where the immediately subsequent narrative refers to a direct interaction with the central object, the initial image may be transformed into a perceptually mimetic one, continuing its life in a new format. While segment [2] in the latter passage bears but a vague resemblance to this scenario (suggesting a hypothetically direct interaction that involves, but is not limited to, the central object), segment [3] provides a more clear-cut example of how mental images from visual description can live a narrative afterlife. In all other cases where visual description is interrupted by narrative, i.e. in the cases represented by segment [1] above, images from visual description appear once and then vanish without extension and the reader's image experience is readily informed by this. The reader thus experiences that, apart from being expected and feeble, images from visual description are essentially finite, in ways that images from narrative are not.

Needed or not as my above observations may have been in themselves, the ultimate aim of this paper is to valorize them for more practical, predictive purposes. They are meant to help determine what it might be that makes a visual description elicit mental imagery, in spite of the lack of perceptual mimesis. However, defined as expectedness, feebleness and finitude, the principal experiential features of images from visual description are still too broad to instruct a text-oriented analysis. In the next section, while I revisit visual description as text-type, a number of sub-features and further observations will be grouped with the two of the above features that are directly relevant to image content, in the following order: finitude (subsection 4.1), feebleness (subsection 4.2).

4/ More on the image and when it arises
In assessing the readerly experience of narrative, it is possible and natural to explain imageability by reference to structural analogies between text and firsthand perceptual experience (Kuzmičová 2012), with a vast body of empirical perception research at one's disposal. In the absence of perceptual mimesis, functional analogies (or functional discrepancies) can only be charted between text on the one hand and visual mental image on the other. Given the general elusiveness of mental imagery, there is by contrast little empirical evidence to rely on, and introspection becomes as indispensable as ever.

Based on introspection, the idea that fiction can be made imageable by emulating the inherent characteristics of voluntary imagery has previously been suggested by aesthetician Elaine Scarry. In Scarry's (1999) valuable account, fiction becomes imageable by virtue of analogy when the predicaments of voluntary imaging are made explicit (e.g., when a character is struggling to visualize a cherished face), or alternatively, when objects of certain qualities (e.g., translucence, floral supposition) are represented. Even if Scarry did take notice of the idiosyncratic mode of visual description, there would still be significant differences between her approach and mine. Most notably, Scarry singles out imageable particulars such as the visual properties of being translucent or flower-like. Meanwhile, my subsections 4.1 and 4.2 aim at distinguishing between markedly imageable and non-imageable classes of visual properties, or parameters (e.g., color, shape), regardless of value (e.g., blue or yellow, rectangular or circular). The respective presence or absence of each and one of the selected parameters in an instance of visual description will be set against the default parameters and limitations of the visual mental image (voluntary or prompted by visual description), and its effect on description imageability will be predicted.

4.1/ Default parameters (finitude)
The experienced finitude of imagery from visual description is closely related to its experienced feebleness. The former will now serve as a background for positive characterization. The latter will subsequently frame an account of what properties a mental image from visual description does not, and in some cases even cannot have.

The kind of image finitude discussed here may be further conceptualized by comparison to a picture. Having no intention to take sides with either the descriptivist or pictorialist camp of the age-old imagery debate in cognitive neuroscience,[9] my suggestion is that mental images from visual description are *picture-like* at least in two relevant respects: Firstly, because of their static nature, they are experienced as two-dimensional (see also Casey 2000: 92). It may be by virtue of this resemblance that one of the most prominent types of so called *ekphrasis* (i.e., the ancient rhetorical device of visual rendition) was the verbal representation of (more or less) two-dimensional visual artworks. As objects, such artworks are largely defined by their complex pictorial surface, while they tend to be uniform in overall contour shape. Interestingly, the mundane objects visually described by modern fiction that are presently

---

[9] Arguing about the pre-experiential cognitive format of mental imagery, the descriptivists posit that mental imagery comes down to propositional structures, while the pictorialists reject the possibility of such a reduction. (See e.g. Thompson 2007 for a review.)

in focus—brooms, cups, flower pots—depend more heavily on contour shape for their identity than on surface. This fact is reflected in the makeup of the correspondent mental image. When I read about a flower pot or simply fancy to image one out of the blue, I may or may not be able to tell afterwards how porous the earthenware was, but I will always roughly know the slope of its wall. The contour of the flower pot may be incomplete (there may be no way of telling whether or not there was a rim at the upper edge), but it will always be there and it will always be perceived as final because the flower pot will be given to me in two dimensions. By contrast, the contour shape of a flower pot imaged in the processing of narrative will be perceived as open to modification due to the possibility of interaction, by means of which a virtual third dimension is brought into existence.

Secondly, mental images from visual description tend to be oriented in a way resembling of certain canonical types of pictorial representation. If their contour is to adhere to the object they represent, they cannot be, and obviously are not, multiperspectival in the manner cubist paintings are. In their feebleness, they can hardly be said to comply with the standards of realist perspectival painting. They are imaged under a perspective nevertheless, and most often a markedly pictorial perspective at that, namely the one optimally revealing the distinctive contour shape of the object in question. When imaging a broom decoupled from perceptual experience, i.e., when processing its visual description, the broom as an entity is given to me in the most perspicuous way: vertically, perhaps in a slight angle to the orthogonal axis, its bristles facing the bottom of my mental visual field (see Figure 1). This is how a broom is normally depicted when immediate comprehension is at stake, e.g., in pictograms or illustrated dictionaries.

Object orientation in involuntary images or in images prompted by narrative, by contrast, is always situated. For instance, should I image the same broom as part of a perceptual experience, e.g. in emulating the act of sweeping, the broomstick would become, in a rather compelling manner, disproportionately short and thick in my mental image and the overall contour of the broom would alter.[10] Moreover, the image as a whole would no longer symmetrically occupy the center of my mental visual field, but rather gravitate toward its lower right hand side (I am right-handed). Albeit compelling in the mental, such a broom image would seem highly indefinite and ambiguous as to its content if transposed into an actual two-dimensional picture (see Figure 2). There are of course instances of perceptual mimesis in which brooms appear under the same perspective as depicted in pictograms or as imaged during visual description processing. The difference is that in mental imagery from visual description, brooms are rarely oriented otherwise.

An approximate contour filled with a sketchy surface as afforded by an initial orientation is all there is to visual mental images of isolated objects such as brooms, cups or flower pots. That is to say, they are all there is by default, at the very instant a reader has pre-reflectively understood that an object description is about to begin unfolding, but before any post-posited visual attributes have been taken in. This particular stage of imagery is what I call the *default mental image*. It arises, for instance, with the underlined portions of the following examples:

---

[10] The perspective thus assumed would coincide with what cognitive psychologists call "canonical perspective", i.e., a perspective by which typical interaction is facilitated (Palmer, Rosch, and Chase 1981).

Fidelity Without Mimesis

[T]hree dirty mattresses, each rolled up in a blanket: which occupied one corner of the room during the day, and formed a kind of slab, on which were placed an old cracked basin, ewer, and soap-dish, of common yellow earthenware, with a blue flower[.] (Dickens 1998: 551)

My Austrian sniper's rifle with its blued octagon barrel and the lovely dark walnut, cheek-fitted, *schutzen* stock, hung over the two beds. (Hemingway 1962: 11)

The tablecloth was thick, smooth and blue. Heavy Indian cotton, a thin turquoise line through blue checks. Small frayed holes here and there. (Roberts 1993: 14)

Whatever parameters the reader brings in on top of contour shape and orientation pertain less to the image as such (but see below, section 4.2) than to the reader's preconceived notion of the object in question. If the reader lives in a world where most brooms are brown, or if the reader assumes that most brooms are brown in the particular world of the particular piece of fiction, then it is sheer conceptual knowledge that makes the reader tacitly believe that a fictional broom is brown. Obviously, the particular contour and orientation imposed on one's default mental image of a broom are mediated by conceptual knowledge as well. They happen to coincide with what one's culture knows as prototypical. The main difference from other visual parameters, e.g. color, is that contour shape and orientation alone are necessary for manufactured objects such as brooms to appear as what they are. As far as mental images of manufactured objects are considered, the other parameters are accidental. A purple emerald will no longer be an emerald, but a broom made of purple china will still appear as a broom unless its practical function is considered, which anyway never happens in visual description proper, where appearance is the only thing at stake (see also section 2).

A strawberry turned upside down will lose nothing of its essence, but a flower pot turned upside down will suddenly appear somewhat less like a flower pot. This, along with a fair deal of introspection, is what lies behind the above suggestion that contour shape and orientation is all one really sees in, rather than reads into, the default mental image.

But what does the particular status of the two closely interconnected parameters of contour shape and orientation imply for imageability in cases when contour shape or orientation are explicitly mentioned in a visual description? Paradoxically, nothing much. Their centrality to the definition of each object category (and the relatively low variability of shape within each object category) seems to make the two parameters relatively useless, and perhaps even relatively little used, in visual descriptions.

That a particular contour shape or orientation is mentioned at all, usually implies that several different contour shapes or orientations are afforded by the object category in question. While less typical contour shapes (rectangular flower pots) need not cause difficulty for imagery, less typical orientations (chairs lying on their backrests) tend to be more treacherous but mostly viable thanks to our ability to perform mental rotation (Shepard and Metzler 1971). Importantly, unless the object in the specific contour shape and orientation is highly unexpected (spheric brooms, banana shaped coffee cups), it is accommodated by the initial mental image without resistance, but also without the reader taking particular notice.

It has been noted by Michael Burke (2011: 145), and partly also by the proponents of the classical theory of literary estrangement (Shklovsky 1990: 1–14), that mental contents really become noticeable only when a mismatch takes place between the reader's top-down preconceptions on the one hand

and bottom-up textual input on the other. Once we adopt the same idea for visual mental imagery, the following conclusion avails: if contour shape and orientation are the only two default parameters in mental images of isolated objects, then explicit references to these parameters should represent the only kind of textual input that can induce a match or mismatch proper, i.e. a match or mismatch concerning the image as such. Yet paradoxically, match or mismatch seems to make little difference to contour shape and orientation. Mentioned or unmentioned, matching or mismatching, it is as if the two parameters were rarely noticed in their own right exactly because their presence in the mental image is inevitable anyway. Compare for instance the following passages:

> She carried the Quimper dish on her upturned hands. ... A big dish, roughly oblong in shape, with rounded shoulders. Its thickness and heaviness were emphasized by the bold strokes of its painted decoration, dark orange, dark pink, and navy blue. (Roberts 1993: 91)

> Gary ... took the last of the six signs that a Neverest representative had sold to him. Considering the cost of a Neverest home-security system, the signs were unbelievably shoddy. The placards, roughly oblong in shape, were unevenly painted and attached by fragile aluminum rivets to posts of rolled sheet metal[.] (Franzen 2001: 225)

Above, a contour shape qualifier ("roughly oblong in shape") was removed from the former passage and planted in the latter passage. Neither one of the two mental images (of the dish, of the home-security sign) lost or gained any of its initial power, in spite of the fact that home-security signs are more likely than dishes to be roughly oblong in shape, and in spite of "roughly oblong" suggesting slightly different shapes for the two objects: an oval one for the dish, a rectangular one for the home-security sign. This is not to say that certain contour shapes or (especially) orientations are not more likely to be imaged than others. The point is simply that there is nothing about visual descriptions referring to contour shape or orientation *per se* that makes them either imageable or non-imageable. This is not the case for those parameters for which any possible match or mismatch pertains not to the level of the image, but to the level of invested conceptual knowledge. Those are the non-default parameters. Among them, I will argue, some truly have the power to make a visual description imageable, while others are for various reasons detrimental to description imageability. Tapping firmly into the conceptual, the non-default parameters overall seem more likely to become noticed, to capture one's attention in the course of reading. The ones listed in the following subsection tend also to make a noticeable difference for one's mental imagery.

Figure 1
Broom contour prompted by visual description

Figure 2
Broom contour prompted by narrative

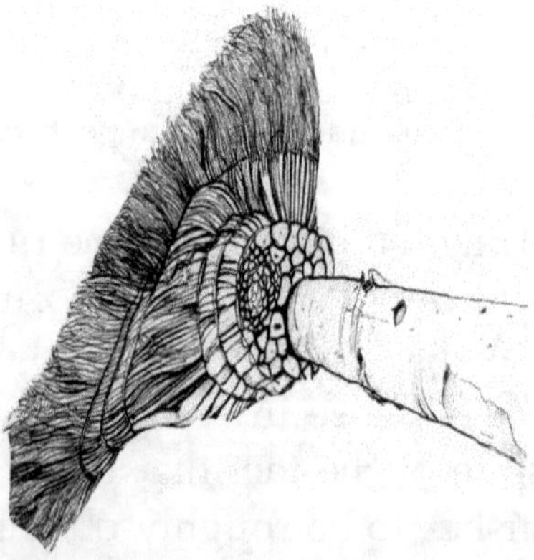

© Jim Shaw

© Schünnin

4.2/ Other parameters, limitations (feebleness)

The absence of each one of the below visual parameters adds to the perceived feebleness of the default mental image from visual description. By recounting these parameters, I will thus continue recounting the many ways in which mental images from visual descriptions, especially in the default, are experienced as feeble. However, there are countless aspects to what meets the eye in perception and I have no ambition to offer a comprehensive overview of all conceivable visual parameters. Rather, my intention is to propose a general way of classifying visual parameters according to their imageability, while identifying salient representatives of each category. Throughout the proposal, new distinctions will need to be drawn between the various levels of the notion of imageability that are at play. A diagrammatic summary will finally be provided in Figure 3, where further examples of each category will also be proposed.

My ultimate aim is to pinpoint visual parameters that have a pronounced impact, be it positive or negative, on the imageability of a visual description of an object as encountered in a piece of fiction. In this respect, the only thing I have been able to establish thus far is that the parameters of contour shape and orientation do not seem to have much impact. On the other hand, the parameters of contour shape and orientation obviously are imageable, even more so than any others, given their privileged status in mental imagery. The ubiquitous notion of imageability thus begins to bifurcate: First, there is the *basic imageability of a particular parameter* in itself. In this sense, a parameter either is or is not imageable depending on whether it can be readily represented in a mental image. Then, there is the impact the same parameter may or may not have on the *imageability of a visual description*. Unlike contour shape and orientation, all the below parameters have a pronounced impact. It is assumed in what follows that a negative score on basic imageability automatically entails a negative impact on description imageability. Meanwhile, a positive score on basic imageability does not, interestingly enough, guarantee a positive impact. But let us begin with the easy cases.

Some visual parameters simply cannot be represented in an image from visual description. Their presence in a visual description is then necessarily a hindrance to mental imagery. Rather than contributing to a visual presentation, the words referring to these parameters leave other sorts of imprints on the reader's consciousness, thus disturbing the mental image; they are reflected upon *qua* higher-order concepts or *qua* verbal expressions, or simply skimmed or skipped. Size is a salient example of this class of parameters. In explaining why size cannot be imaged, I will once more revisit Elaine Scarry. In her treatise, Scarry argues that blossoms are amongst the most easily imageable of all possible contents. For explanation, Scarry (1999: 47) refers to the typical size of a blossom, which she says is commensurable with the size of the physical space occupied by mental images, i.e. with the size of one's forehead.

Even though I do not share Scarry's passion for flowers, and even though I do not posit that the mental visual field is experienced to span a stretch of physical space, my assumption about the non-imageability of size is grounded in a similar premise, namely, that the spatial magnitude of visual mental images is invariable across contents. That is to say, no matter how small or big an object in reality, its visual mental image is readily enlarged or diminished as if to nicely fill the blank of the mental visual field, leaving a perfectly proportionate margin (see also Casey 2000: 54). Evidence from empirical studies on experimenter guided mental imagery concurs with this intuition. People have been found to consistently image smaller objects as if they were closer and vice versa (Kosslyn 1978). Because the blank to be filled is not physical in any respect, I am more inclined to view mental images as sizeless rather than uniformly sized. Either way, explicit reference to size, especially when absolute (e.g., "one foot long") as opposed to relative (e.g., "long"), seems ostentatiously useless and distractive in visual description as far as the content of mental imagery is concerned. In the following examples, for instance, any hitherto conceived mental image may recede or even disperse as soon as the reference to size is processed:

> He showed me one of [the guns], a smoothly jagged piece of metal <u>over a foot long</u>. It looked like babbitting metal. (Hemingway 1962: 182)

> Beyond stands the lamp, in the right corner of the table: a square base <u>six inches on each side</u>, a disk tangent with its sides, <u>of the same diameter</u>, a fluted column supporting a dark, slightly conical lampshade. (Robbe-Grillet 1965a: 144)

Yet other visual parameters are imaged with great ease and tend to have a positive impact on the imageability of a visual description. Color is a salient example of this class of parameters. That visual mental images prompted by names of manufactured objects are generally experienced to appear in shades of white and achromatic grey unless a color is explicitly mentioned, is an insight based on introspection (see also Scarry 1999: 22). There are, however, empirical indications toward such a view of the default mental image. For instance, a brain imaging study of embodied cognition (Simmons et al. 2007) has identified a neural substrate common to the processing of object-color word pairs (e.g., "eggplant-purple") and actual color processing. Interestingly, the same study has shown that object words decoupled from explicit color attributes do not activate the cortical areas in question. Pre-consciously, objects seem to be processed as colorless. Nevertheless, while the stimuli in the above study consisted in both natural and manufactured object words, my own introspective hypothesis regarding conscious and near-conscious imagery does not extend beyond the latter. Rather, I am inclined to describe mental images prompted by names of natural objects — "eggplant", "strawberry", "emerald" — as tinted by the color typically associated with the object (see also section 4.1). To be more precise, I am inclined to thus describe mental images prompted by the names of any objects which are very strongly associated with one particular color. These objects (and the specific colors they are associated with) vary in part across cultures and individuals. The group happens to coincide largely, but far from entirely, with the category of natural objects. It probably includes bricks, but not bell peppers.

Whether default mental images of manufactured objects really are entirely achromatic or just extremely feeble in hue, the parameter of color is essentially different from the parameter of size in that its experienced absence from the visual mental image is no necessity. Not only can color be easily accommodated by a visual mental image. It is often accommodated with benefit, boosting the image beyond the threshold of the reader's attention. The rare potential of externally induced color to inform visual imagery is further confirmed, as it were, by empirical research into the so called Perky effect. In the initial Perky (1910) experiment, participants were asked to produce mental images of diverse objects (e.g., a banana, a book) while unknowingly facing a white screen on which dim pictures of the same kinds of objects were being projected. The original data suggests that exposure to pictures, generally speaking, affects the content of concurrent mental imagery. Further research (Reeves 1981) has shown, however, that the Perky effect is up to six times stronger when the target picture is colored compared to when it is achromatic.

Finally, the basic imageability of color being beyond doubt, its positive impact on description imageability is perhaps most easily avowed by recourse to practical examples. In my view, any mental image produced by these randomly chosen visual descriptions fades drastically when references to color are thought away:

> Right at the back would be a narrow bed covered in ~~ultramarine~~ velvet and stacked with cushions ~~of all colours~~. (Perec 1990: 24)

> The sofa was upholstered in ~~yellow and blue~~ satin, shiny and tight, finished with rolled ~~gold~~ cord and tassels. A hard little matching satin bolster tucked in at either end. ~~Gold~~ claws at the end of twisted wooden legs. (Roberts 1993: 54)

> To encourage him, Baxter at last takes the knife from his pocket. As far as Perowne can tell, it's an old-fashioned French kitchen knife, with ~~an orange~~ wooden handle and curved blade with no sheen. (McEwan 2006: 215)

The third and final category of parameters is those that may be perfectly imageable in themselves, but have a negative impact on the perceived imageability of a visual description. The fact that such discordance is possible at all suggests that the notion of imageability, bifurcated as it already was for the purpose of the preceding analysis, in fact trifurcates. In between the basic imageability of each individual parameter and its impact on overall description imageability, there is the mediating variable of a parameter's respective *possibility or non-possibility to be accommodated in the general object image*. This possibility or non-possibility comes down to the inherent makeup of the mental image as described above. Namely, it derives from the prominence of contour shape in object imagery, and from the feebleness of the surface filling the space delineated by a mentally imaged contour. More specifically, the category encompasses whatever can be imaged in its own right but cannot meet the mind's eye when an object is imaged *as a whole*. The parameters belonging to this third category all reduce, in one way or another, to surface detail and to non-contour shape, i.e. to aspects of shape that do not inform the general object contour (as projected into the two dimensions of a mental image). One salient representative of this category is what I will henceforth call, for lack of a better expression, the parameter of visual complexity. The underlined portions of the following descriptions all roughly amount to visual complexity:

> The table is a metal disc pierced with innumerable holes, <u>the largest of which form a complicated rosette: a series of S's all starting at the center, like double-curved spokes of a wheel, and each spiraling at the outer end, at the periphery of the disk.</u> ¶ The base supporting the table consists of a slender triple stem whose strands separate to converge again, coiling (in three vertical planes through the axis of the system) into three similar volutes whose lower whorls rest on the ground <u>and are bound together by a ring placed a little higher on the curve</u>. (Robbe-Grillet 1965b: 94–95)

> A local craftsman had made the buffet for Thérèse's grandparents. ... A solid piece in worn pine, darkened with age, satin-smooth. Its top pair of doors <u>was carved with reliefs of oakleaf garlands. Two fat swags that hung down</u>, one on each door. (Roberts 1993: 11)

> The placards were unevenly painted and attached <u>by fragile aluminum rivets</u> to posts of rolled sheet metal[.] (Franzen 2001: 225)

It is fair to say that reference to visual complexity, the verbal rendition of the detailed architecture of things, is over-represented in literary visual descriptions. Visual complexity thus adds to why visual descriptions, in aggregate, end up appearing so surprisingly non-imageable, given the reader's intuitive readiness to see with the mind's eye. It has previously been suggested by literary scholars and cognitive psychologists alike that in order to be imageable, visual descriptions of various kinds (descriptions of faces; descriptions of complex spatial settings) need to preserve a holistic (Jajdelska et al. 2010) and unitary (Lopes 1995: 23) view of what is being described. Visual complexity obviously flouts these principles, breaking objects into details of structure (such as fragile aluminum rivets) and details of surface (such as perforations forming complicated rosettes). Any initial object image is then broken down accordingly.

Although the reader may not cease to experience visual imagery while processing references to visual complexity, the images experienced are no longer experienced as images of the central object proper. A sense of discontinuity obtains (see also Casey 2000: 91), with negative consequences for the imageability of the visual description overall. Mental imagery from visual description, at least when discrete objects are considered, thus differs from perceptual experience and from perceptually mimetic (e.g., narrative) mental imagery in that nothing can be represented in it without simultaneously being represented as being in focus. And if whatever is in focus optimally fills the visual mental field, then each mental image consists only and exclusively in whatever is in focus. Hence the necessary lack of continuity between mental images of objects and mental images of object parts.

Figure 3

Parameter	By default	Optionally	Separately	Never
Is imaged				
Imageability I: Is imageable	Yes	Yes	Yes	No
Imageability II: Can be accommodated in object image	Yes	Yes	No	No
Imageability III: Has impact on description imageability	Neutral	Positive	Negative	Negative
Salient example	Contour shape	Color	Visual complexity	Size
Further example	Orientation	Luminance/ Texture	Occluded features	Volume

5/ Conclusion

"Fidelity without mimesis," reads the title of this paper. Let us once more recount its main implications. Firstly, visual description as well as the mental imagery it sometimes elicits is non-mimetic with respect to perceptual experience. Secondly, if visual description is to elicit mental imagery in the first place, it depends for its imageability on a different, non-perceptual kind of fidelity than imageable narrative, namely on its fidelity to the experiential makeup of voluntary visual images. When it deviates from this makeup, visual description decreases in imageability. But when mental imagery is elicited after all, it is further distinguished from other forms of fiction-induced imagery by its level of fidelity to what is actually encoded in the text. Hence a second way of reading "fidelity".

There is of course much more to visual descriptions than visual parameters. Not only are there parameters relevant to vision that have a strong potential to engage embodied, interactive processing (e.g., weight, surface texture). Attached to the third fundamental feature of mental imagery from visual description, i.e. to its inherent expectedness, there are also the countless issues of visual descriptive style. It would be untenable to posit that description imageability is unaffected by stylistic variation. But a detailed inquiry into imageable and non-imageable descriptive lexicon and syntax remains to be carried out. Moreover, a call for a yet larger enterprise lurks in the conceptual network of the above argument, namely the call for a systematic, positive analysis of all the other attentional foci that can piggyback on visual description processing. For instance, when is a visual description more likely to address conceptual reflection or draw one's attention to its linguistic structure rather than elicit visual imagery? What are the mutual relationships between the three? What are their respective relationships to mimesis, and what kind of mimesis are we talking about? Such a systematic analysis, should it be viable, would significantly contribute to the charting out of the regularities of prose fiction reading overall. Literary theorist Philippe Hamon's aphoristic remark about description "being the crucial point at which the readability (of fiction) is organized" (Hamon 1982: 167) would thus acquire new, clearer significance.[11]

Stockholm University
anezka.kuzmicova@littvet.su.se

REFERENCES

Allington, Daniel. 2011. "'It Actually Painted a Picture of the Village and the Sea and the Bottom of the Sea': Reading Groups, Cultural Legitimacy, and Description in Narrative (with Particular Reference to John Steinbeck's *The Pearl*)." *Language and Literature* 20 (4): 317–332.
Atran, Scott. 1990. *Cognitive Foundations of Natural History: Towards an Anthropology of Science*. Cambridge: Cambridge University Press.
Baker, Nicholson. 1998. *The Mezzanine*. London: Granta.
Bal, Mieke. 1982. "On Meanings and Descriptions." *Studies in 20th Century Literature* 6 (1–2): 100–148.
Barthes, Roland. 1989. "The Reality Effect." In *The Rustle of Language*, trans. Richard Howard, 141–48. Berkeley: University of California Press.
Burke, Michael. 2011. *Literary Reading, Cognition, and Emotion: An Exploration of the Oceanic Mind*. New York: Routledge.
Casey, Edward S. 2000. *Imagining: A Phenomenological Study*. Bloomington: Indiana University Press.
Cobley, Evelyn. 1986. "Description in Realist Discourse: The War Novel in Narrative Poetics." *Style* 20 (3): 395–410.

---

[11] Part of this research was carried out at the University of Alberta during a research stay funded by the Swedish Foundation for International Cooperation in Research and Higher Education.

Dickens, Charles. 1998. *Pickwick Papers*. Hertfordshire: Wordsworth Classics.
Esrock, Ellen J. 1994. *The Reader's Eye: Visual Imaging as Reader Response*. Baltimore: The Johns Hopkins University Press.
Fischer, Martin H., and Rolf A. Zwaan. 2008. "Embodied Language: A Review of the Role of the Motor System in Language Comprehension." *The Quarterly Journal of Experimental Psychology* 61 (6): 825–850.
Flaubert, Gustave. 1995. *Madame Bovary*. Trans. Allan Russell. London: Penguin Popular Classics.
Franzen, Jonathan. 2001. *The Corrections*. New York: Picador.
Gallagher, Shaun, and Dan Zahavi. 2007. *The Phenomenological Mind: An Introduction to Philosophy of Mind and Cognitive Science*. New York: Routledge.
Grünbaum, Thor. 2007. "Action between Plot and Discourse." *Semiotica* 165 (1–4): 295–314.
Halliwell, Stephen. 2002. *The Aesthetics of Mimesis: Ancient Texts and Modern Problems*. Princeton: Princeton University Press.
Hamon, Philippe. 1981. "Rhetorical Status of the Descriptive." Trans. Patricia Baudoin. *Yale French Studies* 61: 1–26.
———. 1982. "What is a Description?" In *French Literary Theory Today: A Reader*, ed. Tzvetan Todorov, trans. R. Carter, 147–78. Cambridge: Cambridge University Press.
Hemingway, Ernest. 1962. *A Farewell to Arms*. In *Three Novels*, 1–332. New York: Scribner.
Herman, David. 2009. *Basic Elements of Narrative*. Chichester: Wiley-Blackwell.
Jajdelska, Elspeth, Christopher Butler, Steve Kelly, Allan McNeill, and Katie Overy. 2010. "Crying, Moving, and Keeping it Whole: What Makes Literary Description Vivid?" *Poetics Today* 31 (3): 433–463.
Kosslyn, Steven M. 1978. "Measuring the Visual Angle of the Mind's Eye." *Cognitive Psychology* 10 (3): 356–89.
Kuzmičová, Anežka. Forthcoming. "The Words and Worlds of Literary Narrative: The Tradeoff between Verbal Presence and Direct Presence in the Activity of Reading." In *Stories and Minds: Cognitive Approaches to Literary Narrative*, ed. Lars Bernaerts—Dirk De Geest—Luc Herman—Bart Vervaeck. Lincoln: University of Nebraska Press.
———. 2012. "Presence in the Reading of Literary Narrative: A Case for Motor Enactment." *Semiotica* 189 (1–4): 23–48.

Labov, William. 1972. *Language in the Inner City: Studies in the Black English Vernacular*. Philadelphia: University of Pennsylvania Press.

Lopes, José Manuel. 1995. *Foregrounded Description in Prose Fiction: Five Cross-Literary Studies*. Toronto: University of Toronto Press.

Martin, Alex. 2007. "The Representation of Object Concepts in the Brain." *Annual Review of Psychology* 58: 25–45.

McEwan, Ian. 2006. *Saturday*. New York: Anchor Books.

— — —. 2011. *Solar*. New York: Random House.

Mosher, Harold F. 1991. "Toward a Poetics of 'Descriptized' Narration." *Poetics Today* 12 (3): 425–45.

Noë, Alva. 2006. *Action in Perception*. Cambridge, MA: The MIT Press.

Nünning, Ansgar. 2007. "Towards a Typology, Poetics and History of Description in Fiction." In *Description in Literature and Other Media*, ed. Werner Wolf and Walter Bernhart, 91–128. Amsterdam: Rodopi.

Palmer, Stephen E., Eleanor Rosch, and Paul Chase. 1981. "Canonical Perspective and the Perception of Objects." In *Attention and Performance IX: Proceedings of the Ninth International Symposium on Attention and Performance, Jesus College, Cambridge, England, July 13–18, 1980*, 135–51. Hillsdale: Lawrence Erlbaum.

Perec, Georges. 1990. *Things: A Story of the Sixties*. Trans. David Bellos. Boston: Godine.

Perky, Cheves West. 1910. "An Experimental Study of Imagination." *The American Journal of Psychology* 21 (3): 422–52.

Reeves, Adam. 1981. "Visual Imagery Lowers Sensitivity to Hue-Varying, but not to Luminance-Varying, Visual Stimuli." *Attention, Perception, & Psychophysics* 29 (3): 247–50.

Riffaterre, Michael. 1981. "Descriptive Imagery." *Yale French Studies* 61: 107–125.

Rizzolatti, Giacomo, and Vittorio Gallese. 1988. "Mechanisms and Theories of Spatial Neglect." *Handbook of Neuropsychology* 1: 223–46.

Robbe-Grillet, Alain. 1965a. *In the Labyrinth*. In *Two Novels by Robbe-Grillet*, trans. Richard Howard, 139–272. New York: Grove Press.

— — —. 1965b. *Jealousy*. In *Two Novels by Robbe-Grillet*, trans. Richard Howard, 33–138. New York: Grove Press.

Roberts, Michèle. 1993. *Daughters of the House*. London: Virago.

Rosch, Eleanor, Caroline B. Mervis, Wayne Gray, David M. Johnson, and Penny Boyes-Braem. 1976. "Basic Objects in Natural Categories." *Psychology* 7: 573–605.

Scarry, Elaine. 1999. *Dreaming by the Book*. New York: Farrar, Straus and Giroux.

Shepard, Roger N., and Jacqueline Metzler. 1971. "Mental Rotation of Three-Dimensional Objects." *Science* 171 (3972): 701–3.

Shklovsky, Viktor. 1990. *Theory of Prose*. Trans. Benjamin Sher. Normal: Dalkey Archive Press.

Simmons, W. Kyle, Vimal Ramjee, Michael S. Beauchamp, Ken McRae, Alex Martin, and Lawrence W. Barsalou. 2007. "A Common Neural Substrate for Perceiving and Knowing about Color." *Neuropsychologia* 45 (12): 2802–10.

Thompson, Evan. 2007. "Look Again: Phenomenology and Mental Imagery." *Phenomenology and the Cognitive Sciences* 6: 137–70.

Westbury, Chris, and Gail Moroschan. 2009. "Imageability x Phonology Interactions during Lexical Access: Effects of Modality, Phonological Neighbourhood, and Phonological Processing Efficiency." *The Mental Lexicon* 4 (1): 115–45.

Wolf, Werner. 2004. "Aesthetic Illusion as an Effect of Fiction." *Style* 38 (3): 325–51.

– – –. 2007. "Description as a Transmedial Mode of Representation: General Features and Possibilities of Realization in Painting, Fiction and Music." In *Description in Literature and Other Media*, ed. Walter Bernhart, 1–87. Amsterdam: Rodopi.

Varieties of Photographic Fiction

Peter Alward

> ABSTRACT: Scruton, in "Photography and Representation", argues that the only sense in which a photograph could be fictional is in virtue of being a photograph of a fiction, and hence that photography—and photo-based cinema—is fictional only in a derivative sense. While acknowledging that photographs can be fictional in Scruton's sense, I argue that there can also be non-derivative photographic fiction as well. In some cases, the photograph itself is part of the fiction; and I argue that, in such cases, appreciators imagine *de re* of the photograph that it is a picture of a fictional photographic subject. And in cases in which the photograph is not part of the fiction, I argue that appreciators imagine *de re* of what is seen in the picture (in Wollheim's sense) that it is a fictional photographic subject.

Roger Scruton, in "Photography and Representation", argues that the only sense in which a photograph could be fictional is in virtue of being a photograph of a fiction:

> Of course I may take a photograph of a draped nude and call it *Venus*, but insofar as this can be understood as an exercise in fiction, it should not be thought of as a photographic representation of Venus but rather as a photograph of a representation of Venus. (Scruton 1981: 588)[1]

If Scruton is right about this, then photography—as well as photo-based cinema—is a fictional medium only in a derivative sense. In a recent paper (Alward 2012), I argued, by modeling

---

[1] It is worth noting that Scruton's target is photographic representation more generally and not merely photographic fiction.

Mimesis: Metaphysics, Cognition, Pragmatics
ed. G. Currie, P. Koťátko, M. Pokorný
316–42. London: College Publications, 2012.

photography on the art of casting actors in theatrical and filmic roles, that genuine photographic fiction is possible: by means of their choices of which photographs to exhibit, photographic artists can express the same range of thoughts as artists working in uncontroversial fictional media, such as painting. Although, in my view, this is correct as far as it goes, by itself it does not establish that photographs can be specifically pictorial fictions as opposed to the merely conventional or "relational" sense in which anything can be used to represent anything else. The central goal of this paper is to show how photographs can be pictorial fictions in a non-derivative sense, that is, not merely in virtue of being pictures of fictions.

The strategy here takes as its starting point the notion of photographic transparency: the idea that one can literally see an object by looking at a photograph of it—in effect, seeing it *through* the photograph (Walton 1984). Insofar as photographic seeing through is a species of indirect perception, it consists in seeing the photographic object by means of more directly seeing something else. And the leading idea here is that what mediates the observer's perception of the photographic object is not the photograph itself but rather what is *seen in* the photograph, in Wollheim's sense (Wollheim 1987, 1998). One sees an object through a photograph by means of more directly seeing an image in the photograph, rather than by merely seeing the photographic surface as such. Non-derivative pictorial photographic fiction is secured by taking it to consist in photographs whose proper appreciation requires imagining *de re* of what is seen in them that they are fictional subjects of various kinds.

This paper consists of three parts. First, the casting model of photography is developed and shown to fall short as an account of specifically pictorial fiction. Second, Walton's account of pictorial fiction is presented and subjected to critical scrutiny. Of particular concern are the difficulties that arise as a result of taking engagement with pictorial fictions to require *de se* imagining of various kinds. And finally, a positive account of photographic fiction—inspired by Wollheim's theory of "seeing-in"—is developed and defended.

1/ Derivative fictions and their discontents

1.1/ Fictional incompetence

The main conclusion of Scruton's argument in "Photography and Representation" is that there cannot be a genuine aesthetic interest in the representational natures of photographs (Scruton 1981).[2] As I reconstruct it (see Alward 2012), the central argument for this conclusion has the following form:

P1: Photographs are not representations.
P2: If photographs are not representations, there cannot be a genuine aesthetic interest in their representational natures.
C: There cannot be a genuine aesthetic interest in the representational natures of photographs.[3]

Of particular concern here is Scruton's P1. According to Scruton, in order to be a representation a picture needs to express a thought—"embodied in perceptual form"—about the

---

[2] Strictly speaking, the target of Scruton's argument is not photography *per se*, but rather "ideal photography," which is characterized by a non-intentional causal relationship between the photograph and the photographic subject—a relationship which entails both that the subject exists and that it is as it appears in the photograph.

[3] I am, of course, presupposing that something can have a representational nature without being a representation in Scruton's more narrow sense.

subject of the picture (Scruton 1981: 581). Hence, a proper appreciation of a representational picture requires attending both to the thought expressed and the means by which it is embodied in the picture. But in order to capable of expressing thoughts, a pictorial medium needs to be fictionally competent: the represented subjects need not exist, and even if they do, they need not appear as represented by their pictures. Since the subjects of paintings, for example, need not exist — and even if they do, painters are not constrained to paint them as they actually appear — the painterly medium is fictionally competent; hence, there is no impediment to the expression of thought via painting.

Scruton argues, however, that photographs are not representations in this sense. Because of the nature of the causal relationship in which photographs stand to their subjects, they are not fictionally competent. In particular, since the subject of a photograph just is whoever or whatever the camera was pointed at and focused on when the picture was taken, photographic subjects necessarily do exist. And since the appearance of a photograph is (predominantly) determined by the appearance of the photographic subject (at the time the photograph was taken), photographic subjects necessarily are (or were) as they appear in their photographs.[4] As a result, photographs simply cannot express thoughts, and even if a photographer intends to do so, "it is neither necessary nor even possible that the photographer's intention should enter as a serious factor in determining how the picture is seen" (Scruton 1981: 588).

---

[4] The appearance of photographs can, of course, be modified by the use of Photoshop and the like; Scruton, however, considers the use of such techniques to involve a departure from the photographic ideal with which he is concerned.

1.2/ *Casting for solutions*

In "Transparent Representation: Photography and the Art of casting" (Alward 2012), I offer a twofold response to charge of photographic fictional incompetence. First, I argue that Scruton's claim that photographic subjects necessarily exist rests upon the failure to distinguish between pictorial subjects and pictorial objects: what a picture is of and what it is about.[5] The object of a picture, if there is one, is something that plays a salient causal role in its production—whose observable properties influence the pattern of lines and colours on the pictorial surface. The object of a photograph is whoever or whatever the camera was pointed at and focused on when the picture was taken. And the object of a painting is the model the artist used when she produced it. The subject of a picture, in contrast, is the entity which the picture represents or expresses a thought (or thoughts) about; as such, it is a function or product of what the picture means or how it is correctly interpreted rather than the causal process by which it was produced.[6] Now, as should be clear, all Scruton has (at most) established is that photographic object must exist. But fictional competence requires only that the photographic subject need not exist. Hence unless there are grounds for thinking photographic subjects and objects must coincide, Scruton has not made his case. And not only is there no reason to suppose that, in general, pictorial objects and pictorial subjects must coincide—painted fictions are often produced using models, after all—Scruton has not given any reason to think this to be so specifically in the photographic case.

---

[5] A similar distinction can be found in Maynard (1997) and Philips (2009).

[6] Of course, the meaning of a picture may, in part, be a function of the process by which it was produced.

Varieties of Photographic Fiction

Second, I argue that Scruton's claim that photographic subjects necessarily are as they appear in their photographs rests upon a failure to distinguish between two methods of producing representations: creating and casting. Creating consists of bringing something new into existence by means of combining and modifying pre-existing raw materials. Within the constraints set by the medium and artistic ability, the features of created objects are fully within an artist's control and, hence, how the subject appears is largely within her control as well. In contrast, rather than bringing something new into existence, casting involves choosing something from among from among a collection of pre-existing objects to represent a subject of some kind—a familiar example is that of casting actors for movie and theatrical roles. What is important to note is that given a large and diverse enough collection of objects to choose from, one can have as much control over how a subject is represented through one's casting choices as can be had via creation. Moreover, even when the represented subject is an existent thing, it can be represented as being other than it in fact is simply by casting an object to represent it whose properties differ from those of the subject. Photography, I argue, can be fruitfully understood as an art of representational casting. Photographic artists normally record large numbers of images from which they choose a small subset to print and display and so are capable of exerting a high degree of control over the appearance of the photographs they use to represent their photographic subjects. And since, as above, a photographer can produce a photograph whose subject is in fact different from how she therein appears by choosing a photographic object whose properties (at the time the picture is taken) differ from those of the subject, there remains no reason to believe that photographs fail to be fictionally competent in Scruton's sense.

1.3/ Non-pictorial photographic representation?

Although this is rightheaded as far as it goes—or so I would argue—there are grounds for thinking it is inadequate as it stands. As Scruton formulates the worry, all that has been heretofore shown is that photography is fictionally competent in the conventional or relational sense in which anything can be used to represent anything else: "I may use a photograph of Lenin as a representation of him, in the way that I might have used a clenched fist or a potato or a photograph of Hitler" (Scruton 1981: 597). But, according to Scruton, paintings—unlike photographs—are (or can be) intrinsic representations in the sense that, like eternal sentences, "[they] can be understood in isolation from the special circumstances of [their] creation" (Scruton 1981: 597). That is, in order to grasp the thought expressed by a painting, a suitably sensitive (and, perhaps, informed) observer need only attend to features of the picture itself and not to extrinsic facts about the context in which it was produced.

But it is far from clear that even paintings are intrinsic representations in this sense. At least insofar as the pictorial subject of a painting is ontologically independent of it—an actual person or thing, or a fictional entity originally from a distinct work—the painting cannot be an intrinsic representation: an observer simply cannot tell what a painting is about just by looking at it. As with photographs, an adequate interpretation of such paintings will require attention to contextual features external to them. Hence, paintings and photographs cannot be distinguished in this way.

In David Davies' reading of Scruton, however, the issue is not whether or not the subject of a picture is an intrinsic matter but, rather, whether or not how the subject is represented is an intrinsic matter (Davies 2009: 349). In the case of painting, because the observable properties of the picture are the products of intentional artistic activity, an observer can determine how the subject is represented—both in the sense of what thought is expressed about it and how it is embodied in the medium—just by looking at the painted surface. But in the case of photography, because so much of the detail is the product of the photographed world rather than any intentional activity on the part of the photographer, an observer cannot discern any thoughts the photographer might have wanted to express about the photographic subject by attending to the detail of the photographic image. As a result, unlike paintings, a photograph "can at best be viewed as a 'sign' of the way the photographer thought about her subject, and never as the *artistic expression* of that thought" (Davies 2009: 348).

Even this reconstruction of Scruton, however, fails to show that paintings are representational—or, more specifically, fictionally competent—in a sense in which photographs are not. Painters do not have absolute control over the observable features of their pictures. Not only are they subject to the general constraints of the medium—which vary with the kinds of paints used, the kinds of surfaces to which they are applied, and the methods of paint application deployed—but they are also constrained by the specific limits of their own painterly techniques. As a result, even insofar as how a painted subject is represented is an intrinsic matter—discernible by visual attention to the painted surface—retrieval of this information by looking at a painting requires knowledge of which details were in the control of the painter and, hence, knowledge of both the general and specific constraints to which she was subject. And given information about the analogous constraints under which photographers find themselves, an observer is equally well-placed to discern how a photographic subject is represented simply by looking at a photograph. That is, an observer who is aware of the general constraints of the photographic medium—which, again, vary with the type of camera used, the developing processes used, and the surface on which the photograph is printed—as well as the specific constraints of photographic technique—the range of images particular photographers are capable of producing and, hence, choosing from among—can visually discern any thoughts expressed by photographs in more or less the same sense (and manner) as can a similarly sensitive and informed painting appreciator.

Although I think I have shown that an equal case can be made for the thesis that photographs are intrinsic representations as can be made vis-à-vis paintings, this falls short of showing that either are (or can be) so. As should be clear, what is really at issue in the discussion of intrinsic representation is the essential sense in which pictorial representation is a visual phenomenon—that the representational properties of pictures can be discerned by looking—rather than a semiotic one. And the casting model, by itself, does not guarantee this. After all, someone could choose from a collection of things something merely to stand for some further object. What remains to be done, then, is to supplement the casting model of photographic fiction with an account of pictorial representation more generally which entails that photographic representation is a visual phenomenon.

To this end, a good starting point is Richard Wollheim's amplified minimal requirement:

(i) If a picture represents something, there will be an *appropriate experience* of it that determines that it does so.

(ii) If a *suitable spectator* looks at the picture, he will (all things considered) have this appropriate experience.
(iii) This appropriate experience will be (or include) a visual awareness of the thing represented. (Wollheim 1998: 219)

For reasons adumbrated above, however, I do not believe that in general what a picture represents is either intrinsic to it or can be discerned just by looking. Rather the pictorial subject is a function of the meaning or correct interpretation of the picture. What can be discerned visually, in contrast — and hence, may well be an intrinsic matter — is how the subject is represented. As a result, for present purposes Wollheim's amplified minimal requirement will have to be adapted as follows:

(a) If a picture represents its subject in a certain way there will be an experience of the picture that determines that it does so.
(b) If a suitably sensitive observer looks at the picture, other things being equal, she will have this experience.
(c) This experience will include a visual awareness of how the pictorial subject is represented.

2/ De se *imagining and its discontents*

2.1/ *Seeing through seeing through*
In this section, Kendall Walton's account of pictorial representation is developed and critically evaluated (Walton 1984, 1990, 2008). Although I argue that Walton's views are ultimately unsatisfactory, consideration of them will help situate the alternative defended in the next section. Of particular interest in this first subsection is Walton's thesis of photographic transparency — the view that an observer can literally see an object through a photograph of it (Walton 1984).

Although I do find this thesis tempting, I do not mean to defend it here. It will, however, prove fruitful to frame and motivate the account of pictorial representation on offer here in terms of it. Nevertheless this account does not presuppose transparency: even if photographs are not transparent in Walton's sense, it yields an attractive picture of non-derivative photographic fiction.

As above, photographic transparency is the view that an observer can see something through a photograph. So, for example, when I look at the one remaining photograph of my maternal grandmother in my possession, I thereby literally see her despite the fact that she is long since deceased. It is worth noting that insofar as a photograph is fictional—and, hence, the photographic subject and object are distinct—it is the photographic object, not the subject, which can be seen through it. Walton's thesis is not strictly about the meaning of the word "see"—he is happy to concede that formulating the thesis in terms of seeing may involve a revisionary use of the term (Walton 2008b: 111). Rather, Walton's concern is to flag certain important similarities between the experience of photographs on the one hand and seeing objects directly, as well as through mirrors, microscopes, telescopes, and the like, on the other, which are not shared by the experience of paintings. The content of one's visual experience is counterfactually dependent on the scene that is experienced—what you see depends counterfactually on what you are looking at; similarly, in both photography and painting, the depicted image depends counterfactually on the scene that is painted or photographed. But in the case of photography and seeing—but not painting—this dependence is belief-independent: although what a painting looks like depends on the artist's beliefs about the scene she paints, neither photographic experience nor more familiar kinds of seeing are belief-dependent in this sense.

Walton concedes that photographic seeing through is a species of indirect perception: "I don't mind allowing that we see photographed objects only *indirectly*..." (Walton 1984: 253). What this means is that there are two objects of perception — a direct object and an indirect object — the latter of which is seen only in virtue of seeing the former. In the case at hand, the direct object of perception is the photograph itself and the indirect object is the photographic object — what the photograph is a photograph of; and the photographic object is seen only in virtue of more directly seeing the photograph. It is worth emphasizing that seeing an object by means of a complex causal process does not by itself guarantee that one's perception of it is indirect; unless something which plays a causal role in seeing the object is also (literally) seen, one's perception of the object in question is direct, not indirect. It is also worth noting that seeing one thing through another also does suffice to establish that the perception of the former is indirect. Consider, for example, seeing a child though one's kitchen window. Although one sees both the child and the window, one does not see the child in virtue of seeing the window, but rather despite doing so. Finally, it is worth emphasizing that in order for an object to be indirectly seen by means of (more directly) seeing something else rather than being inferred or otherwise indicated by such means, the direct and indirect objects have to be appropriately related. Exactly what the nature of this relation is has historically been a matter of some controversy. For present purposes, however, I will assume what is minimally required is belief-independent counterfactual dependence of the direct object on the indirect object. Finally, I am going to assume that the objects of direct experience include familiar macroscopic entities such as chairs, trees, and human beings—and not just mental images or sense-data—and that indirect perception is a comparatively rare phenomenon. To my mind, the least controversial example of indirect perception is mirror seeing; hence, I will use that as my model in what follows.

2.2/ Making (believe) your way into photographic worlds

According to Walton's well known theory of artistic representation, representational artworks are props in games of make-believe—rule governed activities whose participants are prescribed to imagine or make-believe various things (Walton 1990). Just as the rules of a sword-fighting game might prescribe imagining *de re* of a stick that it is a sword, the rules governing authorized games in which an art object serves as a prop also prescribe imagining of it that it is thus and so.[7] An important feature of Walton's view, to which we will return later, is that appreciators are reflexive props in the games they play with art objects: not only are they prescribed by the rules of these games to imagine *de re* various things of art objects—as well to imagine *de dicto* various propositions—they are also required to imagine *de se* being and doing various things.

According to Walton's theory of pictorial representation, pictures are props in specific kinds of games of make-believe. What these pictorial games have in common are prescriptions that appreciators both imagine *de re* of their actual experiences of pictures that they are visual experiences of the subjects of those pictures and imagine *de se* seeing those subjects: "[a] picture of a turtle is a prop in games in which viewers imagine seeing a turtle, and imagine their actual visual experience of the

---

[7] Authorized games are those in which it is the function of an art object to serve as a prop (Walton 1990: 72).

picture to be their seeing of a turtle" (Walton 2008a: 275). Hence, although it is not in fact true, it is fictionally true that appreciators see the pictorial subjects of the pictures they observe.[8] It is worth noting that this account of pictorial representation at least arguably satisfies the adapted amplified minimal requirement presented above. After all, having a visual experience of a picture which you imagine to be an experience of the pictorial subject while imagining seeing this same subject seems to involve a kind of visual awareness of both the subject and how it is represented by the picture.[9]

Walton's account of photographic representation in particular can be viewed as a combination of his accounts of pictorial representation in general and photographic transparency. In the case of photographs that are non-fictional, an appreciator actually sees the photographic object indirectly while imagining seeing it directly: "[observing] a family photograph of Judy Garland, one imagines seeing her directly, face to face, while actually seeing her indirectly, via the photograph" (Walton 2008b: 114). An in the case of photographic fiction, an appreciator actually sees the photographic object indirectly, while imagining seeing the fictional photographic subject directly: "[the] viewer of *The Wizard of Oz* imagines seeing Dorothy in the magical kingdom of Oz directly, while actually seeing Judy Garland and movie set via the photographic film" (Walton 2008b: 114). But in addition, as with photographic non-

---

[8] Equivalently, it is true in the worlds of the games they play with pictures that they see their subjects. It is, however, not true in the worlds of the pictures themselves that appreciators exist, let alone that they see anything.

[9] And if Walton is right about what the appreciation of pictorial art consists in, then what it is to be a suitably sensitive observer just is to participate in the imaginative activities at issue.

fiction, the appreciator may imagine seeing the photographic object directly as well: "[so] the spectator may imagine seeing Garland and the movie set face to face, and also imagine seeing Dorothy and the Land of Oz face to face" (Walton 2008b: 115). In effect, on Walton's view, when an appreciator is engaged with photographic fiction, she simultaneously participates in two distinct games of make-believe: one in which she imagines seeing the photographic subject and one in which she imagines seeing the photographic object. Although Walton does not explicitly address the point, one way of simplifying the picture on offer here would be to take the former game to consist in imagining *de re* of the object the appreciator imagines seeing in the latter that it is the subject: rather than participating in an entirely different game from that in which she imagines seeing Garland, the appreciator who imagines seeing Dorothy does so by imagining of Garland that she is Dorothy.

2.3/ You don't (de) se

There are two lines of criticism I wish to raise against Walton's account of pictorial representation here. Since the first objection presupposes the simplification of Walton's view offered above which Walton himself never endorses, it is best formulated as a dilemma. Either Walton accepts the offered simplification of his account of photographic representation or he rejects it. If he rejects it then his view entails that the appreciation of photography involves an unrealistic psychological complexity. Rather than consisting of participation in a single game of make-believe in which an appreciator imagines *de se* seeing the photographic object while imagining *de re* of the object that it is the photographic subject, as the simplification would have it, on this view appreciation involves the simultaneous participation in two distinct and independent games of make-believe—one in which the appreciator imagines *de se* seeing the photographic object, and the other in which she imagines *de se* seeing the subject. And it is far from clear that this is even psychologically possible.[10] But if he accepts the simplification then his view entails photographic appreciators imagine seeing photographic subjects only in virtue of imagining of photographic objects that they are these subjects and, hence, that photographs represent fictional subjects only because their objects represent fictional subjects. As a result, he would be stuck with Scruton's unpalatable conclusion that photography and photo-based cinema are fictional media only in a derivative sense.

The second objection stems from the fact that Walton's account entails that photographic appreciators engage in *de se* imaginings of various kinds and, hence, imaginatively enter into worlds inhabited by fictional photographic subjects. Insofar as you imagine *de se* seeing a fictional subject, you imaginatively co-habit a world with said subject. In my view, however, except in special cases—such as role playing games, first-person shooter video games, theatrical productions involving audience participation, and the like—there is no reason to believe that fiction appreciators generally engage in any kind of *de se* imagining; rather, appreciative phenomena can be wholly explained in terms of imaginative projects requiring only *de re* and *de dicto* imagining of participants (Alward 2006). Moreover, there are grounds for thinking that the supposition that photographic appreciators engage in *de se* imaginings of the kind Walton suggests has unpalatable consequences. Gregory Currie, for example, argues that this

---

[10] It might, of course, be possible to toggle back and forth between the two games, but this suggestion brings with it a whole host of its own problems.

entails that Walton's view entails that given the various perspectives on the action sequential film shots can jump between, a film appreciator who imagines seeing the action from these various locations would have to imagine herself jumping between these perspectives as well (Currie 1995: 172).[11] It also runs afoul of what I call the "problem of the urbane backwoodsman" (Alward, forthcoming). Insofar as a photographic appreciator, who imaginatively enters into a fictional world, feels sympathy for the plight of a fictional co-habitant, we should expect her to desire to intervene on his behalf and experience feelings of frustration at her inability to do so. But as with the experience of jumping between filmic perspectives, this is something we do not commonly find.

3/ Photographic seeing-in and its contents

3.1/ Pictorial fictions as fictional pictures

Before developing a positive account of non-derivative photographic fiction, it will prove fruitful to rehearse the constraints to which, on my view, such an account is subject. First, photographic fiction is a species of pictorial representation and as such is a visual phenomenon. As a result, an adequate theory of photographic fiction will have to satisfy the adapted amplified minimal requirement; hence, it must entail that, other things being equal, the experience of suitably sensitive observers of fictional photographs includes a visual awareness

---

[11] Walton (2008c) rejects Currie's argument by claiming an appreciator can imagine seeing something from one perspective and subsequently imagine seeing it from another without imagining seeing it from the first and the second perspective. Walton's manoeuvre here seems plausible as far as it goes, although it might run afoul of the "transcendental unity of fictional apperception."

of how the fictional photographic subject is represented. Second, photographic fiction involves *de re* but not *de se* imagination: the appreciation of a work of photographic fiction requires imagining *de re* of what you see that it is thus and so but does not require imagining *de se* seeing anything. One of the central concerns of this section is exactly what is this object of *de re* imagination. And third, I will simply be assuming that photographs are transparent—that an observer can literally see the photographic object through a photograph—but that photographic seeing through is a species of indirect perception. Moreover, the natural assumption—which I will be making here—is that the object which mediates our visual awareness of photographic objects in photographic seeing through is the very same object which we imagine *de re* to be thus and so in the experience of photographic fiction.

As a first pass, one might take the object which both mediates photographic seeing through and is the object of *de re* imagination to be the photograph itself. The suggestion that the photograph occupies the former role is relatively straightforward. To treat photographic seeing through as a species of indirect perception is to take it to involve seeing the photographic subject by means of more directly seeing something else. And according to the suggestion on the table, this "something else" just is the photograph itself. The latter suggestion—that the photograph itself is the object of *de re* imagination in the case of photographic fiction—however, requires further comment. After all, to say it is the object of *de re* imagination is one thing, but to say exactly what it is we imagine *de re* of it is another. And the suggestion that we imagine of a photograph that it *is*—in the sense of theatrical identification—the fictional photographic subject is simply a nonstarter.[12] The alternative is to suppose that we imagine *de re* of the photograph that it is *of* the photographic subject, that is, that the actual photographic subject is the pictorial object.[13] Consider, for example, a photograph in fact of Sean Astin portraying Samwise Gamgee. Insofar as this a work of photographic fiction—rather than a photograph documenting Astin's portrayal of Gamgee—then, on the view at issue, appreciation of the photograph as such requires imagining *de re* of it that its pictorial object is the hobbit Sam Gamgee. And it is worth emphasizing that doing so does not require imagining *de re* of Astin that he is Gamgee (or anything else for that matter). As a result, on this picture photographic fiction need not be derivative in Scruton's sense.

As it stands, however, taking the photograph itself to be the object of *de re* imagination in this way is inadequate. The main problem is that it yields a picture of photographic representation which is insufficiently general. In particular, it applies only to cases in which the photograph itself is part of the fiction—a fictional picture of a fictional subject. After all, imagining a photograph to be a picture *of* something requires imagining it to be a picture. And while this is certainly true of some works of photographic fiction—*The Blair Witch Project* is a familiar filmic example—it is hardly true of all such works. In addition, it is not entirely clear that this suggestion satisfies the adapted amplified minimal condition to which we are beholden here.

---

[12] This would be akin to treating fictional photographs as props in theatrical productions in which inanimate objects, rather than actors, occupy the character roles.

[13] It is important that the photographic subject is imagined to be the pictorial object and not the photographic object. After all, there are photographic subjects who occupy fictional worlds which lack photographic technology.

Since there seems to be no requirement that in imagining the seen photograph to be of the photographic subject one must imagine it to be as the actual object there appears, there is no guarantee that the experience of a fictional photographs will involve a visual experience of how the photographic subject is represented.

3.2/ *Mirroring fiction*

The alternative to taking the fictional photograph itself to be the object of *de re* imagination I wish to explore here involves taking instead what is *seen in* the photograph, in (more or less) Wollheim's sense, to play this role. Before considering the phenomenon of photographic—and more generally, pictorial— seeing-in, it will prove fruitful to discuss the more familiar phenomenon of seeing in mirrors. After all, not only are mirrors transparent in sense we are assuming photographs are, mirror seeing is similarly indirect: one sees oneself—or something in one's vicinity—by looking at a mirror only by virtue of more directly seeing something else. And this visually mediating "something else" is neither the mirror itself nor the pattern of lines and colours on the mirror's surface; rather, it is an image one sees in the mirror.

Now, of course, one does not literally see anything in a mirror; after all, there is no "there" there for anything to be in. Instead, seeing an image in a mirror is better understood as a way of experiencing a mirror which is phenomenologically very similar to seeing something behind a window or other mirror-like surface. One might worry, however, that this gloss on images runs afoul of the various roles they are supposed to play in the theory on offer here: as mediators of indirect perception and potential objects of *de re* imagination. After all, both roles seem to require mirror—and photographic—images be entities of some kind which seems to be ruled out by characterizing the experience of seeing images in various media in terms of a kind of experiencing as opposed to an experience of a kind of thing. Although a detailed response to this kind of worry would take us too far afield, there are two strategies worth mentioning here. First, mirror images could be identified with the perceptual contents of what might be called "seeing-images-in" experiences of mirrors. This would, of course, require a theory of perceptual content which does not simply take the contents of such experiences to be the mirrors themselves—or propositions concerning the same. One might, for example, take the contents of such experiences to be non-existent intentional objects or, perhaps, something akin to Fregean senses. Alternately, mirror images could be identified with properties of the mirrors themselves. For example, they might reasonably be identified with the (sometimes fleeting) dispositions of mirrors to produce the relevant kinds of experiences in suitably sensitive and situated observers. Although I do not mean to endorse either strategy, I hope to have shown, at least, that the worry is not an intractable one.

Mirror observers see mirror images. They also thereby see themselves or, perhaps, things in their vicinity. But the images observers see in mirrors are distinct from the observers themselves. Hence, they see themselves and things in their vicinity indirectly by means of seeing images of them. What is also worth noting is that these very same images can be objects of *de re* imagination. One could, of course, imagine of an image of oneself that it is an image of someone else, just as one could imagine of a photograph that it is of someone other than the actual photographic object. But what is of interest here is imagining *de re* of the image itself that it is someone other than oneself—right in front of you or, perhaps, in an alternate reality of some kind. One might, for example, imagine having experiences like those of Alice in Lewis Carroll's *Through the Looking Glass*. And while who you imagine the image to be is not a visual matter, how the subject of some such mirror fiction is represented is something of which you are visually aware. After all, the fictional subject is simply represented as being how you appear (to yourself) in the mirror. Hence, at least in the case of mirror fiction the adapted amplified minimal requirement is satisfied.

3.3/ In through the re *door*
What remains to be done is to adapt the picture of mirror representation developed above to the case of photography. This requires, however, that sense can be made of seeing images in photographs in the same (or a similar) sense in which observers can see images in mirrors. And Wollheim has offered exactly such an account (Wollheim 1987, 1998). According to Wollheim, pictorial seeing-in is a kind of experience—distinguished by a distinctive phenomenology—which is prompted by presence within the visual field of a surface containing a pattern of lines and colours (Wollheim 1987: 46).[14] This experience is characterized by what Wollheim calls "twofoldedness." What this means is it is an experience with two distinguishable but inseparable aspects: one configurational, the other recognitional. The configurational aspect consists of a visual awareness of the pictorial surface and the pattern of shapes and colours upon it. The recognitional aspect, in contrast, consists of an awareness of one thing in

---

14   Wollheim acknowledges that not all "differentiated surfaces" produce this experience but expresses skepticism about the prospects of a general account of what features a surface requires to do so.

front of or behind another: "...I recognize a naked boy, or dancers in mysterious gauze dresses, in front of ... a darker ground" (Wollheim 1987: 46).

My intention here is to simply appropriate Wollheim's account of pictorial seeing-in—but with two caveats. First, Wollheim claims that both particular subjects and general kinds of subjects can be seen in pictures:

> [for] what I see in a surface is subject to precisely the same cross-classification as what a painting represents: objects versus events, and particular objects-or-events versus objects-or-events that are merely of a particular kind. (Wollheim 1987: 71)

On my view, however, only general kinds of subject can be strictly seen in pictures; any particular subject a picture might have is a product of interpretation. After all, given that any picture can be used to represent any subject whatsoever, one would be hard-pressed to claim that the subject in a given case can be discerned by looking. Of course, having an interpretation already in hand when viewing a picture may impact your experience of it; but even in such a case, my inclination is describe this as a case of seeing the photographic image as a particular subject rather than literally seeing the subject in the picture. And second, while Wollheim properly acknowledges that there are typically a plurality of things that can be seen in a representational picture, he claims that the criterion of correctness is determined by the artist's intentions: "...the experience of seeing-in that determines what it represents, or the appropriate experience, is the experience that tallies with the artist's intention" (Wollheim 1998: 226). Although I am willing to concede the point in the case of painting, in the case of photography there seems to be an independent causal standard: the appropriate experience of a photograph involves seeing in it a general subject of the kind (or kinds) of which the photographic object is an instance.[15] Note: in what follows, I will speak of seeing photographic images in photographs; as above, we might identify a photographic image with either the perceptual content of the experience of photographic seeing-in or with the dispositional properties of photographic surface which give rise to it.

The central thesis here is that, in photographic seeing through and photographic fiction, photographic images play the same roles as mirror images play in mirror seeing and fiction. First, insofar as we do literally see objects through photographs, we do so by means of more directly seeing photographic images of such objects in photographs of them. Since, arguably, seeing-in is a species of seeing, observers do literally see photographic images. And insofar as belief-independent counterfactual dependence is sufficient, photographic images and the photographic objects they are images of are appropriately related in order for observers to be able to indirectly see the latter by means of more directly seeing the former. Second, the general thesis regarding photographic fiction is that it is the photographic image—and not the photograph *per se*—that appreciators imagine *de re* to be thus and so in the experience of photographic fiction. More specifically, however, the view is that appreciators imagine of the general photographic images they see in photographs that they are particular fictional subjects. Recall: on the view at issue, what an observer sees in a photograph is a *kind* of thing rather than any particular thing—*a* dog (or dog-image), for

---

[15] In a case in which a photographic artist intends that something else be seen in her photograph, I am inclined to say there are two distinct correct or appropriate experiences both of which are required for a proper appreciation of the picture.

example, rather than any particular dog. And just as one can imagine *de re* of what one sees in a mirror that it is a particular person—perhaps even yourself there in front of you—rather than a general person-image, one can imagine of the general image one sees in a photograph that it is a particular person.

And it is exactly this feature of the account of photographic representation on offer that allows it to satisfy the adapted amplified minimal requirement and, hence, render it visual phenomenon. What an observer sees in a photograph corresponds to both how the photographic object has been presented and how a photographic subject could be represented. By imagining *de re* of a photographic image that it is a particular thing, an appreciator in effect supplies a subject to be represented in that way. Moreover, a similar manoeuvre can be utilized to show how the adapted amplified minimal requirement can be satisfied in cases in which the photograph itself is part of the fiction. Recall: the worry was that there seemed to be no guarantee that in imagining the photograph to be of (rather than about) the photographic subject an observer would imagine it to be as the actual object there appears. But on the view on offer, rather than imagining a *photograph* to be of the photographic subject, a suitably sensitive appreciator imagines of what she sees in the photograph that it is an image of the photographic (or, more generally, pictorial) subject. And hence she imagines of what she sees in the photograph that it corresponds to how the subject appeared when the picture was taken.

4/ Varieties of photographic fiction

Scruton argued that the only sense in which a photograph could count as a work of fiction is in virtue of being of a work of fiction, thus rendering photography and photo-based cinema fictional media in only a derivative sense. While it is of course true that such fictions do exist, there are two other non-derivative varieties of photographic fiction, both of which involve photographic seeing-in. The first includes works in which the photograph itself is part of the fiction. In such cases, appreciators imagine *de re* of what they see in photographs that they are images of photographic subjects. The second and more common variety consists of photographic works in which the photograph itself is not part of the fiction. In such cases, appreciators imagine *de re* of what they see in photographs that they are fictional subjects. But in neither case does the fictional status of the photographic work depend on or even require the fictional status of the actual photographic object.

University of Lethbridge
peter.alward@uleth.ca

REFERENCES

Alward, Peter. 2006. "Leave Me Out of It: *De Re*, but not *De Se*, Imaginative Engagement with Fiction." *Journal of Aesthetics and Art Criticism* 64 (4): 451–60.
— — —. 2012. "Transparent Representation: Photography and the Art of Casting." *Journal of Aesthetics and Art Criticism* 70 (1): 9–17.
— — —. Forthcoming. *Empty Revelations: and Essay on Talk About and Attitudes Toward Fiction*. Montreal: McGill-Queen's University Press.
Currie, Gregory. 1995. *Image and Mind*. Cambridge: Cambridge University Press.
Davies, David. 2009. "Scruton on the Inscrutability of Photographs." *British Journal of Aesthetics* 49 (4): 341–55.
Maynard, Patrick. 1997. *The Engine of Visualization*. London: Cornell University Press.
Philips, Dawn. 2009. "Photography and Causation: Responding to Scruton's Scepticism." *British Journal of Aesthetics* 49 (4): 327–40.

Scruton, Roger. 1981. "Photography and Representation." *Critical Inquiry* 7 (3): 577–603.
Walton, Kendall. 1984. "Transparent Pictures: On the Nature of Photographic Realism." *Critical Inquiry* 11 (2): 246–77.
— — —. 1990. *Mimesis as Make-Believe*. Cambridge: Harvard University Press.
— — —. 2008. *Marvelous Images: On Values and the Arts*, New York–Oxford: Oxford University Press.
— — —. 2008a. "Pictures and Hobby Horses: Make-Believe beyond Childhood." In Walton 2008: 63–79.
— — —. 2008b. "Postscripts to 'Transparent Pictures'. Clarifications and To Do's." In Walton 2008: 110–16.
— — —. 2008c. "On Pictures and Photographs: Objections Answered." In Walton 2008: 117–32.
Wollheim, Richard. 1987. *Painting as an Art*. Priceton: Princeton University Press.
— — —. 1998. "On Pictorial Representation." *Journal of Aesthetics and Art Criticism* 56 (3): 217–26.

MIMESIS AND SHOWING

James R. Hamilton

ABSTRACT: This paper is a study of one way that theories about theater have ignored the actual practices of theater. I start by setting forth a conception of mimesis as "showing", a conception that owes its provenance to Plato. The Platonic account of the mimesis/diegesis distinction is presented, with mimesis construed as showing and diegesis as telling, and two questions regarding it are raised: Is the distinction useful in thinking about the phenomena of theater? And, if not (and it is not), why do so many of us persist in accepting the distinction? My effort is to show that the distinction, as Plato makes it out, is actually in conflict with the very matters it is designed to explain and to explain why the distinction persists among us nonetheless. The second half of the paper presents an alternative conception of theatrical performance that is more nearly faithful to the actual practices of theater. The conception appears to agree with Plato because it relies upon a characterization of theatrical performance as display, or "showing". The conception is, however, fundamentally at odds with Plato's view and a plausible account of the alternative conception reveals there is still work to be done by the term "mimetic", but not the work Plato's view has in mind.

The Greek word *mimêsis* is translated into English in a number of ways: as "imitation", "fiction", "make-believe", "reproduction", "resemblance" and even "representation". The most common translation is "imitation". This raises the question whether there is a properly preferred translation. To avoid taking a position on the scholarly debates about the translation of *mimêsis* in this paper, I will continue to employ the transliteration, *mimêsis*, for the Greek word and provisionally use the English word, "mimesis", i.e., without diacritical markings or translation, for the concept itself. However, I will be exploring the concept under only a few of its possible senses.

Among the alternatives already mentioned, the most popular translations of the term are "imitation" and "resemblance". Those translations seem to be what drive the idea that mimesis is "unpurgeable in performance" (Blau 2007: 97). Another permissible and deeply influential English translation is "showing". In this sense mimesis has long been used as a term to mark off a crucial feature of theatrical performances and dramatic literature. It is primarily this latter sense of "mimesis" and "mimetic" that I will focus upon in this paper.

Accordingly, the focus of this essay, as many readers will readily see, is already well-traveled ground and much of it by my betters. I only hope to demonstrate a small set of points here.

1/ Background

A number of scholarly commentators have suggested that we face two alternatives regarding how to understand the Greek word *mimêsis*. One is that the word is not translatable with exactitude in any of the ways just mentioned. The other is that both Plato and Aristotle used the word inconsistently and, moreover, they each used the word differently. And, of course, both of these alternatives are possible.

For example, in Book III of the *Republic*, Plato treats *mimêsis* as a kind of deception, claiming that Homer gives the reader/hearer the impression it is, for example, Chryses who is speaking and not Homer himself. At 393a he just about defines *mimêsis* as "impersonation", and at 392d he compares it with *diêgêsis,* which is usually translated as "telling". In contrast, in Book X, it is not *mimêsis* as deception that is the root of what is wrong with epic poetry, but rather its very access to the truth, and its importance in teaching. In Book X *mimêsis* seems to mean "imitation", and the back-story developed in Books VI-VIII is that the young are to learn how to behave correctly by imitating good examples. What has to be justified, of course, is that they *are* good examples, and that comes to this: one must know that the sources of the examples are reliable. But poets are not reliable sources about the virtues and vices of the people they tell about. That is, they do not *know* what makes one man virtuous and another vicious. They merely copy them. So, following the examples the poets give is following copies of copies that—so far as the copier (the poet) knows—are mistaken. Thus, the poets and at least epic poetry are not to be trusted.[1]

To illustrate the claim that Plato and Aristotle use the word differently, consider the following. As already noted, in his taxonomy of poetic forms (of different forms of *lexis*), Plato uses the term *mimêsis* in constrast to *diêgêsis*, to mark the differences among various modes of poetry. In contrast, when Aristotle describes the modes of poetry, he only seems to be drawing the same distinction; and a reading that takes him to be making the same contrast appears to be a misreading of Aristotle. Both of the modes of "making" (*poêtikê*) discussed in chapter three of the *Poetics* – the mode (a) in which the poet speaks as another character or in which he speaks as himself, or that (b) in which he represents a character doing something – are forms of *mimêsis* as Aristotle uses that term at 1448a2-24. This is especially obvious if the first two of these are in fact, as the Greek grammar suggests, a single mode (Kosman 1992: 52-53). Perhaps the popular misreading of Aristotle is induced by

---

[1] Woodruff (1992) demonstrates a similar point about Aristotle's inconsistency in using the term.

the desire to see Aristotle as responding directly to Plato who, famously, derided *mimêsis,* at least in Book III of the *Republic,* as a form of deception involving "impersonation" (see Woodruff 1992: 74–76 and 78–80). Moreover, Plato did divide the arts of making into three, only one of which (that in which the poet speaks as another character) involves *mimêsis.*

I am not entirely sure of this explanation. Nor do I rely upon it. Suffice to say, however, that whether this Platonic reading of Aristotle's use of *mimêsis* is mistaken, as I am now convinced it is, the distinction between showing and saying that it has been employed to draw has had an important history. And I do not wish to dispute that distinction in this essay. In fact, it is that very distinction itself — whether Aristotle was marking it or not — that I wish to understand. So, as I understand it, the distinction that will be at the center of our attention in the essay is this:

A mimetic presentation is one that *shows* what it presents; a diegetic presentation is one that *tells* what it presents, where what the latter presents is not necessarily distinct or distinguishable from that which the former presents.

A first question is this: should this distinction give us moral qualms?

Jon Erickson notes (2009: 23) the fact that in contemporary theories of theater "the idea of *mimêsis* is read as an ineluctably Platonic one", that on this Platonic reading of *mimêsis* it is usually taken "to subtend the worst features of exclusionary social and political practices in the West", and that "the category of truth is undermined by the apparent subversion of this Platonic idea of *mimêsis.*" His use of the word "apparent" suggests that Erickson is not on board with some elements of this way of thinking. And in fact, he rejects the whole package.

But this quite prominent way of thinking about *mimêsis* is instructive for several reasons. So, let us rehearse it.

As Plato uses it in Book III of the *Republic*, a mimetic presentation is non-narrative and a diegetic presentation is narrative (because it involves a narrator speaking in her own voice). Secondly, mimesis yields theatre, while diegesis yields non-theatrical presentations. So, we have this pair of alignments:

(a) mimesis (showing) ≡ non-narrating (yielding non-narratives) ≡ theater;
(b) diegesis (telling) ≡ narrating (yielding narratives) ≡ literature (or at least non-theatrical presentations).

I will demonstrate in the next two sections of this paper that this set of alignments, whether or not it is morally compromised, is simply mistaken. I will also speculate as to what might still be driving this mistaken view. And, although prehending from the moral/political issue, I will attempt to arrive at one explanation for its persistence.

The following two sections of the paper demonstrate the continued need for a distinction that allows for some performances to be regarded as properly mimetic and others as non-mimetic. The distinction will not be explicable in terms of the Platonic concept because the comparison class is not that of presentations that tell, but rather of a particular class of elements shown in a performance. I will also show why the justification for the distinction lies within the critical practices of both performers and spectators to any theatrical performance.

In the final section, I briefly present and assess an interesting line of objection to the view I have adopted and proposed in this paper.

2/ Theatrical performances

In pursuing the first task of the paper, I present a sketch of theatrical practices, focusing on the reception of performances and the practical distinction between narrative and non-narrative theatrical performances.[2] The sketch benefits from using practices within Western Europe's avant-garde theatrical traditions that are recognizable analogs of theatrical practices outside of Western Europe.

If we cast the net of what counts as theater widely enough—so as to include much of what goes on in cultures other than our own and to include important developments in our own theatrical avant-garde—we shall arrive at two surprising results. Against that background, the showing/telling distinction yields a picture that is in two ways significantly different from that to which we have become accustomed by accepting Plato's distinction.

2.1/ Grasping any theatrical performance – a basic sketch

Spectators grasp whatever it is that they get from and about a theatrical performance largely by attending to performers during their performances. Attending to performers always involves watching for signs of their states and actions and being physically ready to react, where those reactions themselves are frequently also physical. In some cases the attention involved may take the form of empathic reactions. But *if* there is empathy in *this* attention, it is with performers, not with characters.

Performers, in their turn, draw attention to some features of themselves—and attempt to remove focus from others—so that, if attended to, spectators will grasp that which the

---

[2] Parts of this section were first developed for inclusion in Hamilton (2007) and Hamilton (2009b).

performers intend them to grasp. This is an extremely brief statement of what performers do, of course. But thinking of performers as choosing which features of themselves to present is a good place to start.[3]

For, in contrast, even though one has to learn to watch actors, much of the "attending to" that spectators do is unlearned. Spectators must learn to respond to performers *qua* performers, but their learned responses recruit a variety of unlearned dispositions to respond and unlearned and automatic response mechanisms.

How do most spectators usually go on with the attention they pay to performers? The short answer is that they build a representation of the object of the performance. They do this by projecting the object from the features performers have chosen to display to them. If, for example, it is a narrative performance, the object they build will be a story. That is, they will come to be able to tell the story presented to them. But what if it is not a narrative performance?

2.2/ Non-narrative theatrical performances
What is a non-narrative theatrical performance? For those accustomed mainly to mainstream Western European theater, some examples can help.

Consider first what happens when Curly McClain enters singing "Oh what a beautiful morning" in the musical theater

---

[3] Performers can fail in a variety of ways to bring it off that spectators will track what they intend them to grasp. And some complications arise from the fact that the routines performers develop are difficult and exacting. We should also add that performers will react physically to the attention of spectators and, so, they must choose how to display those reactions, if at all. These facts bring out all the more vividly that performing requires discipline and focused attention.

show *Oklahoma!* (Rogers and Hammerstein 1944). This was an early "book musical" in which songs and dances are fully integrated into a "well-made" plot (Sears and Riis 2002: 137). Nevertheless, and certainly by now, it is a rare spectator who thinks of this song as contributing to the plot of the play. Rather, the plot feels suspended at this moment for the sake of the song. Think of this as a non-narrative moment in an otherwise narrative theatrical performance. It is familiar even to those accustomed to a diet of mostly narrative performances.

Similarly, Bertolt Brecht famously used songs and other theatrical means to "distance" spectators from narratives, seeking thereby to undermine various effects of what he regarded as a growing and pernicious dominance of narrative in theater (Hamilton 1982). These are moments again, but not *mere* moments, because they affect whether the resulting performance is genuinely narrative or the degree to which a performance possesses "narrativity" (Carroll 2001; Currie and Jureidini 2004).

Further along in the same direction, Samuel Beckett employed vaudeville routines to entertain while no story was unfolding in his very first play, *Waiting for Godot* (1948/1954). And his late plays—for example, *Not I* (1973), *That Time* (1976), *Footfalls* (1976)—only suggest underlying narratives but neither present nor even always refer to them. And, finally, consider Gertrude Stein's short play, *WHAT HAPPENED. A Play in Five Acts.* Here is how the play begins:

ACT ONE
(one)
Loud and no cataract. Not any nuisance is depressing.
(five)
A single sum four and five together and one, not any sun a clear signal and an exchange.
  Silence is in blessing and chasing and coincidences being ripe. A simple melancholy clearly precious and on the surface and mixed

> strangely. A vegetable window and clearly and most clearly an exchange in parts and complete.
> A tiger a rapt and surrounded overcoat securely arranged with spots old enough to be thought useful and witty quite witty in a secret and in a blinding flurry. (Stein 1922/1993: 205)

Whatever you imagine when considering how this bit and the rest of the play might look and sound like in performance, in this final example we have moved beyond non-narrative *moments* within narrative performances to *full-on* non-narrative performances.

These samples are taken from fairly recent Western theater and to varying degrees they are exceptions within it. But the examples are instructive because they reflect what many standard and unexceptional examples of theater are like in the rest of the world (Beeman 1993; Edgar 2009: 65; Zarrilli et al. 2006: 18 and 24). So, even if characters are not present in anything like the ways they are in narrative performances, nevertheless, events, images, and objects do appear, need to be picked out and recognized as the same later in any performance. Presumably, the mechanisms by which this happens in all theatrical performances will be the same.

What is different is both the nature of the performance and the correlative non-narrative structure "built" by spectators. That structure might more nearly resemble the presentation of a sonata than that of a novel, or more like that of a poem than that of a short-story. But, if spectators are watching a narrative performance, the object they build will be the presentation of a story. But what is a story?

2.3/ "Stories" and narrative theatrical performances
The characterization of stories that we need for the purposes of understanding narrative theatrical performances must be weak

enough that it does not preclude clear examples of narrative performances that happen to possess richer structures. For example, we need not insist a story must have a beginning, middle, and end, at least if coming to an end entails full-stop closure. Nor should we insist—as Aristotle may have done—that it set forth a causal chain leading from the first events to the last. Nor should we demand that a story set forth a sequence of events a description of which seems to organize and explain the solution to some sort of problem (Brook 1984; Livingston 1999). There are three reasons for allowing greater latitude about what counts as a story.

One general reason is that there is so little theoretical agreement on what a proper account of narrative looks like. As Paisley Livingston remarks,

> Theorists arguing for a favored usage of "narrative" typically appeal to our "intuitions" concerning which examples should and should not count as a story. It is far from clear, however, that any detailed and coherent bed of intuitions awaits any of the theories. (Livingston 1999: 277)

Another reason is that performers may choose to present a narrative in a way that goes against the grain of an audience's richer expectations regarding stories. The performers could have a view about what particular narrative structure they wish the performance to achieve and that may be a view they take explicitly in recognition of and despite the richer expectations they anticipate their audiences will have. This is the sort of thing performers of pieces influenced by Bertolt Brecht might seek to achieve if they know their audience is expecting a Naturalistic performance. We should not foreclose on those performance strategies by adopting a richer conception of narrative structure. We want an account of narratives that allows for unanticipated kinds of things to count as narratives.

The most important reason for adopting a weak characterization of what counts as narrative is that it leaves room for audiences to discuss and debate which rich narrative structure a performance has actually displayed. The ability to have that kind of discussion would seem to be crucial to whatever account we come to give of audience appreciation of theatrical performances. Insisting on a rich conception of narrative could preclude exactly these kinds of discussion.

On the other hand, the characterization of narrative must be strong enough to allow us to make meaningful the distinction between narrative and non-narrative performances. The question is how to get enough into the characterization to allow this without putting too much into it.

For example, although many narratives have structures that might induce a feeling of directionality, cases of non-narrative theatrical performances may easily give us the same feel. Consider the structures of Mabou Mines' *The Gospel at Colonus* (1985) and Peter Handke's *Self-Accusation* (1966).

Lee Breuer of Mabou Mines structured *The Gospel at Colonus* by using a musical or visual analog of the classic structure of problem-development-climax-denouement for organizing the sequence of images developed by the company while reflecting on Sophocles' text of the same name. The company blended that structure with the call-and-response ecstatic singing structure employed by the Alabama Blind Boys who, along with the Chancel Choir of the Abyssinian Baptist Church in Harlem, collectively portrayed Oedipus. We could think of that company as aiming at creating the tension and release patterns characteristic of narrative theater but without (very much of) the narrative (Fischer 2011).

James R. Hamilton

In the preface to his *Sprechstücke*, of which *Self-Accusation* is one, Handke informs any performing company to adopt musical forms such as theme and variations, classical ABA sonata form, or forms of popular music discovered by listening to the Beatles and watching *A Hard Day's Night*, or forms of sound they learn by listening to trains arriving and leaving a station. He then instructs companies to rehearse with the aim of creating the kind of a sonic experience one gets from music (Handke 1966).

Neither of these performances will have had a clearly narrative structure, but each has a structure that is likely to give auditors a feeling of directionality and momentum.

Nor do we want to adopt a characterization of narratives in which causal connections within sequences of events constitutes a sufficient condition for a narrative. Were we to do so, any presented sequence of events having any sort of explicit and effective causal structure would be a narrative and we would be committed to holding that many performances we take to be paradigmatically non-narrative would be narrative theatrical performances after all (Velleman 2003). And we would lose the very distinction we are trying to sort out.

But we are on the right track. For this much seems right: most stories have agents whose actions and changing traits together constitute whatever movement or lack of movement the story possesses. This is enough to get us a generous, but precise, idea of "a story" that we can use in discussing narrative performances.

Accordingly, I propose we provisionally adopt the following: a story—the telling of which demonstrates a spectator possesses basic understanding of a play—is the presentation of a series of events where the events are either the actions or inactions of agents or are the results of the actions or inactions of agents (Currie and Juriedini 2004; Currie 2006).[4]

Accordingly, just as events, images, and objects appear, need to be picked out and recognized as the same later in a non-narrative performance, so also agents and their doings and non-doings need to be picked out and recognized later as the same agents in a narrative performance. Presumably, again, the mechanisms by which this happens in all theatrical performances will be the same.

What is different is, first, what is made salient in the performance, and second, the correlative narrative structure "built" by spectators. And accordingly, if spectators are watching a narrative performance, the object they build will be a story.[5]

This sketch of theater practices, broad enough in scope to capture practices outside our own culture, shows that Plato seems to have gotten the whole business wrong, and in two ways. First he incorrectly thought that mimesis tracks non-narratives and diegesis tracks narratives. And he also seems to have thought that, incorrectly, mimesis (as showing) tracks the theatrical while diegesis (as telling) tracks the non-theatrical.

Both of these are wrong. There are clear instances of mimetic behavior (showing behavior) in non-narratives. Moreover, there are also clear instances of diegetical behavior (telling behavior) in theatrical performances.

---

[4] Currie and Juriedini (2004), as will the later Currie (2006), develop a somewhat similar account. The focus of much of that work is the defense of the idea that "narrativity" is a graded term, in contrast to more categorical analyses of the concept of a "narrative connection" (Carroll, 2001). I do not take a stand on that issue here.

[5] This account is modeled on that given in Hamilton (2007: ch. 4).

It is tempting here to point out that, in most performances, much of the time spent by characters presented in a narrative theatrical performance involves them "diegetically" telling *their* stories. They do not enact them. So it is even with Oedipus. But this is an irrelevant consideration here since it is not the behavior of the characters that is at issue at this point, but the presentation of those characters in the performance by performers. It is the latter that is supposed to be mimetic rather than diegetic. But that is also not always so.

Brechtian theater practice alone would provide sufficient examples to prove that point. But perhaps an even clearer example is Spalding Gray's *Swimming to Cambodia*, in which Gray, alone on the stage with a table, a glass of water, and some devices that enabled him to show film clips and slides, tells the tale, among others, of his part in the making of the movie *The Killing Fields*. Perhaps it was because this was staged in the Performing Garage, but more likely simply because it could hardly be mistaken as anything but theater, that it makes clear how little use the idea of mimesis is here. A second relevant example is given in this description:

> You could argue that a play written in the author's narrative voice, like David Hare's one-person, self-performed *Via Dolorosa*, is essentially diegetic, as are those verbatim plays that employ direct quotation. (Edgar 2009: 65)

What exactly has gone wrong in Plato's account? Is it that he has construed what he calls mimesis and diegesis too narrowly? Is it that he has, as the foregoing seems to show, just gotten the whole business *exactly* wrong? As we shall see, the story is more complicated.

3/ "The classic picture" of theatrical performance

One thing that appears to continue driving an acceptance of Plato's mimesis/diegesis distinction is what I will call "the classic picture" of theatrical performances, derived from reflection on the genuine importance of the literary tradition in theatrical production. That importance, however, stems from the success of the local contents of literary theater, not from the nature of theater itself (Hamilton 2009a and 2007: 3-22). Instead, in this section, I present a contrasting characterization, beginning with phenomena about performance, that gets us the story we need and analyzes all performance, including theatrical performances, as a kind of showing.

Moreover, this contrasting characterization divides the narrative from the non-narrative in performance (within what is shown) by reference not to the writing of the piece and the voice of the author but by reference to what spectators undertake to present by way of demonstrating they have understood a performance. (If spectators tell a story, the performance is/was narrative. If they relate a sequence of images or other objects developed in the performance — even if those are thematically or even causally related to each other — the performance is/was not narrative.)

The "classic picture" is associated with the literary theatrical tradition of late European culture. The features of that picture are the following:

(a) Playwrights have stories to tell that on principle they could tell in their own voices.
(b) But they choose instead to present those stories by dramatic writing, writing that shows rather than tells the stories, that is, writing that has characters speak, rather than writing in which the playwrights tell their stories themselves.

(c) Theatrical performances are then instances of "fleshing out" the showing of a story.

The classical picture matches up well with the practice of theater within the Western literary tradition of theater and is fully consistent with the Platonic division between mimesis and diegesis.[6]

In contrast, if we broaden our conception of theater to include theater that is done in the rest of the world, as well as theater that has been developed in the European theatrical avant-garde, we get an empirically more adequate picture that looks like the following:

(a) Theatrical performances are narrative, non-narrative, or mixed.
(b) If narrative, they present information in patterns that are presented and received as having the nature and structure of stories. If non-narrative, they present information in patterns that are presented and received as having the nature and structure of image sequences, or the sequences of notes or movements, musical or dance phrases, rhythms, and so on, or patterns based on other forms of human behavior and interaction.
(c) Writing that is done for theatrical performances is done for the purpose of assisting in forming the pattern presented in the performance and recording those elements that are crucial to a successful repetition or reproduction of the performance (Hamilton 2009a).

---

[6] Moreover, as the former has come under attack for its ideological commitments, so too has the latter, rightly or wrongly.

Mimesis and Showing

In light of this empirically more adequate picture of theatrical performance, the Platonic mimesis/diegesis distinction is seen to be at best orthogonal to the practices we had wished it to help us explain and at worst utterly beside the point. Understood on the classic picture, Plato's distinction predicts that narrative (because it employs a narrator, real or implied) *tells* a story and that theater in which a story will be *shown* is non-narrative. But what we have seen in the previous section is that, in actual practice, non-narrative theater eschews the presentation of stories altogether. Narrative theater presents stories. And, whether either form of performance is conducted by showing or can also be done by telling is left completely undetermined.

The contrast of the two pictures, then, allows us to see more precisely what is wrong with Plato's deployment of the mimesis/diegesis distinction. The important comparison classes that need to be explained are these:

(A) performance versus writing,
(B) narrative versus non-narrative performances, and
(C) mimetic versus non-mimetic practices.

Plato attempted to explain both (A) and (B) by means of (C), taking the latter to be a distinction between showing and telling. He mistakenly assumed that (A) and (B) referred to the same comparison classes. But they do not. Further, (A) cannot be explained by his interpretation of (C) because performances may — and often do — involve both "showing behavior" and "telling behavior". And (B), likewise, cannot be explained in that way because both narrative and non-narrative theatrical performances may involve showing behavior and telling behavior.

I will argue in a later section that this thesis, insofar as it appears to abandon (C) altogether, is too quick and that, suitably understood, theatrical performances involve a different distinction, one that we actually employ in thinking about performances we have seen, one that allows us to express important differences between some performances and others, and one that seems fair to regard as a distinction between mimetic and non-mimetic performances.

To get a handle on this and move forward, I now turn to what "showing" is when it is done in a theatrical performance.

4/ What "showing" is

In the next two sections, we take a step back and take another run at the issues. For we still need a distinction—to capture, for example, Brecht-like theatrical practices, in which actors display both what their characters do and say, for example, and what the actors themselves think about what the characters do and say.[7] I doubt the distinction falls within the range of what Plato was after with his idea of the showing/telling distinction. But, whether or not that is the case, the distinction we need, which can be fairly labeled a distinction between mimetic and non-mimetic performance, is a distinction between showing what is done and said as well as a showing of how it is done and said, on the one hand, and a kind of *critical* showing of how it is done and how it is said, on the other.

---

[7] It is a completely separate question, and one about which I venture no view here, whether Brecht could have succeeded by these means in achieving the sort of political or politically aware theater he was after. The contrast is still important, even if only because it helps mark a distinction between pre-Naturalist and Naturalist theater.

Mimesis and Showing

The "step back" referred to just now consists in developing a fuller picture of what theatrical performance consists in, based upon the metaphor of theater as "showing".

4.1/ An information-transfer account of theatrical performances
In this section, I sketch the idea of performers showing—displaying—the features of characters (and other objects) they portray. To develop the sketch, I ask you to consider three explanations of the importance of the performer.

On the first, performers are important because they the sources of power in theatrical performances (Chaikin 1993). On the second, performers are important because they are sometimes the source of the contents of performances (Davies 2011: 149-164). Much that is illuminating can, and has been, said regarding these explanations of the importance of performers. The view I now present you, however, is more general (more inclusive) than either of these, less mystifying than the first, and begging fewer ontological questions than the second. On this view, performers are important because they are the sources of whatever information is transferred in a performance to any spectator. And it is this view I now sketch for you.

The view owes its provenance to the work of early theorists in performance studies (Schechner 1988; Schechner and Turner 1985; Kirschenblatt-Gimblet 1976; and others to be found in Bial 2007). Like those views, it finds the ontogenetic base of performance, including theatrical performance, revealed by important ethnological and anthropological studies of the 1960s and 1970s (Lorenz 1966; Huxley 1964; Goodall 1971; Goffman 1961, 1963, 1974; Geertz 1973, 1974). As such, it relies on conceptions of "information" and "information transfer" that do not privilege the occurrent intentions of performers but rather focus upon the publicly available information in the signals performers produce. Unlike those early performance theories, however, the view is not prescriptive, nor does it regard early forms of performance as more authentic than later forms. The fact that our ancestral performers, human and non-human, displayed information (signals) in ritualized behaviors and pursued various ends having to do with power relationships, gods, demons, rites of passage, and so forth, does not entail one should return to performing rituals or performances about gods, for example, in order to perform authentically. If the view is right, the performances of plays in the literary tradition are also displays in the same sense as those others and analyzable *qua* displays in much the same ways as early human rituals or ant and chimpanzee displays.[8]

The idea of theatrical performances as information systems has excited one novel form of rejection, in a recent article, due to the way it is espoused by one of mainstream theater's current darling playwrights. Tom Stoppard, the playwright in question, opined in a number of interviews in 2007 (Singer 2007) that the key for the playwright is to dispense information at the right time, to control the flow of information. In response, Jeff Jones (2007) correctly grasped that one consequence of Stoppard's presentation of the view is that spectators become blind to other forms of theater in which information is not controlled by playwrights. Jones confuses his correct objection with the more general position that theatrical performances are simply not information transfer systems. He is right to object to Stoppard's formulation; he is wrong about performance.

---

[8] One important and influential way to think about how signal theory can contribute to theories underlying the kind of analysis I am giving is found in Dretske (1999: ch. 2).

4.2/ Demonstration, display, acting

On another occasion (Hamilton 2009b), I argued in some detail that the display theory has important, probably even decisive, advantages over at least a behavioral version of the pretense theory of acting. In particular, it is able to resolve a suite of problems about the nature of acting that one has to strain to solve, often by extraneous stipulation, on the pretense view.[9] Among those advantages are that it yields the better story about each of the following desiderata of an adequate theory of theatrical performance:

— What is the ontogenetic base of the behavior called "acting"?
— How do performers determine who does/says what, when, and how?
— Why does an actor say the next line or do the next thing prescribed in a script?
— Why are the construction principles employed in developing a performance spectator-centered?
— In what does theatrical portrayal (acting) consist and how is it different from not-acting? (see Kirby 1972)

---

[9] The "pretense theory" of acting is, roughly, that actors in theatrical performances are pretending to be the characters they portray, doing and saying things that count as the doings and sayings of their characters. The view rests on a natural ontogenetic story, namely, that acting grows out of ordinary games of pretense, the playing of which is ubiquitous in the species. That, and the fact it gets the right story for most of the mental states of performers, gives it real purchase among contemporary philosophers interested in the mental mechanisms that, for at least the last 50,000 years or so, have made art-making and art-reception possible in human beings. I think the make-believe story about mental states comes apart from the pretense story about the behavior we call "acting". The former might possibly be true or on the right track, even about acting: the latter is what I have shown to be false.

— Why do narrative performances typically involve particular characters?
— Why does something an actor does/says count as a different thing a character does/says?
— What accounts for portrayal-failure?
— How do we account for those many elements of performances that are non-imitative or non-resembling, or partially so?
— What role do conventions play in constructing and in receiving performances?
— How do conventions with subdoxastic elements function and how are they appreciated? (see Hamilton 2007: 75–78)
— What is the right story about the mental states of performers?

Some elements of this display theory are relevant to the present paper, and so I rehearse them for you briefly.

First, elements of the display theory resemble parts of several recent analyses of demonstration, analyses that were crafted in the service of theories of quotation. Although it is not part of my project to endorse or argue for a particular theory of quotation, we can exploit these resemblances to get started.

Consider two cases used to suggest a demonstrative theory of indirect discourse, of saying *that*. Heal's (2001) is a case of showing someone how a tune goes. Récanati's (2001) is a case of showing someone the particular way in which his sister, Elizabeth, drinks tea. Similar examples have been deployed in discussing demonstrative theories of *direct* discourse as well, by Herbert H. Clark and Richard J. Gerrig (1990), Paul Saka (1998, 2005, 2006), and Douglas Patterson (2005). The details of these positions, and most of the differences among them, are not relevant here. I am using these investigations only as jumping-off points for showing how a display theory of acting can be developed.

Imagine Angela telling you about a conversation she overheard between two actors who Angela designates "He" and "She". Angela reports the conversation thusly: "He said, 'I'm going to play Gertrude', and she went {*eyes rolling accompanied by a barely articulate gurgle*}."[10] Patterson claims that in such cases there is *no* difference between the references; for, he observes, in neither case is there reference to words. That is, he urges, we may safely ignore the Davidsonian thought that what is referred to must be something *linguistic* (Davidson 1979). Instead, both references can be construed as references to behavior that is immediately displayed. Whether or not Patterson is right about quotation,[11] his claim provides us with an important heuristic device for understanding what goes on in theatrical performances.

So here is a crude starting place: we might think of the institution of theater as functioning like the matrix of a quotation, where quotation is demonstratively understood and where demonstration is understood to be conducted by means of behavioral display. People who go to the theater recognize it is a place of demonstration (or, if you like, of presentation); stories are often presented there; and this just means that, on many particular occasions, one or more performers will demonstrate how a particular story goes.

---

[10] I adopt Heal's (2001) convention of putting descriptions of the relevant non-linguistic behavior in brackets {}.

[11] Ultimately, as I understand it, Patterson's argument depends on an analysis of Davidson's reasons for thinking the interior material in a quotation has to be compositional. But Patterson's reasons for rejecting compositionality "all the way down", so to speak, are beyond the scope of this paper.

Second, if anyone engages in display behavior, there is always a context consisting of those for whom the display is constructed. This is an inherent fact about the general kind of behavior that acting is said, on the display theory, to be a species. Acting is that form of display in which a performer portrays a person—often, but not necessarily, distinct from herself. She does this by selection of her own features (both what is to be seen and heard, and what is to be hidden) and thereby presents many of the features of that person, called "*her character*" (Hamilton 1982, 2004, 2007). An interesting and immediate consequence of this view is that the sincerity of the actor's wish that her audience grasp the content in what she presents is readable directly from the fact she intends to display that content.

Third, how do we explain what actors do when they engage in non-imitative or resembling or only partially imitative or resembling display? For example, suppose a killing is presented this way: actor A makes gestures imitative or resembling of slashing with a sword, while actor B makes moves imitative or resembling of being cut (and then collapses). Simultaneously, however, actor C makes the sounds of being cut, actor D makes the sounds of a sword swishing through the air and cutting through flesh, while actor E wails a brief dirge. Imagine they are standing two meters apart from each other, arrayed across the stage. This is one way a company may portray a killing.

Think of this kind of staging as analogous to the following. You ask me "What did the judge say?" and I go "eehhhh {while jerking my thumb in a gesture of dismissal}."[12] I do not imitate the judge. The judge did not *say* what I said. The judge did not *do* what I did. I may, in short, never have

---

[12] I owe the example to Doug Patterson.

imitated anything the judge has done, nor need my behavior resemble anything he did or would do. Nevertheless, I may have conveyed to you — displayed to you — what the judge said and did.

Fourth, to provide a further analysis of display, we might do worse than to borrow some of the apparatus Nelson Goodman employed (Goodman 1968: 52-57) in discussing "exemplification". To exemplify is to make prominent certain features of a putative sample that are the relevant features for demonstrating the target information to another person, for example a tailor's swatch of cloth.[13] More precisely, to exemplify is both to present names or labels of selected properties that the target has and to make some sort of reference to them. What governs the selection of a swatch of fabric, for example, is often just the fact the other person is interested only in certain features of the swatch and not others — the color and texture as opposed to the size — because the other person is interested in how the fabric will look when it covers her sofa. But, as Mary Sirridge (1980: 392) points out, the size may well be the very feature selected and exemplified in the context of a school for tailors. The selection of features is, then, context dependent, just as the features of samples in indirect discourse are. The fact of context-dependency is also what explains how I might succeed in conveying to you what the judge said and did by going "eehhhh {while jerking my thumb in a gesture of dismissal}".

There is no important difference between the appeal to relevant contextual information in order to explain the conveyance of information in the case of reporting what the judge said and the appeal to contextual information to explain

---

[13] This is a favored example of Goodman's and of many commentators on the passage cited above.

how our four or five performers convey that a killing is taking place. Each will misfire if either the performer has chosen only putatively relevant features for exemplification or of the audience is insufficiently prepared or knowledgeable about how the information is being conveyed.

Contextual resolution of which features are relevant to a given act of exemplification does break down in some circumstances, to be sure. When exemplification is aimed at abstractions that are put in place to facilitate communication rather than being aimed at presentations to facilitate, say, contemplation, the problem of which features are relevant—what generates the relevant sample of features—is particularly pressing (Zillman 2009: 74). In that kind of circumstance a favored, although disputed, solution is

> to attach quantitative information to specific exemplars. The typicality of particular occurrences within a group of events would be defined in frequencies or proportions. (Zillman 2009: 77)

Since we are discussing a very different use to which exemplification is put, it is not clear we need to resolve this, especially not in that way. In those cases it seems plausible that establishing prior purposes suffices, despite the fact that mistakes are possible (and in amateur performances, very likely).

Finally, we might wonder whether the view I propose here does not ignore an obvious fact. The worry may be put this way: "But do theatrical performances not also express *meanings* in addition to transferring information?" And of course they do. But, whereas a Platonic account of mimesis—either as imitation, resemblance, or showing—has exactly the same problem with no solution in view, in following Goodman we do at least have an answer to this worry. Moreover, the answer stresses an already noted important benefit of the information-transfer view, namely that what is presented in a performance is not constrained by intentionalist concerns about the particular reasons performers have for what they present. As Mary Sirridge (1980) put the point,

> What an object exemplifies or expresses is ... for Goodman a matter of which of a contextually determined range of names or labels apply to or denote it literally *or metaphorically*. On Goodman's account, then, neither expression nor exemplification is tied to any kind of act on the part of a producer. Nor is expression restricted a priori to any special group of expressibles. (Sirridge 1980: 392; emphasis added)

This natively plausible approach puts crucial elements of success conditions for theatrical performances squarely where they belong—in the reception of spectators. And it provides, as we shall shortly see, a fairly direct solution to the remaining puzzle regarding how to think of mimetic performances as distinguishable from the non-mimetic ones.

5/ Mimetic display

Earlier I remarked that, given an empirically adequate account of theatrical performance, the showing/telling distinction seems entirely orthogonal to the non-narrative/narrative distinction. For on that broader and more adequate picture, all theatrical performances are cases of showing. But we can now see why that was not sufficiently nuanced.

If we take all theatrical performances as cases of demonstration or display, then all performances *are* cases of showing. But there is still the issue of *what* is shown and *how* it is shown. Reflection on two examples helps us see the point.

— I might demonstrate to someone how the Beatles' song "She loves me" goes by playing the score on a piano, whistling it, or simply by singing the lyrics.
— I might demonstrate to someone how the Gettysburg Address goes by reciting it.

But in each case, I may *also* show someone what *I* think of the thing I am demonstrating to them. So, we actually have another pair of examples to consider.

— If I am demonstrating to you the Beatles' song I might sing "yeah-yeah-yeah" in a derisive tone. And, in doing so, I may deride the Beatles, or that song, or pop music in general. Or I might do so in a context in which it is clear that I am for some reason deriding *you*, the person to whom I am demonstrating how that song goes.
— I might recite the Gettysburg Address in explicit tones of awe, attempting to suggest to my audience that I think they should feel its profundity (or that they should feel the silliness and vapidity of words being said over the dead).

And a crucial final example is this: an actor might demonstrate to someone how Hamlet behaves by various acts of display, including saying what he is called upon or prescribed to say in Shakespeare's script for the play. And in thereby presenting a portrayal of Hamlet, an actor might *also* try to say the words or do the deeds prescribed in the script for Hamlet in a manner that allows for the audience to think about whether Hamlet made the right decision, for example, in the scene in which Hamlet chooses not to kill Claudius.

Thus there appears room, even a requirement, for a distinction between those displays or portrayals in which the performer reveals her own stance with respect to what is being displayed or portrayed and those in which she does not. If I understand how most scholars have wished to use the notion of mimesis—and of course I may not—it would appear they are referring to something like the latter kind of case.

That is, on a standard critical appraisal of a performance it is more likely to be called "mimetic" if the performers stance regarding what she is presenting is hidden from the spectator's view. And it is more likely to be called "non-mimetic" if her stance or viewpoint is not so hidden. Thus the view, in brief, is this:

—Mimetic performances are those in which performer's own stances towards what it is they present are rendered invisible to spectators.
—Non-mimetic performances are those in which performers' own stances towards what it is they present are allowed (or made) to be visible to spectators.

If this way of drawing the distinction is right, there are three things of note about it. First, what counts as mimetic is not encompassed by performance (where the comparison class is writing). Second, what counts as mimetic is not encompassed by narrative performance (where the comparison class is non-narrative performance). And finally, what counts as mimetic is not identical to showing (where the comparison class is telling). The correct account of the mimesis/non-mimesis distinction lies in a different direction altogether.

6/ A final thought
At the outset I remarked that among the alternative translations of *mimesis*, the most popular are "imitation" and

"resemblance". Those translations seem to be what drive the idea that mimesis is "unpurgeable in performance" (Blau 2007: 97) and the suspicion there is something especially problematic about theatrical performance.

One burden of this paper has been to show that, suitably understood, theatrical performance *is* a species of showing. It follows trivially that showing, understood as display, is "unpurgeable in performance".

But that is not true for mimesis and the mimetic, as I have sketched them out in the previous section. Nor is it true for imitation and resemblance. Those *are* purgeable in performance.

However, there is a consideration that seems to cut against this view. I turn to that now. In an essay cited earlier, Jon Erickson tells this little story:

> Years ago I discovered in the process of playing with my baby daughter, that is, when I made the faces she was making back at her, or when I made sounds that she made back again to me, that I sometimes encountered a problem of interpretation. That is, I believed that I was engaging in simple mimesis, mimicking her sounds, so that it would encourage her to make more, and it would seem as if we were actually engaged in a kind of conversation. But I also noticed that at certain points, I felt as if she might be experiencing my mimicry as mockery, and was not always clear when it appeared to her I had crossed a line. ... [E]ven when she was making happy sounds, the *insistence* with which I made those sounds back at her ... was perhaps taken as something aggressive. (Erickson 2009: 27; emphasis in original)

From this story, Erickson says we might draw the following conclusions: (a) it is not clear where the line between mimicry and mockery is nor how we are to draw that line; (b) it is not clear what it is in "the context of reception" that causes the blurring of the line to occur; (c) it is clear that "there can be no perfect intentional control over this interpretation"; and (d) since mockery involves not taking the agent at her word, the difficulty we have with drawing the line between mimicry and mockery entails that mimicry is committed to the "fictive", that is, the falsifying (Erickson 2009: 27–28).

Erickson's first conclusion, (a), appears to contain two distinct claims. First, Erickson claims that when an agent displays features such as those described in his story, features that mimic those of the agent's audience, the line between playful and inclusive display, on the one hand, and aggressive and non-inclusive display on the other, may easily get blurred. Second, Erickson seems to claim that because the line between them can become blurred, we do not know how to explain the difference between mimicry and mockery. In the evaluation to follow I will include a formulation of both claims.

The second conclusion is ambiguous. We might take (b) to hold that contextual markers—the ones displaying agents typically rely upon when determining what features to make salient to their audiences—do not reliably enable such determinations. Or (b) might be taken to mean both that some contexts are certain to cause a blurring of the line between mimicry and mockery and that we do not know what it is about such contexts that causes this blurring. Once again, for purposes of evaluating these claims, I will include both of these conclusions.

I take (c) to mean that when an agent mimics, her intention to mimic rather than mock does not fully control what she is going to be taken as doing.

Finally, notice that (d) is also ambiguous. It could mean that there is a tendency for mimicry to become mockery, and so there is a tendency for mimicry to become fictive, or it could mean that if mimicry cannot be distinguished from mockery and mockery is fictive then mimicry cannot be distinguished from the fictive. And once again, I will include a formulation of both claims. Here then is the full set of claims to deal with:

(A1) When an agent displays features such as those described in Erickson's story, features that mimic those of the agent's audience, the line between playful and inclusive display, on the one hand, and aggressive and non-inclusive display on the other, may easily get blurred.

(A2) Because the line between mimicry and mockery can become blurred, we do not know how to explain the difference between simple mimicry and mockery.

(B1) Contextual markers, the ones displaying agents typically rely upon when determining what features to make salient to their audiences, do not reliably enable such determinations.

(B2) Some contexts of reception seem certain to allow for a blurring of the line between simple mimicry and mockery and we do not know what it is about such contexts that causes the blurring.

(C) When an agent mimics, her intention to simply mimic rather than to mock does not fully control what she is going to be taken as doing.

(D1) Since mockery involves not taking the agent at her word, the difficulty we have with drawing the line between mimicry and mockery entails that mimicry has a tendency to become "fictive", that is, falsifying.

(D2) Since mockery involves not taking the agent at her word, the difficulty we have with drawing the line between mimicry and mockery entails that mimicry cannot be distinguished from the "fictive", that is, the falsifying.

The point now is to investigate whether Erickson's story and the conclusions he draws from it give us reason to think that display—the form of "showing" that I have urged is involved in all performance kinds, including theatrical performances—inherits the same ambiguities, the same worries, and the same practical and theoretical problems that "imitation" and "resemblance" have long been thought to occasion. A second question to ask is whether, to the degree that this inheritance does hold, this poses a serious problem for the theory of theatrical performance I have proposed or the distinction between mimetic and non-mimetic performance I have built upon that theory.

First, however, let us set aside a line of objection that neither I nor Erickson find promising. Although he is wrong to think that children the age his daughter was at the time of the story "would not make use of [the] use-content distinction" in order to grasp what he was doing (Rakoczy et al. 2004),[14] Erickson is right to note it is too easy to dismiss these points by referencing the fact it is a child who is the audience in the context of reception described. For, presumably, these observations and questions can arise within contexts that include all and only adult audiences as well. Ultimately, Erickson's response, like mine, will reject (D) in some form. The route to that rejection is different, however, so I turn now more explicitly to the full range of claims we need to deal with.

So, what are we to make of these claims? Well, first, (A2) is false.[15] Erickson himself describes the difference pretty plainly,

---

[14] Although the paper I cite here addresses a different question, I believe that, if Erickson has in mind what I take him to be claiming, the evidence in this paper shows he has seriously underestimated the capacities of very young children.

[15] Technically, only the second clause of (A2) is false. But because (A1) is true and it figures as the antecedent of (A2), (A2) is a false conditional, containing a true antecedent and a false consequent.

and locates it in the distinction he draws between "an apparent action *with* and an apparent action *toward*" an audience. In the one, an agent is playing with her audience, in the other, she is playing at their expense. A further consideration is that, were (A2) true, we would not be able even to express (C), (B2), and (A1), let alone to evaluate their truth or falsity.

Claims (C) and (A1) do seem to be true.

Nor should we be too concerned about that, I think, at least as a theoretical matter. However, these claims do pose practical problems for performers. And this is what makes these claims important for an understanding of theater. So, a few comments about them are in order.

Performers shape their choices — of the kind referenced in (B1) — with a view to eliciting certain kinds of responses from spectators. In one broad kind of case, for example, what they hope will happen is that spectators will, by attending to them, track a story (which may or may not be about them, and frequently is not).

Claim (B1) is sometimes true. Anyone's knowledge of which context they are in, and a performer's knowledge of which features will be salient to spectators given her understanding of the context she believes herself to be in, are matters of estimation. Some people are better at these estimation tasks than others. Training, perhaps training in a style known to be accessible to a given set of spectators, is useful for reducing the likelihood of error in some of these estimates. That is, performers might have to put in a fair amount of work to prevent the problems described in (A1) from arising. And that observation can be generalized to refer to correlative choices of features that do not involve imitation. Moreover, there are limits to what performers can control by means of their feature selections, just as (C) suggests. And (C) is an important reminder—although not needed, perhaps, by those who have seen too much amateur theater in the Naturalist tradition—that in order effectively to display (for example) the emotion states of a character, what it takes is good actor-training, added to intelligence and a lot of hard work. Even then, it may not be successful.

Finally, (B2) seems to me to be an important empirical question standing in need of research. Is the first clause true? I don't know. But it suggests an interesting research program. We might speculate that, by discovering whether there are circumstances of reception especially prone to this blurring and which ones are so prone, the answer to the question posed in the second clause will simply fall out of the same research. But, again, I do not know that.

What I think I know is that the claims examined so far do not pose significant challenges to the theory of theatrical performance I have proposed nor to the distinction between mimetic and non-mimetic performances I have built upon that theory.

So what, then, of (D)? Well, in either of its forms it proposes an argument. Let us re-write this so that the consequents of the original (D1) and (D2) are represented as the conclusions (D1*) and (D2*). This will enable us to see that the original claims contain arguments and what those arguments are. The arguments go like this:

(1) Mockery involves not taking the agent at her word, that is, the fictive.
(2) We have difficulty drawing the line between mimicry and mockery.

Therefore, either

(D1*) Mimicry has a tendency to become "fictive", that is, falsifying.

or

(D2*) Mimicry cannot be distinguished from the "fictive", that is, the falsifying.

Now, how should we assess them?

The second premise of each is recognizable as the false (A2). For that reason alone we should reject both arguments. And the fact that (A2) is false is also a decisive consideration against (D2*), quite apart from the issue of how well the premises might otherwise have supported the conclusion.

This may not seem satisfactory, if only because (D1*) has an air of independent plausibility to it. Is it true? Possibly. But, if so, it will be true only in circumstances like those referred to in claim (B2). And (B2), you may recall, is a claim whose truth is an empirical matter standing in need of investigation. Finally, even if we are to assume (B2) is true, it will be so only of some circumstances, clearly not all, perhaps not even many.

So, once again I conclude that none of the claims poses a significant challenge to the theory of theatrical performance I have proposed nor to the distinction between mimetic and non-mimetic performances I have built upon that theory. That is, even if display — the form of "showing" that I have urged is involved in all performance kinds, including theatrical performances — inherits some of the same worries and practical and theoretical problems that "imitation" and "resemblance" have long been thought to occasion, and if these claims considered so far express those problems at all fairly, then these are not genuine problems for the theory at all.

Kansas State University
hamilton@ksu.edu

REFERENCES

Beeman, William O. 1993. "The Anthropology of Theater and Spectacle." *Annual Review of Anthropology* 22: 369–93.
Beckett, Samuel. 1948/1954. *Waiting for Godot*. New York: Grove Press.
— — —. 1976. *Ends and Odds: Eight New Dramatic Pieces*. New York: Grove Press.
Bial, Henry (ed.). 2007. *The Performance Studies Reader*. London, New York: Routledge. 2nd edition.
Blau, Herbert. 2007. "Inescapable Mimesis: *JDTC* in the Mortal Coil." *The Journal of Dramatic Theory and Criticism* 22 (1): 95–97.
Brooks, Peter. 1984. Reading for the Plot. In *Reading for the Plot: Design and Intention in Narrative*, 216–37. New York: A.A. Knopf.
— — —. 1984. "Narrative Transaction and Transference." In *Reading for the Plot: Design and Intention in Narrative*, 216–37. New York: A.A. Knopf.
Carroll, Noël. 2001. "The Narrative Connection." In *Beyond Aesthetics*, 118–33. Cambridge–New York: Cambridge University Press.
Chaikin, Joseph. 1993. *The Presence of the Actor*. New York: Theatre Communications Group.
Clark, Herbert H., and Richard J. Gerrig. 1990. "Quotations as Demonstrations." *Language* 66 (4): 764–805.
Currie, Gregory. 2006. "Narrative Representation of Causes." *Journal of Aesthetics and Art Criticism* 64 (3): 309–16.
Currie, Gregory, and Jon Juriedini. 2004. "Narrative and Coherence." *Mind & Language* 19 (4): 409–27.
Davidson, Donald. 1979. "Quotation." *Theory and Decision* 11 (1): 27–40.
Davies, David. 2011. *Philosophy of the Performing Arts*. Oxford: Wiley-Blackwell.
Dretske, Fred. 1999. *Knowledge and the Flow of Information*. Stanford: CSLI Publications.

Edgar, David. 2009. *How Plays Work*. London: Nick Hern Books.
Erickson, Jon. 2009. "On Mimesis (and Truth) in Performance." *The Journal of Dramatic Theory and Criticism* 23 (2): 21–38.
Fischer, Iris S. 2011. *Mabou Mines: Making Avant-Garde Theater in the 1970s*. Ann Arbor: University of Michigan Press.
Geertz, Clifford. 1973. *The Interpretation of Cultures. Selected Essays*. New York: Basic Books.
— — —. ed. 1974. *Myth, Symbol, and Culture*. New York: Norton.
Goffman, Erving. 1961. *Encounters. Two Studies in the Sociology of Interaction*. Indianapolis: Bobbs-Merrill.
— — —. 1963. *Behavior in Public Places. Notes on the Social Organization of Gatherings*. Westport: Free Press of Glencoe.
— — —. 1974. *Frame Analysis. An Essay on the Organization of Experience*. London: Penguin.
Goodall, Jane. 1971. *In the Shadow of Man* (with photographs by Hugo van Lawick). London: Collins.
Goodman, Nelson. 1968. "The Sound of Pictures." In *Languages of Art*, ch. 2, 45–95. Indianapolis: Bobbs-Merrill Company, Inc.
Gray, Spalding. 1985. *Spalding Gray's Swimming to Cambodia*. New York: Theatre Communications Group.
Hamilton, James R. 1982. "'Illusion' and the Distrust of Theater." *The Journal of Aesthetics and Art Criticism* 41 (1): 39–50.
— — —. 2007. *The Art of Theater*. Oxford: Wiley-Blackwell.
— — —. 2009a. "The Text Performance Relation in Theater." *Philosophy Compass* 4 (4): 614–29.
— — —. 2009b. "Narrative, Fiction, Imagination." In *Fictionality – Possibility – Reality*, ed. Petr Koťátko – Martin Pokorný – Marcelo Sabatés, 157–83. Bratislava: Aleph.
Handke, Peter. 1970. *Kaspar and Other Plays*. Trans. Michael Roloff. New York: Hill and Wang.
Heal, Jane. 2001. "On Speaking Thus: The Semantics of Indirect Discourse." *The Philosophical Quarterly* 205 (51): 433–54.
Huxley, Julian. 1964. *Essays of a Humanist*. New York: Harper & Row.
Jones, Jeffrey M. 2007. "The Play Considered as an Information Engine." *The Commonplace Blog of Jeffrey M. Jones* (March 31), online at <http://jeffreymjones.blogspot.com/2007/03/play-considered-as-information-engine_31.html>.
Kirby, Michael. 1972. "Acting and Not-Acting." *The Drama Review: TDR* 16 (1): 3–15.

Kirshenblatt-Gimblett, Barbara. 1976. *Speech Play: Research and Resources for Studying Linguistic Creativity*. Philadelphia: University of Pennsylvania Press.

Kosman, Aryeh. 1992. "Acting: Drama as the Mimēsis of Praxis." In *Essays on Aristotle's Poetics*, ed. Amélie Oksenberg Rorty, 51–72. Princeton: Princeton University Press.

Livingston, Paisley. 2001. "Narrative." In *Routledge Companion to Aesthetics*, ed. Berys Gaut—Dominic M. Lopes, 275–84. London—New York: Routledge.

Lorenz, Konrad. 1966. *On Aggression*. Trans. Marjorie Kerr Wilson. New York: Harcourt, Brace & World.

Patterson, Douglas. 2005. "Comment on Paul Saka, 'Quotation Matters'." Delivered to the Central Division of the American Philosophical Association, Chicago, April 2005 (manuscript from the author).

Rakoczy, Hannes, Michael Tomasello, and Tricia Striano. 2004. "Young Children Know that Trying is Not Pretending: A Test of the 'Behaving-As-If' Construal of Children's Understanding of Pretense." *Developmental Psychology* 40 (3): 388–99.

Récanati, François. 2001. "Open Quotation." *Mind* 439 (110): 637–87.

Sears, Ann, and Thomas L. Riis. 2002. "The Successors of Rodgers and Hammerstein from the 1940s to the 1960s." In *The Cambridge Companion to the Musical*, ed. William A. Everett—Paul R. Laird, 137–66. Cambridge : Cambridge University Press.

Saka, Paul. 1998. "Quotation and the Use-Mention Distinction." *Mind* 425 (107): 113–35.

— — —. 2005. "Quotation Matters." Delivered to the Central Division of the American Philosophical Association, Chicago, April 2005. Online at <http://www.uh.edu/~psaka/cv/Qmatters.pdf>.

— — —. 2006. "The Demonstrative and Identity Theories of Quotation." *The Journal of Philosophy* 103 (9): 452–71.

Schechner, Richard (author), and Victor Turner (Foreword). 1985. *Between Theater and Anthropology*. Philadelphia: University of Pennsylvania Press.

Schechner, Richard. 1988. *Performance Theory*. London: Routledge. 2nd edition.

Singer, Mark. 2007. "Pacing It." *The New Yorker*, March 17.

Sirridge, Mary. 1980. "The Moral of the Story: Exemplification and the Literary Work." *Philosophical Studies* 38 (4): 391–402.

Stein, Gertrude. 1922/1993. "WHAT HAPPENED. A Play in Five Acts." In *Geography and Plays*. Madison: University of Wisconsin Press.
Turner, Victor. 1974. *Dramas, Fields, and Metaphors. Symbolic Action in Human Society*. Ithaca: Cornell University Press.
― ― ―. 1982. *From Ritual to Theatre. The human seriousness of play*. New York: PAJ Publications.
Velleman, J. David. 2003. "Narrative Explanation." *The Philosophical Review* 112 (1): 1–25.
Woodruff, Paul. 1992. "Aristotle on *Mimēsis*." In *Essays on Aristotle's Poetics*, ed. Amélie Oksenberg Rorty, 73–95. Princeton: Princeton University Press.
Zarilli, Phillip B., Bruce McConachie, Gary Jay Williams, and Carol Fisher Sorgenfrei. 2006. *Theatre Histories: An Introduction*. New York: Routledge.
Zillman, Dolf. 2009. "Exemplification Theory: Judging the Whole by Some of its Parts." *Media Psychology* 1 (1): 69–94.

How to Reconcile Seeing-as with Seeing-in (with Mimetic Purposes in Mind)

Alberto Voltolini

ABSTRACT: In this paper, I will try to show that seeing-as doubly grounds seeing-in. First, I will urge that a seeing-as of a certain kind, what I will call illusory seeing-as, partially constitutes the twofold experience of seeing-in, by being what the proper seeing-in fold of that experience really amounts to: the experience of illusorily yet consciously seeing the picture's image as the picture's subject, in other terms, an experience of conscious misrecognition of the picture's image as the picture's subject. Secondly, I will argue that such an illusory seeing-as rests upon a seeing-as of another kind, which I will call organizational seeing-as. This latter seeing-as consists in grasping certain grouping properties of the picture's image while facing that image, where the grouping properties of the image equal the properties of the image's elements to be grouped, or organized, in a certain way, i.e., under a certain orientation. I will indeed claim that entertaining a seeing-as of the latter form explains why one recognizes — although (knowingly) incorrectly — the picture's image as a certain subject. For such a seeing-as consists in grasping roughly the same properties one would grasp when facing that subject. From this, a further interesting result follows: objective resemblance, or mimesis, in grouping properties between the picture and its subject is a necessary condition of pictoriality, of what makes a representation a pictorial representation, and hence ultimately it is a necessary condition of depiction.

Introduction

Following Richard Wollheim (1980, 2nd ed.), among those who hold that an experiential or at least a subjective factor is needed to account for depiction, i.e., for something to be a *pictorial representation* of its subject, many claim that having the experience of *seeing* that subject *in* a picture when facing such a picture is a necessary condition of depiction. For that *seeing-in* experience accounts for the figurativity or *pictoriality* of a picture, i.e., for what makes a pictorial representation *pictorial*.

Notoriously, this idea brought Wollheim to argue against Ernst Gombrich (1960). For Gombrich is taken to have maintained that *another* experience so accounts for depiction, namely a certain *seeing-as* experience. Moreover, the two experiences seem to be not only different, but also antithetic. For seeing-in is mainly characterized by its *twofoldness*: the experience of seeing-in is a complex conscious experience consisting of two equally conscious folds. The first fold consists in literally seeing the physical object that physically constitutes the picture *qua* non-representational entity (the canvas of a painting, the sheet of paper of a photograph, etc.): the picture's *image*, to give it a particular label. The second fold consists in non-literally seeing the picture's subject, what is depicted in the picture (this is the proper "seeing-in" fold). Yet, says Wollheim, seeing-in cannot go along with seeing-as if seeing-as makes it the case that, as Gombrich insists, no such twofold experience can occur when facing a picture. For seeing the picture's image and seeing the picture in its pictorially representational value, i.e., seeing the picture's image as a pictorial representation of the picture's subject, are incompatible, just like any seeing-as experiences that involve a Gestalt switch. In the case of the famous duck-rabbit-figure, one cannot see the figure both as a duck and as a rabbit at one and the same time: if one sees it as a duck, she cannot also see it as a rabbit, and vice versa. Analogously with pictures: if one sees the physical base of the picture, the image, as a pictorial representation, one cannot see it merely as an image, as a physical object devoid of pictorially representational value (see Gombrich 1960: 5).[1]

In fact, however, the theoretical situation is more complicated. First, when originally reflecting on these matters, Wollheim describes the relevant experience in depiction as a seeing-as experience; for instance, when facing a painting of Napoleon one sees that painting as a human being, or even as Napoleon.[2] And even more importantly, while explicitly ruling seeing-as out as the relevant factor for depiction, Wollheim adds that the seeing-in experience rests on a certain seeing-as experience, namely, the experience of seeing a picture as a pictorial representation. Nevertheless, for him it remains the case that the two experiences are different. For the former is the experience of seeing a *certain y* (a subject) in an image x, while the latter is the experience of seeing the same x, the very same image, as *another y* — a pictorial representation. As Wollheim puts it, "seeing y in x may rest upon seeing x as y, but not for the same values of the variable y" (Wollheim 1980: 226).

In what follows, I will try to substantiate these scattered remarks by Wollheim, by utterly reinterpreting them. For I will try to show that seeing-as *doubly* grounds seeing-in. First, I will urge that a seeing-as of a certain kind, what I will call *illusory seeing-as*, partially constitutes the twofold experience of seeing-

---

[1]   As Peetz (1987: 230) and Wollheim himself (1980: 214) originally suspected, the incompatibilty of the duck aspect and the rabbit aspect of the duck-rabbit figure is not the right model for understanding the "seeing canvas"/"seeing nature" disjunction in the form in which Gombrich put it. We will see later how to assess the former incompatibility within the framework of a seeing-in theory of depiction. In any case, it is clear that twofoldness makes the main difference between Wollheim's seeing-in and Gombrich's seeing-as (see Lopes 1996: 47).
[2]   See Wollheim (1980: 17). He later maintained that this description is incorrect: see again Wollheim (1980: 17).

in, by being what the proper seeing-in fold of that experience really amounts to: the experience of illusorily yet consciously seeing the picture's image as the picture's subject, in other terms, an experience of conscious misrecognition of that image as that subject. Secondly, I will argue that such an illusory seeing-as rests upon a seeing-as of another kind, what I will call *organizational seeing-as*. This latter seeing-as consists in grasping certain *grouping properties* of the picture's image while facing that image, i.e., the properties of the image's elements to be grouped, or organized, in a certain way, i.e., under a certain orientation. I will indeed claim that entertaining a seeing-as of the latter form explains why one recognizes, although (knowingly) incorrectly, the picture's image as a certain subject. For such a seeing-as consists in grasping roughly the same properties one would grasp when facing that subject. From this, a further interesting result follows: objective resemblance, or mimesis, in grouping properties between the picture and its subject is a necessary condition of pictoriality, of what makes a representation a pictorial representation, and hence ultimately it is a necessary condition of depiction.

1/ How to analyze seeing-in

An initial problem that Wollheim's "seeing-in"-theory of depiction notoriously raises is that Wollheim fails to specify what the twofold experience exactly consists in. Pending such a specification, the theory seems to collapse onto the commonsensical description that—from Lucretius and especially Leonardo onwards[3]—everybody agrees on, namely that wherever there is depiction there is also the experience one generically characterizes as the experience of seeing the

---

[3] See on this Janson (1961).

picture's subject in the physical basis of the picture—what I have labelled the picture's image.[4]

My proposal consists in characterizing the proper seeing-in fold of the twofold experience as a seeing-as experience, the experience of seeing the picture's image as the picture's subject. For instance, when a perceiver faces a picture of a human being, over and above literally seeing the picture's image the perceiver properly sees one such being in that image iff she sees that image as such a human. Let me say about this seeing-as experience a bit more.

First of all, it is an *illusory* experience, notably an experience of *mis*recognition, for obviously the image is *not* the subject. In the previous example, the image seen as a human being is obviously not such a being. In this respect, I call this experience an experience of *illusory* seeing-as.[5] Moreover, it is an experience of *conscious* misrecognition, for the perceiver *knows* that the image is not the subject. Finally, this experience is unlike a typical illusory conscious seeing-as experience such as for instance the Müller-Lyer illusion, in which the perceiver not only illusorily sees two segments as being different in length but she also knows that the segments are not thus different. Firstly, in our case the experience is precisely a fold of the complex twofold experience. Its conscious character is brought up by the fact that the other fold of the experience—the literal seeing of the picture's image—is conscious as well. In an alternative formulation, once the perceiver realizes that when facing a picture she is literally seeing its image, she also realizes that she is illusorily seeing the image as the picture's subject. Secondly, the awareness of the illusory seeing-as experience in the pictorial case has a phenomenal import. In the case of a

---

[4] Lopes (1996: 50) precisely formulates the problem in this way.
[5] Hermerén (1969: 34–38) labels it "as-if seeing-as".

typical illusory conscious experience—for instance, in the Müller-Lyer illusion—it is the case that even once the perceiver realizes that things do not stand as she perceives them—i.e., that the segments are not different in length—her experience remains phenomenologically the same. In our case, however, once she realizes that things do not stand as she perceives them—i.e., the picture's image is not the picture's subject—the whole experience that she entertains undergoes a change. In this case, as I said, such a realization is prompted by also realizing that one is literally seeing an image. This latter realization in its turn entails having that literal seeing the image as one phenomenologically relevant fold of a new whole experience. Such a fold indeed adds itself to the other experience of seeing the image as the picture's subject, which thereby immediately becomes another fold of the new whole experience. In result— as Wollheim insisted (see Wollheim 1980: 214-15 and 1987: 46)—the new twofold experience has a new specific phenomenological character. This character indeed differs not only from the experience one would have of the picture if she ignored the picture's pictorially representational value, i.e., from the experience of the mere picture's image, as many people have stressed (see e.g. Hopkins 1998: 15). It also differs from the character the seeing-as experience would have if it stood alone as an experience of *non-conscious* misrecognition.[6] This can be clearly seen if one compares the pictorial situation to a normal, three-dimensional case in which a misrecognition becomes conscious. Once one realizes that the thing she has been seeing as a snake is a rope, or that she has been seeing the

---

[6] Hopkins implicitly recognizes all this when he says: "unless my experience represented a surface as before me, I would take myself to be confronted not with a picture, but with a gesturing man", i.e. its subject (Hopkins 2011: 152).

rather ordinary John McCain—one of the many George Clooney look-alikes—as the Hollywood star George Clooney himself, her whole experience changes. For such an experience now results from her going on seeing the rope as a snake plus the fact that she now consciously sees the rope, or from her going on seeing McCain as Clooney plus the fact that she consciously sees McCain.[7]

This is, then, the first manner in which seeing-as grounds seeing-in: by partially constituting, in its illusory form, the twofold experience of seeing-in as its proper seeing-in fold. Clearly enough, this already reduces the gap between Wollheim's and Gombrich's theory. In a charitable interpretation of Gombrich's position, we can see the seeing-as experience required for depiction precisely as the experience of illusorily seeing the picture's image as the picture's subject. This is not a deeply illusory experience of misrecognition, based on the erroneous belief that the image is that subject. For, as I said, it is an experience of conscious misrecognition of the image as that subject, which is definitely not so belief-based. If there is a belief that goes hand in hand with *this* experience, it is the belief that the image is *not* the subject.[8] Yet unlike any standard conscious

---

[7] In point of fact this is more than a mere comparison—the two situations are pretty much alike. For seeing-in occurs both in two-dimensional cases, as typically exemplified by pictures, and in three-dimensional cases, as we will see in the case of *trompe l'oeils*. Thus, the outcome of the McCain–Clooney case is, I hold, legitimately described as a case of Clooney's being seen *in* McCain.

[8] For a similarly sophisticated understanding of Gombrich's theory see Schier (1986: 10–11). Newall ascribes to Gombrich the naïve illusionistic version of the theory based on a deeply illusory experience, but reserves to himself the possibility of defending the idea that at least in some cases of depiction, the relevant experience is, precisely, the experience of a merely illusory seeing-as (cf. Newall 2011: 23–24 and 26–30).

illusory experience of seeing-as, this experience—*pace* Gombrich—is merely a fold of a twofold experience that also includes the conscious literal seeing of the image.

To be sure, the seeing-as experience that Gombrich presents as characteristic of the pictorial experience and as radically alternative to the experience of the mere picture's image and that Wollheim considers as more fundamental than the whole seeing-in experience is the experience of seeing a picture as a pictorial representation. Now, Gombrich is surely right in taking *this* experience as phenomenologically alternative to the experience of the mere image. Puzzle-pictures vividly show this point. For a long while, say, we were facing a mere jungle of patches; then all of a sudden a picture of something emerges precisely at the moment when we see that very something in that jungle. In a rather famous case, once our experience is opportunely focused, we see a dalmatian in a series of black and white spots that we were facing; or, as we can alternatively say, we see a certain image (the whole amount of such spots) as a picture of a dalmatian.[9] Thus it is slightly misleading to hold, as Wollheim urges, that *this* experience is more fundamental than the whole seeing-in experience. For the two experiences actually coincide. Seeing a picture as a pictorial representation—seeing what is actually the image of such a picture as having a pictorially representational value—amounts to seeing the picture's subject in it, and hence to having a twofold seeing-in experience.

Let me now go back to the idea that the proper seeing-in fold of the twofold experience has to be analyzed in terms of what I call illusory seeing-as. Granted, this idea is definitely not

---

[9] This example is so discussed in Lopes (2005: 167–68).

new (see Levinson 1998).[10] Yet people appealing to such an analysis go along with Wollheim in failing to explain how the proper seeing-in fold relates to the other fold, i.e. the conscious literal seeing of the picture's image. Let me call this the relatedness problem of seeing-in. Some other commentators, while appealing to the same analysis, yet deny that the alleged seeing-in fold (once it is so interpreted) *has* to be just a fold in a more complex experience. Sometimes this is the case, yet some other times—typically, in the *trompe-l'oeil* examples—this is not the case. In these latter situations, they say, the conscious illusory seeing-as experience stands alone as the only relevant pictorial experience, there is no twofold experience to appeal to (see Newall 2011: 23-26). I will call this the non-necessity problem of seeing-in. Let me now address the two problems separately, starting from the latter—for once I will have refuted the latter group by showing, as I hope, that there is no pictorial experience without a seeing-in experience constituted by its two folds, I will also be able to show not only that the second fold—the illusory seeing-as experience—arises out of the first fold, i.e. the conscious literal seeing of the picture's image, but also how it so arises.

2/ There are no exceptions to seeing-in qua *the relevant pictorial experience*
On behalf of Gombrich, many people have claimed that *trompe-l'oeils* constitute an important counterexample to Wollheim's

---

[10] Hopkins (2011: 167-68) interprets Lopes's (1996) understanding of seeing-in along similar lines, by taking the second fold as an experience of the picture's subject. Yet in Lopes's framework the latter experience is an experience of a very general kind, covering not only illusory experiences (of the image as the picture's subject) but also hallucinatory experiences (of the subject alone when it is not there).

seeing-in theory. For although *trompe-l'oeils* are pictures as any other, their point is precisely to prevent their perceivers from entertaining a twofold experience. A *trompe-l'oeil* is working insofar as it tricks its perceiver into illusorily perceiving *just* its subject and not the image that physically constitutes it. In being so deceived, the perceiver even believes that she is facing such a subject (see e.g. Levinson 1998: 228; Lopes 1996: 49).

In addressing this objection, Wollheim bites the bullet and argues that since *trompe-l'oeils* prompt no twofold experience, they are no pictures (see Wollheim 1987: 62). However, such a reply is evidently ad hoc, and thus rather implausible. Fortunately enough, there is another way out at Wollheim's disposal, namely to say that *trompe-l'oeils* display no pictorially representational value until they are not recognized as such.[11] For recognizing a *trompe-l'oeil* as such precisely means passing from the experience of non-conscious misrecognition, in which one non-consciously sees the *trompe-l'oeil*'s image by seeing it as its subject, to the experience of conscious misrecognition of the *trompe-l'oeil* as its subject, prompted by a conscious seeing of the *trompe-l'oeil*'s image, and hence to a genuinely twofold experience. *Pace* Lopes (see Lopes 1996: 49–50), this other move is *not* ad hoc. For recognizing a *trompe-l'oeil* as such is just a particular case of recognizing a picture as a picture, of seeing a picture as a pictorial representation, and *this*, as I said before, is nothing but entertaining a twofold experience.

To see that the above is the case, let me start from a three-dimensional case. Suppose that you are facing a dummy figure, say, a dummy of Madonna, unaware that it is a dummy. You will be non-consciously misled, while seeing it, into seeing it as Madonna and even believing that Madonna is what you see. All

---

[11] This reply is envisaged—but not entertained—by Levinson (1998: 228) and critically discussed in Lopes (1996: 49–50).

of a sudden, you realize that you are facing a dummy. You then undergo a phenomenological change. For now you consciously see the dummy, in its plastic and lifeless features. This prompts you to consciously misrecognize the dummy as Madonna, to illusorily see the dummy as Madonna, while at the same time *not* believing anymore that Madonna is what you see. All in all, you now see Madonna *in* the dummy. From then on, the dummy will count as a *sculptural* representation of Madonna. As one can easily see, the situation here is structurally identical to the aforementioned case when all of a sudden you realize that you are facing John McCain rather than George Clooney. Before the realization, you non-consciously saw McCain by mistaking him as George. Once you realize that you are seeing McCain, it prompts a phenomenological change that leads you to see George *in* McCain, by also now consciously yet illusorily see McCain as George.

I claim that that there is no important change when we pass over to a two-dimensional case. Suppose you are facing a *trompe-l'oeil* of a flower vase without knowing that it is a *trompe-l'oeil*. You will be non-consciously misled, while seeing it, into seeing it as a flower vase, even believing that a flower vase is what you see. All of a sudden, you realize that you are facing a *trompe-l'oeil*. You then undergo a phenomenological change. For now you consciously see the *trompe-l'oeil*, in its lack of mass and life. This prompts you to consciously misrecognize the *trompe-l'oeil* as a flower vase, to illusorily see the *trompe-l'oeil* as a flower vase, while at the same time *not* believing anymore that a flower vase is what you see. All in all, you now see a flower vase *in* the *trompe-l'oeil*. From then on, the *trompe-l'oeil* will count as a *pictorial* representation of a flower vase.

On behalf of Gombrich, one could reply that there are other cases of pictures which are no *trompe-l'oeils* and yet prompt no twofold experiences. In such cases—for instance in the case of Van Eyck's *The Arnolfini Portrait*, which is taken to be paradigmatic in this respect—one undergoes no deeply illusory perception—i.e., one does not believe that one is facing the picture's subject, as would be the case with a *trompe-l'oeil*—and yet one entertains no twofold experience either. For one limits herself to a conscious and illusory seeing of the picture's image as its subject, just like in any case of perceptual illusion of the Müller-Lyer- kind (see Newall 2011: 26).

Yet it seems to me that this way of putting things misdescribes the situation at stake. In the Müller-Lyer-situations, it is a *non*-visual factor which prompts the awareness that one is illusorily seeing something as having features that it does not have. In the Müller-Lyer case, one knows that the two segments are equal in length either by testimony or by exploiting a non-visual experiential modality (typically by touching the segments). However, in *all* pictorial situations, what prompts the awareness that one is illusorily seeing a picture's image as the picture's subject is a *visual* factor, namely the fact that one consciously sees the image. Realistic pictures of the van Eyck kind present no exception to this predicament. In order to argue for twofoldness, Wollheim originally pointed out that visual attention can, or rather must, be simultaneously focused both at features of the picture's image and at features of the picture's subject (see Wollheim 1980: 213). It seems to me that this also holds of the allegedly problematic cases. It would be extravagant, yet not utterly uncomprehensible, to say while reflectively facing *The Arnolfini Portrait* something along the lines of "This, which is made of oak, is Mrs. Arnolfini", and thus shift the perceptually based demonstrative reference from (a portion of) the picture's image to (a part of) the picture's subject.[12] Yet it would definitely be much more extravagant to limit oneself to saying something along the lines of "How strange! I can see a wall, a frame on it, and within the frame a minuscule flat Mrs. Arnolfini, even though I know that she cannot be there, for she is neither so small nor flat". In contrast, a similar description would be justified in the Müller-Lyer-cases—however, precisely with the proviso that it would contain no reference to a perception of three-dimensional entities squeezed into two-dimensional entities, for we would simply say: "How strange! Although I know that the two segments are equal in length, I still see one as shorter and one as longer."

3/ How to account for the relatedness problem of seeing-in: grouping properties

Another criticism often raised against Wollheim's theory is that it does not account for the problem of how the two folds of the twofold experience are related. In reassessing his view, Wollheim said that—in contrast to what he originally believed—the two folds are not distinct experiences but rather two aspects of one and the same experience (see Wollheim 1987: 46). However, this reassessment provides no real explanation, since the question of how the two aspects are related simply arises once again. Yet there must be an answer to this question, especially once we notice, with Podro (1998), that (at least a significant part of) seeing-in is *inflected*, which—at the minimum—means that some of the seen features of the picture's image force us to grasp the subject *qua* depicted in that

---

[12] For similar cases where anaphora does not sustain co-referentiality but rather goes along with referential transfer—like "He drank the whole bottle and smashed it on the floor", where the pronoun refers to the bottle itself rather than to its content—see e.g. Sainsbury (2010: 139).

picture as having features that trace back to those features of the image.

In order to address the problem, one has to start from the following question: How is it possible that the pictorial experience contains the seeing-in fold *qua* fold of conscious misrecognition of the image as the picture's subject? In other words, what—in our conscious seeing of the image—prompts such a recognition, even if it is consciously illusory?

People adhering to the so-called recognitional theory of depiction (Schier 1986; Lopes 1996) hold that the answer to the latter question has to be ultimately found in our mind/brain. Lopes holds that it is one and the same ability that allows us to both recognize individuals when we face them and to (mis)recognize them when we see them in pictures. For him, we have to defer to cognitive scientists—psychologists, and possibly neurologists—and leave the explanation of why we have such an ability to them (see e.g. Lopes 2003 and 2005: 161). This conception surely suits Gombrich, who often insists on our subjective powers as the basis of our being in a sense deluded by pictures (see e.g. Gombrich 1960: 304).

Certainly, the fact that many animals are unable to understand pictures the way we do, i.e., by consciously misrecognizing the pictures' images as the pictures' subjects, ultimately depends on how they are hard-wired. If you want to learn your kitten to understand her mirror-image, change her brain. Yet if it were simply a hardware issue, the possibility would be open that, if only *we* were differently hard-wired, we could understand as pictures even entities that we do not actually understand as such, notably non-pictorial representations such as verbal signs. But this sounds very implausible. If we do not understand non-pictorial representations as pictures, this ultimately depends on how those representations are made, not merely on our capacities. As a matter of fact, therefore, animals do not understand pictures because their brains are unable to capture the relevant features which qualify pictures *qua* pictures. By way of analogy, it is certain that the reason we fail to see ultraviolet is that our brains leave us unable to do so — yet if a change in our brain could enable us to see such a colour, it would certainly *not* enable us to *see* odors, smells or sounds.

To see that, as far as picture recognition is concerned, *the picture itself* counts at least as much as our cognitive abilities, consider the following two points. First of all, let us take the so-called ambiguous figures, e.g. the aforementioned duck-rabbit figure. Not just *any* change in seeing-in prompts a phenomenological change in experiencing such a figure. This is to say, as far as phenomenology is concerned we can see, say, a rabbit in the figure (we can consciously see the figure and consciously yet illusorily see it as a rabbit) as well as a hare in it; no phenomenological change occurs. In order to prompt one such change, a change that makes all such previous seeing-ins no longer phenomenologically available at the same time, one has to see a *duck* in the figure, to consciously see the figure and consciously yet illusorily see it as a duck.[13] So there must be

---

[13] Wollheim would have declined to consider these cases of ambiguous figures, seen as different things, as cases of seeing-in (cf. Wollheim 1980: 213). His only reason would be, however, that while agreeing with Gombrich that seeing things as having different aspects requires the perceptual incompatibility of these aspects, he thought that such seeing-as could not account for the twofoldness of pictorial experience. Yet a more precise description of the situation at stake with ambiguous figures shows that each of the different illusory seeings-as involved in it is a component of a different seeing-in experience. The illusorily seeing of a figure as a duck is the proper seeing-in fold of the whole experience of seeing a duck in the figure; the illusorily seeing of a figure as a rabbit is the proper seeing-in fold of the — different — whole experience of seeing a rabbit in the figure.

some (re)configuration in the picture that allows for the fact that only when there is a relevant change in the picture's subject, there also is a phenomenological change. Moreover, as regards a certain picture, not any conceivable seeing-in is really possible. Try to see an elephant in the duck-rabbit figure! This again depends on how the picture is configurated.

These facts enable me to provide an answer to the question of how one can consciously misrecognize a picture's image as the picture's subject: one can thusly misrecognize that image insofar as it shares with such a subject some objective yet perceptible properties. Armed with this answer to the question, I can also provide an answer to the relatedness problem. The two folds of the twofold experience are indeed related. It is in virtue of the fact that the perceiver literally sees the picture's image that she non-literally sees the picture's subject (i.e. she consciously yet illusorily sees the image as the subject), for in that literal seeing she grasps those objective perceptual properties that the image approximately shares with the subject. By virtue of grasping these properties in her literal seeing of the picture's image, she can non-literally see the picture's subject, for that subject has roughly the same properties.

Interpretations of Wollheim's seeing-in divide themselves into the *divisive* ones—holding that the two seeing-in folds, although representing aspects of one and the same experience, are distinct components of it and are endowed with different contents—and the *unitary* ones—holding that such folds are only abstractions of one and the same complex and integral experience, endowed with its own structured content.[14] Yet

---

[14] For this way of putting things, see Hopkins (2011: 170), who ranks Wollheim (1980 and 1987) and Lopes (1996) within the first group, Walton (1990) and himself (1998) within the second group.

such an interpretative contrast can be weakened once the relation between the two folds is taken along the lines presented here. For in my view, the two folds can be legitimately said to have (as *divisionists* would say) different contents—the first fold is seeing *the image*, the second fold is seeing *the image as the picture's subject*—yet there is an important qualification which the *unitarists* would probably be disposed to accept as their own: if, while experiencing the first fold, we focus on the image's pertinent objective perceptual properties, this immediately releases the second fold as experientially available; so to speak, the second fold experientially unfolds itself as soon as the first fold is appropriately focused.

Obviously the question now is, what are the properties whose grasp in the picture's image grounds the conscious misrecognition of the picture's subject as roughly having the same properties? In addressing this question, I want to pursue and expand a suggestion originally put forward by Stephen Davies: "the recognition of gestalt or patterns might involve the noticing of similarities" (Davies 2006: 173). My answer—following Davies—is that the required properties are the properties which were originally—by Christian von Ehrenfels (1988)—labelled *Gestalt qualities* and which I will re-label *grouping properties*: for something to have these properties is for the elements in a certain array, either two-dimensional or three-dimensional—hence also a certain picture's image, but even a certain picture's subject—to be grouped or organized in a certain way. Many pictures actually contain just one relevant kind of such properties. Consider the pictorially relevant phenomenological change brought about when we pass from seeing a mere jungle of patches to seeing something in it, e.g. a dalmatian. This change consists in "that you now see the marks as organized in a particular way", as Robert Hopkins (1998: 15) himself acknowledges. Yet—as Gombrich implicitly noticed by pointing out that all pictures are inherently ambiguous (see Gombrich 1960: 249)—pictures may have more than one such kind of grouping properties, and this is documented by ambiguous figures such as the duck-rabbit figure. Indeed, a figure is ambiguous insofar as the elements of its image can be grouped in more than one way. However, pictures do not allow for all theoretically possible groupings, which is why in the duck-rabbit figure one can see both a duck and a rabbit but not an elephant. Now, grouping properties are *perceptual*. In fact, they are orientation-dependent, i.e., they depend on a certain order of the perceived scene. As a result, if different orientations are provided for elements in an array, that array has different grouping properties. Precisely this happens with ambiguous figures. Nevertheless, grouping properties are *objective* properties, i.e., they are properties of the perceived array, not properties of our experience of it. In Michael Newall's recent terminology, even though such properties depend on a point of view, they are *viewer-independent* properties (see Newall 2011: 67).

That grouping properties are objective rather than subjective cannot be taken for granted, since some have maintained the precise opposite (see Peacocke 1983: 24–26). Yet I can argue in favour of their objectivity by relying on the following considerations: first, grouping properties are not perspectival properties, which many people take as the paradigmatic case of subjective properties; second, they are properties that are possessed by entities in an objective rather than in an egocentric space. Let me present these considerations one by one.

First, note that once one grasps such properties, it does not matter from which perspective one grasps them, since one continues to grasp the very same properties. Once one sees a monkey in certain lines dug in the soil around Nazca in Peru, one continues to see that monkey in such lines even if one moves around them—by passing, say, from a top-down perspective to a fore-ground perspective. For one continues to grasp those lines as grouped along the very same orientation.[15] Second, such an orientation takes place in an objective and not in an egocentric space. At first sight, one might think that with an ambiguous figure, such as the duck-rabbit figure, in order to grasp the duck aspect one must let one's attention pass from a dot on the figure's left-hand side to some curved lines on the figure's right-hand side, whereas in order to grasp the rabbit aspect one must perform the opposite attentional operation. Yet if one draws the figure upon a transparent surface, say a glass window, it becomes clear that if one wants to grasp the duck aspect from the other side of the mirror, one has to let one's attention go along the figure from right to left, and vice versa if one wants to grasp the rabbit aspect. This means that the duck aspect of the figure is not individuated in terms of an egocentric orientation, but rather in terms of an objective orientation, i.e., in terms of a geometric ordering pertaining to a direction, whereas the rabbit aspect is individuated in terms of the opposite direction.

Now, the experiential grouping that stems out of the literal seeing of the picture's image, in virtue of which the non-literal seeing of the picture's subject arises, is also a form of seeing-as. A perceiver sees the elements of a certain array as grouped in a certain way; she can often (always?) see the very same elements as grouped in another, or even in many other,

---

[15] Some people believe that perspectival properties are objective properties (see Hopkins 1998; Noë 2002). But this simply strenghtens my point. For then grouping properties are even more objective.

ways. Let me call this form of seeing-as *organizational seeing-as*. As Ludwig Wittgenstein was the first to notice, seeing-as comes in many varieties which are in some sense similar yet may end up to be held for mutually related but distinct notions (see Wittgenstein 2009, II xi, § 155).[16] This is precisely the case here. Insofar as organizational seeing-as ultimately accounts for how the literal seeing of a picture's image can support the non-literal seeing of the picture's subject, it grounds illusory seeing-as *qua* the proper seeing-in fold of the twofold experience. Since, as we have seen, illusory seeing-as further grounds seeing-in by being one of its constituents, we have arrived at the conclusion that seeing-as in general *doubly* grounds seeing-in. *Pace* Gombrich, therefore, seeing-as and seeing-in are definitely not incompatible.

4/ Mimesis vindicated?

I started this paper by saying that I share Wollheim's idea that (once it is suitably analyzed) seeing-in is a necessary condition for depiction. As I have said before, moreover, the grasping of the grouping properties of a picture's image grounds the proper seeing-in fold of the seeing-in experience, the conscious misrecognition of that image as the picture's subject, insofar as image and subject approximately share the same grouping properties. Finally, since—as I have also said—once they are so conceived, grouping properties are objective properties of the perceived item (and not subjective properties of its perceiver), it turns out that the oldest and apparently most intuitive theory of depiction, according to which something depicts something else insofar as the former resembles the latter, is somehow

---

[16] See also Walton: "the problem of the nature of depiction is, at bottom, the problem of the nature of the relevant variety of seeing-as" (Walton 1990: 300).

vindicated. In this last session of the paper, I will try to understand the significance of this "somehow".

To begin with, the theory is quite clearly not vindicated in its full original import. Insofar as depicting something amounts to representing it in a pictorial way, objective resemblance cannot be a sufficient condition for depiction, i.e., for pictorial representation. After Nelson Goodman's criticism to the effect that representing and resembling behave differently with respect to reflexivity and especially symmetry, such a view simply lacks advocates (see e.g. Davies 2006: 173; Newall 2011: ch. 4).[17]

Moreover, once seeing-in comes to the fore, objective resemblance cannot even be a sufficient condition for pictoriality, i.e., for what makes a pictorial representation pictorial. That is, an experience of a particular kind—such as the seeing-in experience—is also needed to account for pictoriality.

Nevertheless, objective resemblance can be a necessary condition for pictoriality, hence a fortiori for depiction (since pictoriality is a necessary condition for depiction) once it is interpreted in the aforementioned way, namely as an objective resemblance in grouping properties between the picture's image and the picture's subject. For, as we have seen, the experiential grasping of such properties allows the picture's image to be illusorily seen as the picture's subject, and hence it allows for seeing-in, which—once suitably interpreted—suffices for pictoriality.

As a result, Goodman was right in further holding that an appeal to resemblance in depictive matters is vacuous, for if it is taken in the abstract, resemblance is ubiquitous: under some respect or other, everything can be similar to everything

---

[17] For Goodman's original criticism see Goodman (1968: 3-4).

else (see Goodman 1968: 5). Yet such a criticism does not apply to the present proposal. For here I have singled out a *precise respect* of similarity between a picture's image and a picture's subject, namely, similarity in grouping properties. Goodman's criticism, moreover, leaves it open that an appeal to resemblance *under a certain respect* may provide a necessary condition for pictoriality. Goodman is simply skeptical that such a respect can be found, for the respects that have been traditionally put forward to this purpose—colour or shape in the old times, aperture colours or occlusion shape in our present times (see respectively Plato 1997; Hyman 2006)[18]—fail to provide such a condition. Yet to my mind, the reason why traditional perspectives were a failure was that they appealed to the wrong respect. As I just said, I claim that the appeal to a resemblance in grouping properties is the right approach, for unlike other strategies—i.e., appeals to other respects—it actually provides a necessary condition for pictoriality.[19]

Finally, appealing to such a respect may dismantle the objection recently raised by Dominic Lopes against objective resemblance theories. According to Lopes, such theories are

---

[18] Occlusion shape is the solid angle an object subtends at a given point of view; aperture colour is a colour as it appears through a reduction screen.

[19] To be complete, this claim must address the problem of generic depictions or depictions of nonexistents, where it seems that no respect of similarity may be invoked, as there is no item a picture is similar to (see Goodman 1968: 25). (These two cases were mistakenly kept together by Goodman, as Hyman (2006: 66 n. 12) has pointed out.) In a nutshell, generic pictures can be similar in their grouping properties to some instance or other of the generic kind depicted (this may be meant as the non-relational sense of "resemblance", see again Hyman (2006: 65–66)); pictures of nonexistent fictional entities can well be similar in their grouping properties to such entities.

unable to simultaneously satisfy two constraints which they ought to fulfill. These constraints are the diversity constraint, according to which there must be different respects under which different pictures resemble their subjects, and the independence constraint, according to which a picture has a pictorial value independently of its representational value, or in other words, one does not have to know what a picture is about in order to know how it depicts. Yet, says Lopes, in order to know under which respect a picture resembles its subject, one already has to know which subject it is about. That is, in order for an objective resemblance theory to satisfy the diversity constraint, it must contravene the independence constraint. Thus, if it satisfies the latter, it fails to satisfy the former (see Lopes 1996: 35). Yet once—as I have stressed—there is just one respect under which *any* picture must resemble its subject in order for the picture to have pictorial value, and hence to depict its subject—namely, resemblance in grouping properties—there is no reason, *pace* Lopes, why (whatever happens to the independence constraint) the diversity constraint would have to be fulfilled by a theory appealing to objective resemblance in the way I have presented here.[20]

University of Turin
alberto.voltolini@unito.it

---

[20] For more details regarding a theory of depiction that simultaneously appeals to seeing-in and to objective resemblance in grouping properties between the picture's image and the picture's subject, see my Voltolini (2012). Preliminary versions of this paper were presented at the Conference on Depiction and Description, National University of Singapore, January 15-16, 2010, Singapore, and at ECAP VII, Seventh European Congress of Analytic Philosophy, Faculty of Philosophy, University Vita-Salute S. Raffaele, September 1-6, 2011, Milan. I thank all the participants for their stimulating comments.

REFERENCES

Davies, Stephen. 2006. *The Philosophy of Art*. Oxford: Blackwell.
Gombrich, Ernst. 1960. *Art and Illusion*. London: Phaidon.
Goodman, Nelson. 1968. *The Languages of Art*. Indianapolis: Bobbs-Merrill.
Hermerén, Göran. 1969. *Representation and Meaning in the Visual Arts*. Scandinavian University Books: Lund.
Hopkins, Robert. 1998. *Picture, Image and Experience*. Cambridge: Cambridge University Press.
– – –. 2011. "Inflected Pictorial Experience: Its Treatment and Siginificance." In *Philosophical Perspectives on Depiction*, ed. Catharine Abell – Katerina Bantinaki, 151–180. Oxford: Oxford University Press.
Hyman, John. 2006. *The Objective Eye*. Chicago: University of Chicago Press.
Janson, Horst W. 1961. "The 'Image Made by Chance' in Renaissance Thought." In *De artibus opuscula XL: Essays in Honor of Erwin Panofsky*, ed. Millard Meiss, 254–266. New York: New York University Press.
Lopes, Dominic. 1996. *Understanding Pictures*. Oxford: Oxford Univerity Press.
– – –. 2003. "Pictures and the Representational Mind." *The Monist* 86 (4): 35–52.
– – –. 2005. "The Domain of Depiction." In *Contemporary Debates in Aesthetics and the Philosophy of Art*, ed. Matthew Kieran, 160–76. Oxford: Blackwell.
Newall, Michael. 2011. *What is a Picture?* Basingstoke: Palgrave.
Noë, Alva. 2002. "On What We See." *Pacific Philosophical Quarterly* 83 (1): 57–80.
Peacocke, Christopher. 1983. *Sense and Content*. Oxford: Clarendon Press.
Peetz, Dieter. 1987. "Some Current Philosophical Theories of Pictorial Representation." *British Journal of Aesthetics* 27 (3): 227–37.
Plato. 1997. Cratylus. In *Plato: Complete Works*, ed. John M. Cooper. Indianapolis: Hackett.
Podro, Michael. 1998. *Depiction*. New Haven & London: Yale Universty Press.
Sainsbury, R. M. 2010. *Fiction and Fictionalism*. London: Routledge.
Schier, Flint. 1986. *Deeper into Pictures*. Cambridge: Cambridge University Press.
Voltolini, Alberto. 2012. "Towards a Syncretistic Theory of Depiction." In *Perceptual Illusions. Philosophical and Psychological Essays*, ed. Clotilde Calabi. Basingstoke: Palgrave (in press).

Von Ehrenfels, Christian. 1988. "On Gestalt-Qualities." In *Foundations of Gestalt Theory*, ed. Barry Smith, 82–117. München—Wien: Philosophia.
Walton, Kendall L. 1990. *Mimesis as Make-Believe. On the Foundations of the Representational Arts*. Cambridge, MA: Harvard University Press.
Wittgenstein, Ludwig. 2009. *Philosophical Investigations*. Oxford: Blackwell. 4th ed.
Wollheim, Richard. 1980. *Art and its Objects*. Cambridge: Cambridge University Press. 2nd ed.
— — —. 1987. *Painting as an Art*. Princeton: Princeton University Press.

Sound in Film: Design versus Commentary

Jerrold Levinson

ABSTRACT: What are the different possibilities for assigning a source or responsibility to the sounds that form part of a film, according to the nature of the sounds, the nature of the film, and the nature of the narrative, if any, that is unfolding? That question is not one to which one can respond by citing the film's sound editor. The question is rather one of determining, in the course of adequately comprehending a film that one is viewing, what position the sounds heard in the film occupy in relation to the fictional world that is constituted, in the main, by the film's image track. Motivating that question, and setting out some basic distinctions concerning film sound, occupies the first part of the paper. In the second part of the paper I explore that and related questions with special reference to Jean-Luc Godard's 1965 *Masculin-Feminin*, which I subject to an episode-by-episode analysis.

Part One

1/ Film is essentially a visual medium. That is to say, a succession of visual images is a *sine qua non* for something to be considered a film. In film one can have images without sound, but not sounds without images; a sequence of sounds can be music, or sound sculpture, or acoustic environment, but it cannot constitute a film.

The relation of sound to film is thus in one sense problematic from the outset, since the visual is necessarily dominant in the cinematic sphere. What, then, does sound do to, or with, or for, the visual image?

That is too big a question to be addressed in the present essay. So the more specific question I will be concerned with

Mimesis: Metaphysics, Cognition, Pragmatics
ed. G. Currie, P. Koťátko, M. Pokorný
408–34. London: College Publications, 2012.

here is this: What are the different possibilities for assigning a source or responsibility to the sounds that form part of a film, according to the nature of the sounds, the nature of the film, and the nature of the narrative that is unfolding? As I emphasized in an earlier essay devoted to film music (Levinson 2006), that question is not one to which one can adequately respond by citing the film's sound editor. In other words, it is not a question about the causal history or actual making of the film, but one that concerns the interpretation and appreciation of the film. More specifically, the question is one of determining, in the course of following and comprehending a fiction film, what position the sounds heard in the film occupy in relation to the fictional world that is constituted, in the main, by the film's image track.

2/ I begin by recalling some important distinctions in this domain: diegetic versus non-diegetic sound; music versus non-music; speech versus non-speech; noise versus non-noise; narrative sound versus non-narrative sound. The last of these distinctions was a focus of the essay alluded to above, in which I proposed that narrative music was music that made something fictional in the story being related by the film. Presumably the same would hold more generally for narrative sound, that it is sound that makes something fictional in the film's story. The other distinctions mentioned are fairly unproblematic, with the exception of the first one, that of diegetic vs. non-diegetic sound. That distinction, a staple of film theorizing, deserves a bit of comment.

Sound is said to be diegetic when it appears to emanate from the situation visually represented by the image track, whether understood as fiction or as documentary. In most cases this is a straightforward matter, but in some cases it is not. For sometimes the sounds on the soundtrack can be understood as originating in the situation visually represented only with a shift or delay of time; sometimes only as an analogue, modification, or refinement of what could conceivably have issued from the visually represented scene; and sometimes only as the audible counterpart of sounds occurring in the consciousness of a depicted character. In such cases the sounds involved might reasonably be classified as *quasi-diegetic*. And in that light, non-diegetic sound might usefully be characterized as sound that cannot *in any form or at any remove* reasonably be understood to have its source in the situation being visually represented.

3/ I now propose a distinction of wide scope that I hope will prove theoretically fertile, one that cuts across many of the familiar distinctions recalled above. It is that of *sound as design* versus *sound as commentary*. Sound as design means sounds considered as part of the complex audiovisual aesthetic object constructed by the filmmaker. Sound as commentary means sounds considered as conveying or suggesting something about the image track or visual portion of a film, where this can be either commentary on the sequence of images itself or, more often, on what is represented by such a sequence.

This distinction can be related to, though not identified with, what one might propose as the two most basic functions of sound in film. The first is to add to the experiential *realism* of what appears to be happening in the film in virtue of the image track. The second is to add to the film as a total perceptual *configuration*. Film sound understood under the first function is sound that we take to inform us directly, by resemblance, of the audible facts of the story being unfolded. Film sound understood under the second function, by contrast, is sound that is to be taken, not as a transparent semblance of reality and, as it were, heard through, but as an object of aesthetic attention in its own right. The second function is usually not very prominent in standard narrative fiction film, though it is more so in some modes of documentary film, and in non-standard narrative films, such as those of Jean-Luc Godard, one of whose films I will examine in the second part of this paper.

Now though it is clear that sound as contributing to the total perceptual configuration of a film is roughly congruent with that of sound as design, sound as contributing to the experiential realism of a film does not coincide, even roughly, with sound as commentary. The most obvious discrepancy is perhaps in relation to standard dialogue, which clearly contributes to the realism of scenes in which persons are speaking, but which is not comfortably ranged under sound as commentary, being in effect too internal to, or too obviously a constituent of, a film's narrative.

So where does standard dialogue stand in relation to the distinction between sound as design and sound as commentary? In one sense, it stands outside it. Dialogue is normally part of the very substance of the fictional world, rather than something sonic imposed on that world from the outside. That is to say, ordinary dialogue is clearly diegetic sound, and the design vs. commentary distinction applies most naturally to non-diegetic sound. But what of non-standard dialogue, that which doesn't seem to be part of the evolving situation, of the interaction between characters, of the fictional world centrally presented by the film? I will take that up again in the second part of this essay.

4/ In characterizing some film sound as commentary, rather than design, one is in principle committed to answering at least three questions that arise in the wake of that characterization, those of: (a) *what* such sound is commenting on; (b) what *agency*, for instance, a cinematic narrator, the implied filmmaker, or the actual filmmaker, should be held to be responsible for, or viewed as the source of, the commentary; and (c) what the *content* of the commentary is. That these questions are always pertinent does not, of course, mean that answers to them are always readily forthcoming.

So what is the relation between (a) commentative sound, (b) narrative sound, that is, sound that makes fictional something in the story, and (c) non-diegetic sound, that is, sound that appears to emanate from outside the situation visually represented? In short, it is one of partial overlap. First of all, there is commentative sound that is non-narrative, such as film music attributable to the implied filmmaker, isolated sound effects, and voice-overs of a didactic or dadaistic sort. Second, there is narrative sound that is not commentative, such as ordinary diegetic dialogue. Third, there is narrative sound that is non-diegetic, such as film music attributable to the cinematic narrator. Fourth, there is commentative sound that is diegetic, as when a character observes something about the developing story in which he or she is involved, or in a more postmodern vein, about the very film that is charged with narrating that story.

5/ Before continuing with my illustration of the various functions of sound in film and the agents to which we attribute such sounds I will revisit an argument advanced in my essay on film music in light of a subsequent, more careful formulation of the argument due to George Wilson (see Wilson 2007).[1] It is an argument for the existence of cinematic narrators in films that

---

[1]   For Wilson's earlier treatment of these issues, see Wilson (2006).

turns on the need to avoid incoherence in conceptualizing the relation between real viewers and the cinematic fictional worlds into which they imagine seeing and hearing. Though I did not so label it, the argument has come to be known as the "ontological gap" argument.

First, here is Wilson's concise summary of the basic issues in the debate about the existence of narrators in literary and cinematic fiction:

> In literary works of narrative fiction, the story or narrative consists of a sequence of fictional or fictionalized characters, objects, situations, and events. The narration consists in the fictional presentation of those narrative constituents, and the presentation, in these literary instances, is a mode of a linguistic recounting. The critical point for present purposes is that such works have at least two dimensions of fictionality: there is the fictional narrative and there is the fictional narration that presents as actual the relevant narrative events. It is generally accepted that many and even most works of literary fiction involve both a fictional narrative and narration in this way ... but there continues to be a dispute about whether every work of literary fiction involves narration qua fictional recounting of the narrative events. In the case of narrative cinema there is no comparable consensus that films generally involve an analogue of this sort of two-tiered fictionality. It is highly controversial whether a film that presents a fictional narrative normally involves a fictional audio-visual narration of the story, that is, a fictional presentation of the sights and sounds of the narrative world. (Wilson 2007: 73–74)[2]

Second, here is what Wilson has to say about the argument in question:

> The fact that actual people, including actual authors, can fictionally recount a story is why I find Levinson's "ontological gap" argument difficult to construe... If the conclusion of the argument is that, in the

---

[2] For an earlier treatment of these issues, see also Wilson (2006).

work, there must be an implicit agent recounting the story who is *merely* a fictional construct of the work, then the argument is unsound and the conclusion false. But there is another way of looking at the considerations that Levinson provides. In the reading of a work of narrative fiction, it is fictional in the reader's game of make believe and in the work itself that the narrator asserted that P, and it is fictional in the reader's game that the reader, in reading, learns that the narrator has asserted that P. Finally, it is fictional in this game that the reader thereby learns, by a defeasible inference, that P is true. So it is in this way that the reader "gains access" to the facts that belong to the fictional work, but of course it is only a *fictional* mode of gaining access. It is fictional in the reader's game of make-believe that he thereby comes to know the story facts. Clearly, it makes no difference to the account whether the narrator here is a fictionalized version of an actual person or merely a fictional character created by the text.

Perhaps Levinson is simply arguing (a) that this is the most natural and reasonable account of what it is for a reader to gain access to the fictional world of a literary work, and (b) that this preferred account directly presupposes the existence of a fictional or fictionalized narrator. His idea would be that we cannot make coherent sense of a reader's epistemic access to the fictional facts without assuming that it is fictional in the work that some narrator asserts that these facts obtain. The force of this argument depends centrally on the truth of (a), and it is plain that skeptics about the existence of effaced narrators will reject this assumption.. Nevertheless, (a) and (b) may be all that Levinson intended to establish in his "ontological gap" argument. If so, then I agree with him about both theses. (Wilson 2007: 79-80)[3]

Transposing from the literary to the cinematic case, what Wilson's charitable reconstruction of my argument shows is this. Although it is a mistake to suggest, as my original argument may have done, that the cinematic narrator of a fiction film can only be a fictional entity, on the same fictional

---

[3]   For Wilson's fuller defense of the thesis of the ubiquity in narrative film of highly effaced narrators or minimal narrative agents, see Wilson (2011).

plane as the persons and situations presented to us by the narrator—because the cinematic narrator can certainly be a really existing person, such as the filmmaker—a real person occupying the role of cinematic narrator can only coherently occupy it *in a fictionalized guise*, so that causal and cognitive relations between the narrator and the fictional events the narrator presents make sense in relation to the viewer and his imaginative involvement in the fictional world displayed on screen. Otherwise put, even when the cinematic narrator has the identity of a real individual, that narrator is not the real individual *simpliciter*, but rather, as Wilson suggests, a *fictionalized version* of that individual, so that it can be fictional in a univocal sense that the events of the narrative are as they are, and that that individual knows of them, has access to them, and presents them to us.

Still, objections to the positing of cinematic narrators as being unmotivated, unnecessary, metaphysically extravagant, and so on, are rather common.[4] In partial response to such objections, it is important to note at least two things. First, the appeal to cinematic narrators in fiction film might be defended as something categorically required or inescapable, given the phenomenology of our appreciative involvement in such film, but it need not be defended at that pitch. The cinematic narrator, presenter, or shower can instead be understood as more like a *standing postulate* for interpretation of fiction films, that is, as an option that is always intelligible and available, but which there may sometimes be not much critical or interpretive profit in invoking. Second, in many cases the cinematic narrator, when recognized, has little of the character of an *agent* in a robust sense. It is better thought of more abstractly, as

---

[4] See Kania (2005), Gaut (2004), Wartenberg (2007), Carroll (2006), Thomson-Jones (2007), and Davies (2010).

perhaps the agency of the narration, the rationale of its style, an intelligence of some sort that appears to shape and convey the story in a particular way. Of course, as Wilson rightly observes, the more minimal, the more generic, the more recessive the narrative agency that appears to operate in a given film, the less critical or interpretive interest there will be in remarking its presence and querying its character or functioning:

> Suppose, then, that fiction films presuppose only the existence of implicit minimal narrating agencies. Such a result would contrast sharply with the case of works of literature, in which narrators, portrayed as characters of various types and degrees of complexity, abound. Surely, a part of the interest of noticing that a novel has an effaced narrator lies in the fact that the strategy of effacement represents an artistic choice about how the narrative is best conveyed. If in general only minimal narrators are involved in movies, then the importance of their implicit presence to the appreciation and understanding of the narrative cinema is seriously less clear. (Wilson 2007: 87)

Fair enough. But Wilson's caveat still leaves in place as always legitimate an appeal to a cinematic narrative agency distinct from that of the director, cinematographer, sound engineer, and the rest of the real individuals who actually construct the film, wherever and whenever such an appeal enables a fuller interpretation and appreciation of the cinematic work of art. My suspicion is that this is much more often than opponents of the appeal to cinematic narrators suppose to be the case, something a focus on the audible component of a film can make particularly evident, as I hope to have shown in my essay on film music. So before leaving the question of the legitimacy of positing narrative agents in film I take the liberty of quoting from that essay a reminder that the important issue regarding a viewer's understanding of a fiction film's soundtrack persists, regardless of how one resolves the question of internal narrators in film:

> What I want to say about assigning non-diegetic music to narrative agents as opposed to implied filmmakers can be translated so as to require instead only the assumption of narrative processes or mere appearances of being narrated. Thus, even if one does not regard the positing of internal narrators or presenters in film as inevitable, the issue will still remain whether soundtrack music is to be thought of as an element in the narrative process or an appearance of narrative presentation, as opposed to an element in the construction of the film by a filmmaker standing outside both the story and its narration. (Levinson 2006: 147)

And the same naturally goes, *mutatis mutandis*, for the non-diegetic but non-musical components of the soundtrack, with which I will be particularly concerned in what follows. How do such sounds function, how are they categorized, often unreflectingly, when heard, and to what or to whom does the spectator implicitly attribute them?

Part Two

1/ I now take a close look at the use of sound in one of the most emblematic and successful of the films of Jean-Luc Godard from his "golden era", namely, *Masculin-Feminin* (1965). I will first catalog the kinds of sounds employed in the film, and then go on to think about them in relation to the distinctions sketched in the first part of this paper, namely, those of diegetic vs. non-diegetic sound, narrator-attributable sound vs. director-attributable sound, and sound as commentary vs. sound as design. My hope is that a selective exploration of the uses of sound in Godard's film will serve, if you'll pardon the cross-modal metaphor, to shed some light on this dark terrain. I begin with the promised catalogue:

— Voice-over: Frequent, with the speaker often not clearly identified, and even when identified, his or her discourse has little or no manifest connection to the image track. And such voice-over rarely serves a narrative function.
— Dialogue: Frequent, but the person speaking is often not visible; more often the person being addressed is on screen. Also the dialogue is often pointedly obscured, even obliterated, by ambient noise, with which it competes and almost ends up seeming on a par with.
— Music: Intermittent, but only diegetic, though sometimes not synchronous. Ambient sound: Almost throughout, most often issuing from the urban environment. The sounds include those of traffic, honking, gunshots, shouting, footsteps. Virtually no natural sounds—for instance, birds, wind, rain, ocean—are to be heard.
— Artificial sounds, or Sound effects: Fairly frequent, and most obviously, the screechy sound-bursts that announce the various sequences or *"faits précis"* that constitute the film, providing a kind of aural punctuation.

An initial reflection concerning those repeated sound-bursts is this. The fact that it is natural to ask of these sound-bursts whether they serve a narrative purpose or make something fictional in the story, or else merely constitute part of the total audiovisual canvas or cinematic package, suggests, once again, that there is always an issue in the background as to who or what should be thought of as responsible for those sounds in terms of their functioning in the film. And the fact that it is fruitful to pose that question in the attempt to understand the film underscores that those interpretive options regarding the sound-bursts—options that seem to presuppose something like the distinction between directorial and narratorial agency—are very much on the table from the very start.

2/ *Masculin-Feminin* begins with one of Godard's signature word screens, or intertitles, accompanied by two sound-bursts. This first intertitle offers the title of the film with the word "MASCULIN" broken into three parts while the word "FEMININ" is presented whole, followed by the subtitle, "15 FAITS PRECIS". Those harsh and arresting sound-bursts are not clearly identifiable as deriving from this or that real-world sound source, though they call to mind something like a rifle shot or car crash, or perhaps the operation of a massive camera shutter mechanism. In any case, those sound bursts have a pronounced metallic and industrial character, and seem the very paradigm of a filmic "sound object". Those sound bursts—either one, or two, or three, or sometimes four—are heard at every intertitle announcing a new episode. Thus their main function, at least ostensibly, is syntactic. But they also subtly yet unmistakably impart a tone to the film from the outset, one of impersonal objectivity and analytical ruthlessness, while at the same time possibly reflecting the truncated and unsatisfactory relations that constitute the largest part of the interactions between characters to which we are witness. In short, those sound-bursts are arguably heard *both* as design—and more specifically, punctuation—*and* as commentary.

3/ In the first episode,[5] or *"fait précis"*, Paul, a politically

---

[5] Perhaps "segment" would be a better designation than "episode" for the units of which Godard's film is constituted, because implying less in the way of narrativity.

engaged journalist, reads from an unseen text that he is in the process of composing between drags on his cigarette, against intrusive car sounds from the street. The sentences of Paul's text, possibly a poem, are hard to follow, oddly broken up in his utterance of them, and his slow and deliberate pronunciation of individual words makes them hang in the air like lead balloons. The net effect is to foreground the words uttered as mere sounds, such as a machine might emit, and not as vehicles of sense.

Madeleine, an aspiring pop singer and magazine employee, enters and sits at a neighboring table. They converse, Madeleine somewhat reluctantly, with Paul almost entirely off-screen, even when after some initial chitchat he launches into a political screed. This provides a first example of Godard's tendency to disconnect sound and image: what one sees on screen is often not the source of what one hears on the soundtrack, and sometimes has no obvious relation to it. One might see this penchant for sundering sound and image as a way of underscoring the artifactuality and artificiality of a film regarded as a composition, a contrivance, an exercise in audiovisual design, rather than a slice of life, window onto reality, or transparently unfolding story. And that notwithstanding that such sundering is also an echo of the themes of social alienation and male-female misunderstanding central to the film.

Then a couple with a young child in tow at another table begins a domestic fight, whereupon the woman takes out a gun, follows the man into the street, and shoots him. The soundtrack goes silent for a few seconds after that. This silence, the abolition of the expected urban sounds, in fact speaks more loudly than the gunshot, and shows how silence can sometimes be a prominent element in the sonic patterning of a film. But perhaps it is also a mode of thought about the violence that has just transpired on screen. The unexpected silence, in other words, may be an aspect of both sound as design and sound as commentary, though whether it is the implied director or an internal narrator that is responsible for that commentary may be impossible to determine.

The second episode offers us Paul and his friend Robert in a café, bringing each other up to date. A loud car horn obliterates part of their conversation. In this case, Godard's indifference to the drowning of the dialogue by the car horn illustrates a partiality for the real, prior to polishing or varnishing, an unwillingness to shape the actual to artistic or narrative ends. There follows an incident with a busty girl at the next table, in which Robert instructs Paul in a tactic of feeling a woman's breasts in the course of reaching for sugar without her recoiling or taking offense. This somehow seems a nice trope for the difference between masculine and feminine — at least as viewed from the masculine side.

The third episode opens with a salient voice-over spoken by a woman who is probably Madeleine, though it is at first difficult to determine that, especially as she and Paul appear on screen, bustling about an office, while the voice-over is being heard. Her discourse treats of various deficiencies of modern life, the difficulty of reconciling love and everyday working conditions, concluding with the observation that the average Frenchwoman doesn't exist (*"les Françaises moyennes n'existent pas"*).

This voice-over is typical of the film in that there is no obvious connection between the discourse and the images, nor any apparent narrative function to the discourse. Clearly, such discourse falls under sound as commentary if any does. But first, on what does such discourse comment? Surely, not on the specific events that happen to pass on screen, but on the world of the film generally, little conducive to romance or fantasy. There is also the question of who should be considered the real owner of that commentary. The character Madeleine is its ostensible owner, yet it seems more analytical and reflective than the thoughts to which she gives voice in dialogues in the rest of the film. One possibility, already adumbrated, would be to ascribe the commentary ultimately to the implied filmmaker, the Godard-of-this-film, expressing his own views though one of his characters. Another is to ascribe the commentary to the narrative agent implicit in the film's manner of narration, which could be described as dispassionate and detached, not so far removed from the character of the commentary offered. It is of course unclear which of these three possibilities is most apt, but that is partly because such interpretive matters can only be settled, if at all, in the context of a comprehensive interpretation of the film.

This *"fait précis"* continues with a conversation between Paul and Madeleine in the washroom of her workplace. He tries to make a date, remarks flirtingly on her lying, his nose, her prettiness, her age, the difference between going out with and sleeping with, her parents; she asks whether he has ever gone with a prostitute. Paul then says: "It would give me pleasure to sleep with you. And you?" Madeleine replies: "Never thought about it." This exchange appears to epitomize, once again, all the difference between *"masculin"* and *"feminin"*, as does the succeeding exchange: Madeleine: "What is the center of the world?" Paul: "Love, I would say." Madeleine: "Funny, I would have said 'me'." The masculine, in short, gravitates toward the abstract property, the feminine toward the concrete individual.

Throughout this scene we generally see, not the person talking, but the person listening, and no attempt is made to mask the background noise from the workplace, which at one point almost drowns out the conversation between the protagonists.

The fourth episode offers another typical disconnect between image and sound, as we hear Paul intone a political tract while we see him and Robert walking towards a car. They meet Madeleine and her two flatmates, Catherine and Elisabeth, and a happy mood prevails: Paul runs off, holding a suitcase, almost falls, the others follow. This is a silent episode, an obvious homage to classic comic silent film. Silent segments such as this in a sound film naturally have the effect of drawing attention to the normal role of ambient sound in film, and highlight, as it were for intellectual consideration, the wholly constructed nature of cinema. Another such short silence occurs in the sixth episode, where we see Paul nick a book from an outdoors bookstall without breaking stride, then put it in his coat, then start to read it a few moments later; the silence here may function as an ironic invitation to reflection on Paul's action in relation to the high-minded ideas to which he subscribes as regards culture and society.

The fifth episode opens with Madeleine heard in voice-over, while we see only a metro train and railroad bridge, and then subsequently, from the perspective of the railroad bridge, four persons, one of whom is probably Madeleine, walking at ground level. As we view the images set before us we are privy to Madeleine's musings on how her life is going at present. "Paul kissed me for the second time." "I'd like for Paul to be in love with me, and eventually to sleep with him." "But I hope he doesn't become a bother and a bore."

This is followed by a night scene on an elevated metro train, initiated with yet another arresting silence of about five seconds. Paul and Robert are on the train, Madeleine is at the window of her apartment, by which the metro passes, with Paul circling in the train to catch a glimpse of her each time around.

First a sad, solitary male passenger is seen, and then we see the trio—a blonde woman, probably a prostitute, and two well-dressed black men—who enact a version of Leroi Jones' play *The Dutchman*, with increasingly tense exchanges. She: "You know what you are, you blacks? Assassins, at bottom. And you know it." He: "And you want only to be like those whores of Hollywood. You only think about money, right?" Paul and Robert look apprehensively at the trio, though without interfering. Now there is a close-up of the woman's lap, showing that she has just taken out a gun. Noticing Paul looking at her, she shouts at him: "This is none of your business!" It will not have escaped a viewer's attention that this is the second time in this film that a woman has pulled out a revolver to resolve a problem with a man.

Next there is a medium shot on the evolving drama from outside the moving train, whereupon we hear a sound that could be a gunshot, possibly masked by the train sounds, or could even be the signature sound-burst used for punctuation. Godard here plays on the ambiguity, the indecipherability, of that sound-burst. One now thinks, ah, perhaps that's what it was all along, that bit of sonic punctuation, the transmogrified sound of a gunshot. And so one's take on the commentative value of that singular sound object undergoes a subtle mutation, and one is perhaps more inclined to attribute it to the posturing leftist implied director—the Godard-of-this-film—than to the more distanced and dispassionate narrative agency that seems rather to govern the desultory unfolding of the story of Paul, Madeleine, and company.

In the sixth episode we hear a conversation without immediately grasping who is speaking, though shortly we see that it is two half-dressed girls, Catherine and Elisabeth, who are Madeleine's roommates, talking in a bathroom. Godard, by this sort of dislocation technique, manages to make dialogue, at least temporarily, into a free-floating sonic object, rather than a fully diegetic element of the unfolding narrative — until we get our bearings and can connect the abstract, ghostly word sequence to characters in the story. The subject of discussion is how men and women connect, and two rather different perspectives are expressed. Catherine: "For me the skin is very important. The contact between two persons is, first and foremost, via their skins. As soon as two people hold hands, they feel, or transmit, something." Elisabeth: "No, for me it's the eyes, the look."

After a few rounds of sound-bursts the seventh episode begins with Paul and Madeleine in a café-cum-pool-hall. Prominent are sounds of billiard balls clacking, and saloon doors swinging. Paul wanders around the space, unable to find a place that suits him. We hear various conversations off-screen whose sources are subsequently revealed on-screen: two weird guys, perhaps gay, reading together from a magazine, something with sexual content; then a man and a woman having a serious talk.

Whereas dialogue in an ordinary film is an integral part of the developing story, transpiring between personages central to the story, in this film many conversations, such as the ones just mentioned, strike one either as purely decorative, or else as epitomizing some aspect of social reality. Such conversations do not so much serve to flesh out a fictional world or advance a narrative, as they are simply part of the soundscape of modern urban life, both alienated and alienating. In Godard's characteristic treatment of dialogue, and also in his regular recurrence to interview and survey formats, the filmmaker's critical, Marxian-Brechtian motivations are very much to the fore. But in light of our concerns in this essay, what is most interesting is the way Godard manages to make of dialogue something that in a standard narrative film it rarely is, namely, at the same time an element of sound as design and an element of sound as commentary; in standard narrative film, with its focus on story development and transparency of presentation, it is usually neither.

As the episode proceeds we briefly hear one of Madeleine's bouncy pop songs as she and Paul leave the café, but he stops her just before the door and says: "What I wanted to say is, would you like to become my wife?" She replies, incongruously: "Maybe later. I'm in a hurry. *Au revoir*." Anyway, what I want to draw attention to about those pop songs as they occur in this film is that they are substantially just "sound objects", not so different from the sound-bursts on which I have repeatedly dwelt: when heard they are often not diegetically anchored, and their commenting relation to what is passing on-screen is often opaque.

Paul, Madeleine, and Elisabeth are dancing at a club, then have drinks at an outdoor stand nearby. After Madeleine and Elisabeth leave, Paul chats with a girl who soon asks if he wants to take a photo with her. They go into a photo booth together. "If you want to see my breasts it's 15,000 francs." Paul declines this offer, the girl leaves, then Paul enters the adjoining recording booth to record a disk for Madeleine. "I want to live with you. Please give me a date this evening. The stars fly off. Madeleine, here I am in town. Madeleine, imagine that it's written… Look, air travel, we go to Jerusalem, you hold yourself close to me, we take off. There is a transmission from the control tower... 'Control calling Boeing Flight 123'... 'Paul calling Madeleine!'"

Paul pockets the disk, leaves the recording booth, then enters the pinball parlor. Next, while we hear Madeleine's pop song on the soundtrack, Paul somehow gets into trouble with a knife-wielding youth, who first threatens Paul, making him recoil, and then suddenly stabs himself in the stomach and collapses. The viewer connects this, if indeterminately, with the two preceding incidents of deadly violence, the common denominator being a man who ends up dead, though this time by his own hand. And that gratuitous death will be complemented in episode thirteen by an incident off-screen of self-immolation on the part of someone protesting the war in Vietnam, and in the final episode, by Paul's accidental death, which is reported but not shown.[6]

The eighth episode, which takes place in a laundromat, is largely a conversation between Paul and Robert, two topics of which are the then-emerging "Vietnik" Bob Dylan, and a contrast between what can be found in the word *"masculin"* (*"masque"* and *"cul"*) and what can be found in the word *"feminin"* (nothing). At this point we hear, with no preparation, the opening of Mozart's *Clarinet Concerto*, which effects a segue to the ninth episode.

At the beginning of this episode we hear persons intoning statements whose flavor is reminiscent of both Karl Marx and Aldous Huxley, while we are offered city views with no obvious connection to what's being said. Man: "It's not man's consciousness that determines his social existence, but rather his social existence that determines his consciousness." Woman: "In twenty years everyone will be equipped with an electronic

---

[6] So by the film's end the score in the battle of the sexes stands thus: Women: 5, Men: 0.

device for reliably delivering pleasure and sexual satisfaction." Then we see Paul eating with Catherine, one of Madeleine's roommates. Paul: "Can I speak frankly with you?" She says yes, but continues reading, eating a banana, not looking at him. Paul: "I don't believe you. Your behavior is a mode of defense." Paul then puts the slow movement of Mozart's *Clarinet Concerto* on the phonograph, with Catherine listening attentively. At this point we can recuperate the unmotivated and non-diegetic bit of Mozart heard earlier as some sort of adumbration of the bit now being heard, from the same composition.

Most of the tenth episode, which bears the title "*Dialogue Avec un Produit de Consommation*", involves a pretty young woman being interviewed by Paul, who remains off-screen throughout, the most extended example of Godard's technique of dislocating sound and visual source. "You're a friend of Madeleine's?" "Yes, I know her well." "How did you meet?" "At the magazine." "Which one? Mademoiselle Scandale? What did you do at the magazine?" "It was special. I was named 'Mademoiselle Nineteen'. But why all these questions?" "It's a sociological survey." "I was lucky to be chosen 'Mlle 19'. Lots of benefits. Such as money, a car…" "What did you do before?" "My studies for the *bac*." "Do you want to continue your studies?" "No, no." "According to you, socialism is the wave of the future or no?" "What? I'm not qualified to respond." "Well, what is socialism to you?" "I can't explain." "And for you, what does 'The American Way' mean?" "Life at a rapid pace, and very free." "I visited the U.S. It was great, extraordinary, so much to do." "What does the word 'reactionary' mean to you?" "Well, reacting against things." "It's good, or it's bad?" "Oh… it's good." "Do you want to have children?" "Yes, but not now. I want to live, and with children it's not possible." "You know what birth control is?" "Yes, more or less." "Do you know what it amounts to in practical or concrete terms?" "I don't want to answer… all right, the pill, for example, or the diaphragm." "Do you fall in love often?" "No, no." "You don't like being in love." "No, that's not it, it's not something you seek, it just happens." "Do you know where in the world there is a war at this moment?" "No." "Really, you don't know?" "No, that doesn't interest me."

A nice example of a "sound object" devised by Godard that functions, once again, both as design and as commentary, occurs in what appears to still be the tenth *"fait précis"*. We see the date 1965 in bold numerals, then these numerals disappear one by one, leaving only the numeral 9, while one hears the sound of at least what appears to be a cash register ringing. This sound-object, which is both non-diegetic and non-narrative, arrests attention as a sound whose character intrigues in its own right, while at the same time expressing, in the condensed form common to poetic art, the implied filmmaker's critique of capitalist and consumerist society.

The rest of episode ten features more conversational interactions in cafes of the sort remarked earlier, ones observed by Paul and Madeleine, but entirely tangential to their own story. First we see a Nordic type with a blonde at a neighboring table. Madeleine says it's the one who shot her husband on leaving the café on that earlier occasion. Their conversation reveals that he's German, that she's neither German nor French but East European, and that she hates the Germans because her parents perished in a German concentration camp. He says that's got nothing to do with him, he was ten years old at the time. After that we see Brigitte Bardot—yes, Brigitte Bardot!—at another table, rehearsing the text of a play entitled *Le Prodige* with a man in a Greek sailor's cap, probably a stage director. After dutifully listening to the man emphatically lecture her on how to do the scene, she then reads out loud from the text while unrelated city shots pass on screen.

The eleventh episode is one of the most interesting in the film, and involves the trope of a film-within-a-film. Paul and Catherine enter a cinema, joining Madeleine and Elisabeth who are already there. Paul sits next to Madeleine, then Elisabeth changes seats, coming between them, whereupon Paul moves to a seat at Catherine's right, away from Madeleine. This is followed by a brief close-up of Madeleine watching the screen.

We then see an outdoor scene, it's snowing, a man catches up to a woman on a staircase. It's not clear what to make of what we are seeing, how to relate it to the main narrative. Paul goes into bathroom of the cinema, sees two men kissing in a toilet stall. They notice him, tell him to clear off, then close the stall door. Paul uses the urinal, then scrawls on the stall door, the two men still inside: "Down with the republic of cowards!"

Now we see the film that Madeleine and the others are viewing. We understand finally that that outdoor scene in the snow belongs primordially to that film, and only secondarily to Godard's. The film is a somber example of Swedish eroticism, with mild sadomasochistic undertones. The images of the Swedish film fill the whole screen, thus effectively displacing Godard's film, or otherwise regarded, fusing with it. Tension and violence between a man and a woman in an apartment gives way to sexual interaction. Suddenly Paul notices that the correct aspect ratio is not being maintained by the projectionist, so he leaves his seat, runs around to the back of the theatre, enters the projection booth, and gives the projectionist a lesson in aspect ratio, quoting from a book of regulations for film screening. Then he spray paints something about De Gaulle on a wall, briefly regards a man and a woman in the street who are making love, then returns to his seat in the cinema.

On screen the male actor repeatedly grunts in an animalistic fashion, while the woman actor slowly undresses, prodded by his animal sounds. Paul: "Okay, let's go, this is stupid." Catherine: "No, I want to watch." Elisabeth: "Let's go, eroticism disgusts me." Catherine: "Not me." Paul: "You want to stay?" Madeleine: "Yes, I'm staying." The couple on screen kisses passionately in front of a round mirror.

Paul, in voice-over: "One goes to the cinema often. The screen goes blank, one shivers. But more often, Madeleine and I, we are disappointed." Now we see the Swedish couple in bed, the man still communicating by grunting, then taking the woman's head in his hand and, from what one surmises, forcing her to perform oral sex. Paul's voice-over continues: "But more often, we are disappointed, and sad. It's not the film we dreamt of, not the film we would have liked to see, not the film each one of us carries inside himself, or perhaps most secretly, not the film we would have liked to live."

The fourteenth episode gives us the recording studio where Madeleine, the aspiring pop artist, is cutting one of her records. We witness this first from the control booth, where one hears the instrumental accompaniment, with Madeleine's voice, coming from the isolation booth, heard over that. Then we see and hear Madeleine singing in the isolation booth without hearing the instrumental accompaniment. Now Paul enters the isolation booth, and listens to Madeleine singing solo, with her small voice, which has a thin, washed-out quality in contrast to the effect of her singing with full accompaniment. This scene is arguably a sort of trope for the making of a film by combining or assembling different elements, separately constructed, manufactured, or recorded.

On leaving the studio Madeleine is accosted by a radio journalist with cassette recorder and microphone in hand, to whom she accords an interview. He asks what music she prefers, she says the Beatles, and as regards classical music, Johann Sebastian Bach. She doesn't see any conflict between that and the sort of pop song she herself produces. And she agrees, prompted by the journalist, that she is part of the "Pepsi Generation". While she is describing her preferences in clothes, at one point something like a gunshot is heard. But is that sound diegetic or non-diegetic? It remains indeterminate. One effect of a film like *Masculin-Feminin* is to unsettle, or even dissolve, the distinction between diegetic and non-diegetic sound, because the film unsettles and dissolves, to a degree, the distinction between fiction and reality, storytelling and reportage, invention and documentation.

Completing this episode, Paul speaks in voice-over, intoning a series of survey questions, while unrelated city scenes unfold, but without the diegetic sounds that one would expect to hear. Once again, this is both an homage to silent film and a way of underlining the mutual independence and detachability of sound and image, and hence the fundamental artificiality-artifactuality of film. "Why do vacuum cleaners break down?" "Do you like cheese that comes in a tube?" "If you see an accident, what do you do?" "If your fiancée dumped you for a black guy, would you be okay with that?" "Are you interested in poetry?" "Do you know what a communist is?" "Do you read much?" "To avoid having a child, do you prefer the pill or putting something in your vagina?" "Do you know there's a war on in Iraq?" "How much do you earn per month?"

Paul: "I realized that these surveys don't serve to reveal the collective mind, that the responses are generally insincere. I was fooling my subjects, and they were fooling me. Such surveys pass insidiously from simple observation or recording of behavior to outright judgments of value. And the answers to those questions, I realized, did not reflect current ideology, but rather that of the past. I knew I had to remain vigilant."

Our last view of Paul finds him in a café, the natural habitat of a French intellectual, writing in a notebook: "A philosopher is someone who opposes his consciousness to opinion. To be a consciousness is to be open to the world. To be faithful is to act as if time didn't exist. And wisdom consists in being able to see, to really see, life as it is."

That last remark is meant to serve, perhaps, as the motto of the film, though it relates ironically to what we learn in the following and final episode, episode fifteen, namely, that Paul has died of an accident while visiting an apartment in process of renovation where he and the pregnant Madeleine were thinking of setting up house together. How? By backing up too far and falling in the attempt to take a photo of Madeleine in the half-finished apartment—a classic example of being insufficiently conscious of one's surroundings and of the life going on around one.

4. The very end of the film offers a last, double-edged word screen:

FEMININ
F   IN

This belies a remark made by Paul's pal Robert in an earlier scene to the effect that there was nothing contained in the word "FEMININ", while also underlining that, given the sad state of male-female relations in modern capitalist society, men are fated to find their sorry ends in women. A harsh judgment that seems only to be confirmed by the very last perceptual datum offered to the viewer, a final instance of Godard's harsh and resonant signature sound-burst.

University of Maryland
august@mdu.edu

REFERENCES

Carroll, Noël. 2006. "Introduction to Part IV." In *Philosophy of Film and Motion Pictures*, ed. Noël Carroll—Jinhee Choi. London: Blackwell.

Davies, David. 2010. "Eluding Wilson's 'Elusive Narrators'." *Philosophical Studies* 147 (3): 387–94.

Gaut, Berys. 2004. "The Philosophy of the Movies: Cinematic Narration." In *Blackwell Guide to Aesthetics*, ed. Peter Kivy, 230–253. Oxford: Blackwell.

Kania, Andrew. 2005. "Against the Ubiquity of Fictional Narrators." *Journal of Aesthetics and Art Criticism* 63 (1): 47–54.

Levinson, Jerrold. 2006. "Film Music and Narrative Agency." In *Contemplating Art*, 143–183. Oxford: Clarendon Press.

Thomson-Jones, Katherine. 2007. "The Literary Origins of the Cinematic Narrator." *British Journal of Aesthetics* 47 (1): 76–94.

Wartenberg, Thomas. 2007. "Need There Be Implicit Narrators of Literary Fictions?" *Philosophical Studies* 135 (1): 89–94.

Wilson, George. 1997. "*Le Grand Imagier* Steps Out: On the Primitive Basis of Film Narration." *Philosophical Topics* 25 (1): 295–318.

———. 2007. "Elusive Narrators in Literature and Film." *Philosophical Studies* 135 (1): 73–88.

———. 2011. *Seeing Fictions in Film*. Oxford—New York: Oxford University Press.

VIDEOGAMES AND THE FIRST-PERSON

Jon Robson — Aaron Meskin

ABSTRACT: When playing videogames it is common practice to describe events in first-person terms; "I was bitten by the zombie", "I hit Bison with a Shoryuken" and so forth. What are we to make of this tendency? Are these first-person locutions a matter of the ordinary sort of make-believe that is involved in our engagement with standard fictions, or is there some better way of making sense of them? We begin this paper by briefly rehearsing some criticisms we have previously directed at Grant Tavinor's claim that the nature of our interactions (and especially our first-person engagement) with videogames undermines a key element of Kendall Walton's account of fiction and make-believe. We then turn to an extended discussion of David Velleman's recent claim that in virtual environments, like those found in *Second Life* as well as standard videogames, we do not fictionally perform actions (as Walton would have it) but rather "literally perform" fictional actions (Velleman 2008: 407). We argue that the challenge to Walton presented by Velleman is unsuccessful and, furthermore, that the alternate account of videogame engagement posed by Velleman misrepresents Walton's account of make-believe. However, we conclude by arguing that there are still important lessons concerning first-person interaction with videogames to be drawn from the work of Tavinor and Velleman.

1/ Introduction

Videogame players say the strangest things; "I invaded heaven with a band of demons", "I keep getting killed by the men in very dark brown" and even "I travelled back in time to save my fellow dolphins".[1] How should we account for such comments?

---

[1] Such remarks are to be expected from players of *Destroy all Humans!*, *Disgaea* and *Echo the Dolphin: Defender of the Future* respectively.

One obvious suggestion is that such remarks are part of a fiction. If we are to make sense of such remarks along these lines then one of the most promising places to turn is Kendall Walton's book *Mimesis as Make-Believe*, which presents by far the most influential contemporary account of the nature of fictional representations. Walton outlines a very broad notion of fiction which includes anything which has the function of serving as a prop (i.e., something which mandates imaginings in virtue of various principles) in a game of make-believe (Walton 1990: 69). Walton, then, counts not only ordinary or canonical examples such as horror novels, Hollywood movies and Shakespeare plays as fictions but also such unexpected items as toy trucks, patterned wallpaper and, for reasons having to do with his account of depiction, all pictures (Walton 1990: 293-352). We take it as obvious that videogames, or at least the vast majority of videogames, are fictions in this minimal sense. Videogames and their displays are designed to mandate all manner of imaginings: that there are zombies, that ghosts are chasing Pac-Man, that we are serving an ace in tennis, etc. As we will argue below, this claim when properly understood should not be in the least bit controversial. In addition to this minimal claim, though, we believe that (most) videogames are Waltonian in a more full-blooded sense; that is, that they display all the features of fictions that are laid out in *Mimesis as Make-Believe*.

Recently, however, there have been several challenges to construing videogames (and other virtual environments) as fictions in such robustly Waltonian terms. The strongly interactive nature of videogames and the level of first-person engagement involved in videogame play have seemed to some to mark them as importantly distinct from ordinary fictions. One relevant difference is that while it is common practice amongst players of videogames to describe certain goings on in the videogame environment in first-person terms ('I crashed my car on the final corner", "I was bitten by the zombie", "I hit Bison with a Shoryuken") it is far rarer, though if Walton is right not as rare as you may think, to describe our interactions with canonical fictions in this way. How are we to account for this disparity? Is this merely an accidental surface feature of our engagement with videogames, or does it highlight some deep difference between videogames and canonical fictions? In an earlier paper (Meskin and Robson 2012) we discussed and criticized one answer to this question, Grant Tavinor's contention that our first-person engagement with videogames "smudge" (Tavinor 2005: 34) a key aspect of Walton's account of fictions. This article briefly surveys these concerns but focuses primarily on a second, more radical, suggestion, by David Velleman, that in videogames we do not fictionally perform actions (as Walton would have it) but rather "literally perform" fictional actions (Velleman 2008: 407). We hold that while Velleman is right to claim that there are some important differences between videogames and most other fictions with respect to first-person involvement, he is mistaken in claiming that this undermines attempts to construe our engagement with videogames as a matter of make-believe with fictions.

In section 2 we examine some key aspects of what it is to be a fiction in the full-blooded Waltonian sense and say a little about how this applies in the case of videogames. In section 3 we briefly summarize our discussion of Tavinor's claim that first-person interaction with videogames challenges some key aspects of the Waltonian account of fiction. In sections 4 and 5 we focus on a recent article by David Velleman which puts forward a more fundamental challenge to construing videogames in terms of make-believe and argue that

Velleman's account also fails to undermine the claim that videogames are Waltonian fictions of a perfectly standard kind. In section 6 we survey some genuine differences between videogames and canonical fictions which are highlighted in the work of Tavinor and Velleman. We argue that, when properly understood, these differences are important and deserve to be taken into account in our theorising concerning videogames, but that there is no reason to think that they undermine the claim that videogames are full-blooded Waltonian fictions.

2/ Videogames as fictions

The nature of fiction is a deeply contested one, so any attempt to explore the question of how videogames stand in relation to the category of fiction requires some sort of specification as to how that category will be understood. We shall follow Tavinor and Velleman in focusing on Kendall Walton's influential account of fiction and asking whether that theory can make sense of videogames and our interactions with them.

As stated above, fictions on Walton's account are all those objects "possessing the social function of serving as props in games of make-believe" (Walton 1990: 69) and it is hopefully clear from the last section that most (perhaps all) videogames belong to this category. It is important, though, to be clear on just how innocuous this claim is, especially given the ongoing controversies amongst games theorists (and others) as to how videogames are best classified. Videogames being fictions in this sense is compatible with their failing to be fictions in various other senses. Perhaps videogames are not fictions in the everyday sense of that term (if there is such) or according to some other theoretical sense highlighted by those games theorists who deny that videogames are fictions. We think that many videogames (*Bioshock, Sonic the Hedgehog, Resident Evil 5* etc.) are not only fictions in Walton's sense but also under any plausible classification while others (*Wii Sports, SingStar, Project Gotham Racing* etc.) may only be fictional in Walton's highly permissive sense. However, we will not argue for these claim here since our arguments only require videogames to be fictions in Walton's sense and this is perfectly compatible with the claim that they belong (perhaps in some more fundamental sense) to some other category. As such we can remain neutral with respect to disputes amongst games theorists concerning whether videogames are best seen as belonging fundamentally to the category of the fictional or the virtual.[2] For those not convinced by such reassurances, or by our brief arguments in the last section, we offer a more complete defence of the claim that videogames are Waltonian fictions elsewhere (Meskin and Robson 2012: 5-14). For the rest of this paper, though, we will focus our attention on defending the claim that videogames are Waltonian in the full-blooded sense; that is, that they have all the features of fictions as laid out in Walton's *Mimesis as Make-Believe*. Or, rather, we will argue that if videogames fail to be fictions in this stronger sense this is only because of some general flaw in Walton's theory and not because of some feature specific to videogames. It is not our purpose to defend or criticize Walton's overall theory, so from this point on we will merely assume that a full-blooded Waltonian theory can be adequately applied to canonical fictions.

Obviously it will not be possible for us to discuss all, or even most, of the claims Walton makes concerning fictions in *Mimesis as Make-Believe*, so for the most part we will merely highlight those points of Walton's theory which have been subject to specific objections in the case of videogames. Most of

---

[2] Tavinor (2009: 34-60) presents an opinionated overview of these debates.

these aspects will be discussed in later sections when the objections themselves are raised, but it is worth pausing here to discuss one important feature at length, namely Walton's distinction between the work world and the game world, since it will play a vital role in a number of the objections we consider below.

It is not hard to get one's head around the notion of a fictional world (i.e., the "world" composed of, or at least associated with, the fictional truths explicitly or implicitly determined by a fiction). The fictional world of *Doctor Who*, for example, is associated with, or composed of, what is fictional (or fictionally true) in that series. For example, the fictional world of *Doctor Who* contains Cybermen and a time-machine that looks like a 1960s London police-box, and it is true in that world that the Doctor has recently claimed to be 1103 years old. But Walton (1990: 58–61) proposes a novel distinction among fictional worlds—he suggests that we must distinguish the worlds of fictional works and the worlds of the games associated with those works. Work worlds are those fictional worlds associated with representational works or fictions (such as the worlds of *Doctor Who* and *Buffy the Vampire Slayer*) but in addition to those work worlds, there are what Walton calls "game worlds" — fictional worlds associated with games in which those representations serve as props. That is, in addition to the world associated with *Doctor Who*—the work itself—there is also the world associated with our imaginative interactions with *Doctor Who*.

Why talk about game worlds? In short, because there are things made fictional by our interaction with representations that are not fictional in (or according to) those representations. So, for example, according to Walton it is fictionally true when we see the *Doctor Who* Christmas special "The Doctor, the

Widow and the Wardrobe" that we are seeing the Doctor himself ("Look at what the Doctor is doing" we say to the rest of the family gathered around the television). And similar fictional truths are generated by other audience members' viewings. But it is not true in the world of *Doctor Who* that we or any other audience member is seeing him. Rather, Walton suggests, we might say that these fictional truths belong to game worlds (i.e., the games of make-believe we play using the television show as prop). Similarly, albeit controversially, Walton argues that in the case of responses to fictions, it is typically only fictional that audience members have emotional responses that are directed towards the inhabitants of such fictions (though it is true, and not merely fictional, that we have certain affective responses which Walton labels "quasi-emotional" aroused by those fictions) (Walton 1990: 241-49). But it is not standardly the case that such things are fictional in the worlds of the fictions themselves. It is not true, for example, in *Doctor Who* that we are scared of the Weeping Angels; our fear of the Angels is part of the game world associated with our watching of *Doctor Who*—not part of the work world associated with *Doctor Who* itself.

Among game worlds, we may usefully distinguish between the authorised and non-authorised (Walton 1990: 60). We could, after all, imagine just about anything we wanted while watching *Doctor Who*; that is, we could play all sorts of imaginative games while watching the show; imagining that The Doctor was really a travelling carpet salesman, that the Cybermen are just misunderstood, etc. But the function of the show is not to be used in such a way. Game worlds associated with such odd imaginings are unauthorised, whereas those game worlds that accord with the function(s) of the representation (e.g., imagining ourselves to be afraid of the Angels) are authorised.

This allows us to begin spelling out the relationship between work worlds and game worlds. So, for example, there is significant overlap between work worlds and their related game worlds since it is typically the case that what is fictional in a work world is fictional in the game worlds that are associated with it (e.g., it is fictional both in the work world of *Doctor Who* and the vast majority of *Doctor Who* game worlds that the Doctor is a Time Lord). Work worlds are (roughly) composed of those fictional truths that are fictional in all authorised game worlds.[3]

With this understanding of the nature of work worlds and game worlds in place we can now look at an objection to a Waltonian account of videogames put forward by Grant Tavinor.

3/ Tavinor on work worlds and game worlds

In his various discussions of the nature of videogames Grant Tavinor is generally sympathetic to treating videogames as Waltonian fictions (Tavinor 2005: 25; Tavinor 2009: 40-41). However, he also claims that one key aspect of Walton's theory — namely, the work world/game world distinction discussed above — is undermined or "smudged" with respect to videogames (Tavinor 2005: 34). In a previous paper (Meskin and Robson, 2012) we argue that Tavinor is mistaken and that the work world/game world distinction is as robust with respect to videogames as it is with canonical fictions. In this section we briefly recap this debate and consider its application to the particular issue of first-person representation.

---

[3] Though only roughly; see Walton (1990: 60) for a more complete account.

Videogames and the First-Person

Although Tavinor is not opposed to our making the work world/game world distinction with respect to canonical fictions, he believes the distinction is more problematic in the case of videogames (Tavinor 2005: 34). Why is this? In the case of canonical fictions there is a clear distinction between the game world and the work world. In particular, self-referential fictional truths of the game world (e.g., that Aaron sees the Dalek, that Jon admires the Doctor) are not typically true in the work world since (sadly) neither Aaron nor Jon appear in the world of *Doctor Who*. As was mentioned above, only things that are true in all authorised games are true in the relevant work world. And none of us see the Dalek in every authorised game associated with the relevant television show since none of us are involved in every authorised game associated with it (there are other viewers after all). We do not, then, contribute to the truths of any *Doctor Who* episode. But according to Tavinor "players contribute to the truths of the work world of videogames" (Tavinor 2005: 33). Player characters make "many new things fictionally true of that fictional world" (Tavinor 2005: 33) including things about their role in that world. So "the game world of the [videogame] fiction interposes on the work world" (Tavinor 2005: 34). In brief, the smudging or blurring that Tavinor identifies arises from the way in which players may affect work worlds of fictions through their actions and responses rather than just affecting game worlds associated with those works. This strikes him as radically different from the case of ordinary fictions where audiences, their actions and their responses are typically isolated from the fictional (work) world.

Tavinor makes two important claims here (i) that, in contrast to consumers of standard fictions, players of videogames can often influence what is true in a work world

443

and (ii) in videogames there is no clear distinction between what is true in the work world and what is true in the various (authorised?) game worlds associated with it. We believe that the first of these claims, when correctly interpreted, provides an important insight into the nature of videogames and we will discuss this further in section 6. The second claim, though, we take to be demonstrably false and have previously presented (in Meskin and Robson 2012: 21-28) a number of counterexamples to it—instances where what is fictional in an authorised game world is not fictional in the work world. So, for example, we argued that in the recent *Bioshock* series, certain player decisions may make it the case that it is true in the authorised game world associated with a particular playing that the player feels guilty for their actions but there is no reason to believe that any character feels guilt in the world work associated with that playing (and, in particular good reason to think that the player character does not feel such guilt).

So, Tavinor's second claim concerning videogames does not hold. However, in section 6 we will argue that it would be a mistake to dismiss Tavinor's argument completely. Although his position is ultimately mistaken, it highlights some important features of videogames which set them apart from other fictions. Before discussing this, though, we will look at a more radical denial of Walton's theory as applied to videogames.

4/ Velleman on artificial agency

Like Tavinor, David Velleman also believes that videogames do not conform to the standard Waltonian account of fiction. (Velleman presents his proposal primarily with regards to the virtual world *Second Life* but given his repeated emphasis on "virtual play" (Velleman 2008: 407, 408 and 413) and some of the examples he chooses (Velleman 2008: 424) it seems clear that he intends the point to apply to many videogames as well.)[4] However, Velleman's scepticism on this account goes much deeper than Tavinor's, and rather than merely suggesting that we abandon or amend one feature of Walton's theory to account for our agency in videogames, he advocates a wholesale abandonment of attempts to construe videogames in Waltonian terms and to interpret videogame play as a matter of pretend play or make-believe. The second part of this claim is particularly striking since a refusal to accept our interactions with videogames as instances of make-believe would disbar them from being fictions not only on Walton's view but also on a number of other influential accounts of fiction, such as those of Currie (1990) and Davies (1996), which treat fiction as essentially a matter of make-believe. Velleman's central claim is, to put it starkly, that when engaging with virtual play we do not fictionally perform actions but "literally perform" fictional actions (Velleman 2008: 407).

We are not sure exactly how to interpret Velleman's claim, that we literally perform fictional actions, and are especially puzzled by Velleman's insistence that our display of genuine agency differentiates engagement with the virtual from engagement with the merely make-believe. When we engage with fictions we pretend to do certain things—to see a unicorn, to read the diary of Lemuel Gulliver, to hide from the monster—but, of course, we are also genuinely performing certain actions in doing these things: looking at a picture of a unicorn, reading *Gulliver's Travels*, and hiding from a friend who is pretending to be a monster. So it seems that in these cases we are still employing genuine agency.

---

[4] We take no stance here as to whether it is appropriate to classify *Second Life* as a videogame but for convenience will refer to it as such for the remainder of this paper.

To motivate the supposed difference, Velleman highlights a number of features which he believes distinguish videogames, and our interactions with them, from Waltonian fictions. In this section we will address three types of feature which seem to be key to Velleman's account: (i) the phenomenology of our engagement with virtual worlds, (ii) the nature of our discourse concerning such engagement, (iii) the robustness of virtual truths. In the following section we will examine a series of claims which Velleman makes concerning aspects of the uniquely close relationship between the player and their avatar. We will argue that none of these features support Velleman's view that videogames are not Waltonian fictions. We will show that many of the problems Velleman raises can be easily addressed by the Waltonian since they draw their initial plausibility from a focus on childhood games of make-believe rather that canonical fictions (and in many cases misrepresent the nature of childhood make-believe). Velleman does, however, highlight some important distinctions between videogames and canonical fictions; we will address these in section 6 but argue that they provide no reason to abandon the Waltonian view.

The first feature that we will address is the allegedly unique phenomenology which we encounter in virtual environments such as videogames. As an example of this Velleman claims that

> players who send their avatars into unknown regions of the virtual word are genuinely curious about what they will find; they do not attribute a fictional curiosity to their avatars to account for their fictional explorations. (Velleman 2008: 412)

This is, we take it, intended to stand in contrast to the merely fictional curiosity we display concerning make-believe games and canonical fictions. This example, though, appears to rest on a mistaken equivocation of being curious about a fiction and being fictionally curious. We are often curious as to how a novel or film will end; this is curiosity concerning a fiction but it is not fictional curiosity. When reading *Pride and Prejudice and Zombies* for the first time we may be genuinely curious to know how the book turns out. Of course it is only fictional, at least on a standard Waltonian account, that we are curious as to what happens to Elizabeth, Darcy and their undead opponents, and there is nothing preventing a Waltonian from putting forward parallel claims concerning our videogame interactions. When playing *Xenoblade Chronicles*, much of the characters' time is spent exploring the Bionis (the colossal creature on which the majority of the game's character's live). The Waltonian can accept that the player will most likely be genuinely curious to know about the game's layout, what features the programmers have added to the virtual environment and so forth. They will, however, maintain that it is only fictional that the player is curious as to the location of hidden treasure or lurking enemies. Even in the case of childhood games of make-believe, on which Velleman largely bases his contrast, we can see the same phenomenon. Let us imagine, taking one of Walton's classic examples, that we are playing a make-believe game in which any tree stump counts as a bear. In such a case, the Waltonian will claim, we may be generally curious as to what is true in this fictional world; there are so many places where stumps could (genuinely) be uncovered after all and as such so many places where we could (fictionally) stumble upon a hidden bear.

Velleman goes on to make a second claim concerning the phenomenology of our emotional involvement with fictional and virtual entities. With respect to an individual's attitude to the former Velleman claims that "a monster that he has imagined and is aware of being able to kill by means of further imagining does not frighten him as a real monster would" (Velleman 2008: 411). Such a claim is, of course, perfectly in line with Walton's view that our attitudes to such creatures would be one of quasi- (as opposed to genuine) fear. With respect to virtual monsters, though, Velleman proposes that we hold a different, "more realistic" attitude based on our understanding that the world they occupy, while fictional, is not subject to our control.

Again, though, it is clear that Velleman has failed to establish any contrast between virtual horrors and standard fictional ones. The ghosts and ghouls of films and novels are at least as recalcitrant as those in videogames. Further, it is clear that our standard reaction to videogame monster is not "realistic" in the sense of being anything like as intense as our likely reaction to encountering real life monsters. One of us has, today alone, encountered giant spiders, killer robots and murderous ogres in virtual environments but has no need for the extensive post-traumatic counselling that encountering any of these things in the real world would likely necessitate. Indeed all of Walton's arguments that our fear in watching the green slime approaching is not genuine (our desire to repeat such experiences, the fact we don't get up and leave the cinema, our continued belief that the object of our fear does not exist etc.) seem readily applicable, with slight adaptations, in the virtual monster case. Are our emotional (or quasi-emotional) responses to virtual horrors, as Velleman claims, typically more intense than our attitudes towards standard fictional ones? This is an interesting question, and one which we suspect cannot be solved from the armchair; however, it is also not necessary for us to answer it here. Assume that Walton is right and that our "emotional" reactions to fictions are only quasi-emotions, this account is perfectly compatible with the truth of Velleman's claim. It should be clear that our degree of quasi-fear can vary considerably depending on the stimulus; some fictions are merely quasi-unnerving, others are quasi-terrifying. If it transpired that videogame peril was, *ceteris paribus*, more quasi-frightening than peril in games of make-believe or Hollywood movies then this would be an interesting psychological fact but not one that casts any doubt on Walton's account.

Another feature which Velleman highlights in order to support this contrast is the way in which people describe their interactions with virtual environments. Consider, for instance, Velleman's own example concerning players' descriptions of falling in love in virtual worlds (Velleman 2008: 412). There have been numerous, sometimes well publicized, cases of people carrying out whole relationships—meeting, striking up a friendship, dating, falling in love, cheating on their partners and separating—entirely, or at least primarily, within virtual worlds such as *Second Life*. These, Velleman stresses, are not like cases where we become fictionally enamoured with the protagonist of a novel or even, we assume, the complex and often tumultuous romantic relationships you can pursue with the computer controlled characters in a game like *Dragon Age II*. Those involved in such virtual relationships "describe themselves as being in love, not as authoring a fictional romance" (Velleman 2008: 412). Of course, someone who accepts a Waltonian account of our emotional engagement with fictions will not typically take such avowals at face value; after all people will generally claim that they (or at least their less stalwart friends) are genuinely afraid of the fictional monsters on the screen. However, in the virtual romance case we are happy to grant that the emotions experienced are genuine; since they are not directed at fictional objects. The people involved do not love their partner's avatar (assuming they are not suffering from some mental illness and except in the extended sense that you might love some other reflections of your partner's personality such as their music collection or their wardrobe) but their partner themselves. The relationship then is not between fictional or virtual entities, or as Velleman sometimes suggests, between hybrids of the real and the fictional (Velleman 2008: 423), but between two genuine flesh-and-blood people.

Now of course, Velleman will argue, such relationships will make no sense if they are founded on entirely fictitious actions. Relationships based on merely pretended displays of affection and make-believe professions of love (that are known by both parties to be such) are unlikely to get off the ground. However, this response overlooks an important aspect of Walton's theory: the claim that we can, and often do, genuinely perform certain acts by pretending to perform others. We can genuinely display a lack of sympathy for your plight by pretending to play a tiny violin and can genuinely display affection by pretending to blow a kiss. It is not problematic then, on a Waltonian theory, to claim that person A genuinely professes their love for person B by pretending to have their avatar profess love for hers. Falling in love with someone after only communicating via avatars is certainly a curious thing, just as it would be curious to fall in love with someone with whom you had only previously communicated via the medium of sock puppets. Neither, though, presents any theoretical problems. It may well be that in certain contexts we standardly perform the genuine action of asserting P by performing the fictional act of having our avatar, or our sock puppet, assert that P.

Similar considerations apply to other activities one might undertake in certain virtual environments. A law professor may genuinely educate others about the intricacies of property law in virtual environments by pretending to have her avatar lecture theirs on the subject (and indeed, as Velleman points out (Velleman 2008: 424 n. 1), such activities have been undertaken). Clearly, though, not all virtual activities are reflexive in this way. It is often the case in a virtual environment, such as those found in the *Call of Duty* series, that players will make-believe that they are lying in wait to shoot their friends or setting a deadly trap for their brother. Typically a player will not feel resentment if their friend acts in such a way, and indeed would likely be far more worried if they discovered their friend had been spending their time indulging in private games of make-believe concerning their untimely demise.

A more promising candidate for Velleman to appeal to here may well be entirely virtual relationships such as those in *Dragon Age II*. In such cases the player may say things like "I love Merrill" in reference to one of the possible love interests for the game's protagonist, just as some will say when watching *Doctor Who* "I love Amy". Both of these can be accounted for in standard Waltonian terms where the player/viewer engages in a (possibly authorised) game world where they are in love with the character in question. However, in the *Dragon Age II* case the player will frequently say things like "I kissed Merrill", "I bought Merrill a gift", "I helped Merrill summon a demon" (we do crazy things for love), the equivalents of which would be clearly unacceptable in the *Doctor Who* case. In section 6 we will have something more to say about such cases.

A third respect in which Velleman claims that "virtual play differs from typical make-believe is that players cannot make stipulative additions or alterations to the fictional truth of the game" (Velleman 2008: 407). The thought here, we take it, is that while what is fictional in a game of make-believe is entirely within the stipulative powers of the players, those engaging in virtual play need to undertake certain antecedently prescribed actions to make certain outcomes occur. When pretending to be a racing car driver a child can make it (fictionally) the case that they win a race merely by stipulating that they do or, if they are playing with other children, by persuading the group to assent to this stipulation. By contrast, you cannot make it true-in-the-fiction that you won a race in *Project Gotham Racing* merely by stipulating that you did, even if fellow players are happy to go along with this stipulation. You can, of course, make-believe that you won the race, just as you can imagine that virtual dragons are really friendly kittens or that a virtual shack is a castle, but such imaginings are unauthorised.

Even if this contrast holds, though, it fails to motivate the view that videogames are not Waltonian fictions. Compared to many standard fictions, videogames are remarkably open to alteration by the player. Consumers of canonical fictions are rarely able, by stipulation or otherwise, to affect what is true in those fictions. By taking certain actions in *Mass Effect* 2 one *can* make it the case that certain crew members survive the final mission (or, in a more malevolent frame of mind, that they don't). By contrast, we are famously unable to affect what is true in many other fictions; we cannot save Romeo and Juliet no matter how much we may like to.[5] Again, we will have more to say about this in section 6.

5/ *Velleman on avatars*

In addition to the three claims discussed above, Velleman also motivates his alleged disparity by appealing to a series of related claims regarding the unique relationship between the player and their avatar. Firstly, he claims that there is an

---

[5] For a detailed discussion of this fact see Walton (1990: 191–95).

intimate link between the player's view of the virtual world and their avatar's; that the player

> cannot learn about a part of the virtual world unless his avatar goes there. He sees only from the avatar's perspective, and he cannot see around corners unless the avatar turns to look. (Velleman 2008: 408)

Secondly, he argues that the identities of online players are importantly opaque in that "there is no way for players to emerge from behind their avatars to speak or act as their actual selves" (Velleman 2008: 410). Finally, he argues that in virtual environments players typically read off their own emotional attitudes towards the contents of such worlds whereas in make-believe cases the player is "likely to have invented this attribution rather than read it from his own feelings" (Velleman 2008: 411).

Velleman's first two claims may well be correct with respect to some virtual environments but they seem at most to be contingent features of that medium and notably neither actually holds with respect to Velleman's chosen example of *Second Life*. Taking the first claim first it is just not true (even disregarding the concession Velleman makes in a footnote that the players typically view the events of *Second Life* from "slightly behind and above their avatars" (Velleman 2008: 425 n. 6) that the player only sees what their avatar sees. In various sections of *Second Life* the player can view all manner of things- menus, statistics etc. which we assume they are not authorised to imagine their avatar seeing (such items are similar in this respect to thought bubbles in comics and subtitles in films).[6]

---

[6] Of course there are rare instances of comics and films which break this convention. For instance the comic book character Deadpool appears to have an (intermittent) ability to perceive his own thought bubbles.

Even leaving aside such exotica, the player in *Second Life* is able to manipulate the in-game camera away from its default position, while their avatar remains stationary, viewing the action from a number of different angles. In fact it is a relatively simple matter for the player to move the camera so as to view events from a perspective hundreds of feet away from their avatar and to observe objects completely out of their avatar's line of sight.[7] There are, however, extant examples of videogames which come much closer to realising the model Velleman suggests, including the *Metroid Prime* series and *Mirror's Edge*, though even these are not perfect examples (for instance the saving and loading sections of *Metroid Prime* are viewed from a third person perspective). We do not deny that an example perfectly matching Velleman's description is possible, or even that such an example actually exists (though we cannot think of one); what we want to make clear is that this feature is very far from being typical of the kind of virtual world which Velleman discusses. Velleman's point is undermined yet further when we note that there are extant canonical fictions where the action is seen entirely (or almost entirely) from the viewpoint of a fictional character (for instance, the film *Lady in the Lake*).

The second claim concerning opacity is more typical with regards to virtual worlds such as *Second Life*. Two players in such a virtual world may engage in co-operative and competitive activities (building virtual castles, racing virtual vehicles, starting a virtual business etc.) for huge swathes of time without ever learning the other's real names or discussing any matters relating to the real world. By contrast it would be

---

[7] To enable this level of freedom the player must disable camera constraints or, in newer versions of *Second Life*, adjust the default "draw distance".

extremely odd for two children who spent hours playing together in the real world to never discuss issues outside of their make-believe games. Similarly Velleman is correct that players in online games normally "don't see one another's faces" (Velleman 2008: 411) whereas those engaged in traditional game of make-believe typically do. However, this difference is not—as Velleman suggests—a "significant difference between virtual and pretend play" (Velleman 2008: 410) but merely, as we will see below, a generalisation about the kinds of choices made by those taking part in (and setting up) these games.

Velleman's next claim concerning avatars is that in virtual worlds player cannot, within "the venue or the medium of the game" (Velleman 2008: 410), communicate with other players except through their avatars. Again, though, this seems plainly false when applied to Velleman's central example of *Second Life*. There are a variety of ways for players to communicate with each other within the game, and while some of these (for instance communicating via avatar speech bubbles) are clearly intended to be instances where their avatars are speaking, we see no reason to think this of others such as the "in game" chat bar and instant messaging services.[8] A player could choose to only speak "as their avatar" using such methods but this is clearly not prescribed by the makers of *Second Life* and we suspect that, as a matter of empirical fact, such players are very rare. Further, even in cases where plays are exclusively able to communicate via their avatars, for example virtual environments where only avatar speech bubbles are available as means of communication, this does not restrict them to only speaking as their avatars. If two pirate avatars are sailing on a

---

[8] For details of various communication methods available in *Second Life* see http://wiki.secondlife.com/wiki/Communication.

virtual boat and one says "I need to take a break to let the cat out" it seems fairly clear that they are speaking *qua* player rather than *qua* avatar. Similarly if one asks "How do I raise the main sail?" and the other replies "Press control and S", it would be obtuse to imagine that one virtual pirate is giving this advice to another. An online game designer could, perhaps, prevent such activities by limiting the means of communication options available to the players (for instance allowing them a few dozen pre-set commands "Cast a fire spell", "Heal me" etc.). However, such opacity could also be introduced, though it would require significantly greater effort, in real-life games of make-believe. Children could play all their games of pirates in pitch black rooms imagining that the illuminated sock puppets they wear are pirates travelling on a dark ocean and consistently determining to make-believe that any pirate who talked about, for example, "needing to go home to Mummy" (or how another pirate had "cheated") had clearly gone insane and needed to be made to walk the plank.

These features of the player avatar relationship which Velleman highlights, then, seem to be merely stylistic choices with respect to how a particular virtual environment or game of make-believe operates and not ones which, as Velleman would have it, clearly distinguish the two.

Velleman's final claim concerning the player/avatar relationship is that while players in virtual worlds read off their avatar's emotions from their own, players in games of make-believe (and those engaged with canonical fictions) invent their egocentric emotional attributions. However, both aspects of this claim are mistaken. We have argued above, and in more depth in an earlier article (Meskin and Robson 2012: 21–28), that there is a frequent disparity between the attitudes, emotional and otherwise, of players and their avatars. It is also a mistake to think that our emotional, or quasi-emotional, attitudes to fictional entities are typically invented in the way Velleman claims. It is obvious, we take it, that the viewer of a horror film does not merely stipulate that they are feeling quasi-fear as they see the slime approaching but rather, as we discussed earlier, they make-believe certain things (that they are afraid of the monster etc.) based on their (genuine) physiological reactions. Similarly when properly involved with a fantasy or straightforward game of make-believe we need not consciously "make up" our quasi-attitudes but are instead able to, at least partially, read them off our own physiological reactions.

Velleman, then, is mistaken. None of the arguments he raises provide any motivation for denying that our interactions with virtual environments are make-believe in Walton's sense. In the respects Velleman highlights our interactions with videogames are no further away from childhood games of make-believe than are our engagements with canonical fictions.

6/ Videogames and canonical fictions
While we are critical of the arguments put forward by Tavinor and Velleman, and in particular of their claim that videogames are non-Waltonian, we certainly recognize that there are phenomena associated with videogame play which differ importantly from our engagement with canonical fictions. These differences might explain, at least in part, why a number of philosophers have been tempted to treat videogames as not falling within the category of full-blooded Waltonian fictions. In this section we will briefly survey some of these differences and suggest that, while they point to some interesting and underexplored aspects of videogames, they provide no reason to doubt that videogames are fully Waltonian.

One of the most notable differences between videogame play and ordinary engagement with fiction has to do with the *kinds* of first-person discourse they engender. As we have already discussed, certain forms of first-person discourse are not uncommon in our interactions with ordinary fictions. We have not, however, emphasized how pervasive such first-person discourse really is. Consider first-person ascriptions of emotional attitudes towards fictional characters and situations: "I was frightened for so and so", "I felt pity for the heroine", etc. Whatever one's view of such claims (i.e., whether they correctly describe full-fledged emotional states or, rather, must be understood as make-believe), it cannot be denied that they are a common aspect of our engagement with works of fiction. Similarly, we regularly talk, when watching a film for example, of "seeing" and "hearing" fictional characters. The difference between discourse about canonical fictions on the one hand and videogames on the other is not, then, that only the latter engender first-person discourse. We propose that the difference is that videogames engender first-person action talk to a much higher degree than do canonical fictions—when it comes to the former we talk about *doing* things in relation to the fictional world and its characters ("I kissed the elf", "I married the elf"), but this is much less common in the case of the latter where our first-person locutions are almost always mentalistic (i.e., perceptual, affective or cognitive). We may talk of falling in love with the heroine of a novel but we don't talk (or at least not very often) of wooing her and kissing her. We propose, then, that the extent to which we engage in *these* sort of self-attributions—i.e., non-mentalistic self-attributions of fictively directed actions—is a key difference between our interactions with videogames and our interactions with ordinary fictions such as novels and movies.

A further point, concerning the development of automaticity in players, is highlighted by Velleman (2008: 412): although a player may start out by intending to manipulate the mouse and keyboard and to thereby cause her avatar to act, these intentions tend to drop away and she comes to act by means of intentions to do things *with* her avatar—that is, rather than by intending to make her avatar do things. He explicates this contrast by asking us to consider what happens when we develop skills in tennis and come to "treat the racket as under one's direct control" (Velleman 2008: 413). Velleman points out that "as any tennis player knows, trying to make the racket hit the ball is a sure-fire way of missing" and that instead one ought to treat the racket "as an extension of one's arm". Similarly when the proficient *Street Fighter* player wants to swing their virtual fist into Bison's face they no longer (consciously) intend to press certain sequences on the controller or to make their avatar hit Bison but rather to *hit Bison with their avatar*. When they reach this point the player "intends to perform avatar-eye-coordinated actions in the virtual world, not real-world actions of controlling the avatar" (Velleman 2008: 414). We think Velleman has pointed to a significant and interesting phenomenon: videogame players do often develop a high degree of automaticity (though crucially this will also happen in cases where no avatar is involved—*Command and Conquer*, *Lemmings* etc.), and this is a feature that is not shared by our engagement with canonical fictions.

However, neither the preponderance of first person action talk nor the automaticity of virtual action gives us any reason to doubt that videogames are full-blooded Waltonian fictions. These features are absent from our engagement with ordinary fictions simply because such engagement does not involve the relevant kinds of intentions and actions. When reading a

Dickens novel or watching a Tarantino film, we do not act in a manner which, even fictionally, can be appropriately thought of as hitting a character or kissing them. As such it is no surprise that we do not typically speak of interacting with such fictions in this way and, of course, if we do not perform these actions we do not (*a fortiori*) perform them automatically. A different example, on the other hand, shows that Walton's theory has no problems accounting for these features. In children's games of make-believe it is not uncommon that, at some point, the children stop intending, for example, to manipulate the mud balls and start intending (or pretending to intend) to do things with the pies those mud balls represent. Similarly it would not be at all out of place for a child to proclaim, after making certain motions with their empty hand, "I stabbed the pirate". The ubiquitous presence of such features in childhood games of make-believe, then, clearly shows that they fail to provide even a prima facie reason for regarding videogames as non-Waltonian.

A final difference relates to Tavinor's claim (i) from section three that, in contrast to consumers of standard fictions, players of videogames can often influence what is true in the work world of the videogame. In one sense, of course, this claim is clearly false: the plot of *Resident Evil 5*, for example, was written in its entirety by a group of game developers at Capcom long before any of us ever get our hands on it.[9] Nevertheless,

---

[9] An interesting exception to this claim might be found in MMORPG's (Massively Multiplayer Online Role Playing Games). Here it seems that what is true in the work world can straightforwardly be influenced by the player; as famously happened in the "Corrupted Blood" incident (http://news.bbc.co.uk/1/hi/technology/4272418.stm). Such cases are extremely interesting and worthy of further discussion but for now we will focus our attention on a way in which the player can affect fictional work

there is a more charitable interpretation of Tavinor's claim which correctly describes our interactions with videogames. To understand this we will need to return to an analogy we have made in previous articles (Meskin and Robson 2010: 557-59; Meskin and Robson 2012: 28-31) between performances of plays and playings of videogames. Consider a performance of the play *Othello*; the lead actor's physical appearance and actions will often determine what is true in that performance (as well as the production of which that performance is an instance); if the actor wears an earring we are likely authorised to imagine of Othello that he wears an earring, if the actor is tall then we imagine that same applies to Othello. (This tendency will have its limits; we are not to imagine that in various past performances of Othello it was fictional that he was a white man "blacked up".) But while it might be fictional in the performance that Othello wears an earring, these things are not made fictional in *Othello* as such (that is, in the dramatic work written by William Shakespeare). The same will apply to many other aspects of a performance. Various different interpretations of Iago's character may be true according to some performances and false according to others, Othello's ethnicity may vary, and so forth. These things are true in the work worlds of their respective performances (and productions) of *Othello*, and not just in game worlds associated with those performances, but they are not true of the work world of *Othello* itself.

In a like manner we suggest a distinction to be made between what is fictional in a videogame and what is fictional in various "playings" of that videogame, with Tavinor's proposal correctly applying only to the later. It is true in

---

worlds not only in MMORPG but also in more traditional videogame formats.

Resident Evil 5, the game itself, that Chris Redfield sets off to Africa to investigate a mysterious Biohazard outbreak and that he is aided by Shiva Aloma. However, many things which are not true in the game simpliciter will be true according to the work worlds of various playings of it. According to some playings, Chris fails in his task and is killed in all manner of unfortunate ways, and even those "successful" playing in which Chris survives and defeats Wesker will vary in all manner of ways: which enemies Chris fought and in what order, what weapons he used to dispatch each of them and so on.

Crucially, the player has an ability to make things true in a particular playing of *Resident Evil 5* which the audience of a play like *Othello* does not have.[10] We can make things true in our particular game worlds associated with a performance of *Othello* but we are unable to make anything true in the work world of that performance. Our rushing on stage to save Desdemona, for instance, is famously not able to make anything fictional in the work world of (even that particular performance of) the play. By contrast in taking certain actions, such as inputting commands on a controller, we can make it true in a particular playing of *Resident Evil 5* that Chris kills a snake with

---

[10] It could be objected that the distinction which follows holds only when we (mistakenly) treat the player of a game as analogous to the audience of a play whereas, in fact, the player's role is much closer to that of a performer. While there is some truth to this, it is certainly not correct to view the player in strict analogy to a performer. The role of the player in a typical videogame will, we believe, be most strongly analogous to the role occupied in a semi-scripted interactive play by an audience member who is also a performer. However, plays which allow for individuals to take on such roles are certainly atypical and, crucially for our purposes, are not examples of canonical fictions. We thank Greg Currie for raising this objection.

his knife.¹¹ That this happens is true in the work world of the playing and not just the game worlds associated with it. As such we take Tavinor's claim (i), when properly interpreted, to be the claim that the players of videogames, unlike the audiences of canonical fictions, can affect what is true in the work world of a particular playing of a game. Yet again, this gives us no reason for regarding videogames as non-Waltonian.

Videogame play and the use of other computer-based virtual environments such as *Second Life* often exhibit a very high degree of user involvement. We seem, somehow, to "enter" the world of those games and literally do things in them. This is reflected in the phenomenology of game play and in ordinary discourse about game play which is filled with rich action talk about what we do in the virtual world. These phenomena have led philosophers such as Tavinor and Velleman to argue that videogame play is not completely consistent with Walton's account of our engagement with canonical fictions. We have argued that careful attention to the ways works of fiction involve make-believe shows that Tavinor and Velleman are mistaken in thinking that one must give up or alter the Waltonian framework in the case of videogames.¹²

University of Nottingham — University of Leeds
jonvrobson@gmail.co.uk — a.meskin@leeds.ac.uk

---

11   This claim is, of course, importantly distinct from the false claim that it is fictional in that playing that those actions caused Chris to kill the snake.

12   This work was supported by a generous grant from the Arts and Humanities Research Council of the UK. A version of this paper was presented at a Centre for Aesthetics seminar at the University of Leeds. We thank the audience there for helpful comments. Thanks also to Greg Currie and Alice Kay.

REFERENCES

Currie, Gregory. 1990. *The Nature of Fiction*. New York: Cambridge University Press.
Davies, David. 1996. "Fictional Truth and Fictional Authors." *British Journal of Aesthetics* 36 (1): 43–55.
Meskin, Aaron, and Jon Robson. 2010. "Videogames and the Moving Image." *Revue Internationale de Philosophie* 64 (4): 547–63.
— — —. 2012. "Fiction and Fictional Worlds in Videogames." In *The Philosophy of Computer Games*, ed. John Richard Sageng — Tarjei Mandt Larsen — Hallvard Fossheim. Berlin — New York: Springer.
Tavinor, Grant. 2005. "Videogames and Interactive Fictions." *Philosophy and Literature* 29: 24–40.
— — —. 2009. *The Art of Videogames*. Oxford: Wiley-Blackwell.
Velleman, David. 2008. "Bodies, Selves." *American Imago* 65 (3): 405–26.
Walton, Kendall. 1990. *Mimesis as Make-Believe: On the Foundations of the Representational Arts*. Cambridge: Harvard University Press.

Connecting Worlds: Mimesis in Narrative Cinema

Enrico Terrone

ABSTRACT: When we see a narrative film, we perceive a series of pictures and sounds that provide us with information about a fictional world. On one hand, the supporters of the "impersonal imagining thesis" (Currie 1995, Gaut 2004) argue that the spectator uses images and sounds as prompts for the imaginative construction of a fictional world, but this account does not fit well with the actual experience of films. On the other hand, the supporters of the "imagined seeing thesis" (Levinson 1996, Wilson 1997) argue that the film spectator imagines to perceive the fictional events in a first-personal way, but in order to do this, the spectator must first imagine *being* in the fictional world, with some paradoxical consequences. I claim that these opposing theses both rely on the same ontological fallacy, that of conceiving a fictional world as a possible world, causally disconnected from the real one. Conversely, I will argue that fictional worlds are artifactual, that is, essentially created and therefore essentially connected to our reality. This ontological account allows us to explain how the spectator can imagine to perceive the fictional events without the need of imagining to be in the fictional world. What ensues is a new concept of cinematic mimesis, which focuses not only on the similarity between the fictional world and the real world, but especially on the accessibility of the former from the latter. Mimesis in narrative cinema is not only the act of setting up a fictional world, but most importantly the act of giving us a perceptual access to it.

The "imagined seeing thesis" and its problems

When we see a narrative film, we perceive a series of pictures and sounds that provide us with information about a fictional world. Most philosophers of cinema agree about this issue. The disagreement focuses on how this information is conveyed.

Mimesis: Metaphysics, Cognition, Pragmatics
ed. G. Currie, P. Koťátko, M. Pokorný
466-80. London: College Publications, 2012.

For philosophers such as Gregory Currie (1995) and Berys Gaut (2004), the spectator uses the pictures and sounds of a film in the same way as the reader uses the words of a novel, i.e. as prompts for the imaginative construction of a fictional world; this is called the "impersonal imagining thesis". On the other hand, philosophers such as Kendall Walton (1990 and 1997), Jerrold Levinson (1996) and George Wilson (1997 and 2006) state that the film spectator imagines to perceive the fictional events in a first-person way; this is called the "imagined seeing thesis". It is worth noting that the use of the expression "imagined seeing" (or "fictional seeing") instead of simply "seeing", in order to refer to this thesis, comes from the consideration that a spectator in the real world is unable to perceive events that happen in the fictional world: she can only imagine to perceive them. Yet in order to do this, the spectator must first imagine *being* in the fictional world. Because of this condition, the supporter of the "imagined seeing thesis" has to face two alternatives: either the spectator imagines to be in the fictional world face to face with fictional events ("the face-to-face hypothesis"), or she imagines to attend recordings of fictional events, still inside the fictional world ("the fictional recordings hypothesis").

As argued by Currie (1995: 170-79) and as admitted by Wilson (1997: 295-318), the first alternative is not theoretically defensible because of its paradoxical consequences: the spectator would be forced to imagine herself in a continuous displacement within the fictional world, often in absurd positions. However, for the "imagined seeing thesis" an alternative is available: the spectator does not perceive directly the fictional events but only the recordings of them, that is to say, she imagines herself as a fictional spectator of fictional records of fictional events. This solution solves the problem of the excessive mobility of the fictional spectator, but it raises a new question: who has created these fictional records? Since these are fictional artifacts, they may have been created only by a fictional maker, an "image-maker" that corresponds to the role of the narrator: "the fictional person, in the world of the story, who reports the events of the story" (Gaut 2004: 236).

While the "face-to-face hypothesis" allows us to choose whether to dismiss the narrator or consider it as a fictional guide showing the fictional events to the fictional spectator, the "fictional recordings hypothesis" forces us to postulate the existence of the narrator as a fictional filmmaker. Yet, in this way, the problems of excessive mobility afflicting the fictional spectator in the "face-to-face hypothesis" are now afflicting the fictional filmmaker. Wilson's answer to this objection is that it is a "silly question", an excess of pedantry and intransigence: according to Wilson (1997: 306-9), the spectator imagines to attend the fictional records without worrying about the way in which these records were made, without wondering how ever it could come about that at one time the fictional filmmakers were located on the ceiling and at another they are on a desert island together with the lone castaway. The spectator neglects to notice these positional absurdities just as she neglects to notice many other contradictions that can be found in fictions. But this is unconvincing, as observed by Gaut (2004: 245): although, in engaging with a fiction, the spectator usually has a certain quantity of absurdities to imagine, this is not a good reason to force her to imagine other, avoidable absurdities.

The "impersonal imagining thesis" and its problems
Because of the problems of the "imagined seeing thesis", it seems necessary to turn to the "impersonal imagining thesis".

Enrico Terrone

According to this thesis, proposed by Currie, film does not give us access to the perception of fictional events—it just makes us imagine them via the appropriate prompts (which could be attributed to a real author, to an implied author, or to a fictional narrator, depending on the theoretical frame endorsed). This thesis indeed allows us to avoid the paradoxical consequences afflicting the "imagined seeing thesis". However, the explanation that it provides does not seem to fit well with some intuitions about the experience of films. In particular, there are two phenomena that seem to contradict it: "collapsed seeing-in" and "interpellation".

According to Robert Hopkins (2008), "collapsed seeing-in" is the reason why a spectator does not perceive a narrative film as a photographic representation of a theatrical representation of fictional events; rather, she perceives it directly as a photographic representation of fictional events. While seeing a scene from *Taxi Driver*, we normally consider it *not* as moving pictures of Robert De Niro playing Travis Bickle driving a taxi, but more directly as Travis Bickle driving his taxi. Yet according to Currie's "impersonal imagining thesis", in any scene we should see a moving picture of Robert De Niro driving a taxi, and then imagine Travis Bickle driving his taxi: a cognitive effort that, distributed over the whole film, seems too costly and not very plausible.

Historically, since its very beginning (*La sortie de l'usine Lumière*, 1895) the cinema has accustomed its audience to attend events rather than to imagine them, and the practice of live broadcast has accentuated this use of moving images. Against this background, it seems counterintuitive that the case of fiction requires an extremely different cognitive performance. In other words, the "imagined seeing thesis"—which explains the experience of both the fiction film and the non-fiction moving pictures by referring to different modes of the same kind of performance—seems preferable to the "impersonal imagining thesis" which instead forces the spectator of fiction films to accomplish a radically different performance. Let us consider for instance the case of the mockumentary genre, i.e. fake documentaries that the audience can enjoy either as fiction or as non-fiction (for instance, Peter Jackson's *Forgotten Silver*): a mockumentary can appear unsettling just because it exploits the propensity of the audience to switch between two similar cognitive performance (i. e. seeing and imagining seeing).

The other empirical phenomenon that contradicts the "impersonal imagining thesis" is "interpellation", that is, the spectator's feeling of being observed by the fictional character if the actor looked into the camera during the filming (see Casetti 1986: 25-34). Filmmakers such as Jean Renoir, Ingmar Bergman, Jean-Luc Godard and Woody Allen have used interpellation for their own expressive purposes, but normally, on a film set, looking into the camera is not allowed to the actors precisely in order to avoid that the spectator, while observing a character, have the feeling that she is observed by the character.

According to Currie's account, this prohibition would have no reason to be in place: if the spectator uses the sights and sounds of the film as prompts in order to imagine a fictional world, a look into the camera does not interfere with this imagination. The spectator's disturbing feeling elicited by the look into the camera can only be explained by assuming that the spectator imagines to see the fictional events without in her turn being seen, so that the character's look interferes with her imagination, just as the unexpected gaze of somebody we are spying on interferes with our spying.

A more fundamental ontological problem

At this point, we are facing an antinomy: on one hand, if we adopt the "imagined seeing thesis" we find some paradoxical consequences that can be explained away only by endorsing the "impersonal imagining thesis" — yet if we endorse the "impersonal seeing thesis" we are unable to account for the empirical phenomena of "collapsed seeing-in" and "interpellation", which the "imagined seeing thesis" could explain easily.

I wish to claim that the controversy between the "imagined seeing thesis" and the "impersonal imagining thesis" bears upon a common conceptual fallacy, which consists in conceiving a fictional world as a possible world, parallel to the real one, and therefore (see Lewis 1986: 1-69) causally disconnected from it.

Since perceiving an event is a causal effect exercised by the event upon the viewer, both the "imagined seeing thesis" and the "impersonal imagining thesis" assume that, in order to perceive the fictional event, the spectator should be within the fictional world, and since in fact she is in the real world, she has to imagine her own counterpart in the fictional world. Similarly, since the pictures of an event are a joint causal effect of the event itself and of the action of an image-maker, a fictional event can only be depicted by fictional pictures made by a fictional image-maker. In this way the "imagined seeing thesis", in the discourse both of its defenders and of its opponents, leads to postulating an additional set of fictional entities (such as fictional viewers, fictional pictures, fictional image-makers).

Yet the fictional world *is not* a possible world parallel to the real world and causally disconnected from it. Kripke (1980:

44) rightly claimed that we cannot view a possible world through a telescope, but this is not equally true for fictional worlds. In the movie theater it is precisely as if we viewed a fictional world through a telescope, that is, through the film that is being screened.

Usual statements such as "The fictional world of *Taxi Driver* was created by Paul Schrader and Martin Scorsese", "Travis Bickle is played by Robert De Niro" or "Travis's sentiments for Iris have truly touched me" can be explained only by assuming that the fictional world is causally connected to the real world, and therefore that it is not a parallel world but rather (if we want to insist on the geometric metaphor) an intersecting one; rather than a counterfactual world it is an artifactual one. Starting from the artifactualist account that conceives fictional entities as essentially created (see Thomasson 1999), we can indeed conceive the fictional world as essentially created in its turn, and therefore essentially connected to the real world. The fictional world is an artifactual world created by a filmmaker in the real world and perceivable by an audience in the real world. The fictional world is not a hypothetical alternative to the real world, but rather a mind-dependent entity located in a certain sense (to be explained later) in the real world.

This notion of fictional world allows us to maintain the benefits of the "imagined seeing thesis" without an ontological commitment to the notions of fictional spectator, fictional picture and fictional image-maker. Now we can consider "imagined seeing" as a mental state of imagination that uses the direct perception of pictures and sounds, rather than mental propositions or mental imagery, to represent its imaginary content. And so we can retain the intuitive benefits of the "imagined seeing thesis" without incurring its paradoxical consequences. Above all, we can explain how the spectator can imagine to perceive the fictional events while staying in the real world. Yet, for this purpose, the fictional world must include in its ontological structure some access points that allow a spectator of the real world to look inside the fictional world.

The standard situation of watching films requires that the viewer uses these access points while the character is not aware of their existence. However, the cases of "a look into the camera" — and the "Pirandellian" or "Brechtian" situations that ensue (e.g., in the films of Jean-Luc Godard, Woody Allen or Michael Haneke) — also show that exceptionally the character can gain access to these points through which she turns her gaze from the fictional world to the real world.

So the spectator imagines to see the fictional world, but what she is really asked to imagine is an artifactual fictional world equipped with access points that allow her to perceive the fictional events directly from the real world, without having to imagine a fictional counterpart of herself. Similarly she does not need to imagine a fictional image-maker who shows the fictional world to us or supplies us with its pictures: it suffices to consider the real filmmaker (or at the most the implied filmmaker) as a world-maker, that is, the agent who, from inside the real world, creates the fictional world and equips it with the access points by which a real spectator can perceive it.

Yet in order to carry out the theoretical work that the supporters of the "imagined seeing thesis" have assigned to fictional spectators, fictional pictures and the fictional image-maker, the access points have to connect the fictional world to the real world. It remains to clarify how this connection takes place.

How does an access point work?
An access point is a point of the fictional world imagined as perceptually accessible from the real world. As point of the fictional world, the access point is identified by spatial and temporal coordinates: it is in a given fictional place at a given fictional moment. But as regards the real world, the access point does not have a fixed spatial and temporal localization: it is rather a possibility of access (i.e. an access-point type) which may correspond to multiple circumstances of observation (i.e. access-point tokens), just like a window that gives onto a landscape matches this *single* landscape with all the *many* circumstances under which it was and will be looked at. Moreover, what characterizes the access point as regards the real world is a certain mode of perceptual presentation: just like the landscape is seen through the shape of the window and through its glass, the fictional world is in much the same way perceived through pictures that have a certain shape and a certain visual texture, and also through sounds that can be manipulated and integrated by other elements, like the soundtrack.

So a fictional world can be considered as a landscape that is visible from a window, and which retains its identity while, over time, many observers look out of the window. There are however two crucial differences. First, our landscape is considered only as a spatial entity, while the fictional world also possesses a temporal dimension. Second, our landscape belongs to the space-time of the real world, while the fictional world has its own space and its own time. Yet the access points make the space-time of the fictional world accessible to spectators who are inside the real world, just like the window makes accessible the space of the landscape to the people who are inside the building. In other words, it is true that the fictional world has crucial differences compared to the landscape (it is another world, not simply another space), but it is also true that the access point exhibits crucial differences when compared to the window (it is an interface between two worlds, not simply between two spaces).

The comparisons between the fictional world and the landscape, and between the access point and the window, are also illuminating for another reason: the window does not let us see the landscape but only a part of it, and several windows in the same building let us see different spatial parts of the landscape; likewise, the access point does not allow us to perceive the whole of the fictional world but only a spatio-temporal part of it, and several access points in the same film allow us to perceive different spatio-temporal parts of the same fictional world.

What does the filmmaker make?

The filmmaker is the person in the real world to whom the spectator attributes the construction of the access points that allow her to experience the fictional world. By designing the access points, the filmmaker allows the spectator to survey the space-time of the fictional world, just like the architect by designing the windows of a building allows the visitor to survey the surrounding landscape. Since the fictional world exists as a block of space-time, the filmmaker can at will decide which parts of the fictional world will be perceived through the access points, and in what order they will be perceived. In this sense, our explanatory model of cinematic narration is consistent with the possibilities of film editing: a narrative film is a series of access points to the fictional world, and the filmmaker establishes not only where these access points are and what formal features they possess, but also in what order they are arranged.

What ensues is a new concept of cinematic mimesis, which focuses not only on the similarity between the fictional world and the real world, but especially on the accessibility of the former from the latter. Mimesis in narrative cinema, in short, is not only the act of setting up a fictional world, but especially the act of giving us access to it. So the filmmaker is not only the demiurge who has created the "fictional landscape": she is especially the architect who builds the windows from which the "fictional landscape" is visible to us.

Another useful comparison, in this sense, is that between narrative film and live broadcast. In this latter case, we perceive events distant from the place where we currently are and we perceive them via pictures and sounds that are configured and filtered by the choices of a television director. Similarly, a filmmaker gives us direct access to fictional events, and she allows us to perceive them while they are happening. Once again, however, the comparison has an ontological limit: in the case of live broadcast, the events to which the television gives us access happen at another place of our space and at another moment of our time, while the fictional events to which a narrative film gives us access happen in another space-time. We can find a similar difference in the comparison between narrative film (which—as we have argued—gives us access to events that happen in another space-time) and a documentary or a delayed broadcast, which gives us access to events that have happened at different places of our space and earlier moments of our time.

What does the spectator do?
The spectator imagines to perceive the fictional world through the access points that the filmmaker has set. Since these access points are like windows that overlook the fictional world from

the real world, the spectator does not have to imagine to be in the fictional world and she does not even have to imagine the existence of a fictional narrator who makes the fictional pictures of the fictional events from inside of the fictional world: she has just to imagine that the fictional world contains in its ontological structure the access points that make it perceivable from the real world.

The problem to be addressed at this point is the following: since the access points are at the interface between the fictional world and the real world, they belong both to one and the other. In regard of the fictional world this presents no problems: it is a world imagined by the viewer, so she just has to imagine the access points as its constituents (we could say that this is the cognitive competence necessary to understand narrative cinema). In regard of the real world, however, things are more complicated: in order to belong to the real world, the access points must be real in their turn. But do entities like these really exist in the real world?

A way to solve this problem is to assume that, while seeing a film, the spectator imagines being in a pseudo-real world that is identical to the real world except for the fact that, during the film, the screen contains a number of access points that overlook the fictional world. This is a modified version of Wilson's "imagined seeing thesis": the spectator imagines her own fictional counterpart which is now no longer in the fictional world (with all the ensuing paradoxes) but rather in the pseudo-real world from which it perceives the fictional world via the access points.

Although this solution seems to work properly, we should ask ourselves whether we really need to imagine a pseudo-real world where everything is identical to the real world except for the fact that the narrative film that is being screened becomes an access point to a fictional world, when it would be ontologically more parsimonious (i.e. more consistent with Occam's Razor) to argue that, in the real world, the film that is being screened counts as an access point, since the film that is being screened is an artifact whose function is to offer an access point.

So in the real world, the access point is construed as an artifact, that is, a mind-dependent object (see Thomasson 1999), rather than as a fictional object, and it can be explained like this. Let us consider for instance a pair of scissors: it seems much more intuitive to explain their existence by claiming that in the real world we attribute to them the function of cutting rather than by claiming that every time we use the scissors, we imagine to be in a pseudo-real world where everything is identical to the real world except that instead of the scissors as a material object, we have a cutting tool here. Similarly it seems more intuitive to claim that, because of our practices, in the real world we attribute to the film that is being screened the function of access point to the fictional world, rather than to claim that we imagine to be in a pseudo-real world where everything is identical with the real world except that, instead of the screened film as a material object, we have access points.

This account of narrative cinema preserves the benefits of the "imagined seeing thesis", namely its ability to explain the involvement of the spectator in the film. But now we can explain this involvement without having to postulate a fictional counterpart of the spectator within the fictional world, with all the well-known paradoxical consequences. We can do so, since in our account the spectator imagines to perceive the fictional world through an access point that allows her to perceive the fictional events directly from the real world. And we can do so because we have explained that, in the real world, according to our practices, the narrative film that is being screened counts as an access point to fictional events.

The foundation of our account is the idea that, while watching a film, the spectator does not imagine to perceive a possible world parallel to the real world, but rather imagines to perceive a fictional world connected to the real world. The cognitive performance of the spectator therefore consists in representing two worlds (the real one in which she is, and the fictional one that she imagines to perceive), and in imagining their connection.

In this cognitive performance lies the most basic philosophical value of narrative cinema, which does not require us to turn to the real world (as in a documentary or in a live broadcast) or just to imagine a fictional world (as in a novel), but it makes us learn to shift our gaze from one world to another. In this sense, even the least successful narrative film has something magic.

Università degli Studi di Torino
enriterr@gmail.com

REFERENCES

Casetti, Francesco. 1986. *Dentro lo sguardo. Il film e il suo spettatore.* Milano: Bompiani.
Currie, Gregory. 1995. *Image and Mind: Film, Philosophy and Cognitive Science.* Cambridge: Cambridge University Press.
Gaut, Berys. 2004. "The Philosophy of the Movies: Cinematic Narration." In *The Blackwell Guide to Aesthetics*, ed. Peter Kivy, 230–53. Oxford: Blackwell.
Hopkins, Robert. 2008. "What Do We See In Film?" *Journal of Aesthetics and Art Criticism* 66 (2): 149–59.
Kripke, Saul. A. 1980. *Naming and Necessity.* New York: John Wiley & Sons.

Levinson, Jerrold. 1996. "Film Music and Narrative Agency." In *Post-Theory: Reconstructing Film Studies*, ed. David Bordwell—Noël Carroll, 242-82. Madison: University of Wisconsin Press.

Lewis, David K. 1986. *On the Plurality of Worlds*. Oxford: Blackwell.

Thomasson, Amie L. 1999. *Fiction and Metaphysics*. Cambridge: Cambridge University Press.

Walton, Kendall. 1990. *Mimesis as Make-Believe. On the Foundations of the Representational Arts*. Cambridge, MA: Harvard University Press.

———. 1997. "On Pictures and Photographs: Objections Answered." In *Film Theory and Philosophy*, ed. Richard Allen—Murray Smith, 60-75. Oxford: Clarendon Press.

Wilson, George. 1997. "*Le Grand Imagier* Steps Out: On the Primitive Basis of Film Narration." *Philosophical Topics* 25 (1): 295-318.

———. 2006. "Transparency and Twist in Narrative Fiction Film." *Journal of Aesthetics and Art Criticism* 1 (64): 81-95.

Index of Names*

A
Antiochus of Ascalon__246
Aristotle__2, 8, 15–18, 20*f*., 29–34, 36, 133, 176, 225, 233–42, 244, 251, 344*ff*., 352
Auerbach, E.__4, 6

B
Baumgarten, A. G.__3, 223
Beckett, S.__178&*ff*., 350
Benveniste, É.__264
Bergman, I.__469
Bodmer, J. J.__3
Boghossian, P. 50
Booth, W. C.__35*ff*.
Borges, J. L.__187–92
Brandom, R.__84
Brecht, B.__350, 352, 360
Breitinger, J. J.__2
Buridan, J.__115

C
Cage, J.__192
Capote, T. __69
Carroll, N.__355
Carroll, L.__337
Cicero, M. T.__246*ff*.
Coleridge, S. T. __222
Currie, G.__62, 68, 75, 199*f*., 210–15, 331*f*., 355, 462, 468*f*.

D
Daumier, H.__32
Davidson, D.__110*ff*., 115, 129, 181, 365
Davies, D.__322*f*.
Davies, S.__399
Deleuze, G.__7, 264, 267
Derrida, J.__5, 7
Deutsch, H.__64, 67*ff*.
Dickens, Ch.__274, 460
Doyle, A. C.__73, 209
Duchamp, M.__191

E
Ehrenfels, Ch. von__399
Empedocles__244
Erickson, J.__346, 372–375

F
Fielding, H.__17, 36
Flaubert, G.__10, 36, 276
Fleming, I.__74, 76
Franzen, J. E.__273, 293, 301, 308
Frege, G.__336
Freud, S.__4, 6
Friend, S.__65, 70–80, 83
Fyfe, W. H.__17

G
Galen__245
Geertz, C.__69
Gibson, J.__65, 69, 71*ff*., 76*f*., 80
Godard, J.-L.__408&*ff*., 469, 472
Goethe, J. W.__224
Gombrich, E.__384*f*., 389*ff*., 393, 396*f*., 402

---

* Abbreviations: *f*. for one following page, *ff*. for two following pages, &*ff*. for an entire paper or a section with a separate heading, starting at the given page.

481

Index of Names

Goncharov, I. A. __271
Goodman, N. __18–21, 23, 25–28, 31*f*., 367*ff*., 403*f*.
Gray, S. __356
Gruen, J. __180
Guattari, F. __7

H
Halliwell, S. __16*ff*., 32, 242
Hamon, P. __276*f*., 312
Handke, P. __353*f*.
Haneke, M. __472
Hanley, R. __92
Hardy, T. __199
Hare, D. __356
Hegel, G. W. F. __8
Hemingway, E. __17, 36
Homer __16*f*., 250, 344
Hopkins, R. __19, 388, 391, 398*f*., 468
Husserl, E. __178, 263

I
Ingarden, R. __258–62, 267

J
Jackson, P. __469
Jakobson, R. __4
James, H. __70
Jones, J. __362
Jones, L. __424
Joyce, J. __17, 191
Juriedini, J. __355

K
Kafka, F. __195–200, 208, 215–18
Kant, I. __172, 182
Koller, H. __231
Kripke, S. __90, 116, 470

L
Lamarque, P. __62, 193, 196–199, 201–4, 210
Leibniz, G. W. __2*f*.
Leonardo da Vinci __28, 386
Leslie, A. __72
Lessing, G. E. __251
Lewis, D. __87, 92, 96, 179–82, 198, 206–9, 212
Livingston, P. __352
Lopes, D. M. __387, 391*f*., 396, 404*f*.
Lubbock, P. __16, 35*f*.
Lucretius __386
Lukács, G. __8
Lynch, M. P. __46
Lyotard, J.-F. __7

M
Malabou, C. __269
McEwan, I. __273, 294, 307
Meinong, A. __41
Montague, R. __115

N
Nehamas, A. __86*ff*., 90*f*.
Newall, M. __389, 400
Nietzsche, F. __86–89
Nuttall, A. D. __3–7, 10*f*.

P
Parsons, T. __196
Patterson, D. __365
Peirce, Ch. S. __18, 32
Phidias __246, 248, 250
Philostratus __224*f*., 247–51
Plato __8, 16*f*., 224&*ff*., 344–48, 355–60
Prendergast, Ch. __3, 7–11
Pynchon, T. __70

Index of Names

Q
Quine, W. V. O.__41

R
Renoir, J.__469
Ricœur, P.__8, 256
Riffaterre, M.__285

S
Sainsbury, R. M.__46
Salmon, F.__90
Saussure, F. de__5
Scarry, E.__281, 292, 295, 304
Scruton, R.__316&ff.
Searle, J.__76
Shakespeare, W.__5ff., 83, 164, 211f., 214, 370, 436, 461
Stalnaker, R.__95, 97, 101ff.
Stein, G.__350f.
Stock, K.__64f., 70, 77
Stoppard, T.__362

T
Tavinor, G.__437f., 442&ff., 457&ff.
Tolstoy, L. N.__70, 87, 90, 93, 95-98, 102f.

V
Van Eyck, Jan__394
Velleman, D.__437f., 444&ff.
Vico, G.__5

W
Walton, K.__42f., 52, 77, 198f., 200, 224, 252, 317, 325&ff., 402, 436&ff.
White, R.__138
Wilson, G.__412-16, 466f., 476
Wittgenstein, L.__402f.
Wolff, F.__241
Wollheim, R.__317f., 324f., 335, 337f., 383&ff.

Index of Topics*

A
abstract object__41, 89f.
acting__363, 365f.
action__128ff., 161, 164, 171, 174, 181, 188, 229, 233ff., 238f., 244, 247, 265ff., 269ff., 282, 348, 354f., 376, 435, 437, 443–47, 450, 454, 458f., 460, 462
actor__34, 169, 317, 321, 334, 360, 363–66, 370, 461, 469
actual world__2f., 93, 178f., 189, 204, 283
aesthetics__1f., 8, 14, 16, 18, 30, 191
alethic pluralism__40&ff.
ambiguity__117f., 172, 267&ff., 424
animal__235f., 239, 240, 277, 396, 397, 431
appellation__115
artificial agency__444&ff.
assertive author__70&ff.
audience__31, 33, 66f., 228ff., 233, 245, 331, 352f., 366, 368, 370, 373–76, 441, 443, 462f., 468f., 471
*Ausdruck*__251
avant-garde__3, 348, 358

B
betting__153&ff.
body__30, 277
brain__397

---

* Abbreviations: *f.* for one following page, *ff.* for two following pages, *&ff.* for an entire paper or a section with a separate heading, starting at the given page.

C
casting__320f., 324
character__5, 17, 21, 23, 27f., 30f., 42, 68, 75, 79f., 82, 86&ff., 131&ff., 181, 211, 334, 345f., 348, 351, 356, 360f., 363f., 454, 458, 469
cinematic narrator__412, 414ff.
clarity/un-clarity__258, 260, 262f., 265, 268
coherence__44f.
collapsed seeing-in__468, 470
colour__15, 19, 30, 48–50, 397, 404
competence__184, 207
compositionality__22, 26–29, 32, 34, 123, 365
consciousness__278, 284f., 290, 292, 304, 427, 433
copy__2, 222, 232, 240, 246f., 345
correspondence__16, 39, 44f., 57, 63, 175, 216, 259, 296f., 340

D
dance__15f., 20, 29, 231, 349, 358
deception__344, 346
deflationism__54f.
deictic field__161ff., 165
denotation__21, 23, 26, 30, 286, 369
description__22ff., 34f., 72, 98, 111f., 136f., 184, 190, 200, 273&ff.
diagonal intension__100
diegesis__346f., 355f., 409, 411f., 417f., 432
direct speech__37
documentary__409, 411, 469, 475, 478
drama__20, 229, 234, 344, 357

485

Index of Topics

E

ekphrasis__396
emotion__30, 31, 33, 37, 77, 114, 130, 141*ff*., 165, 201, 208, 215, 238, 272, 377, 441, 447*ff*., 453, 456*ff*.
essentialism__86–91
exemplification__111–14, 367*ff*., 389
expression__30–35, 89, 90, 93*ff*., 103*f*.
extension__109–13

F

fiction__10, 42, 45, 47, 50, 61*&ff*., 86*f*., 90, 92*ff*., 133, 140, 148–51, 162, 170*f*., 174*ff*., 193*&ff*., 252, 295
fictional incompetence__318*&ff*.
fictional work__64–68, 70–78, 84
fictional world__73, 79*ff*., 177, 179*f*., 193*&ff*., 224, 252
fictionality__60*&ff*., 413, 131, 174*&ff*.
fictive utterance__60*&ff*.
fidelity__63, 69, 82, 273*&ff*.
fidelity constraint__63*&ff*.
film__16, 20, 317, 332, 356, 408*&ff*., 447*f*., 453, 458, 464*&ff*.
first person__186, 459

G

game__10, 15, 328*&ff*.
game worlds__440*&ff*.
*Gestalt*__384, 399
grouping properties__386, 399, 400–5

H

history__6*f*., 11, 75*f*., 169
homodiegetic__180
horizontal intension__100

I

iconicity__16, 18–22, 24–29, 32, 34*f*., 37, 136
identity__41, 86, 92, 97*f*., 122*f*., 133, 146*f*., 169, 297, 415, 473
illocutionary force__186
image__18, 221*f*., 236, 248*f*., 273*&ff*., 317, 323*f*., 335–41
imitation__383*&ff*., 408*ff*., 418, 420*f*., 423, 432
incomprehension__260, 267
indexicals__94, 103*f*.
individuals__91, 93, 95, 97*f*., 100, 132*&ff*., 396, 415*f*.
inscription__21, 23, 27*f*.
intension__79, 95, 100, 103, 105*&ff*.
interpretation__5*f*., 18, 196, 338

L

language__8, 11, 20, 56, 58, 107, 112*f*., 120*f*., 188, 200, 280, 288
lie__68*f*., 175
literature__4, 10*f*., 15*f*., 31*f*., 72, 155, 160, 171, 188, 195, 197, 205, 347

M

make-believe__33, 62*f*., 65*f*., 70–76, 80–84, 89, 224, 228, 237, 328–31, 363, 436–39, 441, 445*ff*., 449–52, 455–58, 460, 463

Index of Topics

meaning__52, 54, 109*f.*, 115*f.*, 139, 181*f.*, 195–98, 200*f.*, 204, 248, 251, 258–61, 267, 320, 325, 368
medium, mediation__15, 17, 23, 25, 27, 36, 189, 249, 283, 287, 299, 316*f.*, 319, 321, 323*f.*, 331, 333, 335, 341, 407
metaphor__31*f.*, 369
metaphysics__223, 225*f.*
mimesis__*passim*
mimetic activity__15, 22, 219, 227, 239, 244*f.*, 250
mimetic art__5, 15, 18, 20, 229, 241
model__16, 229, 232, 246, 248, 320
modernism__3*f.*, 10
Müller-Lyer illusion__387*f.*, 394*f.*
music__2, 15*f.*, 18, 29–34, 192, 227*f.*, 230, 231, 235, 354, 358, 408*f.*, 412, 416, 418, 432

N

*Nachahmung*__251
narrative__17, 20, 36*ff.*, 61*&ff.*, 147*f.*, 152*&ff.*, 177*&ff.*, 274*f.*, 278*f.*, 281*&ff.*, 347*&ff.*, 464*&ff.*
narrativity__37, 147, 174*&ff.*, 290, 355, 419
narrator__17, 35, 63, 70, 147, 161, 163, 178*&ff.*, 210, 285, 347, 359, 412, 417, 419, 421, 467*f.*, 476
non-fiction, non-fictional__63, 65, 70*&ff.*, 147*f.*, 329, 469

P

painting__25, 107, 232, 244, 249, 297, 319, 322*f.*, 326, 385
perception__33, 107, 156, 172, 187*f.*, 190, 192, 229, 243, 257, 273*&ff.*, 317, 327*f.*, 333, 336, 339, 383*&ff.*, 410*f.*, 458, 465*&ff.*

performance__179, 181, 186–89, 225*f.*, 228, 230*f.*, 234, 242, 245, 248*&ff.*, 461*f.*
Perky effect__306*f.*
phenomenology__257*&ff.*, 282, 291
photography__25, 316*&ff.*, 468
physics__202, 240
picture__296, 298, 306*f.*, 318–26, 328*ff.*, 332*&ff.*, 382*&ff.*, 465*f.*, 468–73, 475*f.*
pleasure__15, 30, 33, 146, 233, 235*f.*, 238, 241
poetry__15–18, 133, 164, 226, 232, 234, 245
postmodernism__3*f.*, 8, 11
pragmatics__10*f.*, 104, 153*ff.*, 168, 170*f.*, 200
pre-conscious__282, 306
predicate__44, 110*f.*, 172*&ff.*
proper name__77–80, 83, 90*&ff.*, 110*f.*, 125, 133, 138*ff.*

Q

quasi-individuality__159, 165*ff.*

R

reader__33*f.*, 37, 62*f.*, 65, 73–77, 80*ff.*, 97*ff.*, 103, 148*ff.*, 156, 166, 176, 179, 182, 186, 213, 217, 273, 278, 290, 414
real world__70, 73, 148, 198, 200, 213, 448, 454*f.*, 466, 470, 471–78
realism__3*ff.*, 410*f.*
reference__3, 25*f.*, 41, 78*f.*, 89*f.*, 96, 98, 107, 109–12, 115, 138*f.*, 186, 394, 355
representation__2, 4, 6–11, 19*&ff.*, 73, 106*&ff.*, 191*f.*, 200*&ff.*, 220*&ff.*, 258*&ff.*, 285,

487

Index of Topics

296, 318&ff., 349, 383–86, 390, 392f., 396, 403, 440, 468
rigid designators__95, 98f., 102

S
sculpture__32ff., 189, 228, 243, 246f., 250, 393, 408
seeing-as__382&ff.
seeing-in__332&ff., 382&ff.
seeing through__317, 325&ff.
semiotics__18, 20, 22, 27
showing__35ff., 342&ff.
sign__21, 23, 203, 207, 258&ff., 396
similarity__16, 18f., 21, 28f., 404, 464, 475
sound__31, 366, 407&ff., 465f., 473
story__16f., 36ff., 73, 80–83, 87, 91, 94, 96–100, 102f., 134, 144, 156, 158f., 164, 180ff., 277, 279, 349, 351&ff., 410, 412ff., 417f., 425f., 467
story-telling__62f., 67ff., 75, 79, 101, 432
supplementation__42, 194&ff.
symbol__20–23, 26ff., 32

T
teleology__238f., 241, 244f.
telling__37, 355f., 359

temporality__20, 37, 63, 95, 146, 278, 288, 290, 293, 473
theater, theatrical__16, 20, 34, 317, 321, 331, 333, 342&ff., 468
token__28, 67, 125, 127, 136f., 140, 142, 144, 152, 156, 161f.
transparency__317, 325f., 329, 333, 335, 411, 426
*trompe l'oeil*__389, 391–94
truth__18, 39&ff., 72, 96, 110–13, 117ff., 144, 249, 345f., 376, 443, 446
truth in fiction__40&ff., 87, 92, 179, 199, 202f., 206, 210f., 440–43, 451
type__67, 136f., 140&ff.

U
universals__4, 6f., 133

V
verbicture__153&ff.
visual art__15, 32, 296
visuality__218, 272&ff.
voice__227f., 243, 347, 357, 408&ff.

W
work of art__191f.

www.ingramcontent.com/pod-product-compliance
Lightning Source LLC
Chambersburg PA
CBHW060313230426
43663CB00009B/1687